Lecture Notes in Computer Science

Lecture Notes in Artificial Intelligence 16435

Founding Editor

Jörg Siekmann

The series Lecture Notes in Artificial Intelligence (LNAI) was established in 1988 as a topical subseries of LNCS devoted to artificial intelligence.

The series publishes state-of-the-art research results at a high level. As with the LNCS mother series, the mission of the series is to serve the international R & D community by providing an invaluable service, mainly focused on the publication of conference and workshop proceedings and postproceedings.

Shuzhi Sam Ge · Weizheng Yuan ·
Honglong Chang · Yanen Wang ·
Hooman Samani · Hongsheng He
Editors

Social Robotics + BioMed

17th International Conference
on Social Robotics + BioMed, ICSR + BioMed 2025
Xi'an, China, September 26–28, Proceedings

Editors
Shuzhi Sam Ge
National University of Singapore
Singapore, Singapore

Honglong Chang
Northwestern Polytechnical University
Xi'an, China

Hooman Samani
University of Arts London
London, UK

Weizheng Yuan
Northwestern Polytechnical University
Xi'an, China

Yanen Wang
Northwestern Polytechnical University
Xi'an, China

Hongsheng He
University of Alabama
Tuscaloosa, AL, USA

ISSN 0302-9743 ISSN 1611-3349 (electronic)
Lecture Notes in Artificial Intelligence
ISBN 978-981-95-7537-4 ISBN 978-981-95-7538-1 (eBook)
https://doi.org/10.1007/978-981-95-7538-1

LNCS Sublibrary: SL7 – Artificial Intelligence

This Springer imprint is published by the registered company Springer Nature Singapore Pte Ltd.
The registered company address is: 152 Beach Road, #21-01/04 Gateway East, Singapore 189721, Singapore

Preface

The 17th International Conference on Social Robotics + BioMed (ICSR + BioMed) 2025 took place in Xi'an, China, as an in-person event from September 10 to 12, 2025. ICSR + BioMed 2025 was organized under the Global Robotics, Arts, and Science Synergies (GRASS). GRASS hosted two conferences in 2025: ICSR + BioMed in Xi'an, China, and ICSR + AI in Naples, Italy.

This LNCS volume comprises the peer-reviewed proceedings of the conference. From a total of 55 submitted manuscripts that were single-blindly reviewed by an international team of program committee, associate editors, and reviewers, 27 regular papers were selected for inclusion in the proceedings and presented during the technical sessions. Submissions received two reviews each on average.

ICSR + BioMed 2025 focused on interdisciplinary innovation on bioinspired, biomedical, surgical, and AI-integrated bio-mechanical robotics. By fostering the much-needed merging of these disciplines, together with fast-emerging biotech, the conference aimed to blend the lessons learned by these communitiesto unleash the real potential of robots. The conference served as a scientific, technical, and business platform for fostering collaboration, exploration, and advancement in these cutting-edge fields. It showcases the latest breakthroughs and methodologies, shaping the future of robotics design and applications across several sectors, including biomedical and healthcare.

We extend our sincere gratitude to all members of the organizing committee and the volunteers for their dedication, which made the conference a resounding success. We are also deeply indebted to the program committee, associate editors, and reviewers for their rigorous review of the papers. Finally, we are immensely grateful for the continued support from the authors, participants, and sponsors.

November 2025

Shuzhi Sam Ge
Weizheng Yuan
Honglong Chang
Yanen Wang
Hooman Samani
Hongsheng He

Organization

General Chairs

Shuzhi Sam Ge	National University of Singapore, Singapore
Weizheng Yuan	Northwestern Polytechnical University, China

General Co-chair

Honglong Chang	Northwestern Polytechnical University, China

Program Chair

Yanen Wang	Northwestern Polytechnical University, China

Program Co-chair

Hooman Samani	University of the Arts London, UK

Invited Session Chair

Xiangyang Zhu	Shanghai Jiao Tong University, China

Workshop Chair

Jeffrey Koh	Singapore Institute of Technology, Singapore

Award Chair

Jiadao Wang	Tsinghua University, China

Competition Chairs

Bing Xu	Zhejiang University, China

Publication Chair

Hongsheng He	The University of Alabama, USA

Registration Chair

Weiwei Yu	Northwestern Polytechnical University, China

Young Leaders Chair

Haonan Zhang	Northwestern Polytechnical University, China

Finance Chair

John-John Cabibihan	Qatar University, Qatar

Sponsorships/Exhibitions Chair

Chi Zhang	Xi'an Bone Technology Co., China

Publicity Chair

Chenguang Yang	University of Liverpool, UK

Local Arrangements Chair

Xia Zou	Northwestern Polytechnical University, China

Web Masters

Heng Tian	Xi'an Bone Technology Co., China
Zhang Jiaqi	Xi'an Bone Technology Co., China

Standing Committee

Shuzhi Sam Ge	National University of Singapore, Singapore
Oussama Khatib	Stanford University, USA
Maja Mataric	University of Southern California, USA
Haizhou Li	Chinese University of Hong Kong, China
Jong Hwan Kim	Korea Advanced Institute of Science and Technology, South Korea
Paolo Dario	Scuola Superiore Sant'Anna, Italy
Abderrahmane Kheddar	LIRMM Montpellier, France and CNRS-AIST, Japan
Tianmiao Wang	Beihang University, China

Contents

A Review of Performance Optimization of Artificial Bone Scaffolds: Design, Materials, and Manufacturing 1
Yaoxing Hu and Hao Zeng

A Prediction Model for Assessing the Risk of Cognitive Dysfunction in Elderly Patients with Cerebral Small Vessel Disease Was Developed Using Decision Tree Algorithms 12
Wang Xiaojie, Wang Wenxiu, Zhang Qiang, Li Xin, Pang Yi, and Zhang Hong

Apply Human Factors in the Full Life Cycle Design of Wrist Rehabilitation Robot 23
Donglai Lu, Weiwei Yu, Sixiang Fei, and Abderraouf Benali

An Optically Enhanced Nano-Sniffer Based on Au-SnO_2 for Bionic Olfaction in Biomedical Robots 35
Yihui Wang, Ting Yu, Huijun Yin, Shangyi Shen, Zhenqi Yang, Honglong Chang, and Haitao Zhao

A Review of Bone Tissue Engineering Scaffold Design Strategies 43
Haonan Zhang, Yanen Wang, Zhisheng Liu, Bo Ren, Minyan Liu, Xiaohu Chen, Yingchao Song, and Yixiao Guo

The Application and the Development of 3D Printing Technology in Biosensors 54
Maimoona Afzal, Chi Zhang, Ghulam Hassan Askari, Aamir Shehzad, Sidra Aslam, and Nasar Ali

A Review of the Current Researches on the Application of Barrier Membrane Technology in Guided Bone Regeneration in the Oral and Maxillofacial 65
Chi Zhang, Zhewei Liu, Yakuang Zhang, and Xinpei Li

Bidirectional Target Bias APF-RRT* Algorithm for Indoor Path Planning of Epidemic-Prevention Robots 80
Rili Wu, Yuhai Zhong, Xiru Wu, Yi Lu, and Aoliang Xu

Comprehensive Review on Bioceramic Bone Repair Scaffolds with TPMS Lattice Structure Based on Vat Photopolymerization 95
Zhisheng Liu, Yinghao Zhao, Haonan Zhang, Xiaohu Chen, Mengjie Wang, Chunliang Chen, Yanen Wang, and Chi Zhang

Chemical Modification Strategies, Performance Optimization and Challenges of Conductive Hydrogels for Wearable Health Monitoring 108
Lijun Yang, Tuanjie Chen, and Caijuan Li

Evaluation of UAV Crash Risk for Low-Altitude Biothreat Sample Transport Using Fuzzy Bayesian Networks 120
Yichuan Yang, Peng Hu, Weiwei Yu, Xiang Zou, Yi Ai, and Guangyuan Zhang

Deep Motion Physics Model for Parkinson's Motion Deficit Classification 131
Ajay Kishore Ponnada, Hongsheng He, and Fujian Yan

Development of Physiological Temperature Responsive Shape Memory Polymer for Bone Tissue Engineering 141
Xiaolu Zheng, Yanqing Yang, Junchen Zhou, Xun Yuan, Xian Cheng, and Wei Zhu

Employing Soft Robotic Systems to Replicate the Kinematics and Biomedical Properties of Upper Limb Joints 151
Muhsina Muneer, Sarah Arif, and John-John Cabibihan

Eye Movement Recognition and Gaze Point Prediction with Webcam 169
Jiawei Shen, Ruoyu Wang, Weiwei Yu, and Gautam Srivastava

Evaluation of LVA Treatment Efficacy for Secondary Lymphedema of the Limbs in Middle and Advanced Stages Using the LYMQOL Score 181
Zhongyu Jia, Gaofeng Liang, Zonghai Jia, and Chi Zhang

FES in Motor Function Reconstruction for Spinal Cord Injury: A Review 192
Hao Zeng and Yaoxing Hu

Innovations in Electrical Materials for Flexible Sensors: From Metals, Hydrogels to Carbon-Based Materials and Polymer Conductors 204
Caijuan Li and Hongxue Xu

Neuro-symbolic Model for Motion Deficit Detection in Parkinson's Disease Patients 215
Sai Leela Harika Thota, Hongsheng He, and Fujian Yan

Omnisurface: Intention Awareness and Touch-Based Query for Human–Robot Teaming 225
Akhlak Uz Zaman, Hui Li, Tianjun Xu, and Hongsheng He

Personalized Resistance Control Method for Wrist Rehabilitation Robots in Isotonic and Isokinetic Training 238
Weiwei Yu, Donglai Lu, Sixiang Fei, and Abderraouf Benali

Research on Cloud Edge Collaborative Algorithm for Surgical Robots Based on Model Predictive Control 250
Yinghao Zhao, Yaoxing Hu, Hao Zeng, Fan Feng, Xinyu Zhang, and Yingchao Song

Research on the Application of Additive Manufacturing Technology in Precision Electronic Components 260
Sidra Aslam, Chi Zhang, Nasar Ali, Ghulam Hassan Askari, Aamir Shehzad, and Maimoona Afzal

The Competency Assessment of UAV Operators Based on Human-Machine Collaboration 273
Shanshan Wu, Weiwei Yu, Peng Hu, Xiang Zou, Yichuan Yang, and Huan Liu

Schlieren-Based Monitoring and Deep Learning Detection for Volumetric Additive Manufacturing 284
Miaomiao Yuan, Yifei Wang, and Xiaoxiao Han

3D Printed Microstructure Hydrogel for Wearable Sensors and Triboelectric Nanogenerator 296
Tuanjie Chen, Hongxue Xu, and Caijuan Li

4D Printed CNT-Ag/PLLA/TPU Bone Scaffold Having Enhanced Electro-Responsive Shape Memory Properties 308
Feng Yang, Jiye Jia, and Pei Feng

Author Index 319

A Review of Performance Optimization of Artificial Bone Scaffolds: Design, Materials, and Manufacturing

Yaoxing Hu[1,2](✉) and Hao Zeng[1,2]

[1] Department of Industry and Engineering, School of Mechanical Engineering, Northwestern Polytechnical University, Xi'an, Shaanxi 710072, People's Republic of China
huyaoxing@mail.nwpu.edu.cn

[2] Bio-Additive Manufacturing University-Enterprise Joint Research Center of Shaanxi Province, Northwestern Polytechnical University, Xi'an, Shaanxi 710072, People's Republic of China

Abstract. This paper systematically reviews research progress on bioceramic artificial bone scaffolds for addressing the clinical challenge of large bone defects. Currently, bone defects exceeding critical dimensions cannot heal spontaneously, while traditional treatments such as autogenous bone grafting and metal scaffolds still face limitations including restricted availability, inadequate mechanical compatibility as well as non-degradability. Bioceramic materials demonstrate significant application potential due to their composition resembling natural bone, combined with degradability and osteoinductive potential. However, an effective collaborative optimization mechanism has not yet been established between design, materials, and manufacturing processes in this field. This paper reviews the current state of domestic and international research from three perspectives: multiscale structural design, material adaptation, and additive manufacturing. It aims to provide references for over-coming challenges in the integrated design and precision manufacturing of artificial bone structures, performance, and function.

Keywords: Bone scaffold · Additive manufacturing · Biomaterials

1 Introduction

Bone is one of the few tissues in the human body capable of regenerating after trauma without scar formation [1, 2]. It performs vital functions including weight-bearing, haematopoiesis, participation in movement, and organ protection. Bone comprises cortical bone and cancellous bone. Cortical bone exhibits a porosity below 10% and high mechanical strength (3–20 GPa), whereas cancellous bone presents a spongy structure with approximately 50–90% porosity and mechanical strength ranging from 0.1 to 4.5 GPa [3]. However, once the length of a bone defect exceeds 1.5 times the shaft diameter (massive bone defect), it surpasses the critical threshold for self-repair, rendering healing impossible [4]. Presently, the repair of massive bone defect remains a significant clinical challenge [5, 6].

S. S. Ge et al. (Eds.): ICSR + BioMed 2025, LNAI 16435, pp. 1–11, 2026.
https://doi.org/10.1007/978-981-95-7538-1_1

The primary clinical treatment approaches for extensive bone defects encompass autogenous bone grafting and metal artificial bone scaffold reconstruction. Autogenous bone grafting yields the most favourable outcomes, yet it faces limitations in source availability, mouldability, and the potential for secondary injury at the donor site [7]. Metal artificial bone scaffolds achieve favourable osseointegration with host bone post-implantation, yet suffer from drawbacks including excessive mechanical strength, metal ion leaching and non-degradability [8, 9]. In contrast, bio-ceramic artificial bone materials share similar composition and physicochemical properties with natural bone. They promote bone regeneration while gradually degrading, making them a more promising therapeutic strategy [10, 11]. Nevertheless, establishing a synergistic optimisation mechanism between artificial bone design and manufacturing remains a critical unresolved issue and a prominent research focus in the field of bone tissue engineering in recent years [12, 13].This paper therefore reviews the current status and progress of bioceramic artificial bone scaffold research worldwide from the perspectives of design, materials, and manufacturing, aiming to provide reference for related studies.

2 Structural Design Method of Artificial Bone

The design of artificial bone structures often relies on empirical knowledge and simple geometric mimicry, making it challenging to fully replicate the complex multi-level architecture and mechanical properties of natural bone tissue [14, 15]. With advancements in computational mechanics and advanced manufacturing technologies, topology optimisation theory has increasingly been applied to artificial bone design due to its ability to achieve optimal material distribution under specified constraints, which provides a novel approach for precisely regulating structural performance [16–18]. For instance, Park et al. [19] designed complex internal bone structures similar to native bone using a perimeter-controlled topology optimization method. Results showed that the introduction of perimeter constraints can significantly alleviate the checkerboard effect and density islands, while enabling the acquisition of curved surface appearances with various curvatures. This demonstrates that this method has inherent advantages in mimicking the complex geometric structures of natural bone. Zhao et al. [20] proposed a multi-material topology optimization method. By means of a binary-coded parameterization (BCP) scheme, this method enables natural transitions at multi-material interfaces, thereby realizing the topological design of multi-level porous scaffold structures under the condition of separation between the material density field and the porosity field. Results indicated that the optimized structure is less affected by changes in relative density and load, which implies that the scaffold structure design will be subject to fewer constraints.Takezawa et al. [21] designed porous lattice structures based on the multi-scale homogenization theory and analyzed the regulatory mechanism of the structure on mechanical strength. The numerical simulation results showed that the modulus of the optimized optimal lattice structure reached 83% of the Hashin-Shtrikman upper bound performance. Montaño et al. [22] proposed a load multi-scale adaptive scaffold optimization design method. Studies have shown that the optimized irregular scaffolds can respond to boundary and load conditions in a timely manner and exhibit superior mechanical properties (Fig. 1).

Whilst topological optimisation methods advance structural design, some scholars combine optimised designs with experimental validation to facilitate practical application. Yuan et al. [23] employed laser selective melting technology to fabricate porous magnesium artificial bone with diverse structures based on a three-periodic minimal surface optimisation approach. Although its mechanical strength approximates that of cancellous bone, porous magnesium exhibits extreme sensitivity to inherent defects such as porosity and microcracks in metal printing, which seriously compromise the fatigue performance of the artificial bone.

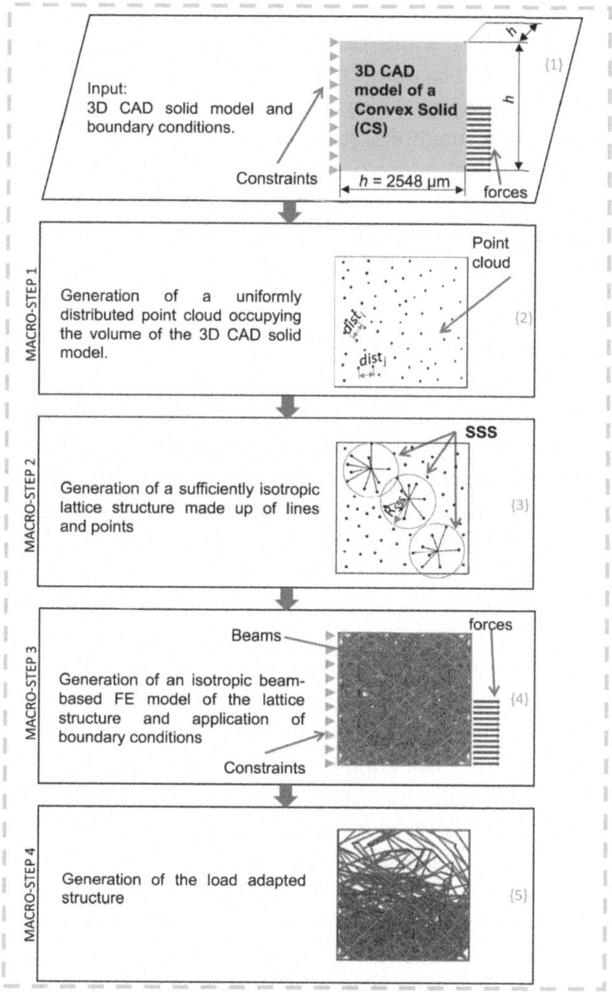

Fig. 1. Algorithmic process for generating skeletonized load-adaptive structures [22]. Copyright 2019, ACS Publications.

Zhang et al. [24] developed a Representative Volume Element (RVE) method to predict the elasto-mechanical properties of lattice structures and introduced geometric defect compensation. The double-cone diamond (DCD) structured scaffolds fabricated via Selective Laser Melting (SLM) could reduce the stress shielding effect as predicted by the RVE method. However, due to the powder adhesion phenomenon, there remains a noticeable discrepancy between the predicted results and the actual results. Zou et al. [25] modelled porous artificial bone structures by simulating loofah-like reticulated patterns, employing ceramic photopolymerisation for fabrication. However, the use of photoinitiators during printing and subsequent high-temperature post-processing rendered the scaffolds incapable of supporting active substances.

Overall, the application of topology optimisation theory in the design of artificial bone structures has significantly enhanced the mechanical adaptability and biomimetic properties of scaffolds [26, 27]. Multiscale optimisation strategies demonstrate considerable potential in simulating the complex architecture of bone tissue [28, 29]. Nevertheless, there are still challenges in existing research concerning the collaborative design of materials, structures and functions, particularly the constraints imposed by manufacturing processes on material properties and biological activity. In the future, further exploration is required into integrated design methodologies that simultaneously address mechanical performance, manufacturing feasibility and biological functionality, thereby advancing the clinical translation of topologically optimised artificial bone.

3 Materials for Artificial Bone

The selection and design of artificial bone materials decisively influence their mechanical properties, biocompatibility and degradation behaviour [30, 31]. An ideal bone substitute material must not only possess a chemical composition and microstructure similar to natural bone tissue, but also achieve favourable biocompatibility and metabolic equilibrium within the body [32, 33]. Bioceramic materials have become a focal point in contemporary bone repair research due to their outstanding biocompatibility and tunable physicochemical properties [34–36]. In this field, bioceramic materials such as hydroxyapatite, β-tricalcium phosphate, and biphasic calcium phosphate have similar compositions to natural bone inorganic salts [37]. The calcium and phosphate ions released during their degradation process can promote osteoblast proliferation and differentiation [38, 39].

Bioceramic scaffolds can be further engineered with favourable pore architecture and high porosity through material composition adaptation tailored to optimised structures. This facilitates tissue and vascular ingrowth while promoting nutrient transport and metabolic activity [40, 41]. For instance, Chen et al. [42] fabricated bioceramic bone scaffolds with microporous shells using calcium silicate (CaSi) materials doped with 4% and 10% magnesium (Mg), and evaluated their mechanical properties, degradability, and in vivo osteogenic capacity. Results showed that while the presence of micropores reduced the compressive strength of the scaffolds, it significantly enhanced their osteogenic capacity and also contributed to the degradability of the scaffolds to a certain extent (Fig. 2a). Ning et al. [43] established a quantitative relationship between the area ratio of high-density/low-density regions and compressive strength by regulating the β-tricalcium phosphate composition ratio based on a biomimetic gradient structure. They successfully fabricated a bioceramic scaffold simulating the composite structure of cortical-cancellous bone, achieving an overall compressive strength of 80 MPa, suitable for weight-bearing bone repair. Aboushelib et al. [44] fabricated HA/ZrO_2 composite biphasic bioceramic scaffolds and evaluated their in vivo biological properties. Results showed that the addition of HA significantly enhanced the biocompatibility and osteogenic capacity of the ZrO_2 scaffolds (Fig. 2b).

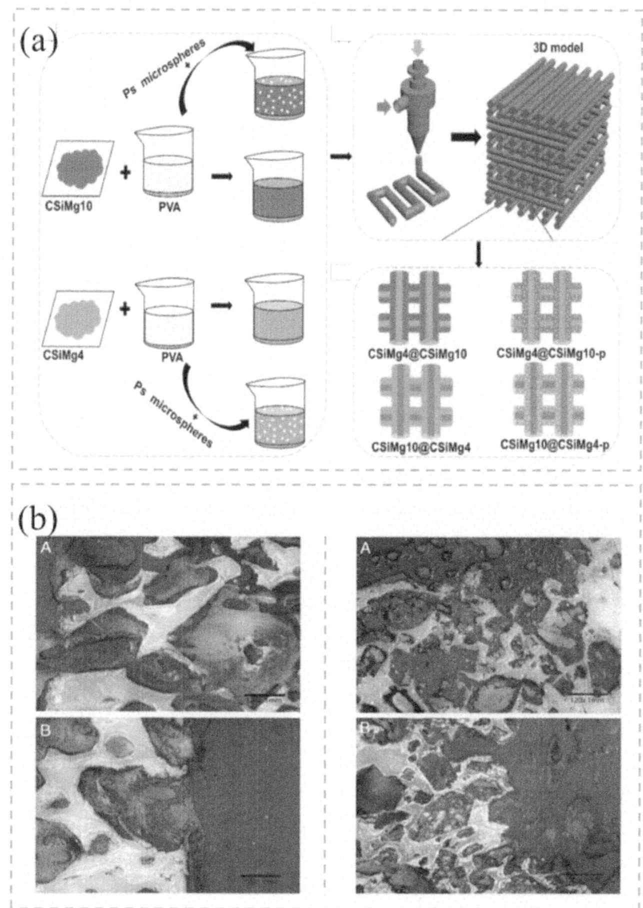

Fig. 2. (a) Mg-doped CaSi ceramic scaffolds with a three-dimensional (3D) structure of microporous shells [42]. Copyright 2021, OXFORD, CC BY 4.0. (b) Comparison of in vivo osteogenesis between ZrO2 (left) and HA/ZrO2 (right) composite scaffolds [44]. Copyright 2017, Springer, CC BY 4.0.

Chang et al. [45] utilised bio-ceramics with diverse nanostructures, employing hydrothermal treatment to enhance surface texture and increase specific surface area. This selectively amplified adsorption of specific plasma proteins, thereby promoting osteoblast adhesion, growth and differentiation. He et al. [46] prepared a composite biomimetic scaffold with excellent degradability and compressive strength up to 120 MPa by regulating the composition ratio of β-tricalcium phosphate and magnesium-doped calcium silicate, achieving strength comparable to human cortical bone. Studart et al. [47] targeted large-scale layered porous ceramics with high strength-to-weight ratios and tunable pore sizes by adjusting ink ratios, achieving stable performance during extrusion moulding.

These studies have broadened the application scope of scaffolds across diverse mechanical environments by optimising the material composition of structurally enhanced bioceramics. However, their performance and architecture still fall short of natural cancellous bone. Although bioceramic scaffolds have been fabricated using various printing techniques, the precise manufacture of biomimetic scaffolds that balance material properties remains challenging, thereby limiting their clinical translation. Therefore, there is an urgent need to establish an integrated research system that combines chemical composition design, structural digital design and ceramic manufacturing processes.

4 Application of Additive Manufacturing Technology in Artificial Bone

With the continuous advancement of precision medicine and the growing demand for personalised bone repair, additive manufacturing (3D printing) technology has emerged as the core technique for fabricating bio-ceramic artificial bone. This is due to its advantages in high-degree-of-freedom shaping, precise form control, and controllable pore structure. Compared to conventional manufacturing methods, additive manufacturing not only efficiently achieves integrated forming of complex macroscopic shapes and microscopic porous structures but also enables individualised customisation of implants based on clinical imaging data. This significantly enhances the fit between artificial bone and defect sites, as well as the biointegration outcome. Particularly in the processing of bioceramic materials, 3D printing facilitates multi-level regulation from macrostructure to microporous channels, which provides a novel pathway for the fabrication of biomimetic bone scaffolds.

Wang et al. [43, 48] employed extrusion moulding and ceramic stereolithography techniques respectively to investigate surface-modified micro/nano-scale hydroxyapatite crystal bone scaffolds and microchannel-structured HA-based bone plates. The former approach was combined with hydrothermal mineralisation (calcination at 1100 °C for 3 h) to construct scaffolds featuring micro/nano-scale HAp surface layers and interconnected porous structures, promoting in vitro osteogenic differentiation and in vivo capillary formation. The latter utilised photosensitive polymers as a binder between ceramic particles to form the HA substrate, followed by debinding (thermal decomposition of the binder) and sintering to obtain dense ceramic components, thereby enabling biological applications. Liu et al. [49] fabricated a low-viscosity β-tricalcium phosphate (β-TCP) bioceramic slurry. The scaffolds printed via digital light processing (DLP) technology exhibited a maximum compressive strength of up to 9.89 MPa at a porosity of 40%.

Bose et al. [50] employed binder-jet 3D printing to fabricate porous tricalcium phosphate (TCP) scaffolds (Fig. 3). This approach enhanced surface roughness and osteoblast proliferation through 3D printing combined with a dense core/porous surface design.

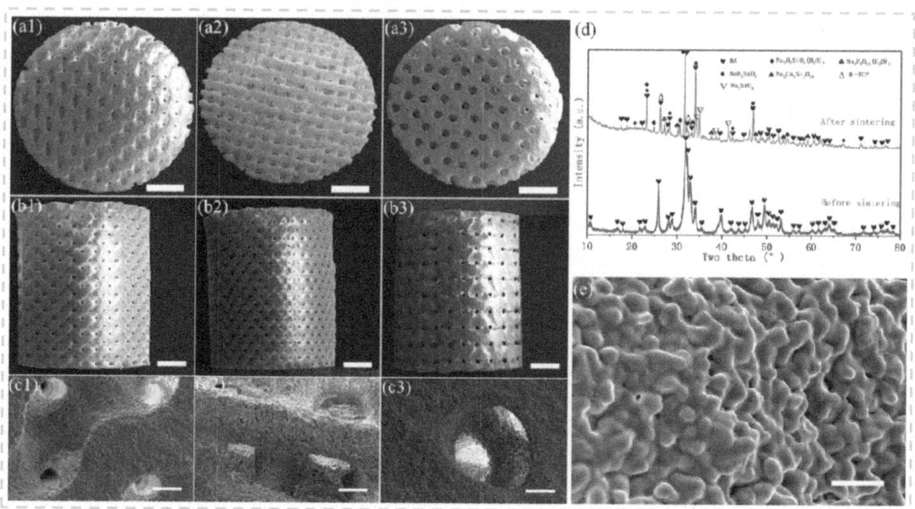

Fig. 3. Scaffold printing structure and X-ray diffraction analysis of the ceramic product [51].

The study encompassed porous surface design, material reinforcement, printing, and post-processing sintering techniques.

Miculescu et al. [52] from the University of Bucharest, Romania, proposed using natural fibres as sacrificial pore-forming templates to construct complex configurations in bioceramic scaffolds. They investigated the pyrolysis capabilities and biocompatibility of common natural fibres, successfully producing porous calcium phosphate scaffolds using loofah fibres. Heat treatment is commonly employed to enhance the mechanical properties of porous structures, yet it proves challenging to achieve functionalisation of artificial bone, such as incorporating bioactive agents. Awad et al. [53] investigated inkjet-printed tricalcium phosphate bioceramic scaffolds, validating the feasibility of this printing process for bone regeneration strategies through in vivo animal experiments (mouse femoral defects).

Additive manufacturing technologies provide robust support for the personalised design and precision fabrication of bioceramic artificial bones, demonstrating particular advantages in complex structural formation, multi-level pore regulation and individualised adaptation. At present, various 3D printing processes (such as extrusion molding, photocuring, and binder jetting) have been widely used to prepare bioceramic scaffolds of different systems and have demonstrated good biocompatibility and osteogenic properties in preliminary experiments. The balance between printing accuracy and surface quality remains to be fully resolved, and the impact of post-processing on the physicochemical and biological properties of the material requires further investigation. In the future, research should focus on developing new functional ceramics and optimizing the printing and post-processing process to accelerate the translational application of additively manufactured bioceramic artificial bones in clinical settings.

Acknowledgments. This study was funded by the National Natural Science Foundation of China (Grant No. 52535008).

Disclosure of Interests. The authors have no competing interests to declare that are relevant to the content of this article.

References

1. Manzini, B.M., Machado, L.M.R., Noritomi, P.Y., da Silva, J.V.L.: Advances in bone tissue engineering: a fundamental review. J. Biosci. **46**, 17 (2021). https://doi.org/10.1007/s12038-020-00122-6
2. Henkel, J., Woodruff, M.A., Epari, D.R., Steck, R., Glatt, V., Dickinson, I.C., Choong, P.F.M., Schuetz, M.A., Hutmacher, D.W.: Bone regeneration based on tissue engineering conceptions—a 21st century perspective. Bone Res. **1**, 216–248 (2013). https://doi.org/10.4248/BR201303002
3. Zhang, X.-Y., Fang, G., Xing, L.-L., Liu, W., Zhou, J.: Effect of porosity variation strategy on the performance of functionally graded ti-6Al-4V scaffolds for bone tissue engineering. Mater. Des. **157**, 523–538 (2018). https://doi.org/10.1016/j.matdes.2018.07.064
4. Dimitriou, R., Mataliotakis, G.I., Calori, G.M., Giannoudis, P.V.: The role of barrier membranes for guided bone regeneration and restoration of large bone defects: current experimental and clinical evidence. BMC Med. **10**, 81 (2012). https://doi.org/10.1186/1741-7015-10-81
5. Vahidi, M., Rizkalla, A.S., Mequanint, K.: Extracellular matrix-surrogate advanced functional composite biomaterials for tissue repair and regeneration. Adv. Healthcare Mater. **13**, 2401218 (2024). https://doi.org/10.1002/adhm.202401218
6. Guo, X., Tao, Z., Dai, Z., Gao, Y., Chu, C., Fan, C., Liu, S., Ma, X., Jin, F., You, Z., Jiang, J.: Magnetically guided mechanoactive mineralization scaffolds for enhanced bone regeneration. Adv. Funct. Mater. 2503903 (2025). https://doi.org/10.1002/adfm.202503903
7. Qi, J., Yu, T., Hu, B., Wu, H., Ouyang, H.: Current biomaterial-based bone tissue engineering and translational medicine. Int. J. Mol. Sci. **22**, 10233 (2021). https://doi.org/10.3390/ijms221910233
8. Vishwakarma, V., Kaliaraj, G.S., Amirtharaj Mosas, K.K.: Multifunctional coatings on implant materials—a systematic review of the current scenario. Coatings **13**, 69 (2023). https://doi.org/10.3390/coatings13010069
9. Ali, M., Mohd Noor, S.N.F., Mohamad, H., Ullah, F., Javed, F., Abdul Hamid, Z.A.: Advances in guided bone regeneration membranes: a comprehensive review of materials and techniques. Biomed. Phys. Eng. Express. **10**, 032003 (2024). https://doi.org/10.1088/2057-1976/ad1e75
10. Romanazzo, S., Molley, T.G., Nemec, S., Lin, K., Sheikh, R., Gooding, J.J., Wan, B., Li, Q., Kilian, K.A., Roohani, I.: Synthetic bone-like structures through omnidirectional ceramic bioprinting in cell suspensions. Adv. Funct. Mater. **31**, 2008216 (2021). https://doi.org/10.1002/adfm.202008216
11. Huang, T., Qiao, S., Wang, J., Lian, J., Yang, B., Zhu, S.: The journey of functional nanoparticles in the human hard tissue mineralization: classification, key functions, and future perspectives. NANO-MICRO small. https://doi.org/10.1002/smll.202504003
12. Prasad, A.: State of art review on bioabsorbable polymeric scaffolds for bone tissue engineering. Mater. Today Proc. **44**, 1391–1400 (2021). https://doi.org/10.1016/j.matpr.2020.11.622
13. Sun, J., Chen, C., Zhang, B., Yao, C., Zhang, Y.: Advances in 3D-printed scaffold technologies for bone defect repair: materials, biomechanics, and clinical prospects. BioMed. Eng. OnLine **24**, 51 (2025). https://doi.org/10.1186/s12938-025-01381-w

14. Tabrizian, P., Davis, S., Su, B.: From bone to nacre—development of biomimetic materials for bone implants: a review. Biomater. Sci. **12**, 5680–5703 (2024). https://doi.org/10.1039/D4BM00903G
15. Foroughi, A.H., Valeri, C., Razavi, M.J.: A review of computational optimization of bone scaffold architecture: methods, challenges, and perspectives. Prog. Biomed. Eng. **7**, 012003 (2024). https://doi.org/10.1088/2516-1091/ad879a
16. Fritz, C., Fischer, L., Wund, E., Zaeh, M.F.: Inner design of artificial test bones for biomechanical investigations using topology optimization. Prog. Addit. Manuf. **8**, 427–435 (2023). https://doi.org/10.1007/s40964-022-00343-1
17. Wu, N., Li, S., Zhang, B., Wang, C., Chen, B., Han, Q., Wang, J.: The advances of topology optimization techniques in orthopedic implants: a review. Med. Biol. Eng. Comput. **59**, 1673–1689 (2021). https://doi.org/10.1007/s11517-021-02361-7
18. Kladovasilakis, N., Bountourelis, T., Tsongas, K., Tzetzis, D.: Computational investigation of a tibial implant using topology optimization and finite element analysis. Technologies **11**, 58 (2023). https://doi.org/10.3390/technologies11020058
19. Park, J., et al.: Design of complex bone internal structure using topology optimization with perimeter control. Comput. Biol. Med. **94**, 74–84 (2018). https://doi.org/10.1016/j.compbiomed.2018.01.001
20. Zhao, Z., Zhang, X.S.: Design of graded porous bone-like structures via a multi-material topology optimization approach. Struct. Multidisc. Optim. **64**, 677–698 (2021). https://doi.org/10.1007/s00158-021-02870-x
21. Takezawa, A., et al.: Isotropic Ti–6Al–4V lattice via topology optimization and electron-beam melting. Addit. Manuf. **22**, 634–642 (2018). https://doi.org/10.1016/j.addma.2018.06.008
22. Rodríguez-Montaño, Ó.L., et al.: Irregular load adapted scaffold optimization: a computational framework based on mechanobiological criteria. ACS Biomater. Sci. Eng. **5**, 5392–5411 (2019). https://doi.org/10.1021/acsbiomaterials.9b01023
23. Wang, Y, et al.: Fatigue and dynamic biodegradation behavior of additively manufactured Mg scaffolds. Acta Biomater. **135**, 705–722 (2021). https://doi.org/10.1016/j.actbio.2021.08.040
24. Zhang, L., et al.: A topology strategy to reduce stress shielding of additively manufactured porous metallic biomaterials. Int. J. Mech. Sci. **197**, 106331 (2021). https://doi.org/10.1016/j.ijmecsci.2021.106331
25. Chen, Q., et al.: 3D printing and osteogenesis of loofah-like hydroxyapatite bone scaffolds. Ceram. Int. **47**, 20352–20361 (2021). https://doi.org/10.1016/j.ceramint.2021.04.043
26. Alsheghri, A., Reznikov, N., Piché, N., McKee, M.D., Tamimi, F., Song, J.: Optimization of 3D network topology for bioinspired design of stiff and lightweight bone-like structures. Mater. Sci. Eng. C **123**, 112010 (2021). https://doi.org/10.1016/j.msec.2021.112010
27. Tuninetti, V., et al.: Biomimetic lattice structures design and manufacturing for high stress, deformation, and energy absorption performance. Biomimetics **10**, 458 (2025). https://doi.org/10.3390/biomimetics10070458
28. Zhang, L., et al.: Investigation of mechanism of bone regeneration in a porous biodegradable calcium phosphate (CaP) scaffold by a combination of a multi-scale agent-based model and experimental optimization/validation. Nanoscale **8**, 14877–14887 (2016). https://doi.org/10.1039/C6NR01637E
29. Colabella, L., Cisilino, A., Fachinotti, V., Capiel, C., Kowalczyk, P.: Multiscale design of artificial bones with biomimetic elastic microstructures. J. Mech. Behav. Biomed. Mater. **108**, 103748 (2020). https://doi.org/10.1016/j.jmbbm.2020.103748
30. Zhang, J., Feng, Y., Zhou, X., Shi, Y., Wang, L.: Research status of artificial bone materials. Int. J. Polym. Mater. Polym. Biomater. **70**, 37–53 (2021). https://doi.org/10.1080/00914037.2019.1685518

31. Huang, Q., Wang, L., Wang, J.: Mechanical properties of artificial materials for bone repair. J. Shanghai Jiaotong Univ. (Sci.) **19**, 675–680 (2014). https://doi.org/10.1007/s12204-014-1565-8
32. Dec, P., Modrzejewski, A., Pawlik, A.: Existing and novel biomaterials for bone tissue engineering. Int. J. Mol. Sci. **24**, 529 (2023). https://doi.org/10.3390/ijms24010529
33. Bongio, M., van den Beucken, J.J.J.P., Leeuwenburgh, S.C.G., Jansen, J.A.: Development of bone substitute materials: from 'biocompatible' to 'instructive.' J. Mater. Chem. **20**, 8747–8759 (2010). https://doi.org/10.1039/C0JM00795A
34. Kumar, R., Pattanayak, I., Dash, P.A., Mohanty, S.: Bioceramics: a review on design concepts toward tailor-made (multi)-functional materials for tissue engineering applications. J. Mater. Sci. **58**, 3460–3484 (2023). https://doi.org/10.1007/s10853-023-08226-8
35. Tanvir, M.A.H., Khaleque, M.A., Kim, G.-H., Yoo, W.-Y., Kim, Y.-Y.: The role of bioceramics for bone regeneration: history, mechanisms, and future perspectives. Biomimetics **9**, 230 (2024). https://doi.org/10.3390/biomimetics9040230
36. Vaiani, L., et al.: Ceramic materials for biomedical applications: an overview on properties and fabrication processes. J. Funct. Biomater. **14**, 146 (2023). https://doi.org/10.3390/jfb14030146
37. Zhu, H., Guo, D., Qi, W., Xu, K.: Development of Sr-incorporated biphasic calcium phosphate bone cement. Biomed. Mater. **12**, 015016 (2017). https://doi.org/10.1088/1748-605X/12/1/015016
38. Ma, H., et al.: 3D-printed bioceramic scaffolds: from bone tissue engineering to tumor therapy. Acta Biomater. **79**, 37–59 (2018). https://doi.org/10.1016/j.actbio.2018.08.026
39. Dong, S., Chen, Y., Yu, L., Lin, K., Wang, X.: Magnetic hyperthermia–synergistic H_2O_2 self-sufficient catalytic suppression of osteosarcoma with enhanced bone-regeneration bioactivity by 3D-printing composite scaffolds. Adv. Funct. Mater. https://doi.org/10.1002/adfm.201907071
40. Zhang, Y., et al.: 3D-printed bioceramic scaffolds with antibacterial and osteogenic activity. Biofabrication **9**, 025037 (2017). https://doi.org/10.1088/1758-5090/aa6ed6
41. von Erlach, T.C., et al.: Cell-geometry-dependent changes in plasma membrane order direct stem cell signalling and fate. Nat. Mater. **17**, 237–242 (2018). https://doi.org/10.1038/s41563-017-0014-0
42. Chen, Y., Huang, J., Liu, J., Wei, Y., Yang, X., Lei, L., Chen, L., Wu, Y., Gou, Z.: Tuning filament composition and microstructure of 3D-printed bioceramic scaffolds facilitate bone defect regeneration and repair. Regen. Biomater. **8**, rbab007 (2021). https://doi.org/10.1093/rb/rbab007
43. Zhang, F., Chang, J., Lu, J., Lin, K., Ning, C.: Bioinspired structure of bioceramics for bone regeneration in load-bearing sites. Acta Biomater. **3**, 896–904 (2007). https://doi.org/10.1016/j.actbio.2007.05.008
44. Aboushelib, M.N., Shawky, R.: Osteogenesis ability of CAD/CAM porous zirconia scaffolds enriched with nano-hydroxyapatite particles. Int. J. Implant Dent. **3**, 21 (2017). https://doi.org/10.1186/s40729-017-0082-6
45. Lin, K., et al.: Tailoring the nanostructured surfaces of hydroxyapatite bioceramics to promote protein adsorption, osteoblast growth, and osteogenic differentiation. ACS Appl. Mater. Interfaces **5**, 8008–8017 (2013). https://doi.org/10.1021/am402089w
46. Shao, H., et al.: Bone regeneration in 3D printing bioactive ceramic scaffolds with improved tissue/material interface pore architecture in thin-wall bone defect. Biofabrication **9**, 025003 (2017). https://doi.org/10.1088/1758-5090/aa663c
47. Minas, C., Carnelli, D., Tervoort, E., Studart, A.R.: 3D printing of emulsions and foams into hierarchical porous ceramics. Adv. Mater. **28**, 9993–9999 (2016). https://doi.org/10.1002/adma.201603390

48. Liu, X., et al.: 3D-printed bioactive ceramic scaffolds with biomimetic micro/nano-HAp surfaces mediated cell fate and promoted bone augmentation of the bone–implant interface in vivo. Bioact. Mater. **12**, 120–132 (2022). https://doi.org/10.1016/j.bioactmat.2021.10.016
49. Liu, S., et al.: DLP 3D printing porous β-tricalcium phosphate scaffold by the use of acrylate/ceramic composite slurry. Ceram. Int. **47**, 21108–21116 (2021). https://doi.org/10.1016/j.ceramint.2021.04.114
50. Ke, D., et al.: Effects of pore distribution and chemistry on physical, mechanical, and biological properties of tricalcium phosphate scaffolds by binder-jet 3D printing. Addit. Manuf. **22**, 111–117 (2018). https://doi.org/10.1016/j.addma.2018.04.020
51. He, J., Xie, M., Luo, S., Tang, G., Zou, Z., Teng, J., Zhao, B., Cui, D., Zhou, T., Yang, L., Ye, C.: ACS Omega **10**(30), 32895–32906 (2025). https://doi.org/10.1021/acsomega.5c01819
52. Mocano, A.C., et al.: Comprehensive analysis of compatible natural fibre as sacrificial porogen template for tailored ceramic 3D bioproducts destined for hard tissue reconstruction. Ceram. Int. **47**, 5318–5334 (2021). https://doi.org/10.1016/j.ceramint.2020.10.113
53. Inzana, J.A., et al.: 3D printing of composite calcium phosphate and collagen scaffolds for bone regeneration. Biomaterials **35**, 4026–4034 (2014). https://doi.org/10.1016/j.biomaterials.2014.01.064

A Prediction Model for Assessing the Risk of Cognitive Dysfunction in Elderly Patients with Cerebral Small Vessel Disease Was Developed Using Decision Tree Algorithms

Wang Xiaojie[1], Wang Wenxiu[2], Zhang Qiang[2], Li Xin[2], Pang Yi[2], and Zhang Hong[2](✉)

[1] Xi'an Medical University, Xi'an 710068, China
[2] Department of Neurology, Shaanxi Provincial People's Hospital, Xi'an 710068, China
doczhanghong@163.com

Abstract. With the increasing number of elderly patients with cognitive impairment due to cerebral small vessel disease (CSVD) and the integration of computer technology in the medical field, there is an urgent need for more effective data analysis methods to reveal the relationships among different medical data features, helping clinicians better understand the disease mechanisms and influencing factors. The wide availability of decision trees in clinical research makes it more feasible to mine disease risk factors. Therefore, a decision tree model is constructed to predict the risk of cognitive impairment.

Keywords: Decision tree model · Cerebral small vessel disease · vitamin B12 · cognitive function

Cerebral small vessel disease (CSVD) is a chronic pathological condition affecting the small blood vessels in the brain and is more prevalent among the elderly. Its incidence increases with age, and it is associated with high morbidity and disability rates [1]. CSVD lacks specific clinical symptoms and progresses insidiously, potentially leading to lacunar infarction, cerebral hemorrhage, and subcortical white matter lesions, making it a significant contributor to cognitive dysfunction [2]. The cognitive impairments associated with CSVD present with diverse clinical manifestations and are often misdiagnosed as age-related neurodegenerative changes. This diagnostic challenge delays appropriate intervention and significantly compromises patients' quality of life [3]. With the increasing integration and effectiveness of computer technology in the medical field [4], there is a growing demand for more advanced data analysis methods. Therefore, it is crucial to identify relevant factors that can aid in the diagnosis and prediction of cognitive dysfunction in CSVD patients, enabling timely and targeted preventive or therapeutic interventions. Vitamin B12 is an essential nutrient for human health. Evidence suggests that vitamin B12 (VitB12) plays a critical role in maintaining nervous system integrity, and its deficiency may result in neurological symptoms such as sensory disturbances and memory impairment [5]. The decision tree model has been widely applied in the medical field, where it can identify key influencing factors, visualize relationships among

S. S. Ge et al. (Eds.): ICSR + BioMed 2025, LNAI 16435, pp. 12–22, 2026.
https://doi.org/10.1007/978-981-95-7538-1_2

variables, and assist in predicting clinical outcomes [6, 7]. However, its application in predicting cognitive dysfunction among elderly CSVD patients remains limited. In light of this gap, the present study focuses on investigating the association between VitB12 levels and cognitive function in elderly CSVD patients and constructing a decision tree model to predict the risk of cognitive dysfunction. The findings are reported below.

1 Objects and Methods

1.1 Subjects

A cross-sectional study was conducted, involving data from 114 patients diagnosed with cerebral small vessel disease (CSVD) who were admitted to the hospital between October 2022 and October 2024. The inclusion criteria were as follows: ① diagnosis in accordance with established guidelines [8]; ② age of 65 years or older; ③ clear consciousness and willingness to participate in cognitive function assessments; ④ provision of informed consent by the patient or their legal guardian. The exclusion criteria were as follows: ① presence of cardiogenic cerebral embolism or large intracranial artery occlusion; ② leukoaraiosis caused by non-vascular etiologies, such as genetic, infectious, or metabolic factors; ③ cognitive impairment resulting from non-vascular conditions, including neurosyphilis, hydrocephalus, traumatic brain injury, or brain tumors; ④ coexistence of other neurological disorders, such as Parkinson's disease or dementia; ⑤ presence of severe psychiatric or psychological disorders; ⑥ use of calcium supplements or vitamin preparations within the past three months; ⑦ recent administration of nootropic agents or immunosuppressive drugs, or a history of recent head trauma or neurosurgical procedures; ⑧ presence of malignant neoplasms; ⑨ significant hepatic or renal dysfunction.

1.2 Research Methods

General Information Baseline demographic and clinical data were systematically collected from all participants upon admission. This included demographic characteristics (e.g., gender, age, and educational level), lifestyle factors such as smoking and alcohol consumption, as well as medical histories of diabetes mellitus, coronary artery disease, and hypertension.

Cognitive Function All patients underwent cognitive assessment using the Mini-Mental State Examination (MMSE) [9], a standardized tool with a maximum score of 30. Cognitive impairment was defined using specific cutoff scores based on educational background: a score below 24 for individuals who completed junior high school, below 20 for those with only primary school education, and below 17 for those without any formal schooling. Furthermore, the Montreal Cognitive Assessment (MoCA) [10], which has a maximum score of 30, was also utilized. In this assessment, a score lower than 26 was considered indicative of cognitive impairment.

Activities of Daily Living (ADL) Functional status was evaluated using the ADL scale [11], which comprises 14 items. A total score exceeding 20 was considered indicative of impaired daily living ability, with higher scores reflecting greater functional disability. The internal consistency of the scale, as indicated by Cronbach's α coefficient, was 0.911, and its validity was reported as 0.845.

Laboratory Measurements On the morning of the second day following admission, a 5 mL sample of fasting venous blood was collected from each patient. The blood samples were centrifuged at 3000 revolutions per minute (radius: 10 cm) for 10 min to separate the serum, which was subsequently stored at appropriate conditions until analysis. Serum levels of total cholesterol (TC), aspartate aminotransferase (AST), triglycerides (TG), low-density lipoprotein cholesterol (LDL-C), alanine aminotransferase (ALT), high-density lipoprotein cholesterol (HDL-C), homocysteine (Hcy), and fasting blood glucose (FBG) were measured using an automatic biochemical analyzer (Ai2000; Chongqing PuMen ChuangBao Biotechnology Co., Ltd., registration number: Yum Mechanical registration standards 20232220139). Creatinine (Cr) levels were determined via immunoturbidimetric assay. Serum vitamin B12 concentrations were analyzed using an automatic chemiluminescence immunoassay analyzer. A serum vitamin B12 level below 180 pg/mL was classified as low, while a level of 180 pg/mL or higher was considered normal [12].

1.3 Cognitive Function Assessment and Grouping Methodology

Upon admission, all patients underwent cognitive function assessment using the Mini-Mental State Examination (MMSE) [9]. According to the MMSE scoring results, the participants were categorized into two groups: a cognitive impairment group ($n = 71$, 62.28%) and a cognitively normal group ($n = 43$, 37.72%). The severity of cognitive impairment was further classified based on the Montreal Cognitive Assessment (MoCA) scores as follows: mild cognitive impairment (21–25 points), moderate cognitive impairment (15–20 points), and severe cognitive impairment (< 15 points). The internal consistency of the scale, as measured by Cronbach's α coefficient, was 0.905, indicating high reliability, and the construct validity was reported at 0.873.

1.4 Statistical Methods

Shapiro-Wilk normal distribution was used to test the normality of measurement data. Measurement data that followed a normal distribution were presented as mean ± standard deviation (±s). For comparisons between independent groups, an independent samples t-test was applied, while a paired t-test was used for within-group comparisons. Data with skewed distributions were described using medians and interquartile ranges [M (P25, P75)]. To compare two independent groups, the Mann-Whitney U test was employed, and the Wilcoxon signed-rank test was used for paired comparisons within the same group. Categorical data were expressed as frequency and percentage (n (%)), and the chi-square test was used for analysis. Logistic regression analysis was conducted to assess the impact of various factors on the presence of cognitive dysfunction in patients with Cerebral Small Vessel Disease (CSVD). Classification and regression tree (CART) nodes were used to generate a decision tree model of cognitive dysfunction in CSVD patients. Parameter setting: (1) Gini coefficient was used as the classification basis; (2)

The minimum sample size of split internal nodes was 10. (3) The maximum depth of the tree is 3; (4) The minimum sample required for leaf nodes is 5; The receiver operating characteristic (ROC) curve was drawn to analyze the prediction efficiency of the decision tree model. The test level $\alpha = 0.05$.

2 Result

2.1 General Information

Compared to the normal cognitive group, the cognitive impairment group exhibited significantly higher proportions of patients with primary school education or below and those with middle and high school education. Additionally, the cognitive impairment group demonstrated higher ADL scores and serum homo cysteine (HCY) levels, as well as lower vitamin B12 (VitB12) levels ($P < 0.05$). No statistically significant differences were observed in other parameters between the two groups ($P > 0.05$). Refer to Table 1 for detailed information.

Table 1. Comparison of general data between the two groups ($\bar{x} \pm$ s/n (%)

Variables of interest		Cognitive impairment group (n = 71)	Cognitively normal group (n = 43)	U/t/χ2 value	P value
Age (years)		67.52 ± 12.03	66.05 ± 10.75	1.107	0.271
Gender	Male	41 (57.75)	21 (48.84)	0.857	0.355
	Female	30 (42.25)	22 (51.16)		
Level of education	Primary school and below	21 (29.58)	5 (11.63)	12.645	<0.001*
	Junior high school	41 (57.75)	21 (48.84)		
	College or above	9 (12.68)	17 (39.53)		
History of smoking	Have	14 (19.72)	14 (32.56)	2.383	0.123
	No	57 (80.28)	29 (67.44)		
History of alcohol consumption	Have	19 (26.76)	13 (30.23)	0.160	0.689
	No	52 (73.24)	30 (69.77)		
Hypertension	Have	33 (46.48)	25 (58.14)	1.457	0.227
	No	38 (53.52)	18 (41.86)		
Coronary heart disease	Have	7 (9.86)	2 (4.65)	0.411	0.521
	No	64 (90.14)	41 (95.35)		
diabetes	Have	11 (15.49)	7 (16.28)	0.012	0.911
	No	60 (84.51)	36 (83.72)		
ADL (score)		[19.00 (18.00, 21.00)]	[17.00 (16.00, 19.00)]	4.262	<0.001*
TC (mmol/L)		3.89 ± 0.92	4.14 ± 1.05	1.343	0.182

(continued)

Table 1. *(continued)*

Variables of interest	Cognitive impairment group (n = 71)	Cognitively normal group (n = 43)	U/t/χ2 value	P value
TG (mmol/L)	[1.10 (0.83, 1.33)]	[1.25 (0.82, 1.79)]	1.085	0.278
LDL-C (mmol/L)	2.16 ± 0.77	2.46 ± 0.83	1.997	0.053
HDL-C (mmol/L)	1.19 ± 0.39	1.15 ± 0.37	0.623	0.528
FBG (mmol/L)	[4.66 (4.21, 5.35)]	[4.56 (4.15, 5.25)]	0.763	0.445
AST (U/L)	[21.00 (18.00, 25.00)]	[20.00 (17.00, 27.00)]	0.047	0.963
ALT (U/L)	[16.00 (13.00, 25.00)]	[17.00 (14.00, 23.00)]	0.662	0.508
Cr (μmol/L)	[105.00 (103.00, 107.00)]	[106.00 (103.00, 108.00)]	0.696	0.486
Hcy (μmol/L)	21.47 ± 3.35	18.41 ± 3.12	4.856	<0.001*
VitB12 (pmol/mL)	152.34 ± 23.64	175.47 ± 24.81	4.969	<0.001*

2.2 MoCA Score

The cognitive impairment group showed significantly lower scores in all cognitive domains as well as in the overall cognitive assessment compared to the group with normal cognition ($P < 0.05$). Refer to Table 2 for details.

Table 2. Comparison of cognitive domain scores of MoCA between the two groups (total score, ± s)

Group of groups	Cognitive impairment group (n = 71)	Cognitively normal group (n = 43)	t/U value	P value
Visuospatial and executive functions	[2.00 (1.00, 3.00)]	[4.00 (3.00, 5.00)]	5.801	<0.001*
Naming	[2.00 (1.00, 3.00)]	[3.00 (2.00, 3.00)]	3.406	<0.001*
Force of calculation	[2.00 (1.00, 3.00)]	[3.00 (3.00, 3.00)]	4.479	<0.001*
Attention to attention	[2.00 (1.00, 3.00)]	[3.00 (3.00, 3.00)]	4.978	<0.001*
Language	[1.00 (0.00, 2.00)]	[3.00 (2.00, 3.00)]	5.402	<0.001*
Abstract	[0.00 (0.00, 1.00)]	[1.00 (1.00, 2.00)]	4.112	<0.001*
Delayed recall	[0.00 (0.00, 1.00)]	[3.00 (0.00, 4.00)]	5.022	<0.001*
Force of orientation	[4.00 (2.00, 3.00)]	[6.00 (5.00, 6.00)]	6.476	<0.001*
Total score	15.13 ± 5.87	24.12 ± 3.48	9.114	<0.001*

2.3 Comparison of Vitamin B12 Concentrations in Patients with Different Degrees of Cognitive Impairment

Patients were categorized into two groups based on their vitamin B12 (VitB12) levels: 65 cases (57.02%) with low concentrations and 49 cases (42.98%) with high concentrations. According to the Montreal Cognitive Assessment (MoCA) scores, 114 patients were further classified into three cognitive categories: 18 cases (15.79%) with normal cognition, 59 cases (51.75%) with mild to moderate cognitive impairment, and 37 cases (32.46%) with severe cognitive impairment. Higher VitB12 levels were predominantly observed in patients with normal cognition and those with mild to moderate cognitive impairment, whereas lower levels were more commonly found in patients with severe cognitive impairment ($P < 0.05$). Refer to Table 3 for detailed information.

Table 3. Comparison of vitamin B12 concentrations in different degrees of cognitive impairment [n (%)]

Group of groups	Cognitively normal (n = 18)	Mild to moderate cognitive impairment (n = 59)	Severe cognitive impairment (n = 37)
VitB12 Low concentration group (n = 65)	4 (22.22)	34 (57.63)	27 (72.97)
VitB12 High concentration group (n = 49)	14 (77.78)	25 (42.37)	10 (23.26)
$\chi2$ value	3.309		
P value	0.001*		

2.4 Comparison of Cognitive Domains of MoCA in Patients with Different Vitamin B12 Concentrations

Compared with the high vitamin B12 concentration group, the low vitamin B12 concentration group had significantly lower scores of visual space and executive function, calculation power and attention, and delayed recall ($P < 0.05$), and there were no significant differences in the scores of other dimensions between the two groups ($P > 0.05$). Refer to Table 4 for detailed information.

Table 4. Comparison of cognitive domains of MoCA in patients with different vitamin B12 concentrations (±s)

Group of groups	VitB12 Low concentration group (n = 52)	VitB12 High concentration group (n = 62)	U value	P value
Visuospatial and executive functions	[2.00 (1.00, 2.00)]	[2.00 (2.00, 4.00)]	2.816	0.005*
Naming	[3.00 (2.00, 3.00)]	[3.00 (2.00, 3.00)]	0.216	0.829

(continued)

Table 4. *(continued)*

Group of groups	VitB12 Low concentration group (n = 52)	VitB12 High concentration group (n = 62)	U value	P value
Force of calculation	[3.00 (1.00, 3.00)]	[3.00 (2.50, 3.00)]	2.594	0.011*
Attention to attention	[2.00 (1.00, 3.00)]	[3.00 (2.00, 3.00)]	2.527	0.009*
Language	[0.50 (2.00, 2.00)]	[2.00 (1.00, 3.00)]	0.595	0.552
Abstract	[1.00 (0.00, 2.00)]	[1.00 (0.00, 2.00)]	0.894	0.371
Delayed recall	[0.00 (0.00, 2.00)]	[1.00 (0.00, 3.00)]	2.347	0.019*
Force of orientation	[5.00 (3.00, 5.00)]	[5.00 (4.00, 6.00)]	0.040	0.968

2.5 Analysis of Influencing Factors of Cognitive Dysfunction in CSVD Patients

The cognitive function of CSVD patients was used as the dependent variable (" 0 " = normal cognitive group," 1 " = cognitive impairment group), and the variables with statistically significant differences in Table 1 were used as independent variables (continuous variables: ADL, Hcy, VitB12; Categorical variables: education level: "2" = primary school OR below, "1" = junior high school, "0" = college or above). Logistic regression analysis showed that primary school or below, junior high school education level, ADL, and high Hcy concentration were risk factors for cognitive impairment in patients with CSVD ($OR > 1$, $P < 0.05$). High concentration was a protective factor ($OR < 1$, $P < 0.05$). See Table 5.

Table 5. Analysis of influencing factors of cognitive dysfunction in CSVD patients

Related factors	β	Standard error	Wald$\chi 2$	P value	OR	95% Confidence interval
ADL	0.338	0.110	9.435	0.002*	1.402	1.130–1.740
Junior high school	1.509	0.652	5.355	0.021*	4.524	1.260–16.249
Primary school and below	2.074	0.847	5.993	0.014*	7.956	1.512–41.866
Hcy	– 0.043	0.012	13.735	<0.001*	0.958	0.937–0.980
VitB12	0.279	0.087	10.182	<0.001*	1.322	1.114–1.569
Constant quantity	– 5.520	2.989	3.410	0.065	–	–

2.6 Decision Tree Model of Factors Affecting Cognitive Dysfunction in CSVD Patients

These identified influencing factors were incorporated into the development of a decision tree model, in which four explanatory variables—ADL, Hcy, vitamin B12, and education level—were selected, there are 4 layers and 8 nodes in total, Among these, vitamin B12 was identified as the most important root node variable and predictor.(see Fig. 1).

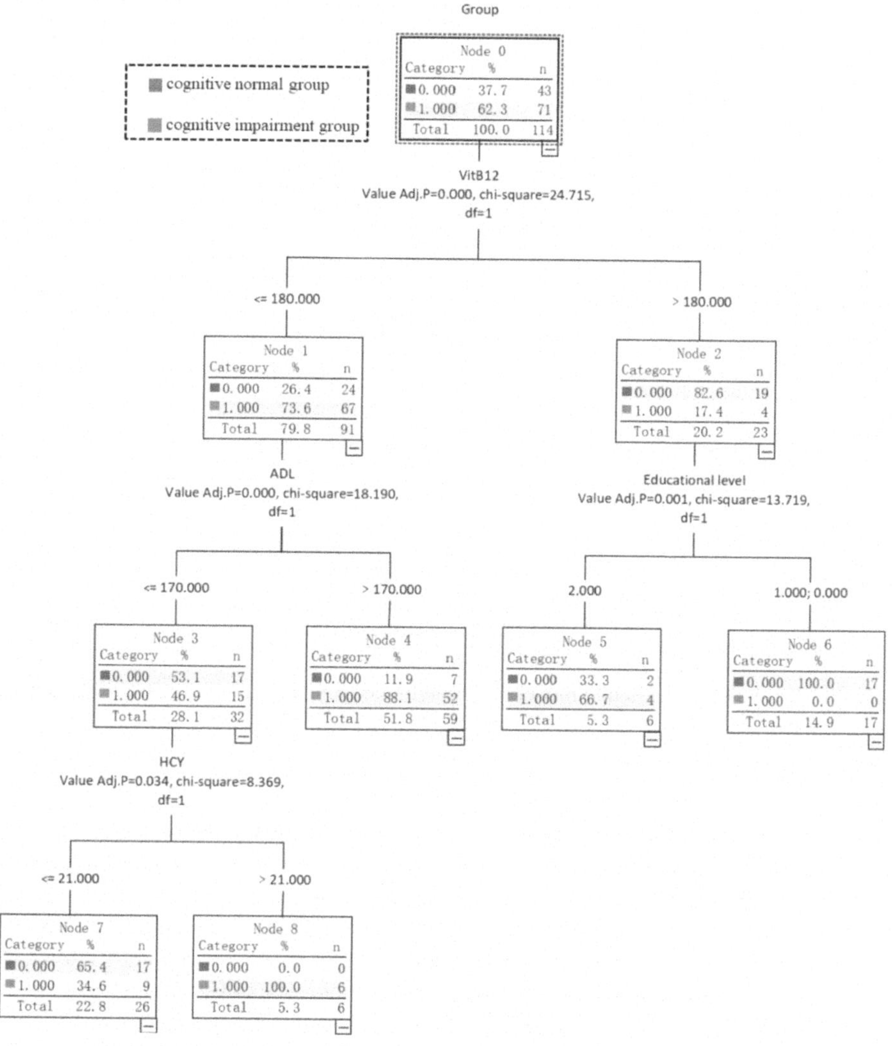

Fig. 1. Decision tree model affecting cognitive dysfunction in CSVD patients

The model demonstrated an AUC of 0.896 (95% confidence interval: 0.833–0.960, $P < 0.001$), with a sensitivity of 0.859 and a specificity of 0.837. The Youden index was calculated as 0.696 (refer to Fig. 2).

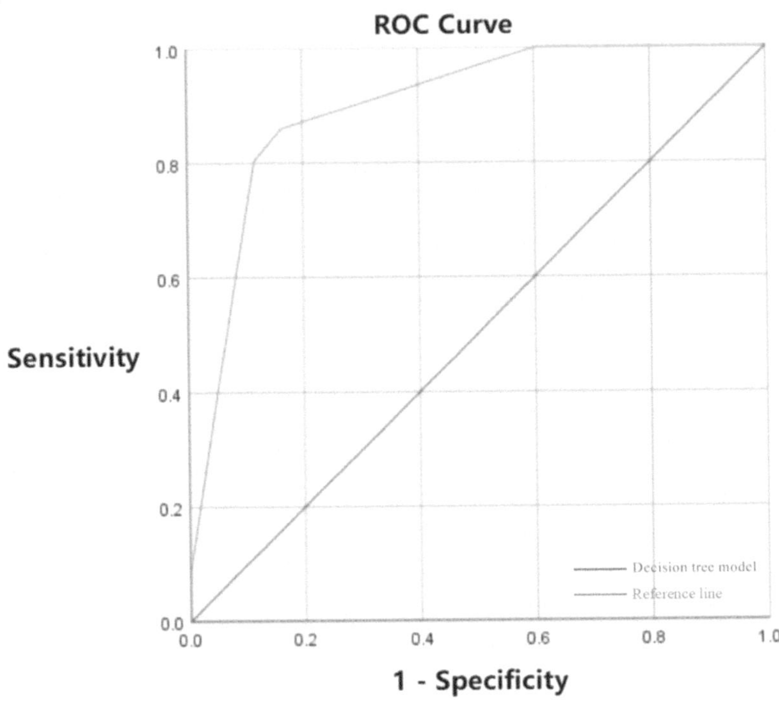

Fig. 2. ROC curve of decision tree model for predicting cognitive dysfunction in CSVD patients

3 Discussion

The decision tree model has gained extensive application in the medical domain, enabling the identification of key influencing factors, the visualization of variable interactions, and the prediction of clinical outcomes. However, its use in studying cognitive decline among older adults with cerebral small vessel disease (CSVD) remains limited.With the accelerating aging of the population in China and changes in work and dietary habits, the number of related risk factors has increased, and the incidence of CSVD has been on the rise year by year [13]. There is an urgent need for efficient data analysis methods to screen for risk factors causing cognitive dysfunction and for early prevention. CSVD is insidious in its early stage and is easily overlooked. As the disease progresses, insufficient blood supply to the brain tissue leads to brain tissue damage and loss of brain cell function, which in turn causes cognitive dysfunction [14]. In this study, 71 patients with CSVD had cognitive dysfunction, with an incidence rate of 62.28%, indicating a high risk of cognitive dysfunction caused by CSVD. If the risk factors for cognitive dysfunction can be detected early and effective measures taken, the incidence of cognitive dysfunction can be reduced.

Therefore, establishing an effective prediction model for early screening of cognitive impairment is of great significance for improving the quality of life of patients and formulating personalized intervention measures. As a classic classification and prediction method, the decision tree algorithm has advantages in predicting cognitive dysfunction, such as intuitive output structure, simple and clear tree structure generated by the decision tree algorithm, which is easy for medical staff to understand and use, flexible data types, the algorithm can handle various types of data, including continuous variables and categorical variables, strong adaptability, high classification accuracy, and the ability to handle multicollinearity problems and improve prediction accuracy. Previous studies mostly used regression analysis methods, focusing on the independent effect of individual factors. However, the decision tree algorithm can present the interaction of multiple factors and comprehensively evaluate the overall predictive performance of the model. By determining key predictive indicators and combining the decision tree algorithm, we can more effectively predict the risk of cognitive dysfunction in patients with CSVD, perform risk stratification, and provide support for clinical decision-making and optimize treatment plans for patients.

In summary, patients with low serum Vitamin B12 levels exhibit more severe cognitive dysfunction. Educational attainment, Activities of Daily Living (ADL) scores, Vitamin B12, and Homocysteine (HCY) levels are identified as significant factors influencing cognitive impairment in patients with Cerebral Small Vessel Disease (CSVD). The decision tree model constructed based on these factors enables risk stratification for cognitive impairment, facilitating early and rapid screening of such patients, which will assist clinicians in better utilizing data for medical prediction and decision support. This study identified four explanatory variables: ADL, Hcy, Vitamin B12, and educational level, with Vitamin B12 being the most critical root node variable and predictor. The model achieved an AUC of 0.896, indicating that the decision tree based on these factors has excellent predictive value. However, as this study is a cross-sectional investigation with a relatively small sample size, the model's representativeness and generalizability require further evaluation. Additionally, the inclusion of influencing factors is not yet comprehensive, lacking elements such as imaging data, long-term dietary habits, and carotid ultrasound findings. Future research should involve multicenter, large-sample studies, along with external validation and adjustments to enhance the model's predictive performance, thereby further aiding clinicians in leveraging data for medical prediction and decision support.

Acknowledgments. This study was funded by Shaanxi Provincial Key Research and Development Program Project (2023-YBSF-569); Shaanxi Provincial Key Research and Development Project (2023-YBSF-033).

Disclosure of Interests. The authors have no competing interests to declare that are relevant to the content of this article.

References

1. Chojdak-Łukasiewicz, J., Dziadkowiak, E., Zimny, A., et al.: Cerebral small vessel disease: a review. Adv Clin Exp Med **30**(3), 349–356 (2021)

2. Markus, H.S., de Leeuw, F.E.: Cerebral small vessel disease: recent advances and future directions. Int. J. Stroke **18**(1), 4–14 (2023)
3. Zanon Zotin, M.C., Sveikata, L., Viswanathan, A., et al.: Cerebral small vessel disease and vascular cognitive impairment: from diagnosis to management. Curr. Opin. Neurol. **34**(2), 246–257 (2021)
4. Zhang, H., Jiao, L., Yang, S., et al.: Brain-computer interfaces: the innovative key to unlocking neurological conditions. Int. J. Surg. **110**(9), 5745–5762 (2024)
5. Markun, S., Gravestock, I., Jäger, L., et al.: Effects of Vitamin B12 supplementation on cognitive function, depressive symptoms, and fatigue:a systematic review, meta-analysis, and meta-regression. Nutrients **13**(3), 923 (2021)
6. Rasouli, S., Dakkali, M.S., Ghazvini, A., et al.: Predictive model for converting optic neuritis to multiple sclerosis; decision tree in focus. PLoS ONE **19**(12), e0309702 (2024)
7. Kuang, J., Zhang, P., Cai, T., et al.: Prediction of transition from mild cognitive impairment to Alzheimer's disease based on a logistic regression-artificial neural network-decision tree model. Geriatr. Gerontol. Int. **21**(1), 43–47 (2021)
8. Chinese Society of Neurology, Chinese Society of Neurology Cerebrovascular Disease Group, Yining, H., et al.: Guidelines for the diagnosis and treatment of cerebral small vessel disease in China 2020. Chin. J. Neurol. **55**(8), 807–818 (2022)
9. Jia, X., Wang, Z., Huang, F., et al.: A comparison of the mini-mental state examination (MMSE) with the montreal cognitive assessment (MoCA) for mild cognitive impairment screening in Chinese middle-aged and older population:a cross-sectional study. BMC Psychiatry **21**(1), 485 (2021)
10. Kang, J.M., Cho, Y.S., Park, S., et al.: Montreal cognitive assessment reflects cognitive reserve. BMC Geriatr. **18**(1), 261 (2018)
11. Mlinac, M.E., Feng, M.C.: Assessment of activities of daily living, self-care, and independence. Arch. Clin. Neuropsychol. **31**(6), 506–516 (2016)
12. Obeid, R., Andrès, E., Češka, R., et al.: Diagnosis, treatment and long-term management of Vitamin B12 deficiency in adults: a Delphi expert consensus. J. Clin. Med. **13**(8), 2176 (2024)
13. Dupré, N., Drieu, A., Joutel, A.: Pathophysiology of cerebral small vessel disease: a journey through recent discoveries. J. Clin. Invest. **134**(10), e172841 (2024)
14. Yang, X.L., Guo, Y., Chen, S.F., et al.: Cerebral small vessel disease is associated with motor, cognitive, and emotional dysfunction in multiple system atrophy. J. Parkinsons Dis. **13**(7), 1239–1252 (2023)

Apply Human Factors in the Full Life Cycle Design of Wrist Rehabilitation Robot

Donglai Lu[1], Weiwei Yu[1(✉)], Sixiang Fei[2], and Abderraouf Benali[3]

[1] School of Mechanical Engineering, Northwestern Polytechnical University, Xi'an 710072, China
yuweiwei@nwpu.edu.cn

[2] Hebei University of Technology, Tianjin, China

[3] Laboratoire d'Ingénierie Systèmes Versailles, Université de Versailles Saint Quentin en Yvelines, Paris, France

Abstract. Stroke patients often have upper limb dysfunction, and the wrist, critical for dexterity and daily life, needs targeted rehabilitation. Robot-assisted rehabilitation outperforms traditional therapist-led training as it avoids reliance on therapists' experience/skills, offers personalized programs per patient, and logs full-cycle data to evaluate rehabilitation. Yet existing robots focus on arm movement, ignoring the wrist's unique physiological and motor traits, and lack full-stage integration in structure, control, and interface. To solve these issues, this paper proposes the NPU-Wrist, a wrist rehabilitation robot integrating human factors and ergonomics, with a robot structure, control methods and interactive system. It adjusts to users' hand, wrist, and forearm size, offering targeted training for patients in different rehabilitation stages (early, middle, late). A pilot study evaluated its usability, and results confirm its good ergonomics, comfort, and safety, satisfying personalized wrist rehabilitation needs.

Keywords: wrist rehabilitation training · human factors · wrist rehabilitation robot

1 Introduction

In rehabilitation medicine, limb motor dysfunction impacts daily life, with many stroke patients suffering from upper limb dysfunction [1,2]. As the wrist is key for dexterous movements and daily life, targeted wrist rehabilitation is vital for regaining motor abilities and independence.

Per Brunnstrom theory, stroke rehabilitation has three stages (early: passive, middle: assisted, late: resistance training) [3–7]. Robot-assisted rehabilitation outperforms traditional therapist-assisted training: it is unaffected by therapists' experience/skills, provides personalized programs per patient status, and records full-cycle data for rehabilitation evaluation [8–10].

S. S. Ge et al. (Eds.): ICSR + BioMed 2025, LNAI 16435, pp. 23–34, 2026.
https://doi.org/10.1007/978-981-95-7538-1_3

To design full-stage rehabilitation robots, human factors are integrated into: 1) mechanical structure (e.g., lightweight/portable/safe design) [11–13]; 2) control modes (e.g., EMG-based safety for passive training, trajectory tracking for active/assisted switching, impedance control for force feedback, position-based resistance) [14–17]; 3) interfaces (e.g., CIL visual interface via participatory design, ergonomics+VR) [18,19]. However, existing robots focus on arm movement, ignoring wrist's individual physiological/motor differences [20–22], and lack full-stage integration into structure/control/interface for personalized needs.

In summary, this paper addresses stroke patients' full-stage personalized wrist rehabilitation needs, integrates human factors into robot structure/control/interface, designs the NPU-WRIST system, and conducts feasibility experiments.

2 Case Study

2.1 Mechanical Structure

The Mechanical Structure Introduction for the NPU-Wrist. This paper's wrist rehabilitation robot mechanical structure has: base, elbow support, wrist support and handle (see Fig. 1). Considering individual differences in hand, wrist and forearm sizes, its elbow support, wrist support and handle are adjustable to fit different users' limb sizes and wrist movement axis spacing, meeting adaptability needs. To use, place it on a suitable-height plane, grasp the handle (via wrist support), rest the arm on elbow support, adjust the structure to fit the user's wrist, then start rehabilitation activities.

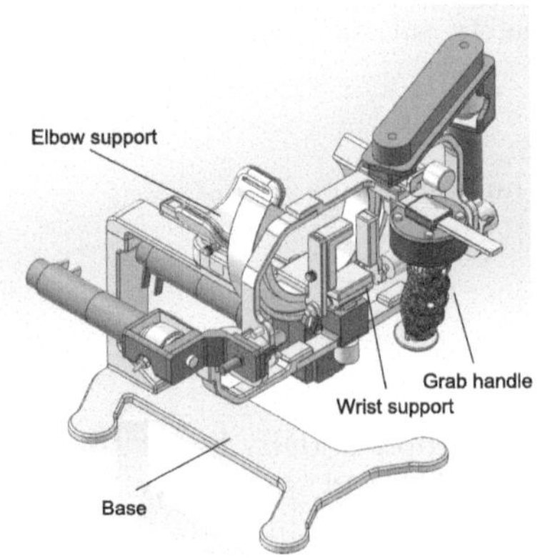

(a) Mechanical structure of the NPU-Wrist

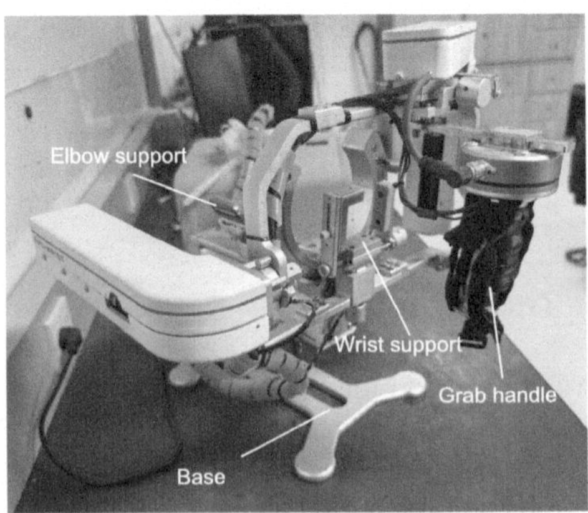

(b) Physical product of the NPU-Wrist

Fig. 1. Mechanical structure and physical product of the NPU-Wrist.

Based on human wrist anatomical structure and motor characteristic studies, any complex wrist movement can be decomposed into three basic forms: flexion-extension, radial-ulnar deviation, and pronation-supination. To achieve auxiliary movement rehabilitation, the wrist rehabilitation robot's mechanical structure simulates wrist motion with three active degrees of freedom, each with activity angles matching normal wrist range. Besides, it supports single- and multi-degree-of-freedom coupled motion to enhance motor function for rehabilitation needs.

Elbow Adjustment Mechanism Design with Anthropometric Factors. The function of the elbow adjustment mechanism is to adjust the spatial position of the elbow cushion, and its model is shown in Fig. 2a. The elbow cushion in the figure is used to lift the user's elbow, and the elbow adjustment mechanism is installed on the base, as shown in Fig. 2b. The base mainly plays the function of supporting the entire wrist rehabilitation robot.

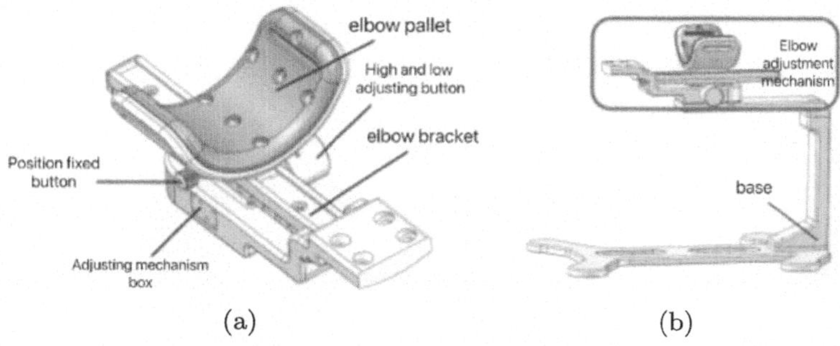

Fig. 2. Elbow adjustment mechanism.

Anthropometric data show that forearm length and diameter vary among individuals, so the wrist rehabilitation robot's elbow contact position needs adjustment. The robot's designed elbow adjustment mechanism has a two-degree-of-freedom adjustable elbow pad.

Horizontally, the pad moves in the bracket slide rail's chute and is fixed via a knob matching the rail's position holes, adapting to forearm length. Vertically, it is displaced and fixed by rotating a height-adjustment knob, fitting forearm diameter. The adjustment's transmission structure is enclosed in the mechanism box.

The elbow adjustment mechanism box's internal structure is shown in Figs. 3a and 3b. Pulling the height-adjustment knob outward separates clutches A and B; turning the knob then makes the spur gear drive the cylindrical rack for vertical displacement, adjusting the elbow bracket's height. To fix the bracket's height, push the knob inward to engage clutches A and B. This design enables the wrist rehabilitation robot to fit users with different forearm sizes.

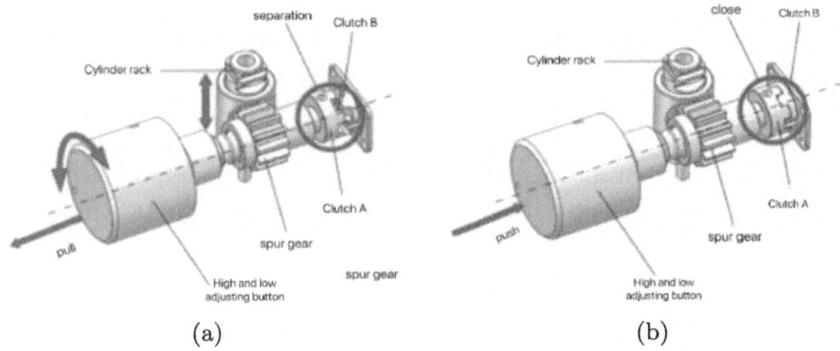

Fig. 3. Mechanism regulating box.

Design of Handle Structure Considering Human-Machine Interaction Comfort. The handle, contacting the hand for human-computer interaction perception and assisting wrist rehabilitation training, has a link structure slidable in flexion/extension to adjust the distance between handle and flexion axes, adapting to and measuring the user's hand length (Fig. 4a).

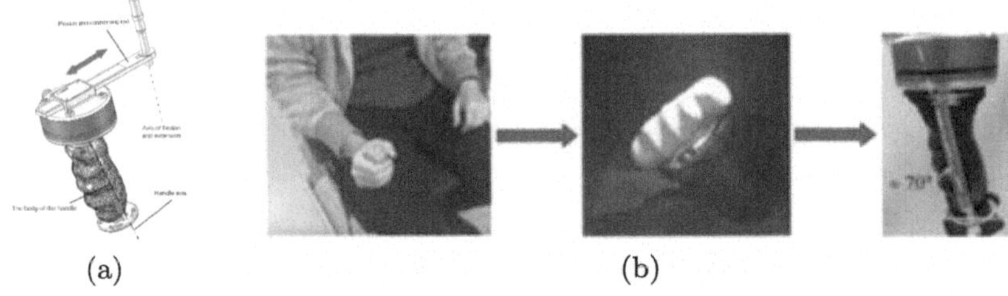

Fig. 4. Handle structure (a) and design process (b) of the Handle.

As the handle contacts the human body for a long time during training, its structural rationality affects users' subjective feelings. To enhance emotional acceptance and rehabilitation enthusiasm, the handle's main structure is designed per Fig. 4b: 1) Select subjects with average hand size (anthropometry) to grasp rod-shaped plasticine (left/right hand alternately) at 60% max grip force repeatedly until comfortable; 2) 3D-scan the indented plasticine for its 3D model; 3) Mold the plasticine, then make the handle's silica gel grip with an internal metal frame.

2.2 Control Algorithm

Different rehabilitation training modes have distinct purposes. Specifically, passive rehabilitation training should incorporate wrist anatomy and functional movement characteristics of the human wrist; assisted training needs to focus on users' movement intentions; resistance training aims to enhance muscle strength, endurance, and coordination.

DTM-Based Control Method for Passive Training. This study emphasizes integrating Dart Thrower's Motion (DTM) laws with rehabilitation robots. First, after identifying DTM angle change rules, the robot system incorporates these into trajectory planning for passive wrist rehabilitation.

A full training cycle trajectory is divided into 8 segments with 9 process points, considering factors like wrist angle ranges and DTM laws. The relationship between process point angles and time is shown in Fig. 5a.

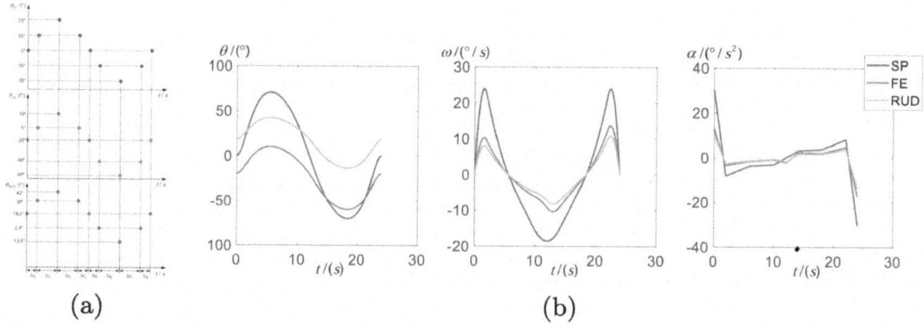

Fig. 5. DTM process points (a) and Multi-DOF coupled passive rehabilitation training trajectory based on wrist DTM motion law (b).

SP, FE, and RUD in the Fig. 5 represent supination-pronation, flexion-extension, and radial-ulnar deviation angles. Continuous cubic polynomial functions are established to solve unknowns. The multi-DOF coupled passive training trajectory based on DTM is shown in Fig. 5b, with different colored curves for angle, angular velocity, and acceleration of SP, FE, and RUD, all continuous.

Practical user needs vary (e.g., movement range, speed). Adjustments are made by modifying angles of the 9 process points based on individual wrist ranges.

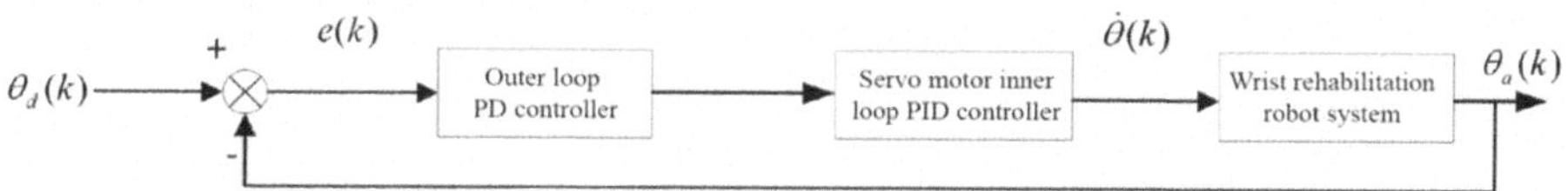

Fig. 6. Position control block diagram with an outer-loop PD controller.

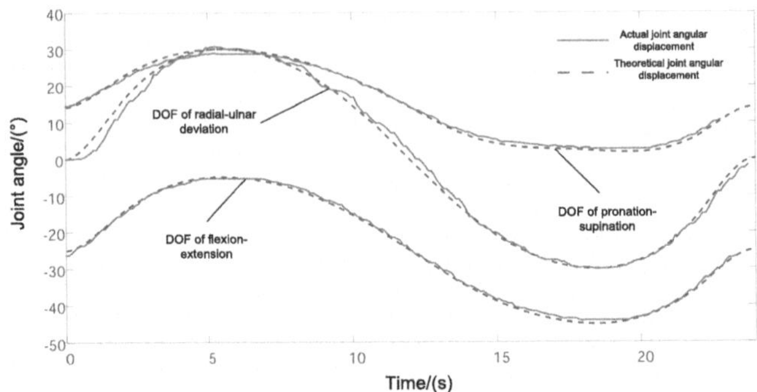

Fig. 7. Ideal trajectory tracking situation with an outer-loop PD controller.

For passive mode, servo motors are used in speed mode (due to better tracking than position mode and lower workload than torque mode). The control block diagram is in Fig. 6: error $e(k)$ between desired $\theta_d(k)$ and actual $\theta_a(k)$ is input to an outer PD controller, driving the robot with angular velocity $\theta(k)$. Ideal trajectory tracking in speed mode is shown in Fig. 7.

2.3 Assistive Training Control Method

For patients in the middle stage of stroke rehabilitation, although they have initially acquired independent motor ability, their muscle strength remains relatively weak; therefore, assistive training is necessary. The key to this assistance lies in enabling the robot to recognize the wrist movement intention, achieve compliant following, and provide assistive force. The 6-axis force sensor equipped on

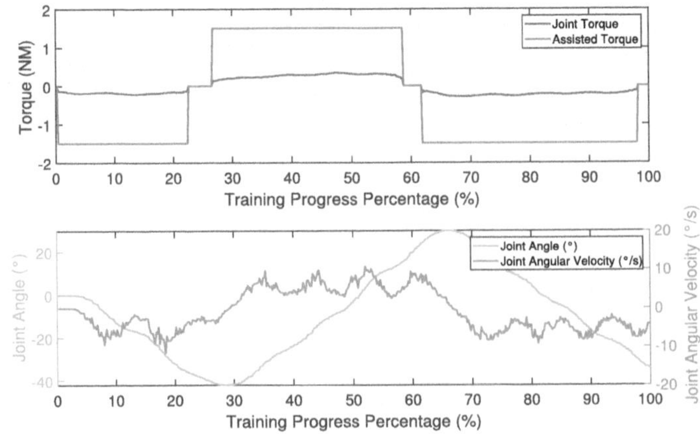

Fig. 8. Results of assistive training. Red: Wrist torque; Blue: Robot assistive torque; Yellow: Joint angle; Green: Joint velocity. (Color figure online)

the NPU-Wrist handle is used to recognize the force and torque exerted by the wrist on the handle. Subsequently, through admittance control, these force and torque signals are converted into the speed and position signals of the motor, as shown in Eq. 1.

$$\mathbf{B}_{\Delta}\dot{\boldsymbol{\theta}} + \mathbf{K}_{\Delta}\boldsymbol{\theta} = \mathbf{J}^{T}\,{}^{0}_{4}\mathbf{R}\boldsymbol{F} + \boldsymbol{T}_{assisted} \tag{1}$$

In Eq. 1, $\boldsymbol{F}$ denotes the force and torque collected by the sensor, while $\boldsymbol{T}_{assisted}$ is the assistive torque. The specific algorithm for the assistive torque is as shown in Eq. 2, and the result of assistive training is shown in Fig. 8.

$$\boldsymbol{T}_{assisted} = Gain/sign(\mathbf{J}^{T}\,{}^{0}_{4}\mathbf{R}\boldsymbol{F}) \tag{2}$$

2.4 Resistance Training Control Method

For patients in the late stage of rehabilitation, their motor function has recovered to a certain extent, allowing them to independently complete basic wrist joint movement such as flexion-extension. However, they still have problems of weak muscle strength and insufficient stability in motor control, making it difficult to bear the training load of conventional intensity. Therefore, Resistance Training is required to gradually enhance muscle strength and improve motor control ability.

For safety, position-based impedance control is chosen. The control flow compares actual F_a and desired F_d contact forces, generates position increment ΔX via an outer impedance controller, and tracks X_d with an inner position controller.

Stiffness and inertia terms in the impedance model are omitted, using damping control (considering slow training speeds and patient autonomy). The impedance control diagram (Fig. 9) shows: $F_h(6 \times 1)$ from the user is collected by a 6D force sensor; $F_b(3 \times 1)$ and $T_b(3 \times 1)$ are decoupled via J^T to joint torques; damping controllers calculate angular velocity changes, with motor desired speed 0 (triggered by user movement).

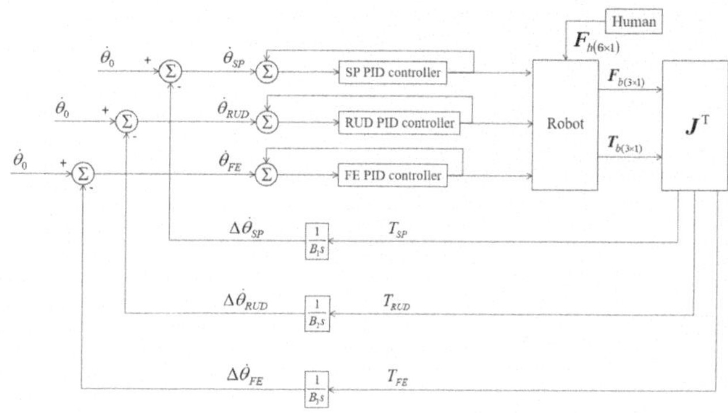

Fig. 9. Impedance control diagram.

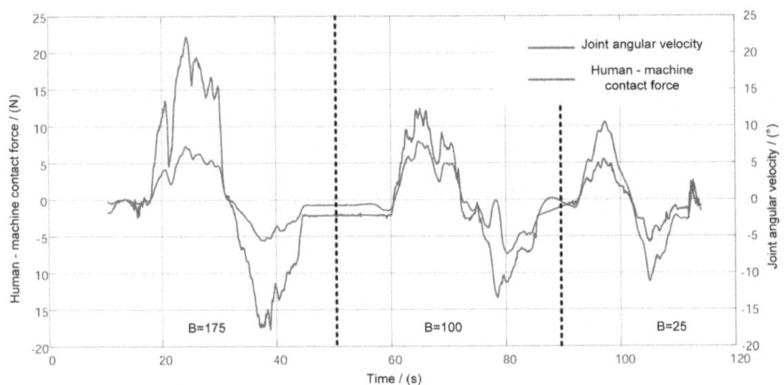

Fig. 10. Result of single degree of freedom resistance training.

The process of a subject performing single degree of freedom (flexion-extension) resistance training is shown in Fig. 10. The force application process in the figure is divided into three stages, and the damping coefficient B decreases successively in each stage, which enables the subject to drive the wrist joint rehabilitation robot with a smaller force. The result verifies the effectiveness of the established damping control algorithm.

2.5 Interactive System

This system introduces the ACT-R cognitive model (simulating human cognitive patterns to study users' cognitive characteristics of interface elements and build the interactive interface framework) and applies interface design principles to develop the human-computer interaction interface (prototype shown in Fig. 11). The interface mainly helps users control the rehabilitation robot

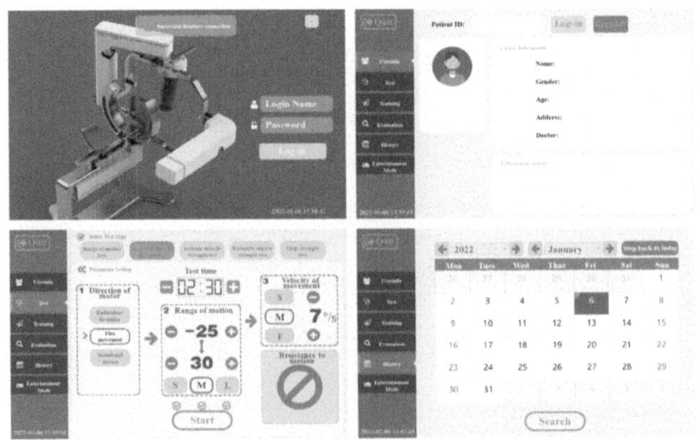

Fig. 11. Prototype interface of NPU-WRIST.

for state detection and training, with expanded functions including creating patients' health/medical records, displaying logged-in user info, accessing historical records, and adding entertainment features to reduce boredom from monotonous wrist exercises. After defining functions, an ACT-R-guided information architecture (aligned with users' cognitive traits) is designed: interaction information is divided into functional modules and detailed into low-overlap pyramid units, with balanced breadth and depth to avoid confusion, and specific interfaces (e.g., username/password login screens, main screens with entries to user info, detection, training, history, and auxiliary info) planned. Visual design covers three aspects: color & icons (simple style like light blue background with dark text for clarity, user-friendly icons), layout (divided into main/secondary menus, main display, and function module areas via Fitts' law, with tailored main display layouts for different functions), and result display (highlighting test goals such as angle limits in range-of-motion tests).

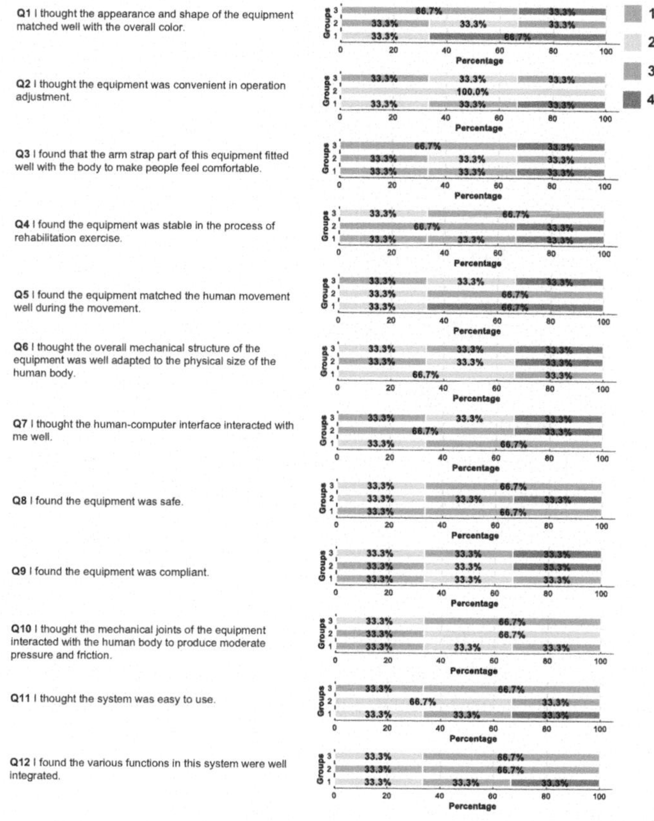

Fig. 12. The distribution of attitudes towards the same question among the three groups

2.6 Usability Verification

To evaluate the NPU-Wrist system's usability, a subjective satisfaction scale with a 5-point Likert scale (responses: "very dissatisfied" to "very satisfied") was developed, including 12 questions in interaction sequence, with 9 participants (3 per group) grouped by rehabilitation training types. Questionnaire contents and response results are shown in Fig. 12 (1–4 scores in different colors).

The boxplot in Fig. 13 shows data median and fluctuation. One-way ANOVA compared group results after normality (Shapiro-Wilk, all $P > 0.05$, normal distribution) and homogeneity of variance (Levene's, all $P > 0.05$, homogeneous) tests via SPSS. ANOVA results (Table 1) showed no significant difference between groups (F significance > 0.05).

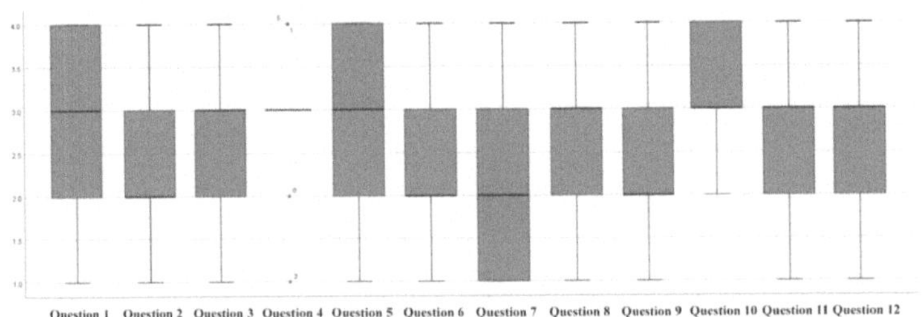

Fig. 13. Boxplot for All Data.

Table 1. ONE-WAY ANOVA

Question	F	P	Question	F	P	Question	F	P
1	2.000	0.216	5	0.583	0.587	9	0.538	0.609
2	1.500	0.296	6	0.364	0.709	10	1.400	0.317
3	1.091	0.394	7	0.176	0.842	11	0.500	0.630
4	0.444	0.661	8	0.375	0.702	12	0.375	0.702

Through analysis, it can be concluded that participants were relatively satisfied with NPU-Wrist, which indicates that the rehabilitation robot system has good ergonomics, comfort, and safety, satisfying personalized wrist rehabilitation needs.

3 Conclusion

In this paper, the design of wrist rehabilitation training robot is carried out with the deep integration of human factors. The structural design of the rehabilitation robot is based on human factors such as the motion characteristics of human wrist joint and the dynamic and static dimensions of human body. The control design is developed according to the needs of patients in different rehabilitation stages. The interactive system is constructed by combining ACT-R model and interaction design principles. Through statistical analysis, the results show that the NPU-Wrist has good adaptability, safety and comfort for patients.

Acknowledgment. This study was supported by National Foreign Expert Program (Grant No. H20251040).

References

1. Gandolfi, M., et al.: eXplainable AI allows predicting upper limb rehabilitation outcomes in sub-acute stroke patients. IEEE J. Biomed. Health Inform. **27**(1), 263–273 (2022). IEEE
2. Lawrence, E.S., Coshall, C., Dundas, R., Stewart, J., Rudd, A.G., Howard, R., Wolfe, C.D.A.: Estimates of the prevalence of acute stroke impairments and disability in a multiethnic population. Stroke, vol. 32, no. 6, pp. 1279–1284 (2001). Lippincott Williams & Wilkins
3. Shah, S.K., Harasymiw, S.J., Stahl, P.L.: Stroke rehabilitation: outcome based on Brunnstrom recovery stages. The Occupational Therapy Journal of Research, vol. 6, no. 6, pp. 365–376. SAGE Publications Sage CA: Los Angeles, CA (1986)
4. Wang, F., Zhang, D., Hu, S., Zhu, B., Han, F., Zhao, X.: Brunnstrom stage automatic evaluation for stroke patients by using multi-channel sEMG. In: 2020 42nd Annual International Conference of the IEEE Engineering in Medicine & Biology Society (EMBC), pp. 3763–3766. IEEE (2020)
5. Jeong, I.-S.: The Effects of CPM (Continuous Passive Motion) on Hand Function and Muscular Strength for Patients with Stroke. Therapeutic Science for Rehabilitation, vol. 3, no. 2, pp. 71–81. Korean Society of Neurological Occupational Therapy (2014)
6. Lee, K.W., Kim, S.B., Lee, J.H., Lee, S.J., Yoo, S.W.: Effect of upper extremity robot-assisted exercise on spasticity in stroke patients. Ann. Rehabil. Med. **40**(6), 961 (2016)
7. Harris, J.E., Eng, J.J.: Strength training improves upper-limb function in individuals with stroke: a meta-analysis. Stroke, vol. 41, no. 1, pp. 136–140. Lippincott Williams & Wilkins (2010)
8. van Dellen, F., Aurich-Schuler, T., Labruy'ere, R.: Within-and between-therapist agreement on personalized parameters for robot-assisted gait therapy: the challenge of adjusting robotic assistance. Journal of NeuroEngineering and Rehabilitation, vol. 20, no. 1, pp. 81. Springer (2023)
9. Parnandi, A., Kaku, A., Venkatesan, A., Pandit, N., Fokas, E., Yu, B., Kim, G., Nilsen, D., Fernandez-Granda, C., Schambra, H.: Data-driven quantitation of movement abnormality after stroke. Bioengineering, vol. 10, no. 6, pp. 648. MDPI (2023)
10. Yang, J., Zhu, Y., Li, H., Wang, K., Li, D., Qi, Q.: Effect of robotic exoskeleton training on lower limb function, activity and participation in stroke patients: a systematic review and meta-analysis of randomized controlled trials. Frontiers in Neurology, vol. 15, pp. 1453781. Frontiers Media SA (2024)

11. Molaei, A., Foomany, N.A., Parsapour, M., Dargahi, J.: A portable low-cost 3D-printed wrist rehabilitation robot: Design and development. Mechanism and Machine Theory, vol. 171, pp. 104719. Elsevier (2022)
12. Xu, D., Zhang, M., Xu, H., Fu, J., Li, X., Xie, S.Q.: Interactive compliance control of a wrist rehabilitation device (WReD) with enhanced training safety. J. Healthcare Eng. **2019**(1), 6537848. Wiley Online Library (2019)
13. Yellewa, M.E., Mohamed, A., Ishii, H., Assal, S.F.M.: Design and hybrid impedance control of a compliant and balanced wrist rehabilitation device. In: IECON 2022–48th Annual Conference of the IEEE Industrial Electronics Society, pp. 1–6. IEEE (2022)
14. Bae, J.-h., Hwang, S.-j., Moon, I.: Evaluation and verification of a novel wrist rehabilitation robot employing safety-related mechanism. In: 2019 IEEE 16th International Conference on Rehabilitation Robotics (ICORR), pp. 288–293. IEEE (2019)
15. Gherman, B., Banica, A., Tucan, P., Vaida, C., Antal, T., Pisla, D.: Inverse dynamic modeling of a parallel wrist rehabilitation robot towards an assistive control modality. In: 2021 25th International Conference on System Theory, Control and Computing (ICSTCC), pp. 284–289. IEEE (2021)
16. Shi, K., Song, A., Li, Y., Chen, D., Li, H.: Cable-driven 3-DOF wrist rehabilitation robot with optimized human-robot interaction performance. In: 2020 8th IEEE RAS/EMBS International Conference for Biomedical Robotics and Biomechatronics (BioRob), pp. 112–117. IEEE (2020)
17. Khor, K.X., Chin, P.J.H., Yeong, C.F., Su, E.L.M., Narayanan, A.L.T., Rahman, H.A., Khan, Q.I.: Portable and reconfigurable wrist robot improves hand function for post-stroke subjects. IEEE Trans. Neural Syst. Rehabil. Eng. **25**(10), 1864–1873. IEEE (2017)
18. Ghods, A., et al.: Iterative design of visual analytics for a clinician-in-the-loop smart home. IEEE J. Biomed. Health Inform. **23**(4), 1742–1748. IEEE (2018)
19. Zhao, Y., Liang, C., Gu, Z., Zheng, Y., Wu, Q.: A new design scheme for intelligent upper limb rehabilitation training robot. Int. J. Environ. Res. Public Health **17**(8), 2948. MDPI (2020)
20. Altamimi, A.R., et al.: Association between carpal height ratio and ulnar variance in normal wrist radiography. BMC Musculoskeletal Disorders **25**(1), 524. Springer (2024)
21. Jais, I.S.M., Wong, Y.-R., McGrouther, D.A., Leo, H.-L.: Investigating the biomechanical behaviour of tendon-loaded wrist joint using web-like kinematic network model. J. Biomech. **172**, 112210. Elsevier (2024)
22. Binder-Markey, B.I., Murray, W.M., Dewald, J.P.A.: Passive properties of the wrist and fingers following chronic hemiparetic stroke: interlimb comparisons in persons with and without a clinical treatment history that includes Botulinum Neurotoxin. Front. Neurol. **12**, 687624. Frontiers Media SA (2021)

An Optically Enhanced Nano-Sniffer Based on Au-SnO_2 for Bionic Olfaction in Biomedical Robots

Yihui Wang[1], Ting Yu[1], Huijun Yin[1], Shangyi Shen[2], Zhenqi Yang[2], Honglong Chang[1], and Haitao Zhao[1,3](✉)

[1] MOE Key Laboratory of Micro/Nano Systems for Aerospace, School of Mechanical Engineering, Northwestern Polytechnical University, Xi'an, China
zhaoht@nwpu.edu.cn
[2] Beijing Institute of Metrology, Beijing, China
[3] State Key Laboratory of Discovery and Utilization of Functional Components in Traditional Chinese Medicine, School of Pharmaceutical Science, Guizhou Medical University, Guizhou, China

Abstract. Nitrogen dioxide (NO_2), a significant atmospheric pollutant primarily emitted from combustion processes, poses substantial environmental and health risks, underscoring the critical need for accurate detection methods. Conventional metal oxide semiconductor sensors often suffer from limitations such as high operating temperatures and insufficient sensitivity. This study addresses these challenges by introducing a synergistic approach that combines noble metal modification with light excitation, enabling high-performance NO_2 detection at room temperature. Au/SnO_2 composites with hierarchical nanosheet architectures were synthesized via hydrothermal and impregnation methods, as confirmed by SEM. Their sensing properties were systematically investigated under light excitation. Among the samples tested, the 2.5 wt% Au/SnO_2 sensor demonstrated superior performance, exhibiting a remarkable response, a low detection limit, and excellent selectivity, long-term stability, and humidity tolerance at room temperature. First-principles calculations reveal that the enhanced sensor performance originates from a synergistic effect between Au nanoparticle decoration, which enhances NO_2 adsorption and charge transfer, and the additional photogenerated carriers induced by light excitation. This study provides novel material design insights for developing high efficiency room temperature NO_2 sensors.

Keywords: NO_2 gas sensor · Room temperature · Au/SnO_2 · Light excitation · First-principles calculations

1 Introduction

NO_2, as one of the primary atmospheric pollutants, not only contributes to the formation of acid rain and photochemical smog, but also poses serious threats to human health. Prolonged exposure to low concentrations of NO_2 has been linked to chronic respiratory diseases, whereas short-term exposure to high concentrations can cause acute

S. S. Ge et al. (Eds.): ICSR + BioMed 2025, LNAI 16435, pp. 35–42, 2026.
https://doi.org/10.1007/978-981-95-7538-1_4

lung injury [1, 2]. Therefore, the development of reliable NO_2 gas sensors is crucial for environmental monitoring and public health protection.

Metal oxide semiconductor sensors have been extensively studied for their cost effectiveness and robust stability [2]. Among them, tin dioxide (SnO_2), as a representative n-type semiconductor, has gained significant attention for NO_2 detection due to its high electron mobility and abundant surface active sites [3–6]. Several studies have demonstrated the NO_2 sensing capabilities of SnO_2-based materials at elevated temperatures, though their operation often requires temperatures as high as 200–300 °C. Despite these promising results, most SnO_2-based sensors reported to date require relatively high operating temperatures, which not only increase energy consumption but also shorten the lifespan of the sensing materials. Therefore, achieving high performance NO_2 detection under low temperature conditions remains a critical challenge in sensor development.

Optical excitation provides an effective strategy to lower the operating temperature of metal oxide semiconductor sensors, serving as a viable alternative to traditional thermal activation. This mechanism leverages photon energy to excite electrons into the conduction band, generating charge carriers that activate surface adsorbed oxygen species for redox reactions, thereby enabling gas sensing at lower temperatures without external heating [7–9]. Several metal oxide-based sensors have demonstrated effective room-temperature gas detection under UV or visible light, highlighting the feasibility of photoexcitation-assisted sensing.

While photoexcitation-assisted methods have enabled significant advances in room-temperature NO_2 sensing, current sensors still suffer from limited selectivity and sensitivity. To address these challenges, noble metals are widely employed as photosensitizers to enhance sensing performance, benefiting from their catalytic activity and localized surface plasmon resonance (LSPR) effects under photoexcitation. The LSPR effect of Au nanoparticles, in particular, has shown promise in improving gas sensing performance in various systems including ZnO, SnS_2, and TiO_2. However, Au/SnO_2 composites remain underexplored for NO_2 sensing applications under light activation. Given SnO_2's well-established performance as a gas sensing material and the pronounced LSPR effect of Au nanoparticles, investigating their synergistic sensing properties under light excitation is highly promising.

This work introduces a novel strategy combining Au/SnO_2 composites with blue light excitation for room-temperature NO_2 detection. Experimental results demonstrate that the Au/SnO_2 sensor exhibits excellent responses at low concentrations (1–5 ppm), along with good stability and humidity resistance at room temperature. To elucidate the sensing mechanism, first-principles calculations were employed to evaluate the adsorption energies of NO_2 molecules on SnO_2 and Au/SnO_2 surfaces, and to analyze the associated charge transfer processes.

2 Experimental Methods

2.1 A Subsection Sample

Hierarchical SnO_2 nanosheets were synthesized via a hydrothermal method. In a typical procedure, 1.0 mmol of $SnCl_4 \cdot 5H_2O$ was dissolved in 40 mL of deionized (DI) water under vigorous stirring. The solution was transferred into a 50 mL Teflon-lined stainless steel autoclave and maintained at 180 °C for 12 h. The resulting white precipitate was collected by centrifugation, washed thoroughly with DI water and ethanol, and dried at 60 °C for 12 hours. Au nanoparticles (NPs) were deposited onto the SnO_2 surface via a wet impregnation method. Aqueous solutions of $HAuCl_4$ were prepared to obtain different Au loadings (2.0, 2.5, and 3.0 wt%). The SnO_2 powder was dispersed in the precursor solution, followed by stirring for 6 h, drying at 60 °C, and annealing in air at 300 °C for 2 h to obtain the Au/SnO_2 composites.

2.2 Sensor Fabrication

The sensing layer was prepared by mixing 1 mg of the as-prepared Au/SnO_2 powder with 100 μL of DI water to form a uniform paste. This paste was carefully brushed onto a commercial gold interdigital electrode (on an alumina substrate), ensuring a thin and even coating. The coated substrate was dried in an oven at 60 °C for 2 h to remove residual moisture and improve adhesion between the sensing material and the electrode.

2.3 Gas Sensing Measurements

Gas sensing measurements were conducted using a CGS-MT system (Beijing Elite Tech Co., Ltd.) under blue light irradiation ($\lambda = 462$ nm) at 25 ± 2 °C and 15 ± 2% RH. The sensor was placed in a sealed chamber with a quartz window, and target gases including NO_2, H_2, and VOCs (ethanol, methanol, ammonia, formaldehyde) were introduced using premixed gas cylinders or a static liquid-dilution method. Gases were injected via syringe or flow controller, and the sensor was allowed to stabilize in air before each cycle. Sensor response was defined as Rg/Ra for oxidizing gases and Ra/Rg for reducing gases, where Ra and Rg are the resistances in air and target gas, respectively. Response and recovery times were recorded as the time to reach 90% of the total resistance change upon gas exposure and removal.

2.4 Computational Method

First-principles calculations based on density functional theory (DFT) were performed using the Perdew-Burke-Ernzerhof (PBE) functional under the generalized gradient approximation (GGA). A vacuum layer of 15 Å was introduced, with a cutoff energy of 571.4 eV, an energy convergence criterion of 1.0×10^{-5} eV/atom, and a k-point mesh of $3 \times 3 \times 1$.

3 Results and Discussion

3.1 Characterization of the Materials

The crystal structures of pure SnO_2 and Au-decorated SnO_2 samples were examined by XRD. All diffraction peaks could be indexed to the tetragonal rutile phase of SnO_2 (JCPDS No. 72-1147), indicating that Au loading did not alter the crystal structure. No obvious diffraction peaks related to Au were observed, likely due to its low loading or small particle size, suggesting high dispersion on the SnO_2 surface.

SEM analysis revealed that the samples exhibited a hierarchical nanosheet morphology assembled into flower-like structures. These architectures are beneficial for gas diffusion and molecule interaction. After Au modification, the overall morphology remained intact, and no aggregation was observed, suggesting uniform loading. TEM and HRTEM images further confirmed the presence of Au nanoparticles (approximately 5 nm), which were well-dispersed on the nanosheet surface. The identified lattice fringes of 0.33 nm and 0.23 nm correspond to the (110) plane of SnO_2 and the (111) plane of Au, respectively, confirming successful composite formation.

XPS analysis provided evidence of elemental composition and chemical states. Compared with pure SnO_2, the Au 4f peaks at ~ 83.7 and ~ 87.5 eV indicate the metallic state of Au. The O 1s spectra showed an increased ratio of oxygen vacancies after Au loading, which plays a key role in enhancing gas adsorption. A slight shift in the Sn 3d binding energy was also detected, indicating electron transfer between Au and SnO_2.

UV–Vis absorption spectra revealed that the optical absorption of Au/SnO_2 composites was significantly enhanced in the visible region due to the localized surface plasmon resonance (LSPR) effect of Au nanoparticles. Additionally, the bandgap of SnO_2 slightly narrowed after Au loading, suggesting improved light utilization.

3.2 Gas-Sensing Properties

As shown in Fig. 1a, the gas response of samples with various Au loadings was measured under blue light ($\lambda = 462$ nm) to 5 ppm NO_2 at room temperature. The response first increased with Au content, reaching a maximum at 2.5 wt%, and then decreased at higher loading. This trend is attributed to the dual effect of Au: while moderate loading enhances charge transfer and gas adsorption via LSPR and catalytic activity, excessive Au may lead to particle aggregation and blockage of active sites.

Dynamic response–recovery curves in Fig. 1b showed that all sensors exhibited typical n-type semiconducting behavior—resistance increased upon NO_2 exposure. The Au/SnO_2 sensor not only showed a higher baseline resistance but also a more significant change upon NO_2 injection, attributed to the Schottky barrier formed at the Au/SnO_2 interface. This barrier amplifies the modulation of resistance under gas exposure.

The sensitivity of the sensors to different NO_2 concentrations (1–5 ppm) is presented in Fig. 1c and d. The response increased nearly linearly with concentration, and the regression coefficient $R^2 = 0.99$ confirmed excellent linearity. Importantly, the detection limit of the Au/SnO_2 sensor reached 0.15 ppm, much lower than that of pure SnO_2 (0.98 ppm), indicating suitability for low-level NO_2 monitoring.

The repeatability of the 2.5 wt% Au/SnO_2 sensor was evaluated through three consecutive exposure cycles to 2 ppm NO_2, as illustrated in Fig. 2a. The response curves remained highly consistent across all cycles, with a relative standard deviation of just 1.0%, indicating excellent reproducibility and signal stability.

To assess the long-term stability, the sensor's response to 2 ppm NO_2 was recorded daily over the course of one week (Fig. 2b). The response values showed only minor fluctuations, demonstrating that the sensor maintains reliable performance over extended periods without significant degradation.

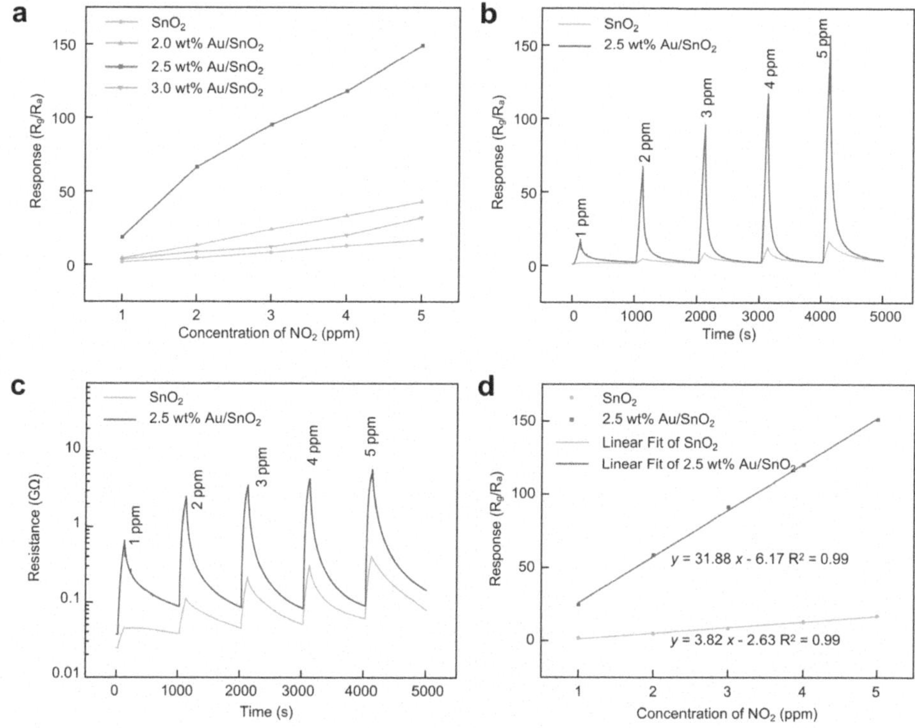

Fig. 1. (a) Response of Au samples with varying mass ratios to different NO_2 concentrations; (b) Transient response curves of SnO_2 and 2.5 wt% Au/SnO_2 at room temperature; (c) Resistance curves and (d) The response fitting curves to different NO_2 concentrations.

In terms of selectivity, Fig. 2c compares the response of pure SnO_2 and Au/SnO_2 sensors toward 5 ppm NO_2 and 1000 ppm of several interfering gases, including H_2, ethanol, methanol, ammonia, and formaldehyde. The Au/SnO_2 sensor exhibited a dramatically stronger response to NO_2 than to any other tested gases. In particular, the response to NO_2 was about 76 times higher than that to methanol, the most reactive interfering gas, highlighting the sensor's excellent discrimination capability. This high specificity is mainly due to the strong electron-withdrawing nature of NO_2 and the enhanced surface reactivity provided by Au nanoparticles.

The sensor's humidity tolerance was also investigated under relative humidity levels of 16, 32, and 48%, as shown in Fig. 2d. Although the response to 1 ppm NO_2 decreased slightly with increasing humidity—primarily due to competitive adsorption between water and NO_2 molecules—the sensor still retained reasonable sensitivity, confirming its suitability for practical applications in ambient environments.

3.3 First-Principles Calculations and Analysis

Based on first-principles calculations, this study systematically investigates the gas adsorption mechanisms of SnO_2 and Au/SnO_2 systems. The (110) crystal plane of SnO_2

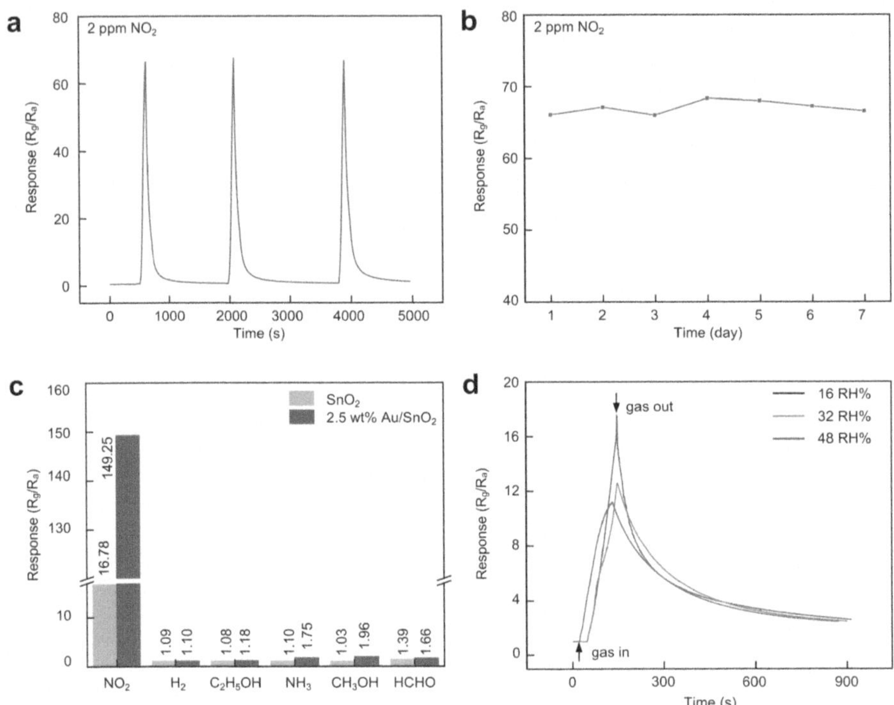

Fig. 2. (a) Cyclic sensing response of 2.5 wt% Au/SnO_2 to 2 ppm NO_2; (b) Long term stability of 2.5 wt% Au/SnO_2 to 2 ppm NO_2; (c) Response of SnO_2 and 2.5 wt% Au/SnO_2 to various gases; (d) Response of 2.5 wt% Au/SnO_2 in different relative humidity.

was selected for subsequent analysis, as supported by material characterization results. Eight potential adsorption sites on the SnO_2 surface were considered, including the top sites of five-coordinated and six-coordinated Sn atoms (Sn5c, Sn6c), two-coordinated and three-coordinated O atoms (O2c, O3c), bridge sites of Sn5c-O3c, Sn6c-O2c, and Sn6c-O3c, as well as the hollow site, with NO_2 molecules adopting an O-up orientation as the adsorption configuration in all cases. The hollow site exhibited the most negative adsorption energy for NO_2 molecules, confirming it as the optimal adsorption position. For Au modified systems, all eight sites were evaluated with NO_2 adsorbed at Au top configurations. Computational results revealed that Au adsorption at the hollow site achieved maximum negative adsorption energy, demonstrating a significant enhancement compared to the pristine SnO_2 system. The lower adsorption energy indicates stronger molecular binding, suggesting that Au modification enhances NO_2 adsorption and lowers the detection limit.

The optimal adsorption configurations of the SnO_2 and Au/SnO_2 systems are those where Au is located at the hollow site of SnO_2, and the NO_2 molecule is adsorbed atop the Au atom. To clarify the charge redistribution between the sensing material and the adsorbed species, charge density differences were computed for both systems. In the resulting maps, red and blue zones indicate electron-rich and electron-deficient regions, respectively. The introduction of Au notably enhances charge transfer, resulting in a significant increase in the response, as observed in the experimental results.

3.4 Light Enhanced NO_2 Sensing Mechanisms

SnO_2, as a typical metal oxide, exhibits a gas sensing mechanism explained by the electron depletion layer (EDL) model. Under light illumination and ambient air, oxygen molecules adsorb on the SnO_2 surface and extract electrons from the conduction band, forming photoinduced oxygen anions and establishing an electron depletion layer (EDL). This process increases the resistance of the sensor.

Upon exposure to NO_2, photogenerated electrons and adsorbed oxygen species react with NO_2, a strong electron acceptor, leading to EDL broadening and a significant increase in resistance. The weak binding between NO_2 and the material facilitates rapid desorption when exposed to air, where photogenerated holes recombine with adsorbed species, resulting in resistance recovery.

The enhanced performance of Au/SnO_2 originates from Au modification. Under ambient air and light excitation, Au modification significantly improves the light-harvesting ability of SnO_2. The LSPR effect generated on the Au nanoparticles resonates with incident photons, producing a localized electromagnetic field that enhances carrier excitation efficiency. The hot electrons excited by LSPR can overcome the Schottky barrier at the Au/SnO_2 interface and inject into the conduction band of SnO_2, forming high-mobility carriers. Meanwhile, Au nanoparticles serve as catalytic active sites that facilitate the dissociation of oxygen molecules into reactive photoinduced oxygen anions, promoting the formation of a wider electron depletion layer (EDL) and lowering the baseline resistance.

Uupon exposure to NO_2, the gas molecules interact with photogenerated electrons and photoinduced oxygen anions on the Au/SnO_2 surface, resulting in a significant expansion of the EDL and a sharp increase in resistance. This enhancement is attributed to the dual role of Au: first, the Schottky junction formed between Au and SnO_2 facilitates charge migration from the oxide surface to Au, enriching electrons at the Au surface and enhancing the polarized adsorption of NO_2; second, light sustains dynamic generation of electron-hole pairs while suppressing recombination losses, ensuring a continuous supply of charge carriers. Furthermore, Au nanoparticles promote the dissociation of oxygen molecules into more reactive species, enhancing the adsorption and redox reaction of NO_2.

In summary, the synergistic effects of Au modification, including chemical sensitization and LSPR induced enhancement, increase the carrier density and surface reactivity under illumination. This leads to a broader EDL, more pronounced resistance change, and ultimately, improved NO_2 sensing performance with higher sensitivity and lower detection limit, consistent with the adsorption enhancement revealed by first-principles calculations.

4 Conclusions

In conclusion, Au/SnO_2 composites synthesized through hydrothermal and impregnation methods demonstrated significantly enhanced NO_2 sensing performance under light illumination. The optimized 2.5 wt% Au/SnO_2 sensor achieved a high response with a low detection limit. The sensor also exhibited excellent stability, as indicated by only 1.0% variation relative to the mean response over one week of continuous operation, and maintained strong selectivity, with a response over 76 times higher than that to other interfering gases. These enhancements are attributed to the synergistic effects of noble metal modification and photoexcitation, which collectively promote charge separation, facilitate reactive oxygen species formation, and strengthen NO_2 adsorption. First-principles calculations supported this by showing that Au decoration lowers the adsorption energy and increases electron transfer. Overall, this study proposes a practical approach for constructing room-temperature NO_2 sensors with enhanced sensitivity, selectivity, and environmental stability.

References

1. Li, Z.K. et al.: Selective quantification of nitrogen dioxide in the presence of interfering gases via electronic modulation of MoS_2 by Ru doping. Rare Metals **44**, 3258–3268 (2025)
2. Li, J. et al.: Fast detection of NO_2 by porous SnO_2 nanotoast sensor at low temperature. J. Hazard. Mater. **419**, 126414 (2021)
3. Jasim, K.E., Dakhel, A.A.: Role of (cu, Al) codoping in tuning the optical, structural and magnetic properties of Co-doped SnO_2 nanostructures: a comparative study. Phys. B Condens. Matter. **614**, 413040 (2021)
4. Mirzaei, A., Janghorban, K., Hashemi, B., Bonyani, M., Leonardi, S.G., Neri, G.: A novel gas sensor based on Ag/Fe_2O_3 core-shell nanocomposites. Ceram. Int. **42**, 18974–18982 (2016)
5. Wang, Z., Han, T., Fei, T., Liu, S., Zhang, T.: Investigation of microstructure effect on NO_2 sensors based on SnO_2 nanoparticles/reduced graphene oxide hybrids. ACS Appl. Mater. Interfaces **10**, 41773–41783 (2018)
6. Lipsky, F. et al.: Effective sensing mechanisms of O_2 and CO on SnO_2 (110) surface: a DFT study. J. Mater. Chem. A. **13**, 918–927 (2025)
7. Xu, F., Lv, H.F., Wu, S.Y., Ho, H.P.: Light-activated gas sensing activity of ZnO nanotetrapods enhanced by plasmonic resonant energy from au nanoparticles. Sens. Actuators B: Chem. **259**, 709–716 (2018)
8. Chang, J. et al.: Visible light enhanced NO_2 sensing performance of au nanoparticles modified SnS_2 hierarchical structure at room temperature. Sens. Actuators B: Chem. **385**, 133633 (2023)
9. Sun, Z. et al.: LSPR effect enabled Ag-TiO_2 nanotube arrays for high sensitivity and selectivity detection of acetone under visible light. J. Alloys Compds. **1003**, 175533 (2024)

A Review of Bone Tissue Engineering Scaffold Design Strategies

Haonan Zhang[1,2], Yanen Wang[1,2](✉), Zhisheng Liu[1,2], Bo Ren[3], Minyan Liu[1,2], Xiaohu Chen[1,2], Yingchao Song[1,2], and Yixiao Guo[4]

[1] Department of Industry Engineering, School of Mechanical Engineering, Northwestern Poly-Technical University, Xi'an 710072, China
wangyanen@nwpu.edu.cn
[2] Bio-Additive Manufacturing University-Enterprise Joint Research Center of Shaanxi Province, Northwestern Polytechnical University, Xi'an 710072, China
[3] Sports Medicine Center, Honghui Hospital, Xi'an Jiaotong University, Xi'an 710054, China
[4] Department of Biomedical Engineering, School of Life Sciences, Northwestern Polytechnical University, Xi'an 710072, China

Abstract. Human skeleton system, weights over 10% of total body weights, plays an important role in blood production, mineral storage, and endocrine regu-lation. Similar to many other body tissues, bones are self-repairing after injuries until bone defects reach critical level. Bone scaffold is one of the most widely used implant type for critical-size bone defect surgery. In this review, the main bone scaffold design strategies are reviewed in three perspectives: the material selections, the structure generation strategies, and the bioactive components. The effect and drawbacks of each choice or strategy will be analyzed in terms of how it would affect bone scaffolds' performance in the inflammation, repair, or remodeling phases of bone defect recovery.

Keywords: Bone scaffold · Tissue engineering · Biomaterial · Bone regeneration · Biocompatibility · Scaffold design

1 Introduction and Background

The human skeletal system, which forms the framework of the human body, accounts for approximately 10% to 15% [1] of a person's total weight. The human skeleton not only functions as the physical support of the human body, but also plays a crucial role in blood cell production, mineral storage, and endocrine regulation [2]. Bone defects caused by injuries or diseases are one of the most common causes of skeletal dysfunction. Although bone tissues have remarkable regeneration potentials. However, when the bone defect reaches critical size, it cannot recover on its own and requires surgical intervention [3]. When autografting or allografting are not suitable, bone scaffolds are usually used as an alternative to fix critical-size bone defects [4]. The strategies to optimize bone scaffold functions can be summarized in three main design dimensions: the material [5], the structure [6], and the integration of bioactive molecules [7].

S. S. Ge et al. (Eds.): ICSR + BioMed 2025, LNAI 16435, pp. 43–53, 2026.
https://doi.org/10.1007/978-981-95-7538-1_5

Critical-size bone defect recovery after surgery includes three phases: inflammation, repair, and remodeling [8]. In past decades, the research focus on bone scaffolds had shifted from pure physical supports to the biological functions of scaffolds [9, 10]. Many emerging bone scaffold design methodologies and ideas aim to prevent infection, promote cell growth, and facilitate bone regeneration in these three phases.

This review focuses on the strategies of bone scaffolds to promote recovery from critical-size bone defects, encompassing the inflammation, repair, and remodeling phases, with consideration of the material, structure, and integrated bioactive components of the scaffold. The advantages and limitations of different materials, structural design methods, and bioactive components will be summarized, and the possible future development of bone scaffold design strategies will be discussed.

2 Materials for Bone Scaffold Fabrication

As a substitute for the original bone, bone scaffolds are usually expected to have similar physical and biochemical properties to the original human bone. Inappropriate properties of bone scaffolds may cause stress shielding [11], unwanted immune responses [12], degradation mismatch [13], and other problems that can result in failure of bone defect regeneration. In recent decades, new materials have been increasingly used in bone scaffold fabrication to address the challenges faced by traditional bone scaffolds.

In this section, we will summarize the advantages and limitations of the four main categories of bone scaffold materials, metals, natural polymers, synthetic polymers, and bio-ceramics [14].

2.1 Metals

Metals are one of the most used materials for bone tissue engineering scaffolds and other implants for their outstanding physical strength and chemical stability [15]. Materials with excellent bio-capability, including titanium and its alloys, are often used for permanent bone scaffolds, which will not degrade [16]. Developing biodegradable metal-based bone scaffolds with biologically metal elements (including magnesium and zinc) is one of the emerging tissue engineering strategies to solve this problem[17].

Zinc, copper, and silver are well-known antibacterial, antiviral, and antifungal elements. Therefore, materials with these metallic elements are widely used for implants to avoid infection [18]. At the repair and remodeling phase, these biodegradable metallic materials are usually integrated into bone scaffolds as part of the composite material to promote new bone formation.

2.2 Natural Polymers

Natural polymers, large molecules composed of many monomers, are one of the most common forms of substance in human body. They are usually components of composite material bone scaffolds [19]. Natural polymers for bone scaffolds can be classified in two main categories: proteins and polysaccharides.

Proteins are large organic compounds which play essential roles as structural components and bio-functional molecules in human body. For example, collagen is one of the most studied proteins in bone tissue engineering for its excellent biodegradability and versatility [20].

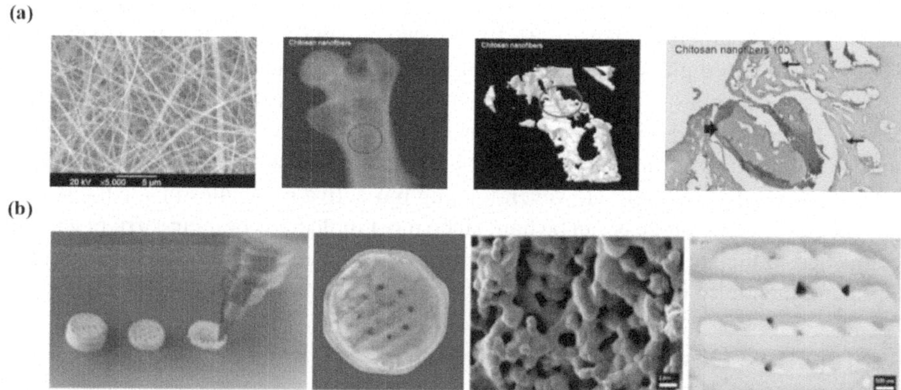

Fig. 1. Bone tissue engineering scaffolds based on different materials: (a) Chitosan nanofiber scaffolds on bone healing and new bone formation after 21 days. Reproduced with permission from ref. [21]. Copyright 2015 Dove Medical Press Ltd. (b) 3D printed HA scaffold and SEM image after sintering. Reproduced with permission from ref. [22]. Copyright 2021 Springer Nature

Polysaccharides are large molecules made of monosaccharides, linked by glycosidic bonds. Chitosan (See Fig. 1a), alginate, and hyaluronic acid are representative examples of this category of natural polymer used in bone scaffolds [23]. They are more usually known as a minor component of composite bone scaffolds instead of a significant structural material, as collagens do.

2.3 Synthetic Polymers

Compared to natural polymers, synthetic polymers are expected to be more flexible and reproducible due to their designed molecular structures. Their outstanding mechanical strength and chemical stability make them one of the most common types of bone scaffold materials. Poly(ε-caprolactone) (PCL), polylactide (PLA), and poly(lactide-co-glycolide) (PLGA) are three of the most commonly used synthetic polymers as the significant component of bone scaffolds [24].

PCL and PLA are widespread 3D printing materials. The complex porous design of bone scaffolds can be fabricated with mature 3D printing technology, which is a significant advantage for PCL and PLA-based bone scaffolds. Lactic acid (at high concentration) can impair immune cell functions and potentially promote cancer progression in the tumor microenvironment [25]. Consider that bone tumor removal surgery is a significant cause of critical-size bone defects; this disadvantage of PLA should be considered seriously. PLGA is a more common bone scaffold material due to its biodegradation tunability [26].

2.4 Bio-ceramics

Human bone is composed of 50 to 70% mineral, which is mostly hydroxyapatite (HA), a type of bio-ceramic [22, 27–29]. Based on this fact, it is easy to understand the high potential of bio-ceramics in bone tissue engineering fields. Currently, most bio-ceramic materials used for bone scaffold fabrication contain calcium, the most abundant element in human bone. The main types of bio-ceramics for bone scaf-folds include HA (See Fig. 1b), β-tricalcium phosphate (β-TCP), octacalcium phos-phate (OCP), and bioactive glasses (silica-based glasses containing calcium and phosphates) [22, 27–29].

Since bio-ceramics are usually brittle with very high melting points, fabricating bio-ceramic-based scaffolds can be challenging. Most bio-ceramic-based bone scaffolds are fabricated with 3D printing methods. For bio-ceramics (mostly in powder form) to fuse, sintering is usually required. However, loading bio-active molecules inside the scaffold after the 3D printing process can be hard since most molecules or their carriers will only be attached to the surface of the scaffold. Thus, a fabrication method without sintering steps can potentially improve the performance of bio-ceramic-based scaffolds.

3 Structure Designs of Bone Scaffolds

The structure of natural bone is complex, as it serves multiple functions, including supporting muscles and organs, providing space for vessels and other soft tissues, and facilitating cell migration, differentiation, and proliferation [4, 30]. Therefore, the structural designs of bone scaffolds need to achieve more than just supporting the bone defect site [31]. The design criteria of a bone scaffold structure can be seen as a balance, with one side comprising the physical and biological functions, and the other side comprising the limitations imposed by the materials and fabrication techniques.

By treating "designing bone regeneration promoting scaffold structure" as a problem, we can classify the design solutions of this problem into three types in terms of problem-solving logic: natural-inspired structures, bone-mimic structures [4, 32], and property-oriented structures [33].

3.1 Natural-Inspired Structure Designs

Evolution, the process by which living organisms change and adapt, can be seen as a natural optimization process. Different organisms may develop structures with similarities for similar purposes (analogous in this case). For instance, cephalopods and vertebrates both have complex eyes that share many similarities, though their eyes have evolved independently [34]. Similarly, bone scaffolds need to achieve many functions, which are also essential for other organisms. Therefore, learning from the structures of different plants and animals can be an efficient way for designing bone scaffolds [32].

Most bone scaffolds are expected to allow cell entry and substance transmission. Thus, bone scaffolds' structures are mostly porous. For example, a lotus seedpod-inspired porous scaffold structure can promote vascularization and thus significantly accelerate new bone formation at the repair and remodeling phase of bone defect recovery (See Fig. 2a) [35]. Another essential feature of human bone is its complex composition. For example, sponge spicules-inspired scaffold can achieve high flexibility and fracture toughness at the same time with a simple, direct ink writing 3D printing method [36].

3.2 Bone-Mimic Structure Designs

Mimicking human bone structure is a direct method for bone structure design to achieve the original bone functions. Bone scaffolds usually need to have a structure matching the target bone defect sites. Most bone-mimic structures are one of the two types, trabecular bone simulation and cortical bone simulation (See Fig. 2b) [37].

Two methods achieve most of the trabecular bone simulation. One method is scanning the natural trabecular bone with micro-CT, rebuilding the 3D model, and 3D printing the structure. The other method is generating a spongiform structure by topology optimization. Since the targets of topology optimization are always specific properties of trabecular bone instead of the overall morphology of trabecular bone, this method will be discussed in the "Property-oriented Structure Designs" session of the paper.

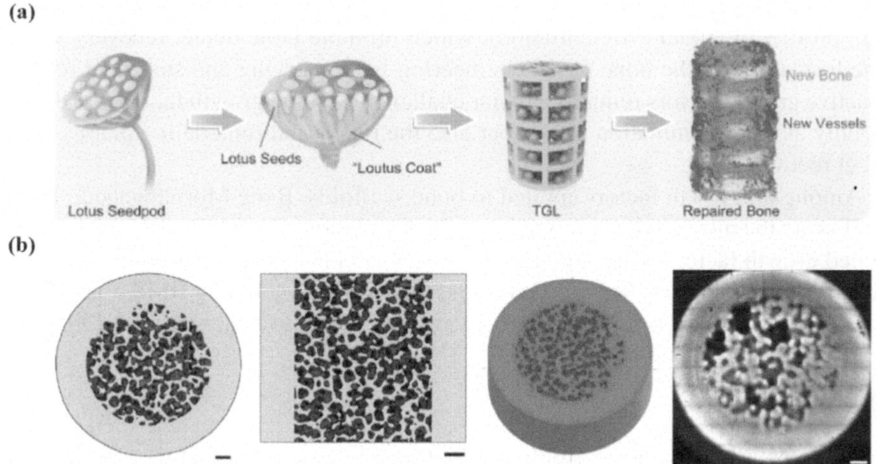

Fig. 2. Examples of bio-inspired and bone-mimic bone scaffold structures: (a) Lotus seedpod-inspired internal vascularized bone scaffold. Reproduced with permission from ref. [35]. Copyright 2021 Elsevier B.V. (b) 3D printed bone-mimic scaffold with both trabecular and cortical bone features. Reproduced with permission from ref. [37]. Copyright 2025 Springer Nature.

3.3 Property-Oriented Structure Designs

Without mimicking existing structures, bone scaffold design can be based on target properties directly. For example, a porous bone scaffold structure can be generated with pure mathematical methods to ensure substance transmission in the bone scaf-fold with a clearly defined porous rate and minimum stiffness [38].

A major example of property-oriented bone structure design method is topology optimization, a computational method that can generate 3D structures with target bone properties. One of the most used topology optimization methods is the triply periodic minimal surface (TPMS). TPMS can generate 3D bone scaffold structures with defined surface thicknesses and given boundaries. Another most popular topology optimization method, solid isotropic material penalization (SIMP), can generate a bone scaffold structure with target properties directly with restrictions.

4 Integrated Bioactive Molecules and Stem Cells of Bone Scaffolds

Growth factors, peptides, small bone mass regulator molecules, drugs, and stem cells that regulate or promote new bone growth are widely utilized in bone scaffolds to enhance their performance [10, 39]. These bioactive molecules are typically used to promote angiogenesis, accelerate osteogenesis, inhibit the growth of cancer cells, and exhibit other biological activities essential for bone regeneration [3, 14].

This section provides an overview of the main bioactive molecules that can be loaded into bone scaffolds. The functions, delivery methods, and challenges faced by these molecules will be discussed.

4.1 Growth Factors

Growth factors, in this review, can be defined as proteins that stimulate cell activities (e.g., proliferation and differentiation), which promote bone defect recovery and new bone formation. In the bone tissue engineering field, carrying and sustained release of bioactive growth factors remains a major challenge as some growth factors are expected not only at the inflammation phase, but also the repair and remodeling phases of bone defect recovery [40].

Among all growth factors applied to bone scaffolds, Bone Morphogenetic Proteins (BMPs) are the most studied growth factor family. Among the BMPs, BMP-2 is the most studied growth factor for its ability to promote osteoblast progenitor differentiation and accelerate osteogenesis (See Fig. 3a) [41]. Other BMPs, including BMP-7 and BMP-9, also draw attention of researchers as bioactive integrates to bone scaffolds [39, 40].

4.2 Peptides

Loading peptides to bone scaffolds is an alternative to growth factors with lower cost and higher stability [10]. A peptide is a compound that consists of more than two amino acids. Peptides derived from growth factors or other bone growth-related proteins may target a specific type of cell and mimic the functions of the whole protein. Peptides can be produced by enzymatic hydrolysis or chemical synthesis.

Enzymatic hydrolysis breaks down peptides from proteins directly and is usually more cost-effective, while chemical synthesis is usually a more flexible method compared to enzymatic hydrolysis for its ability to synthesize peptides with long chains and unnatural amino acids. Chemically synthesized does not necessarily mean the peptides cannot be growth factor-derived. For example, peptide P-15 is widely used in bone scaffold coatings to promote new bone formation (See Fig. 3b) [42].

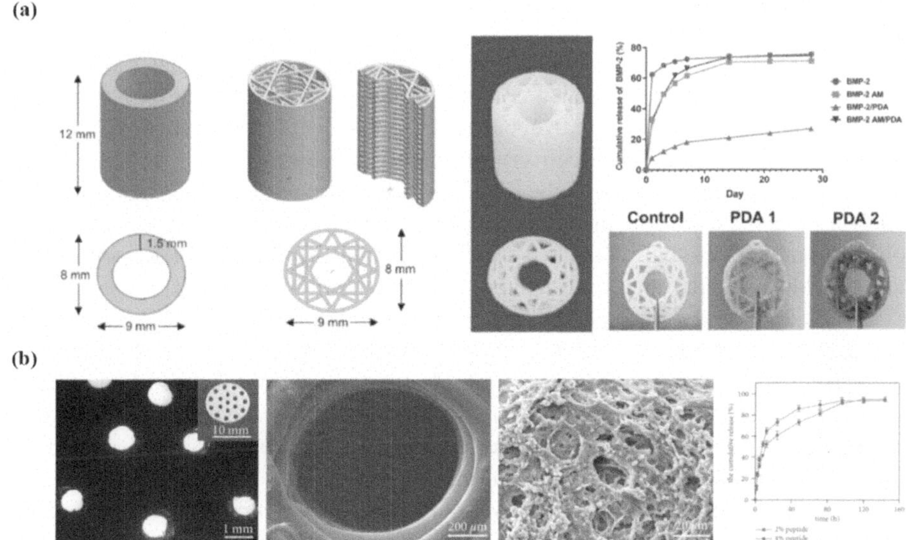

Fig. 3. Examples of growth factor and peptide loaded bone scaffolds: (a). Sustained BMP-2 delivery via alginate microbeads and polydopamine-coated 3D-Printed PCL/β-TCP scaffold. Reproduced with permission from ref. [41]. Copyright 2024 Elsevier B.V. (b). 3D Printing PLGA Scaffold with BMP-9 and P-15 Peptide Hydrogel. Reproduced with permission from ref. [42]. Copyright 2022 Wiley & Sons, Inc.

4.3 Small Molecules, Drugs, and Bone Mass Regulators

Small molecules (including small molecule drugs), which usually have a molecular weight lower than 900 Daltons, are another possible alternative growth factor and peptides [7]. With their low molecular weights and simple structures, these small molecules can usually be osteoinductive at low doses with less immune risk. In the past few decades, numerous small-molecule drugs have been developed and applied to bone scaffolds. For instance, simvastatin (a reductase inhibitor with a molecular weight of 418.6 Da) can be delivered by microspheres loaded on bone scaffolds [43]. Another example is doxorubicin (DXR), which can be delivered by nanoparticles (NPs) in scaffolds to inhibit cancer cells and prevent cancer metastasis.

4.4 Stem Cells

Seeding cells before the bone scaffold implantation is another possible way to improve bone scaffold performance. Currently, there are three main types of stem cells used in bone scaffolds: marrow stromal cells (BMSCs), adipose-derived mesen-chymal cells (ADSCs), periosteum-derived stem cells (PDSCs), and induced pluripo-tent stem cells (iPSCs) [10, 39]. With stem cells seeded on the bone scaffold, bone scaffolds can have much larger potential in restoring bone functions after the surgery, especially for bone tumor removal surgeries.

5 Conclusion

As described above, bone scaffold design is a process combining material selection, structure generation, and bio-active component delivery strategies aiming to improve bone scaffolds' osteoinductivity, osteoconductivity, anti-infection function, and many other critical size bone defects recovery-promoting properties.

Material selection determines the foundation of the bone scaffold design. Metals are widely used as bone scaffold materials for their outstanding mechanical strength; natural polymers and bio-ceramics both have excellent biocompatibility; synthetic polymers are more flexible and reproducible compared to their natural counterparts.

From a structural design perspective, a large number of bone scaffolds have either natural-inspired or bone-mimic structures. Mimicking naturally formed structures is a promising way of designing bone scaffold structures with enhanced bone-forming properties. Opposite to bio-mimic methods, some scaffolds have structures designed with specific properties as targets. Bone scaffold structures can also be designed with topology optimization to have more controllable properties.

Currently, the main types of bioactive molecules loaded into bone scaffolds include growth factors, peptides, drugs, and other bone-forming related molecules. These bioactive molecules can be delivered and sustained released by micro-carriers (e.g., microspheres and micro-tanks) which could be attached to bone scaffolds. Seeding living stem cells to bone scaffolds is also a way to promote new bone formation after bone scaffold implantation surgery.

In conclusion, this review has summarized the designs of bone tissue engineering scaffolds from material, structure, and bioactive component perspectives. Possible design strategies and examples are provided.

Acknowledgments. This work was supported by the National Key Research and Development Program of China (grant number 2022YFB3304000) and the Provincial Special Fund for Science and Technology Development of Shannxi (grant number 2024JC-YBMS-630) and Key Program of the National Natural Science Foundation of China (Grant No. 52535008).

Disclosure of Interests. The authors have no competing interests to declare that are relevant to the content of this article.

References

1. Avtandilashvili, M., Tolmachev, S.Y.: Modeling the skeleton weight of an adult Caucasian man. Health Phys. **117**, 149–155 (2019). https://doi.org/10.1097/HP.0000000000000881
2. Su, N., Yang, J., Xie, Y., Du, X., Chen, H., Zhou, H., Chen, L.: Bone function, dysfunction and its role in diseases including critical illness (2019)
3. Schulze, F., Lang, A., Schoon, J., Wassilew, G.I., Reichert, J.: Scaffold guided bone regeneration for the treatment of large segmental defects in long bones (2023)
4. Jiang, S., Wang, M., He, J.: A review of biomimetic scaffolds for bone regeneration: toward a cell-free strategy (2021)
5. Francis, A.P., Augustus, A.R., Chandramohan, S., Bhat, S.A., Priya, V.V., Rajagopalan, R.: A review on biomaterials-based scaffold: an emerging tool for bone tissue engineering. Mater Today Commun. **34** (2023). https://doi.org/10.1016/j.mtcomm.2022.105124

6. Abdelaziz, A.G., Nageh, H., Abdo, S.M., Abdalla, M.S., Amer, A.A., Abdal-hay, A., Barhoum, A.: A review of 3D polymeric scaffolds for bone tissue engineering: principles, fabrication techniques. Immunomodulatory Roles, and Challenges (2023)
7. Ferracini, R., Martínez Herreros, I., Russo, A., Casalini, T., Rossi, F., Perale, G.: Scaffolds as structural tools for bone-targeted drug delivery, (2018)
8. Lafuente-Gracia, L., Borgiani, E., Nasello, G., Geris, L.: Towards in silico models of the inflammatory response in bone fracture healing (2021)
9. Ghiasi, M.S., Chen, J., Vaziri, A., Rodriguez, E.K., Nazarian, A.: Bone fracture healing in mechanobiological modeling: a review of principles and methods (2017)
10. Ho-Shui-Ling, A., Bolander, J., Rustom, L.E., Johnson, A.W., Luyten, F.P., Picart, C.: Bone regeneration strategies: engineered scaffolds, bioactive molecules and stem cells current stage and future perspectives (2018)
11. Raffa, M.L., Nguyen, V.H., Hernigou, P., Flouzat-Lachaniette, C.H., Haiat, G.: Stress shielding at the bone-implant interface: influence of surface roughness and of the bone-implant contact ratio. J. Orthopaedic Res. **39**, 1174–1183 (2021). https://doi.org/10.1002/jor.24840
12. Wu, L., Liu, J., Qiu, T., Dai, H.: The natural reticular hematoma scaffold modulating inflammatory microenvironment and promoting bone regeneration. Compos B Eng. **295** (2025). https://doi.org/10.1016/j.compositesb.2025.112199
13. Park, S.H., Gil, E.S., Shi, H., Kim, H.J., Lee, K., Kaplan, D.L.: Relationships between degradability of silk scaffolds and osteogenesis. Biomaterials **31**, 6162–6172 (2010). https://doi.org/10.1016/j.biomaterials.2010.04.028
14. Koons, G.L., Diba, M., Mikos, A.G.: Materials design for bone-tissue engineering (2020)
15. Alvarez, K., Nakajima, H.: Metallic scaffolds for bone regeneration. Materials. **2**, 790–832 (2009). https://doi.org/10.3390/ma2030790
16. Liu, J., Wang, R., Gong, X., Zhu, Y., Shen, C., Zhu, Z., Li, Y., Li, Z., Ren, Z., Chen, X., Bian, W., Wang, D., Yang, X., Zhang, Y.: Ti6Al4V biomimetic scaf-folds for bone tissue engineering: Fabrication, biomechanics and osseointe-gration. Mater Des. **234** (2023). https://doi.org/10.1016/j.matdes.2023.112330
17. Jia, B., et al.: In vitro and in vivo studies of Zn-Mn biodegradable metals designed for orthopedic applications. Acta Biomater. **108**, 358–372 (2020). https://doi.org/10.1016/j.actbio.2020.03.009
18. He, J., Li, K., Wu, T., Chen, J., Li, S., Zhang, X.: Research progress in degradable metal-based multifunctional scaffolds for bone tissue engineering (2023)
19. Radha, G., Manjubaashini, N., Balakumar, S.: Nano-hydroxyapatite/natural polymer composite scaffolds for bone tissue engineering: a brief review of recent trend. In vitro models. **2**, 125–151 (2023). https://doi.org/10.1007/s44164-023-00049-w
20. Fan, L., Ren, Y., Emmert, S., Vučković, I., Stojanovic, S., Najman, S., Schnettler, R., Barbeck, M., Schenke-Layland, K., Xiong, X.: The use of collagen-based materials in bone tissue engineering (2023)
21. Ho, M.H., Yao, C.J., Liao, M.H., Lin, P.I., Liu, S.H., Chen, R.M.: Chitosan nanofiber scaffold improves bone healing via stimulating trabecular bone production due to upregulation of the Runx2/osteocalcin/alkaline phospha-tase signaling pathway. Int. J. Nanomedicine **10**, 5941–5954 (2015). https://doi.org/10.2147/IJN.S90669
22. Zhongxing, L., Shaohong, W., Jinlong, L., Limin, Z., Yuanzheng, W., Haipeng, G., Jian, C.: Three-dimensional printed hydroxyapatite bone tissue engineering scaffold with antibacterial and osteogenic ability. J Biol Eng. **15** (2021). https://doi.org/10.1186/s13036-021-00273-6
23. Donnaloja, F., Jacchetti, E., Soncini, M., Raimondi, M.T.: Natural and synthetic polymers for bone scaffolds optimization (2020)
24. Maisani, M., Pezzoli, D., Chassande, O., Mantovani, D.: Cellularizing hydro-gel-based scaffolds to repair bone tissue: how to create a physiologically relevant micro-environment? J Tissue Eng. **8** (2017). https://doi.org/10.1177/2041731417712073

25. Choi, S.Y.C., Collins, C.C., Gout, P.W., Wang, Y.: Cancer-generated lactic acid: a regulatory, immunosuppressive metabolite? (2013)
26. Sun, F., Sun, X., Wang, H., Li, C., Zhao, Y., Tian, J., Lin, Y.: Application of 3D-Printed, PLGA-based scaffolds in bone tissue engineering (2022)
27. Chocholata, P., Kulda, V., Babuska, V.: Fabrication of scaffolds for bone-tissue regeneration (2019)
28. Brochu, B.M., Sturm, S.R., Kawase De Queiroz Goncalves, J.A., Mirsky, N.A., Sandino, A.I., Panthaki, K.Z., Panthaki, K.Z., Nayak, V.V., Daunert, S., Witek, L., Coelho, P.G.: Advances in Bioceramics for bone regeneration: a narrative review (2024)
29. Teterina, A.Y., Smirnov, I.V., Fadeeva, I.S., Fadeev, R.S., Smirnova, P.V., Minaychev, V.V., Kobyakova, M.I., Fedotov, A.Y., Barinov, S.M., Komlev, V.S.: Octacalcium phosphate for bone tissue engineering: synthesis, modification, and in vitro biocompatibility assessment. Int. J. Mol. Sci. **22** (2021). https://doi.org/10.3390/ijms222312747
30. Yang, W., et al.: Biomimetic bone-like composite hydrogel scaffolds composed of collagen fibrils and natural hydroxyapatite for promoting bone repair. ACS Biomater. Sci. Eng. **10**, 2385–2397 (2024). https://doi.org/10.1021/acsbiomaterials.3c01468
31. Ghassemi, T., Shahroodi, A., Ebrahimzadeh, M.H., Mousavian, A., Movaf-fagh, J., Moradi, A.: Current concepts review current concepts in scaffolding for bone tissue engineering (2018)
32. Huang, D., Li, Z., Li, G., Zhou, F., Wang, G., Ren, X., Su, J.: Biomimetic structural design in 3D-printed scaffolds for bone tissue engineering (2025)
33. Polo-Corrales, L., Latorre-Esteves, M., Ramirez-Vick, J.E.: Scaffold design for bone regeneration (2014)
34. Nilsson, D.E., Johnsen, S., Warrant, E.: Cephalopod versus vertebrate eyes (2023)
35. Han, X., et al.: Lotus seedpod-inspired internal vascularized 3D printed scaffold for bone tissue repair. Bioact Mater. **6**, 1639–1652 (2021). https://doi.org/10.1016/j.bioactmat.2020.11.019
36. Yang, Z., Xue, J., Li, T., Zhai, D., Yu, X., Huan, Z., Wu, C.: 3D printing of sponge spicules-inspired flexible bioceramic-based scaffolds. Biofabrication. **14** (2022). https://doi.org/10.1088/1758-5090/ac66ff
37. Kontakis, M.G., Moulin, M., Andersson, B., Norein, N., Samanta, A., Stelzl, C., Engberg, A., Diez-Escudero, A., Kreuger, J., Hailer, N.P.: Trabecular-bone mimicking osteoconductive collagen scaffolds: an optimized 3D printing approach using freeform reversible embedding of suspended hydrogels. 3D Print Med. **11** (2025). https://doi.org/10.1186/s41205-025-00255-0
38. Liu, M., Wang, Y., Wei, Q., Ma, X., Zhang, K., Li, X., Bao, C., Du, B.: Topology optimization for reducing stress shielding in cancellous bone scaffold. Comput Struct. **288** (2023). https://doi.org/10.1016/j.compstruc.2023.107132
39. Bello, S.A., Cruz-Lebrón, J., Rodríguez-Rivera, O.A., Nicolau, E.: Bioactive scaffolds as a promising alternative for enhancing critical-size bone defect regeneration in the craniomaxillofacial region (2023)
40. Oliveira, É.R., Nie, L., Podstawczyk, D., Allahbakhsh, A., Ratnayake, J., Brasil, D.L., Shavandi, A.: Advances in growth factor delivery for bone tissue engineering (2021)
41. Lee, S., et al.: Sustained BMP-2 delivery via alginate microbeads and polydopamine-coated 3D-Printed PCL/β-TCP scaffold enhances bone regeneration in long bone segmental defects. J Orthop Translat. **49**, 11–22 (2024). https://doi.org/10.1016/j.jot.2024.08.013

42. Wang, X., Chen, W., Chen, Z., Li, Y., Wu, K., Song, Y.: Preparation of 3D printing PLGA scaffold with BMP-9 and P-15 peptide hydrogel and its application in the treatment of bone defects in rabbits. Contrast Media Mol Imaging. **2022** (2022). https://doi.org/10.1155/2022/1081957
43. Tai, I.C., Fu, Y.C., Wang, C.K., Chang, J.K., Ho, M.L.: Local delivery of controlled-release simvastatin/PLGA /HA p microspheres enhances bone repair. Int. J. Nanomedicine **8**, 3895–3905 (2013). https://doi.org/10.2147/IJN.S48694

The Application and the Development of 3D Printing Technology in Biosensors

Maimoona Afzal[1](✉), Chi Zhang[1,2], Ghulam Hassan Askari[1], Aamir Shehzad[2], Sidra Aslam[2], and Nasar Ali[2]

[1] Bio-Additive Manufacturing University-Enterprise Joint Research Center of Shaanxi Province, Northwestern Polytechnical University, Xi'an 710072, China
{maimoonaafzal,zhangchi160985}@mail.nwpu.edu.cn

[2] Department of Industry Engineering, School of Mechanical Engineering, Northwestern Poly-Technical University, Xi'an 710072, China

Abstract. The advent of 3D printing has transformed the development of flexible, sticky biosensors for continuous, non-invasive health monitoring. This review examines the integration of 3D printing with metal components such as titanium, stainless steel, and bronze in wearable biosensor design. Key 3D printing methods like Fused Deposition Modeling (FDM), Stereolithography (SLA), and Selective Laser Sintering (SLS) are explored for combining the mechanical strength of metals with the flexibility of polymers and hydrogels. The use of metal-based conductive electrodes enhances sensor accuracy and durability. We discuss the challenges of skin adherence, electrical conductivity, and scalability, along with innovations in materials such as novel alloys and nanomaterials like graphene. The paper also highlights the potential of wearable metal-polymer hybrid sensors in real-time health tracking and concludes with future prospects in IoT and AI integration for personalized healthcare, emphasizing the need for bio-compatible materials and commercialization in the next generation of smart, wearable technologies.

Keywords: 3D printing technology · Flexible biosensors · Metal components · Wearable health monitoring · Biocompatibility

1 Introduction and Background

Biosensors are analytical devices that combine a biological recognition element with a physicochemical transducer to detect chemical compounds, playing a crucial role in healthcare by enabling rapid disease diagnosis and real-time monitoring of vital signs such as heart rate and temperature [1]. These compact, flexible, and self-powered devices offer seamless integration with the human body for personalized health monitoring, significantly improving patient care through accurate and efficient healthcare delivery [2, 3].3D printing, a transformative technology, enables the precise creation of customized biosensors, incorporating flexible substrates, conductive materials, and sensing elements for cost-effective, patient-specific devices [4].

Recent advancements in 3D printing have revolutionized the development of flexible biosensors capable of continuous monitoring [5]. Techniques such as Fused Deposition

S. S. Ge et al. (Eds.): ICSR + BioMed 2025, LNAI 16435, pp. 54–64, 2026.
https://doi.org/10.1007/978-981-95-7538-1_6

Modeling (FDM), Stereolithography (SLA), and Selective Laser Sintering (SLS) have enabled the production of flexible, compact biosensors for multianalyte detection, particularly for clinical applications like rapid diagnostics during the SARS-CoV-2 pandemic [6–8]. Metals such as gold, silver, and titanium enhance biosensor performance due to their excellent conductivity, durability, and biocompatibility, with gallium-based liquid metals offering flexibility and self-healing properties ideal for wearable sensors [8].

This paper explores the integration of 3D printing for the development of flexible, sticky biosensors incorporating metal components for precise measurements of health parameters like heart rate and body temperature. It examines the role of additive manufacturing in creating customized, non-invasive sensors, and discusses challenges related to sensor comfort, wearability, and noise reduction, aiming to advance personalized healthcare solutions.

2 Principles of 3D Printing for Sticky and Flexible Biosensors

2.1 3D Printing Techniques for Flexible Biosensors

3D printing has revolutionized biosensor fabrication by enabling the creation of complex, customized, and flexible biosensors. Among the different 3D printing technologies, Stereolithography (SLA), Fused Deposition Modeling (FDM), and Digital Light Processing (DLP) are the most used (See Fig. 1) [9].

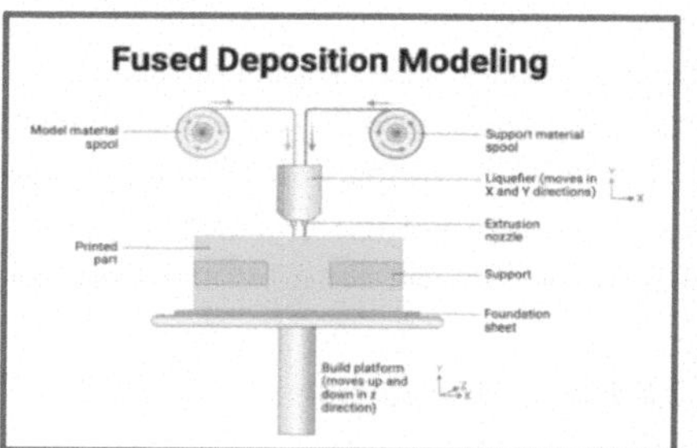

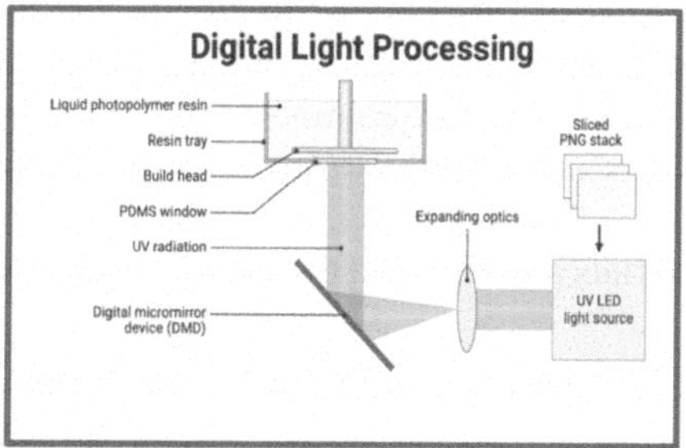

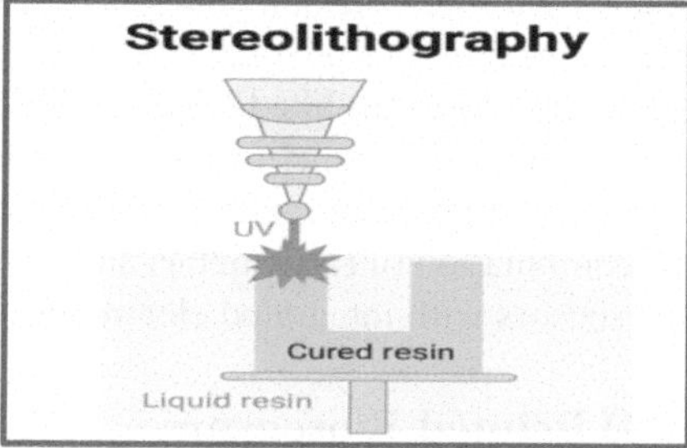

Fig. 1. 3D printing processes [9]. Copyright 2024 Polymers.

SLA and DLP are ideal for creating high-resolution structures by curing photosensitive resins with precision. FDM, known for its cost-effectiveness, is widely used in flexible biosensor production, particularly with substrates like PDMS and PET. Direct Ink Writing (DIW) is gaining attention for printing hydrogels and soft materials, offering advantages in biocompatible flexible biosensors [10, 11]. These techniques enable the integration of microfluidic channels, multi-analyte detection, and flexible substrates for wearable health monitoring devices [12].

2.2 Materials for Flexible Biosensors

Polymers and Hydrogels. Flexible biosensors rely on polymers and hydrogels for biocompatibility, elasticity, and comfort. Polydimethylsiloxane (PDMS) is commonly used for its excellent elasticity, stability, and biocompatibility in wearable biosensors [13]. Other materials like polyimide (PI), polyethylene terephthalate (PET), and poly-urethane (PU) are also used for flexible substrates. Conducting polymer hydrogels are gaining popularity for their high permeability and rapid electron transfer, making them ideal for flexible biosensor platforms with superior sensitivity and biocompatibility [14, 15].

Metals. Metals like titanium, bronze, and stainless steel are essential in biosensor fabrication due to their strength, conductivity, and corrosion resistance. Titanium alloys are used for their low elastic modulus and corrosion resistance in biomedical applications, while stainless steel and bronze provide mechanical strength and flexibility. Noble metal nanoparticles, such as gold (Au) and silver (Ag), enhance sensor performance through their electrical and optical properties. Liquid metals, with low melting points and high conductivity, are emerging as a promising solution for flexible biosensors requiring dynamic properties and self-healing capabilities [12].

Adhesive Properties. Materials with adhesive properties are essential for ensuring that flexible biosensors maintain a secure attachment to the skin or other organs. Silicone-based adhesives are commonly used for transdermal medication delivery and in biosensor designs due to their strong adhesive properties and biocompatibility. Surface modification of nanoparticles is frequently employed to improve the uniform dispersion of materials and enhance the adhesion properties of the final biosensor composite [13].

2.3 Integration of Metal Components with Flexible Materials

Integrating metal components with flexible substrates is crucial for high-performance biosensors. A key challenge is the modulus mismatch between rigid metals (e.g., gold or silver nanoparticles) and flexible substrates like PDMS or PET, which affects adhesion. Strategies such as embedding plasmonic units into flexible matrices and using hybrid 3D printing techniques help improve interfacial adhesion and stability. Multi-nozzle extruders enable seamless combination of rigid metals and flexible substrates, allowing the production of complex sensors with integrated electrodes [14].

3 Development of 3D Printed Biosensors

3.1 Designing Flexible and Sticky 3D Printed Biosensors

3D printing enables low-cost, rapid prototyping, and simple fabrication of biosensors and biomedical devices for microfluidic, optical, electrochemical, and integrated applications [15]. The design of flexible, sticky 3D printed biosensors focuses on material selection, simulation, and fabrication strategies, especially for metal, bronze, and ceramic-based sensors [16]. For example, a customizable fabrication process for carbon-based biosensors uses 3D extrusion printing with conductive inks, achieving high resolution (100 μm) and fast production for applications like smart wound dressings [17]. This technology has revolutionized potentiometric sensor development by enabling customizable, low-cost, and rapid prototyping of analytical devices [18].

3.2 Case Studies and Examples

Case Study 1: Titanium-Based Heart Rate Sensor. 3D-printed titanium electrode-based wearable sensors for heart rate monitoring highlight the use of metal components in flexible biosensors. Titanium alloys are preferred in biomedical applications for their low elastic modulus, corrosion resistance, and high biocompatibility [19]. While human heart rate sensors are still developing, animal studies show the potential of titanium-based implants for vital sign monitoring [20].

Case Study 2: Flexible Bronze Temperature Sensors. 3D-printed flexible temperature sensors made from nanocomposites show reversible temperature responses with linear sensitivity (− 10 °C to 60 °C, + 0.29%°C^{-}1), offering excellent chemical and mechanical stability. Liquid metal-based tactile sensors for simultaneous temperature and force sensing exhibit high sensitivity in the 20–80 °C range [21].

Case Study 3: Metal-Polymer Hybrid Biosensor. A multi-sensory wearable biosensor integrating flexible polymers and metal components has been developed for heart rate and temperature monitoring, incorporating energy harvesters for battery-free operation [22]. Biofriendly ultrathin sensors with gold nanoparticles and elastomeric materials offer high conductivity and stretchability, ensuring stable electrical conduction under strain [13].

4 Applications of Metal-Based Flexible Biosensors

4.1 Heart Rate Monitoring

The integration of metal components in flexible biosensors is crucial for precise heart rate measurement, aiding in early cardiovascular disease diagnosis and mental health assessments. Wearable cardiac biosensors, often using electrocardiogram (ECG) signals, capture heart rate and other vital signs, transmitting data wirelessly to handheld devices [23]. Metal-based electrodes enhance accuracy and durability, while advances in 3D bioprinting have led to adaptable ECG biosensors embedded in clothing or applied as adhesive patches for continuous, non-invasive monitoring LM-based bio-sensors to monitor heart and pulse rate (See Fig. 2) [24, 25].

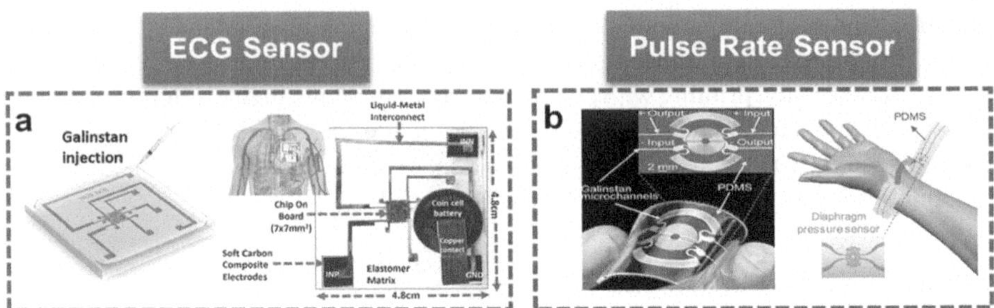

Fig. 2. LM-based biosensors to monitor heart and pulse rate. (a) ECG monitoring analysis [24]. Copyright permission from John Wiley and Sons 2019 Advanced Electronic Materials (b) Pressure sensor for heart rate monitoring [25] Copyright 2017 Adv. Mater.

4.2 Temperature Measurement

Metal-based temperature sensors, known for their high thermal conductivity, are ideal for health monitoring, environmental control, and disease diagnosis. Unlike traditional rigid sensors, flexible, conformal sensors made from conductive materials and temperature-sensitive polymers provide accurate, real-time body temperature monitoring (See Fig. 3) [26].

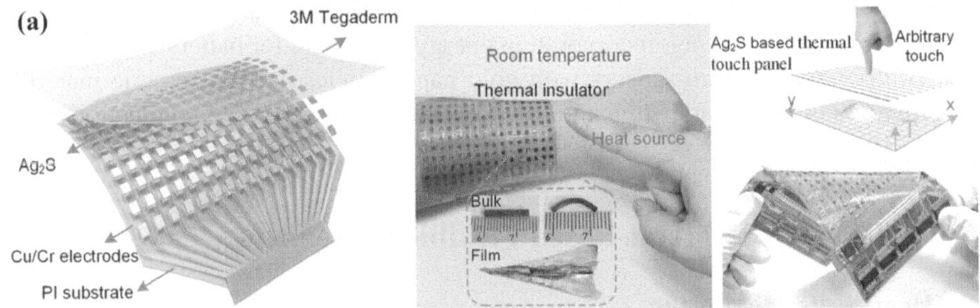

Fig. 3. Metal Sulfide Temperature Sensor Array [26]. Copyright Permission from 2022 Advanced Materials.

4.3 Wearable Health Monitoring

Flexible biosensors play a significant role in wearable health monitoring systems by enabling continuous measurement of physiological parameters such as heart rate, temperature, glucose levels, and hydration status [27–29]. Wearable biosensors allow for real-time, non-invasive, and continuous monitoring, overcoming the limitations of traditional invasive blood tests [3]. For example, microfluidic systems integrated into wearable biosensors collect sweat, which is rich in molecules like sodium, potassium, and chloride, offering valuable medical information. The preparation and detection of wearable sensors (See Fig. 4) [30].

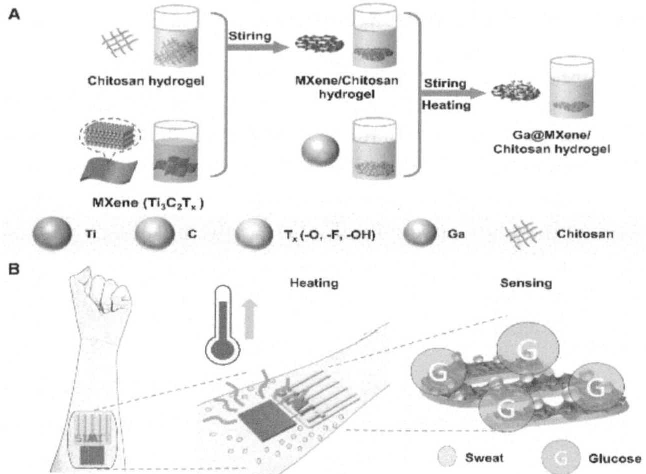

Fig. 4. Wearable sensors (a) Preparation of Ga@MXene/CS (b) Detection principle of Ga@MXene/CS sensor [30]. Copyright 2025 iScience.

4.4 Skin and Organ Attachment

Flexible biosensors for skin and organ attachment enable non-invasive monitoring of bio-signals. 3D printing allows the creation of flexible materials and metal components for conformal attachment to soft, curvilinear surfaces like skin or organs.

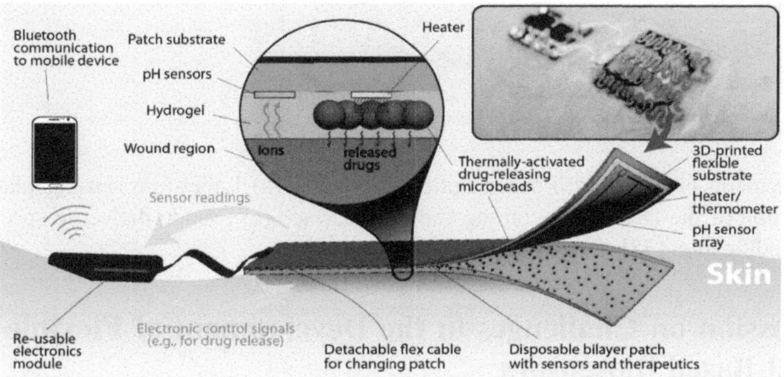

Fig. 5. Schematic of an automated smart bandage with flexible pH sensors, a heater for thermo-responsive drug release [31]. Copyright permission from 2018 Small Journal.

These devices, such as patches, tattoos, or bands, integrate metal components for improved conductivity and flexibility. For example, gold-coated silver nanowires with elastomeric polymers record physiological data from skin or swine hearts [13]. These biosensors detect biomarkers like glucose, lactate, and cortisol in body fluids, offering a non-invasive diagnostic alternative (See Fig. 5) [31].

4.5 Flexible Electronics for Health Monitoring

Metal-based strain and pressure sensors enable continuous, non-invasive health tracking with high sensitivity and flexibility. Noble metal nanoparticles such as gold and silver are used to create highly sensitive, stretchable sensors that maintain excel-lent electrical conductivity while providing flexibility. The integration of these sensors with silicon integrated circuits results in highly efficient, thin-film systems that can monitor a broad range of physiological indicators using biofluids like sweat, saliva, tears, and interstitial fluid. The development of wearable electrochemical biosensors using advanced materials has significantly enhanced their ability to track health metrics continuously, paving the way for more accessible healthcare solutions [32]. (See Fig. 6) [33].

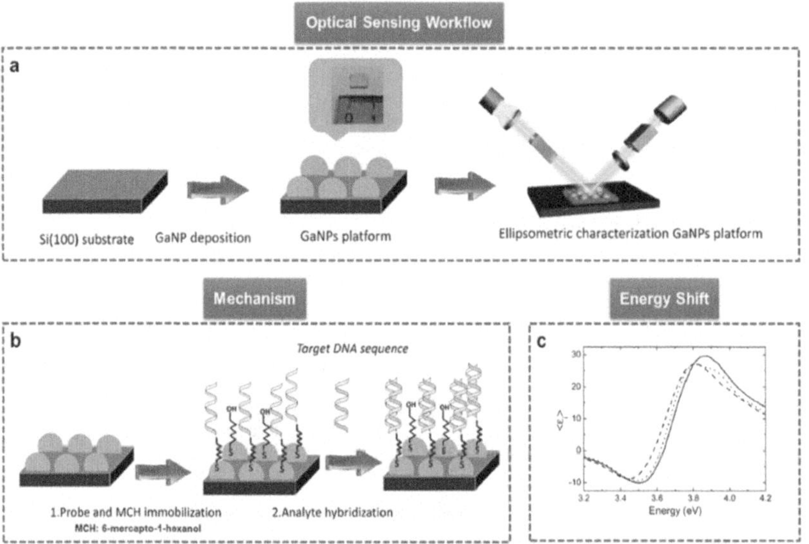

Fig. 6. Schematic of a GaNP/Si-based optical biosensor (a) Label-free sensing platform. (b) Immobilization of the DNA probe on the GaNP/Si surface (c) Pseudo dielectric spectra before and after modification [33]. Copyright 2016 Nanoscale.

5 Discussion on Challenges in the Development of Flexible Metal-Based Biosensors

5.1 Challenges in Development

Material Limitations and Challenges in Achieving Optimal Adhesion. A major challenge in developing flexible metal-based biosensors is ensuring biocompatibility and preventing skin irritation, especially with metals like titanium, bronze, and stain-less steel [34]. While titanium alloys are biocompatible, metals like silver nanowires raise concerns over ion leaching. Integrating rigid metals into flexible designs is difficult due to mechanical mismatches, leading to poor adhesion and compromised sensor performance [35].

Addressing Comfort and Wearability in Flexible Designs. Achieving strong adhesion without skin irritation is a challenge for flexible biosensors. Bio-friendly, adhesive substrates are essential for comfort and safe removal. Wearable sensors must also prevent discomfort and motion artifacts, ensuring reliable data collection. Long-term monitoring requires materials and designs that minimize irritation and allow natural movement [36].

Issues Related to Electrical Conductivity and Signal Quality. Balancing conductivity and signal sensitivity is key for accurate measurements. Optimizing the microstructure and surface properties of metal nanoparticles enhances performance, but zero-dimensional nanoparticles can degrade conductivity and signal quality due to charge scattering, especially during motion. Optimizing sensor architecture is essential to maintain high signal quality without interference from metal components [37].

Challenges in Scaling Up the Manufacturing Process. Scaling up the manufacturing of flexible metal-based biosensors for commercialization requires high standards of accuracy, durability, and safety, as well as cost-effectiveness. Producing high-quality 3D printing filaments at an industrial scale demands advanced technologies and substantial investments. Ensuring consistent performance over time and under varying conditions further complicates scalability and reliability [38].

5.2 Future Directions and Trends

Integration with IoT and AI. Integrating flexible biosensors with IoT and AI enables real-time data analysis and predictive medicine, enhancing accuracy, continuous monitoring, and early disease detection through IoT systems [3, 39].

Personalized Healthcare. Metal-based flexible biosensors are essential for personalized medicine, particularly for chronic conditions. These sensors enable continuous biomarker monitoring, with 3D printing improving accessibility and customization for patient-specific care [40].

Regulatory and Commercialization Challenges. Wearable biosensors with metal components face regulatory challenges in meeting accuracy, durability, and safety standards. Successful commercialization requires extensive testing, addressing reproducibility, shelf-life, and environmental conditions [8, 40].

Advancements in Material Science and Manufacturing Techniques. Progress in biocompatible materials, like titanium alloys and self-healing polymers, enhances sensor performance. Titanium-graphene composites and conductive filaments with gold/silver particles improve durability and functionality for real-world applications [39, 41].

6 Conclusion

This paper highlights the transformative role of 3D printing in developing flexible and sticky biosensors for healthcare monitoring. Unlike traditional methods like photolithography, 3D printing enables the creation of intricate, customizable, three-dimensional sensor architectures that can be printed directly on non-planar surfaces, such as skin or organs, enhancing patient-specific designs and comfort. The use of metals like titanium, bronze, stainless steel, and noble metal nanoparticles (e.g., gold, silver) is crucial for improving the conductivity, durability, and accuracy of biosensors. Hybrid 3D printing techniques that integrate metals with flexible polymers or hydrogels allow for the development of multi-functional biosensors, combining electrical performance with biocompatibility. Additionally, the incorporation of nano-materials such as graphene enhances sensor sensitivity and selectivity, advancing non-invasive, continuous health monitoring. This advancement enables the creation of highly customizable, flexible, and reliable biosensors that can seamlessly interact with the human body, whether as skin patches, tattoos, or potentially integrated with internal organs. These biosensors allow for real-time, non-invasive tracking of vital signs and biomarkers, marking a shift from reactive to proactive healthcare. By rap-idly prototyping patient-specific biosensing systems, this technology democratizes advanced diagnostics, providing tailored health insights and empowering patients and clinicians with continuous, actionable data. This approach enhances early detection, timely interventions, and chronic disease management, reducing hospital visits and improving overall well-being. As such, 3D-printed metal-based flexible biosensors are poised to lead the future of personalized medicine and healthcare delivery.

Disclosure of Interests. The authors have no competing interests to declare that are relevant to the content of this article.

References

1. Tang, L., Yang, J., Wang, Y., Deng, R.: Recent advances in cardiovascular disease biosensors and monitoring technologies. ACS Sensors **8**(3), 956–973 (2023). https://doi.org/10.1021/acssensors.2c02311
2. Kim, J.: (Invited) Wearable electrochemical biosensors for continuous biomarker monitoring in daily-life. ECS Meet. Abstr. **MA2024–02**(54), 3701 (2024). https://doi.org/10.1149/MA2024-02543701mtgabs
3. Bhatia, D., Paul, S., Acharjee, T., Ramachairy, S.S.: Biosensors and their widespread impact on human health. Sensors Int. **5**, 100257 (2024). https://doi.org/10.1016/j.sintl.2023.100257
4. Jose, R.R., Rodriguez, M.J., Dixon, T.A., Omenetto, F., Kaplan, D.L.: Evolution of bioinks and additive manufacturing technologies for 3D bioprinting. ACS Biomater. Sci. Eng. **2**(10), 1662–1678 (2016). https://doi.org/10.1021/acsbiomaterials.6b00088
5. Zhou, F., et al.: Wearable electrochemical glucose sensor of high flexibility and sensitivity using novel mushroom-like gold nanowires decorated bendable stainless steel wire sieve. Anal. Chim. Acta **1288**, 342148 (2024). https://doi.org/10.1016/j.aca.2023.342148
6. Crapnell, R.D., Banks, C.E.: Electroanalysis overview: additive manufactured biosensors using fused filament fabrication. Anal. Methods **16**(17), 2625–2634 (2024). https://doi.org/10.1039/D4AY00278D
7. Wu, T., Liu, G.: Non-invasive wearables in inflammation monitoring: from biomarkers to biosensors. Biosensors **15**(6) (2025). https://doi.org/10.3390/bios15060351
8. Van Tran, V., Phung, V.-D., Lee, D.: Recent advances and innovations in the design and fabrication of wearable flexible biosensors and human health monitoring systems based on conjugated polymers. Bio-Design Manuf. **7**(4), 476–516 (2024). https://doi.org/10.1007/s42242-024-00297-z
9. Pereira, A.C., Nayak, V.V., Coelho, P.G., Witek, L.: Integrative modeling and experimental insights into 3D and 4D printing technologies. Polymers (Basel). **16**(19) (2024). https://doi.org/10.3390/polym16192686

10. Lu, G., Tang, R., Nie, J., Zhu, X.: Photocuring 3D printing of hydrogels: techniques, materials, and applications in tissue engineering and flexible devices. Macromol. Rapid Commun. **45**(7), 2300661 (2024). https://doi.org/10.1002/marc.202300661
11. Li, L., et al.: A nanostructured conductive hydrogels-based biosensor platform for human metabolite detection. Nano Lett. **15**(2), 1146–1151 (2015). https://doi.org/10.1021/nl504217p
12. Li, G., Liu, S., Xu, Z., Guo, J., Tang, S.-Y., Ma, X.: Recent advancements in liquid metal enabled flexible and wearable biosensors. Soft Sci. **3**(4) (2023). https://doi.org/10.20517/ss.2023.30
13. Song, L., Chen, J., Bin Xu, B., Huang, Y.: Flexible plasmonic biosensors for healthcare monitoring: progress and prospects. ACS Nano **15**(12), 18822–18847 (2021). https://doi.org/10.1021/acsnano.1c07176
14. Khan, Y., Thielens, A., Muin, S., Ting, J., Baumbauer, C., Arias, A.C.: A new frontier of printed electronics: flexible hybrid electronics. Adv. Mater. **32**(15), 1905279 (2020). https://doi.org/10.1002/adma.201905279
15. Liang, M., et al.: Designing flexible and sticky 3d printed biosensors: a material-centric approach three-dimensional (3D) printing facilitates the fabrication of biosensors and biomedical detection devices by offering low cost, rapid prototyping, and simple operation meth. ECS Sensors Plus **2**(3), 30604 (2023). https://doi.org/10.1149/2754-2726/ace5bd
16. Song, D., Chen, X., Wang, M., Wu, Z., Xiao, X.: 3D-printed flexible sensors for food monitoring. Chem. Eng. J. **474**, 146011 (2023). https://doi.org/10.1016/j.cej.2023.146011
17. Marculescu, C., et al.: Customizable fabrication process for flexible carbon-based electrochemical biosensors. Chemosensors **11**(4) (2023). https://doi.org/10.3390/chemosensors11040204
18. Zalewska, A., Lenar, N., Paczosa-Bator, B.: 3D printing in the design of potentiometric sensors: a review of techniques, materials, and applications. Sensors **25**(16) (2025). https://doi.org/10.3390/s25164986
19. El-Bassyouni, G.T., Mouneir, S.M., El-Shamy, A.M.: Advances in surface modifications of titanium and its alloys: implications for biomedical and pharmaceutical applications. Multiscale Multidiscip. Model. Exp. Des. **8**(5), 265 (2025). https://doi.org/10.1007/s41939-025-00823-1
20. Vickram, A.S., Infant, S.S., Manikandan, S., Sowndharya, B.B., Gulothungan, G., Chopra, H.: 3D bio-printed scaffolds and smart implants: evaluating functional performance in animal surgery models. Ann. Med. Surg. **87**(6) (2025). [Online]. Available: https://journals.lww.com/annals-of-medicine-and-surgery/fulltext/2025/06000/3d_bio_printed_scaffolds_and_smart_implants_.66.aspx
21. Ang, Y., Jin, J., Lu, Y., Mei, D.: 3D printing of liquid metal based tactile sensor for simultaneously sensing of temperature and forces. Int. J. Smart Nano Mater. **12**, 269–285 (2021). [Online]. Available: https://api.semanticscholar.org/CorpusID:237831335
22. Song, Z., et al.: Flexible and wearable biosensors for monitoring health conditions. Biosensors **13**(6) (2023). https://doi.org/10.3390/bios13060630
23. Das, V., Boothby, A., López, J.J.V., Lie, D.Y.-C.: Design investigations for robust and continuous online heartbeat monitoring using wearable versus Doppler-based non-contact vital signs biosensors (2016). [Online]. Available: https://api.semanticscholar.org/CorpusID:64362719
24. Li, Y., et al.: A stretchable-hybrid low-power monolithic ECG patch with microfluidic liquid-metal interconnects and stretchable carbon-black nanocomposite electrodes for wearable heart monitoring. Adv. Electron. Mater. **5**(2), 1800463 (2019). https://doi.org/10.1002/aelm.201800463
25. Gao, Y., et al.: Wearable microfluidic diaphragm pressure sensor for health and tactile touch monitoring. Adv. Mater. **29**, 1701985 (2017)

26. Zhao, X.-F., et al.: A fully flexible intelligent thermal touch panel based on intrinsically plastic Ag2S semiconductor. Adv. Mater. **34**(13), 2107479 (2022). https://doi.org/10.1002/adma.202107479
27. Sharma, A., Badea, M., Tiwari, S., Marty, J.L.: Wearable biosensors: an alternative and practical approach in healthcare and disease monitoring. Molecules **26**(3) (2021). https://doi.org/10.3390/molecules26030748
28. Vo, D.-K., Trinh, K.T.L.: Advances in wearable biosensors for healthcare: current trends, applications, and future perspectives. Biosensors **14**(2024). [Online]. Available: https://api.semanticscholar.org/CorpusID:274261548
29. Lee, J., Kim, M.C., Soltis, I., Lee, S.H., Yeo, W.-H.: Advances in electrochemical sensors for detecting analytes in biofluids. Adv. Sens. Res. **2**(8), 2200088 (2023). https://doi.org/10.1002/adsr.202200088
30. Zhang, W., Jiang, S., Yu, H., Feng, S., Zhang, K.: Ga@MXene-based flexible wearable biosensor for glucose monitoring in sweat. iScience **28**(2), 111737 (2025). https://doi.org/10.1016/j.isci.2024.111737
31. Mostafalu, P., et al.: Smart bandage for monitoring and treatment of chronic wounds. Small **14**(33), 1703509 (2018). https://doi.org/10.1002/smll.201703509
32. Raymond, D.A., Kumar, P., Goureshettiwar, P.: Wearable electrochemical sensors for real-time biomarkers detection. In: 2024 second international conference on intelligent cyber physical system internet things, pp. 649–655 (2024). [Online]. Available: https://api.semanticscholar.org/CorpusID:273106049
33. Marín, A.G., et al.: Gallium plasmonic nanoparticles for label-free DNA and single nucleotide polymorphism sensing. Nanoscale **8**(18), 9842–9851 (2016). https://doi.org/10.1039/C6NR00926C
34. Morshed-Behbahani, K., Bishop, D.P., Nasiri, A.: A review of the corrosion behavior of conventional and additively manufactured nickel-aluminum bronze (NAB) alloys: current status and future challenges. Mater. horizons (2023). [Online]. Available: https://api.semanticscholar.org/CorpusID:263169228
35. Zhou, N., Liu, T., Wen, B., Gong, C., Wei, G., Su, Z.: Recent advances in the construction of flexible sensors for biomedical applications. Biotechnol. J. **15**(12), 2000094 (2020). https://doi.org/10.1002/biot.202000094
36. Nam, D., Cha, J.M., Park, K.: Next-generation wearable biosensors developed with flexible bio-chips. Micromachines **12** (2021). [Online]. Available: https://api.semanticscholar.org/CorpusID:231587818
37. Chiu, Y.H., Guo, Y.-T., Rinawati, M., Chang, C.-C., Chang, L.-Y., Yeh, M.-H.: Developing flexible carbon nitride quantum dots decorated polyaniline nanocomposite layer for a non-invasive wearable sweat biosensor for glucose monitoring. ECS Meet. Abstr. (2024). [Online]. Available: https://api.semanticscholar.org/CorpusID:272119257
38. Silva, L.R.G., Lopes, C.E.C., Tanaka, A.A., Dantas, L.M.F., Silva, I.S., Stefano, J.S.: Electrochemical biosensors 3D printed by fused deposition modeling: actualities, trends, and challenges. Biosensors **15** (2025). [Online]. Available: https://api.semanticscholar.org/CorpusID:275641437
39. Nagamine, K., et al.: Printed organic transistor-based biosensors for non-invasive sweat analysis. Anal. Sci. **36**(3), 291–302 (2020). https://doi.org/10.2116/analsci.19R007
40. Zhao, Y., et al.: Development of flexible electronic biosensors for healthcare engineering. IEEE Sens. J. **24**(8), 11998–12016 (2024). https://doi.org/10.1109/JSEN.2023.3287291
41. Deka, M., et al.: A review on the surface modification of materials for 3D-printed diagnostic devices. Anal. Methods (2024). [Online]. Available: https://api.semanticscholar.org/CorpusID:266382392

A Review of the Current Researches on the Application of Barrier Membrane Technology in Guided Bone Regeneration in the Oral and Maxillofacial

Chi Zhang[1,2](✉), Zhewei Liu[2,3], Yakuang Zhang[4], and Xinpei Li[2,3]

[1] Department of Industry Engineering, School of Mechanical Engineering, Northwestern Poly-Technical University, Xi'an 710072, China
zhangchi160985@mail.nwpu.edu.cn

[2] Bio-Additive Manufacturing University-Enterprise Joint Research Center of Shaanxi Province, Northwestern Polytechnical University, Xi'an 710072, China

[3] Xi'an BONE Biotechnology Ltd, Xi'an 710026, China

[4] Aerospace and Astronautics Propulsion Research Institute Co., Ltd, Haining 314499, China

Abstract. With the continuous advancement of Artificial Intelligence (AI) technology, its applications in the medical field are expanding rapidly, particularly demonstrating significant advantages in image recognition, data analysis, and predictive modeling. In bone augmentation techniques, AI can be utilized for pre-operative assessment, postoperative monitoring, and the development of personalized treatment plans. Alveolar bone augmentation technology is a technique that increases the volume and density of alveolar bone through surgical means to support dental implants or improve the effectiveness of orthodontic treatment. The core principle is to promote the generation of new bone tissue by implanting bone replacement materials, such as artificial bone materials or autologous bone materials, thereby restoring the normal anatomical structure and function of the alveolar bone. Alveolar Bone augmentation technology relies on the regenerative ability of bone tissue. In the bone defect area, guided bone regeneration (GBR) is a technique that promotes the regeneration of bone tissue in the defect area by implanting barrier membranes and bone replacement materials. This technique is mainly used to address issues such as alveolar bone defects and insufficient alveolar bone volume, helping to restore the stability of bone structure and providing a foundation for subsequent restoration. As an effective method for bone defect repair, GBR is widely used in dentistry and maxillofacial surgery. It guides the growth of new bone through biomaterials, thereby improving bone mass. It is particularly significant in dental implants and bone augmentation surgeries. AI can assist dentists in preoperative planning of surgical pathways, thereby enhancing surgical success rates. Additionally, AI can be employed for postoperative monitoring of barrier membrane stability, bone regeneration processes, and complication risks, thereby improving treatment safety and predictability. This article provides a review of the current application of barrier membrane technologies used in the dental field and explores future research directions.

Keywords: Artificial Intelligence · Alveolar bone augmentation · Guided bone re-generation · Barrier membrane

S. S. Ge et al. (Eds.): ICSR + BioMed 2025, LNAI 16435, pp. 65–79, 2026.
https://doi.org/10.1007/978-981-95-7538-1_7

1 Introduction

Common causes of alveolar bone defects include periodontitis, trauma, tooth loss, tumors or cysts, genetic factors, and systemic diseases (such as osteoporosis and diabetes) [1]. These factors cause alveolar bone resorption or destruction through local inflammation, mechanical damage, metabolic abnormalities, or systemic effects, leading to defects. In the field of dental implants, bone augmentation techniques are primarily used to increase the bone volume of the alveolar ridge to meet the requirements for dental implants. More specifically, bone augmentation can be horizontal or vertical augmentation of the alveolar ridge, or augmentation of the maxillary sinus floor, thereby providing sufficient support and stability for the implant (see Fig. 1). In the field of orthodontics, bone augmentation technology is equally significant. Alveolar bone defects are a common oral problem among ortho-dontic patients and may lead to complications such as root resorption and bone fenestration. Therefore, oral health professionals should assess the patient's alveolar bone condition and promptly develop and implement a bone augmentation plan [2].

Bone augmentation technology is an innovative solution that combines science and dental skills to regenerate and repair bone tissue through a variety of methods. Guided bone regeneration (GBR) is a commonly used technique with a wide range of indications that helps restore the dimensions of the alveolar ridge [3]. By placing a barrier membrane between the soft tissue and bone defect, a closed environment is created that promotes the growth of osteoblast precursors, thereby achieving reparative bone regeneration.

The core principle of GBR is to isolate soft tissue through a physical barrier membrane to prevent fibroblasts from invading the bone defect area too quickly, while using bone substitute materials (such as autogenous bone and artificial bone powder) to provide a growth scaffold for osteoblasts and promote new bone formation.Barrier membranes are divided into absorbable membranes and non-absorbable membranes [4]. The former can degrade on their own, while the latter require a second surgery to remove.

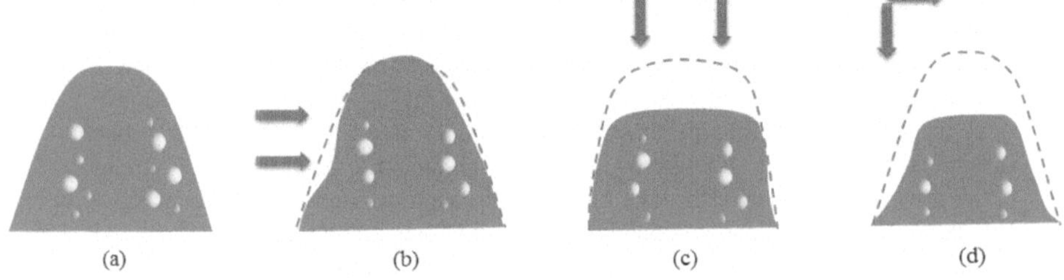

Fig. 1. Types of alveolar bone defects. (a) Normal bone volume. (b) Horizontal bone loss with adequate height, which leads to insufficient bone volume. (c) Vertical bone loss with adequate width, which leads to insufficient bone volume for proper positioning of regular length implants in correct prosthetic corono-apical position for successful placement of regular diameter implants. (d) Vertical and horizontal bone loss that prevents placement of successful implants in all spatial dimensions.

2 Techniques for GBR

Guided bone regeneration (GBR) is a barrier membrane that separates soft tissues from bone defects. It can effectively prevent the growth of epithelial cells and fibro-blasts around bone defects, allowing slow-growing stem cells/bone cells sufficient time to carry out in situ repair and regeneration of bone tissue [5]. Guided bone re-generation technology has been widely used in the restoration of insufficient bone volume in the oral and maxillofacial region, such as alveolar bone defects and reconstruction of bone defects around implants [6]. Studies have reported that up to 40% of implant osseointegration implants require guided bone regeneration surgery [7].

The materials mainly used in GBR technology include barrier membranes and bone graft materials. Barrier membranes are divided into two types: absorbent and non-absorbent. Bone transplantation materials mainly include autologous bone, allogeneic bone and artificial bone materials.

2.1 Classification and Application of Absorption Barrier Membrane

Absorbable membranes are mainly divided into two categories: natural polymer materials and synthetic polymer materials:Natural polymeric materials primarily include Collagen, Silk fibroin, Chitosan, Cellulose, Alginate, Gelatin etc. Collagen membranes have excellent biocompatibility, low immunogenicity, and degradability, making them ideal barrier membrane materials that promote wound healing and bone tissue regeneration [8]. The physical and chemical properties of collagen membranes can be controlled by cross-linking methods to improve their mechanical properties and stability. Synthetic polymeric materials include Polylactic Acid(PLA), Polyglycolic Acid (PGA), Poly(ε-caprolactone) (PCL), Poly (lactic-co-glycolic acid) (PLGA), Ethyl 4-hydroxybenzoate (PDO), Poly(lactic-co-caprolactone) (PLCL), Polyvinyl Alcohol (PVA), Magnesium(Mg) alloy [9–11], etc. (see Fig. 2). These materials are chemically synthesized and have controllable degradation rates and good mechanical properties.

Absorbable membranes gradually degrade within the body, eliminating the need for a second surgery to remove them and reducing patient discomfort and the risk of complications. They are typically made from natural or synthetic materials, exhibit excellent biocompatibility, and promote tissue regeneration [12, 13]. They are easy to cut, suture, or shape to meet different clinical needs. Absorbable membranes can promote angiogenesis and tissue regeneration, acting as scaffolds to provide support and guidance for new tissue growth, thereby aiding wound repair and healing. How-ever, they also have several drawbacks, including uncontrollable degradation rates: the degradation rate of absorbable membranes may vary among individuals, affecting bone formation [14–18]. If the membrane absorbs too quickly, the implant lacks rigid support, and during inflammation, this will affect the integrity of the membrane and reduce the functionality of the barrier membrane. Additionally, these membranes have drawbacks such as poor mechanical properties, particularly natural collagen membranes, which lack self-forming ability and struggle to maintain a stable spatial structure. Postoperatively, they may fold or collapse, interfering with bone regeneration in the surgical area [19–30]. During degradation, absorbable membranes may induce mild inflammatory reactions, though these do not significantly affect bone formation. However, these issues pose potential risks and limit their widespread clinical application [31, 32].

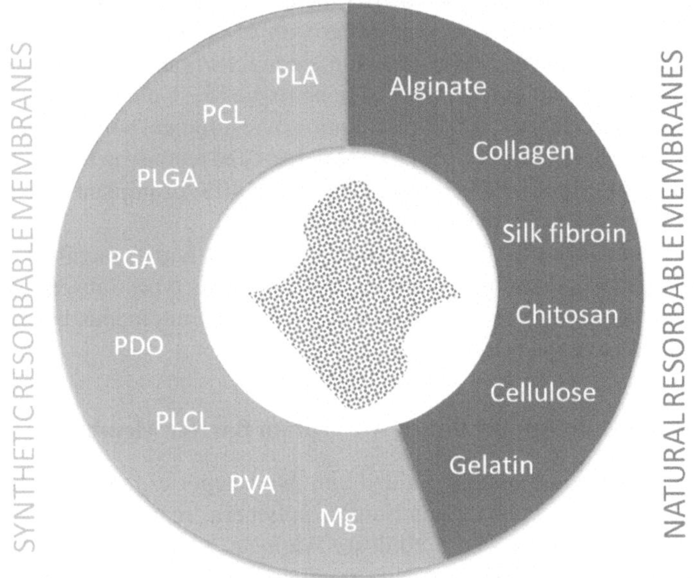

Fig. 2. Classification of resorbable membranes. Synthetic sources (left) and natural sources (right)

Main applications: In periodontal bone defect repair, absorbable barrier membranes are widely used to guide bone tissue regeneration. Studies have shown that absorbable membranes such as Bio-Guide demonstrate good results in periodontal bone defect repair, promoting capillary proliferation and providing a good growth environment for bone cells [33]. Furthermore, collagen membranes, due to their unique bio-logical properties, have become one of the preferred materials in clinical practice, especially in cases where no secondary surgery is required, as they demonstrate higher patient acceptance and lower complication risks [34].

In the preservation of the alveolar ridge site after tooth extraction, the application of absorbable barrier membranes is particularly important. GBR technology, combined with absorbable membranes and bone grafting materials, can effectively maintain the height and width of the alveolar ridge, providing favorable conditions for subsequent implantation. For example, Bio-Guide barrier membranes are widely used in clinical practice. Their main advantage is that they can degrade in vivo, eliminating the need for a second surgery to remove them. Even if exposure occurs during the healing period, they still have a certain degree of anti-infective capacity [33, 35–37].

In both vertical and horizontal bone augmentation, absorbable barrier membranes also play a crucial role. Studies have shown that absorbable membranes are less effective than non-absorbable membranes (such as titanium mesh) in terms of space maintenance [34, 38, 39], but they offer significant advantages in soft tissue healing and bone regeneration [40]. In recent years, the development of digital titanium mesh technology has made non-resorbable membranes highly customizable in clinical practice, further improving the success rate of GBR surgery [12, 34, 39, 41].

Tent bone grafting is an innovative technique derived from GBR that uses different supports to lift the periosteum or barrier membrane away from the bone surface and provides osteogenic space for osteoblasts using bone substitute materials [43, 44]. Tent bone grafting has significant advantages in terms of bone augmentation and is particularly suitable for severely atrophied alveolar ridges. Studies have shown that tent peg technology can achieve high vertical bone increment (e.g., an average of 2.87 ± 0.79 mm) [45]. In this technology, the application of absorbable barrier membranes is particularly important because they can combine with bone replacement materials to form a stable submembrane space that promotes bone regeneration [46].

2.2 Classification and Application of Non-Absorbable Barrier Membrane

In GBR technology, a non-absorbable membrane refers to a physical barrier membrane made from biocompatible materials that are not absorbed or degraded by the human body after surgery. These membranes are typically composed of synthetic materials such as polytetrafluoroethylene (PTFE), which exhibit excellent biocompatibility and mechanical properties. They help maintain the spatial integrity of bone defects, prevent soft tissue invasion, and promote bone tissue regeneration [47]. Non-absorbable barrier membranes are primarily categorized into dense polytetrafluoro-ethylene (d-PTFE), expanded polytetrafluoroethylene (e-PTFE) membranes, titanium membranes, titanium-reinforced polytetrafluoroethylene (TR-PTFE) membranes, and other metallic materials (such as titanium mesh and titanium plates) [36, 46, 48–51], as well as some materials that are not yet widely used or are still in the research stage (such as Janus collagen membranes, alginate, and ceramic membranes)[12, 52, 53]. (see Fig. 3).

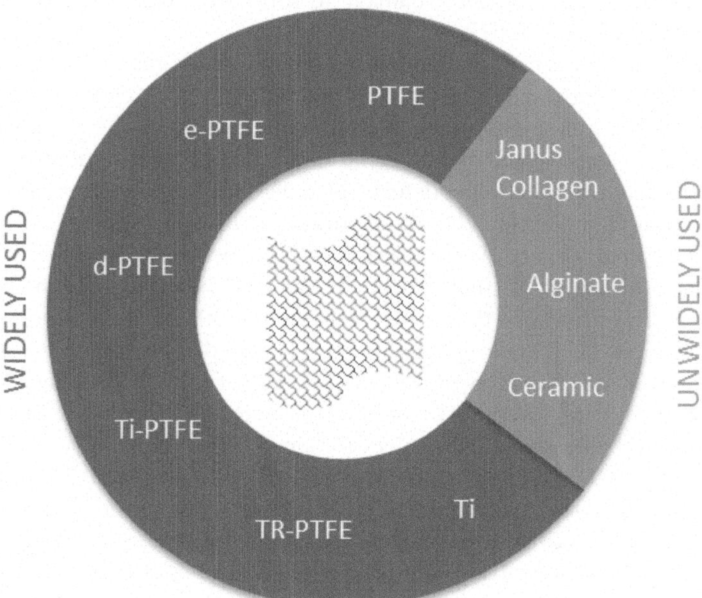

Fig. 3. Classification of non-resorbable membranes. Widely used materials (left) and materials not yet widely used (right)

Non-absorbable barrier membranes, such as e-PTFE membranes and titanium membranes, possess high mechanical strength and stability, effectively maintaining the spatial integrity of bone defect areas and preventing soft tissue invasion. This spatial maintenance capability is particularly crucial for larger or more complex bone defects, facilitating bone tissue regeneration and the stable implantation of implants [48, 54, 55]. Typically made from biocompatible materials such as e-PTFE and titanium, these materials are unlikely to trigger immune or rejection reactions within the body, allowing them to integrate well with surrounding tissues and promote bone tissue regeneration [31, 34, 56]. Non-absorbable barrier membranes can maintain barrier function in bone defect areas for extended periods of time, providing a stable environment for bone tissue regeneration. Numerous studies have demonstrated that e-PTFE membranes maintain good barrier effectiveness for 6–12 months postoperatively [50, 57–61].

Although non-absorbable barrier membranes perform well in maintaining bone defect spaces, their non-degradable nature poses significant clinical challenges. First, since non-absorbable barrier membranes cannot degrade within the body, a second surgery is typically required 4–12 weeks postoperatively to remove them. This not only increases patient discomfort and medical costs but may also lead to complications such as infection and bleeding [62, 63]. In some cases, the barrier membrane may become exposed to the oral environment due to improper handling or displacement during the healing process, thereby increasing the risk of postoperative infection [64, 65].

Non-resorbable barrier membranes are challenging to use during surgery, particularly in the treatment of complex bone defects, requiring a high level of technical skill and experience [60]. Since non-resorbable barrier membranes are directly located at the implant shoulder, they limit the height of bone regeneration, which may affect the long-term stability of the implant [66]. Secondary surgery to remove non-resorbable barrier membranes may cause some damage to soft tissue, potentially affecting bone regeneration and healing [54, 67].

The non-absorbable barrier membrane itself is not biologically active and cannot promote cell proliferation and differentiation, but only provides a physical barrier [68].

Main applications: Non-absorbable barrier membranes have a wide range of applications in dentistry and oral and maxillofacial surgery. They are commonly used to treat large bone defects or vertical bone defects, alveolar ridge preservation, restoration of bone defects around implants, and bone augmentation in aesthetic areas.

In dental implant surgery, non-resorbable membranes are often used in combination with bone graft materials (such as Bio-Oss) to fill bone defects and maintain space [71–79]. In the repair of bone defects around dental implants, non-absorbable barrier membranes also play a crucial role. Studies have shown that the use of non-absorbable barrier membranes can effectively prevent the invasion of epithelial cells and connective tissue, thereby providing favorable conditions for bone tissue regeneration [72]. Additionally, non-absorbable membranes offer prolonged barrier protection in the repair of bone defects around dental implants, reducing the risk of postoperative infection [73].

In the repair of bone defects around dental implants, non-absorbable barrier membranes also play an important role. Studies have shown that the use of non-absorbable barrier membranes can effectively prevent the invasion of epithelial cells and connective tissue, thereby providing favorable conditions for bone tissue regeneration [74].

Additionally, non-absorbable membranes can provide longer-term barrier protection in the repair of bone defects around dental implants, reducing the risk of postoperative infection [54].

Alveolar ridge preservation is a critical component of dental surgery, particularly in cases of multiple tooth loss, as it helps extend the lifespan of dental implants. Non-resorbable barrier membranes have demonstrated excellent efficacy in alveolar ridge preservation, effectively preventing rapid resorption of the alveolar bone and maintaining its height and width. Studies have shown that using non-resorbable barrier membranes for alveolar ridge preservation significantly improves the long-term success rate of implants [75, 76].

In aesthetic zones (such as the anterior region), the use of non-resorbable barrier membranes has achieved significant results in bone augmentation. Non-resorbable barrier membranes, such as e-PTFE and titanium mesh, are widely used in GBR technology due to their excellent biocompatibility, space maintenance capability, and long-term stability. These materials effectively isolate non-osteogenic cells, promote the migration and proliferation of osteogenic cells, thereby achieving bone tissue regeneration [32, 77].

In periodontal regenerative therapy, the application of non-resorbable barrier membranes has been extensively studied, playing a crucial role in guided bone regeneration (GBR) and guided tissue regeneration (GTR). Non-resorbable barrier membranes exhibit excellent biocompatibility, mechanical stability, and space-maintaining capabilities, effectively preventing soft tissue migration into the defect area and thereby providing space for bone cell and periodontal tissue regeneration [78–81].

In alveolar socket preservation techniques, non-resorbable barrier membranes can effectively reduce alveolar bone resorption, maintain the shape and function of the alveolar socket, and provide a good foundation for subsequent implant restoration [76, 82].

2.3 The Application of Artificial Intelligence in GBR Technology

The application of AI in the field of guided bone regeneration (GBR) represents a cutting-edge and rapidly evolving direction. It primarily leverages machine learning particularly deep learning to analyze medical imaging (such as CBCT and X-rays), clinical data, and biomarkers, thereby providing data-driven decision support throughout preoperative, intraoperative, and postoperative stages (see Fig. 4).

2.3.1 Pre-Operative Planning

The application of AI in medical image analysis, surgical planning, material design, and data analysis has become increasingly mature. AI can be utilized to optimize preoperative planning, postoperative monitoring, and personalized treatment design for guided bone regeneration (GBR) surgery. AI-enhanced CBCT analysis is trans-forming dental implant optimization, highlighting its potential in automatically identifying anatomical features, assessing bone quality and volume, and predicting implant success [83]. The study indicates that AI-driven CBCT analysis can reduce operator dependency while enhancing diagnostic accuracy and treatment efficiency. AI algorithms can automatically identify and delineate (segment) bone defect regions within CBCT images, precisely calculating parameters such as volume, morphology, and density. This significantly outperforms the rough estimates achievable by human eyes, providing accurate foundations for graft volume calculation, barrier membrane selection, and trimming [84]. Based on segmentation and analysis results, AI can assist or automatically generate personalized surgical guide designs for guided bone regeneration (GBR) procedures, ensuring precision in implant placement location, depth, and angle, as well as the scope of bone grafting [85, 86].

2.3.2 Post-Operative Monitoring

In postoperative monitoring, AI can quantify the extent of new bone formation and changes in bone density by comparing serial X-rays or CBCT scans, generating objective healing trend reports that reduce subjective judgment differences among physicians [87]. AI models can learn from extensive case data of both successful and failed outcomes (e.g., infections, membrane exposure, abnormal bone resorption), enabling them to identify subtle patterns predictive of complications in early imaging or clinical photographs, thereby facilitating early intervention [88, 90].

2.3.3 Personalized Treatment Design

This represents the most promising field for AI, aimed at achieving precision medicine. Its application manifests in AI models leveraging patient-specific data—such as bone defect type, volume, bone density, imaging data, genomic data, and clinical data—to predict success rates and anticipated osteogenic outcomes under different treatment protocols (e.g., using various brands of bone grafting materials or barrier membranes). This assists physicians and patients in selecting the optimal treatment plan [91]. In the selection and optimization of materials, AI also plays a significant role. By analyzing vast amounts of historical case data, AI can evaluate the performance of different materials—such as autogenous bone, allograft bone, and synthetic bone—in clinical applications, thereby recommending the most suitable material combination for specific types of defects. For instance, autogenous bone exhibits excellent osteoinductive and osteogenic properties but poses challenges related to donor site trauma and limited bone availability. Conversely, synthetic bone materials (such as bioceramics and polymers) offer superior biocompatibility and controllability, though they may lack osteoinductive capabilities [92, 93]. AI can integrate imaging techniques (such as micro-CT) with histological analysis to evaluate material properties including degradability, biocompatibility, osteoconductivity, and osteoin-ductivity [94, 95]. AI can assist in designing novel composite materials that combine the advantages of different substances, such as the combined application of autologous bone and synthetic materials, to enhance bone repair outcomes [92, 96].

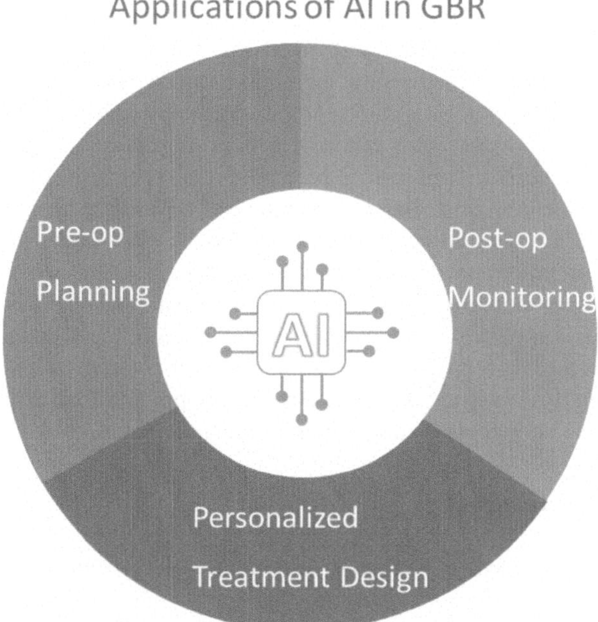

Fig. 4. The main applications of AI in GBR: Pre-operative Planning, Post-operative Monitoring and Personalized Treatment Design

3 Conclusion

AI is revolutionizing the practice of guided bone regeneration (GBR) surgery, transforming it from an experience-dependent "art" into a data-driven "science." Its application in guided bone regeneration is increasingly becoming a significant focus in both research and clinical practice. With the continuous advancement of artificial intelligence (AI) and biomaterials science, future research and applications in the field of GBR will witness multifaceted innovations and breakthroughs.

AI-assisted surgical planning and image analysis technologies enhance the precision and efficiency of surgical procedures. AI-driven image analysis helps clinicians more accurately identify bone defect areas and optimize surgical plans, thereby improving treatment success rates. This demonstrates the immense potential of AI applications in guided bone regeneration (GBR).

In the field of biomaterials, significant progress has been made in recent years in the research of biodegradable magnesium-based metal GBR membranes. These materials exhibit excellent mechanical properties, biodegradability, and osteoinductive capabilities, making them ideal candidates for bone defect repair. Magnesium-based metal GBR membranes not only promote bone tissue regeneration but also possess favorable biocompatibility and degradability, rendering them suitable for treating oral and maxillofacial bone defects. However, several challenges remain, including controlling degradation rates, optimizing mechanical strength, and enhancing biological activity.

Future research directions include developing GBR membranes with functional gradients to achieve more complex biological functions, such as antimicrobial properties and enhanced bone regeneration. Research on AI-assisted design of intelligent bioactive membranes or biodegradable magnesium membranes holds promise for further enhancing GBR outcomes. AI technology can be employed to optimize material structure and properties, thereby improving their efficacy in bone regeneration applications. Concurrently, AI's application in biomaterial preparation and performance evaluation will accelerate the development and clinical translation of novel materials. The integration of AI with biomaterials will emerge as a key research direction in the future.

Future research directions also include exploring the development of novel bioactive materials and smart materials to achieve more efficient bone regeneration and tissue repair. The application of AI in guided bone augmentation holds great promise, with future studies increasingly focusing on integrating AI with biomaterials to advance GBR technology. Through AI-assisted design and the development of smart materials, more efficient and precise bone regeneration therapies are anticipated.

4 Disclosure of Interests

The authors have no competing interests to declare that are relevant to the content of this article.

Acknowledgments. This work was supported by the Technological Innovation Guidance Projects of Shaanxi Province (grant numbers 2023KXJ-038).

References

1. Zhang, F.G., Su, Y.C., Qiu, L.X., et al.: Expert consensus on the bone augmentation surgery for alveolar bone defects [J]. J Prev Treat Stomatol Dis **30**(4), 229–236 (2022)
2. Jiang, Q.S., Lai, W.L., Wang, Y.: Research progress on bone augmentation technique in ortho-dontics [J]. Int J Stomatol **50**(2), 243–250 (2023)
3. Vineetha V, Anwgundi RV, Santhosh S, Karishma A, BJU T, Guided Bone Regeneration-A Comprehensive Review[J].Journal of Clinical and Diagnostic Research. 2021 Apr, 15(4): ZE01-ZE04
4. Bee, S.L., Hamid, Z.A.A.: Asymmetric resorbable-based dental barrier membrane for periodontal guided tissue regeneration and guided bone regeneration: A review [J]. J. Biomed. Mater. Res. B Appl. Biomater. **110**(9), 2157–2182 (2022)
5. Gentile, P., Chiono, V., Tonda-Turo, C., et al.: Polymeric membranes for guided bone regeneration [J]. Biotechnol. J. **6**(10), 1187–1197 (2011)
6. Buser D, Urban I, Monje A, et al. Guided bone regeneration in implant dentistry: basic principle, progress over 35 years, and recent research activities [J]. Periodontol 2000, 2023, 93(1): 9–25
7. Bornstein, M.M., Halbritter, S., Harnisch, H., et al.: A retrospective analysis of patients referred for implant placement to a specialty clinic: indications, surgical procedures, and early failures [J]. Int. J. Oral Maxillofac. Implants **23**(6), 1109–1116 (2008)
8. MD Zhu, XY Zhang, Q Wang, J Zhou. Research Progress of Collagen Membranes Based on Guided Bone Regeneration Applications [J]. Chinese Journal of Practical Stomatology, 2025, Vol. 18 Iss (1): 27–33

9. Riad FARDOUN. Barrier membranes used in guided bone regeneration: A review [J]. International Arab Journal of Dentistry: Vol. 10: Iss. 2, Article 6
10. LW Chen, JM Han, CB Guo.Research Status and Prospect of Degradable Magnesium-based metal-guided Bone Regeneration Membranes [J]. West China Journal of Stomatology, 2024–08 42(4):415–425
11. Abtahi, S., Chen, X., Shahabi, S., Nasiri, N.: Resorbable Membranes for Guided Bone Regeneration: Critical Features, Potentials, and Limitations [J]. ACS Mater. Au **3**, 394–417 (2023)
12. Ren, L.Z., Sun, R.: New progress in the clinical application of GBR membrane materials [J]. Journal of Prevention and Treatment for Stomatological Diseases **28**(6), 404–408 (Jun.2020)
13. PAGANO JN, CARRE E. Biomaterials used for bone regeneration in dental implantology and periodontology [J]. REV.PHARM.DISP.MED. (2024)6–1:1024–1040
14. Bunyaratavej, P., Wang, H.-L.: Collagen Membranes: A Review [J]. J. Periodontol. **72**(2), 215–229 (February 2001)
15. YJ He, WC Chen. The application of intelligent biomaterials in the field of dentistry[J].Journal of Oral Science Research,Jan. 2022,Vol. 38,No. 1:9–12
16. Wang, J.L., et al.: Biodegradable Polymer Membranes applied in Guided Bone/Tissue Regeneration: A Review [J]. Polymers **8**, 115 (2016)
17. Aprile, P., Letourneur, D., Simon-Yarza, T.: Membranes for Guided Bone Regeneration: A Road from Bench to Bedside [J]. Adv. Healthcare Mater. **9**, 2000707 (2020)
18. Zheng, Y.X., Ding, Y.D., Chen, F., Yang, F.: The application progress of silk fibroin as a barrier material for oral tissue regeneration [J]. Stomatology **44**(1), 69–74 (2024)
19. Moghe, A.K.: GuptaBS Pol Rev **48**, 353–377 (2008)
20. Guan, H.D., Tian, K., Niu, L., et al.: Rare Metal Materials and Engineering. **36**, 138–140 (2007)
21. N Wei，P Gong, Y Li et al. Rare Metal Materials and Engineering, 200736:34–36
22. Venugopal, J., MaL, L., Yong, T., et al.: Cell Bio Int **29**, 861–867 (2005)
23. Xu, X.L., Chen, X., Liu, A., et al.: Eur Pol **43**, 3187–3196 (2007)
24. Kim, H.W., Lee, H.H., Knowles, J.C.: Biomed Mater Res A **79**, 643–649 (2006)
25. Bhattarai, N., Li, Z.S., Edmondson, D., et al.: Adv. Mater. **18**, 1463–1467 (2006)
26. Jia, J., Duan, Y.Y., Ju, Y., et al.: J. Biomed. Mater. Res. A **86A**, 364–373 (2007)
27. Pham, Q.P., Sharma, U., MikosA, G.: Biomacroamolecules. **7**, 2796–2805 (2006)
28. Km, H.W., Song, J.H.: Kim HE. Adv. Funct. Mater. **15**, 1988–1994 (2005)
29. Fujihara, K., Kotaki, M., Ramarkrishna, S.: Biomaterials **26**, 4139–4147 (2005)
30. Tian, W.D., Bao, C.Y., Liu, L.: J. Biomed. Eng. **21**(5), 844–847 (2004)
31. Rodriguez, I.A., et al.: Barrier membranes for dental applications: A review and sweet advancement in membrane developments[J]. Mouth Teeth **2**(1), 1–9 (2018)
32. C H.F.HAMMERLE, R E. JUNG. Bone augmentation by means of barrier membranes [J]. Periodontology 2000, Vol. 33, 2003, 36–53
33. Yang, M.D., Tang, Y.: The application of alveolar ridge site preservation after tooth extraction in oral implantology[J]. International Journal of Stomatology **39**(2), 211–213 (2012)
34. Yanru Ren, L., Fan, S.A., Liu, L., Emmert, S., et al.: Barrier Membranes for Guided Bone Regeneration (GBR): A Focus on Recent Advances in Collagen Membranes[J]. Int. J. Mol. Sci. **23**, 14987 (2022)
35. Sun, X.L., Dai, A.N., Huang, J.P., et al.: The application of alveolar ridge preservation in periodontal infection sites: From soft and hard tissue regeneration to subsequent implant restoration [J]. Stomatology **44**(2), 130–138 (2024)
36. Li, P., Xiao, X., Zhang, H.B., Song, J., et al.: Research Progress on the Application of Autogenous Demineralized Dentin Matrix Particles for the Regeneration in Periodontitis Alveolar Defect[J]. Science Discovery **13**(1), 1–5 (2024)

37. Niu, X.Y., Xiao, Y., Gao, Z.J., Sun, J.J.: Safety and efficacy of absorbable silk fibroin film for alveolar ridge preservation after extraction. Chinese Journal of Tissue Engineering Research **23**(6), 906–911 (2019)
38. Y Xie, SH Li, TX Zhang, C Wang, XX Cai. Titanium mesh for bone augmentation in oral implantology: current application and progress [J].International Journal of Oral Science (2020)12:37
39. Funato A, Ishikawa T, Kitajima H, Yamada M, Moroi H. A Novel Combined Surgical Approach to Vertical Alveolar Ridge Augmentation with Titanium Mesh. Resorbable Membrane, and rhPDGF-BB: A Retrospective Consecutive Case Series [J]. Int J Periodontics Restorative Dent. 2013:33(4):437–445
40. Rispoli, L., Fontana, F., Beretta, M., Poggio, C.E., Maiorana, C.: Surgery Guidelines for Barrier Membranes in Guided Bone Regeneration (GBR) [J]. J Otolaryngol Rhinol **1**, 2 (2015)
41. Li, S.H., Cai, X.X.: A retrospective study on the comparative effect of digital titanium mesh and absorbable collagen membrane on bone augmentation [J]. Chin J Oral Implantol **30**(1), 19–26 (February 2025)
42. Alessandro Cucchi, Elisabetta Vignudelli, Debora Franceschi, et al. Vertical and horizontal ridge augmentation using customized CAD/CAM titanium mesh with versus without resorbable membranes. A randomized clinical trial [J]. Clin Oral lmpl Res.2021; 32:1411–1424
43. Li, X.Y., He, J., Wang, X.K., et al.: A case of vertical bone augmentation for continuous loss of maxillary posterior teeth was performed using bone collagen combined with tent technology [J]. Chin J Oral Implantol **28**(2), 97–101 (April 2023)
44. Song, Y.L., Zhao, W.S., Song, S.: Comparison of the clinical efficacy of tent screw technology and conventional GBR in horizontal bone increment [J]. Stomatology. **41**(2), 103–109 (2021)
45. J Wu, ZY Zhao, DH Zou, et al. Application of a tent-pole screw technology in reconstruction of severe alveolar bonedefect: a retrospective study of 30 patients [J]. JOURNAL OF SHANGHAI JIAO TONG UNIVERSITY (MEDICAL SCIENCE). Jun.2022 Vo1.42 No.6:768–777
46. Zhou, D.H., Ling, H., Zhou, G.D., et al.: Application of bone blocks harvested from the lateral wall of the maxillary sinus in horizontal alveolar ridge augmentation using the tenting technique [J]. Chin J Oral Implantol **29**(5), 407–412 (October 2024)
47. Shi, S.J., Ding, F., Song, Y.L.: Research progress of bone regeneration on jaw defect guided by GBR technique [J]. Stomatology **39**(2), 261–265 (2019)
48. Qiu, L.X., Niu, L.X.: Management of vertical bone deficiency in the posterior mandibular region [J]. Chin J Oral Implantol **29**(5), 400–406 (October 2024)
49. Pe S. Baboab, R L Pires, R L. Reis, et al. Membranes for periodontal tissues regeneration [J]. Ciência & Tecnologia dos Materiais 26(2014):108–117
50. Alauddin, M.S., AbdulHayei, N.A., Sabarudin, M.A., MatBaharin, N.H.: Barrier Membrane inRegenerative Therapy: A Narrative Review [J]. Membranes **12**, 444 (2022)
51. Ausenda, F., Rasperini, G., et al.: New Perspectives in the Use of Biomaterials for Periodontal Regeneration [J]. Materials **12**, 2197 (2019)
52. D Yang, ZL Xu, Dou JM Guo, LM Ge, DF Li et al. Immunomodulatory multifunctional janus collagen-based membrane for advanced bone regeneration [J]. Nature Communications (2025)16:4264
53. Wang, Q.N., Shen, T., Song, Z.F.: A clinic observation of GBR biofilm combined with biodegradable coral-hydroxyapatite ceramic and autologous venous blood in treatment of bone partial defect [J]. Stomatology **34**(12), 928–930 (2014)
54. Yang, K.W., Liu, A.P., Wang, X.H., et al.: Research Progress of Dental Implants under Condition of Insufficient Horizontal Alveolar Bone[J]. Medical Recapitulate **26**(22), 4450–4456 (Nov.2020)

55. Wang, C.X., Rong, Q.G., Zhu, N., Ma, T., et al.: Finite element analysis of stress in oral mucosa and titanium mesh interface [J]. BMC Oral Health **23**, 25 (2023)
56. Ma, S.Q., Zhang, X., Sun, Y.C., Gao, P.: Research Progress of GBR Membrane [J]. Journal of Oral Science Research **32**(3), 308–310 (Mar.2016)
57. Ronda M, Rebaudi A, Torelli L, Stacchi C. Expanded vs. dense polytetrafluoroethylene membranes in vertical ridge augmentation around dental implants: a prospective randomized controlled clinical trial [J]. Clinical Oral Implants Research, 08 Apr 2013, 25(7):859–866
58. ST Xu. Clinical Study of Immediate Implantations Using Guided Tissue Regeneration [J]. Journal of Comprehensive Stomatology. May, 2000, 16(2):127–129
59. Kalsi, A.S., Kalsi, J.S., Bassi, S.: Alveolar ridge preservation: why, when and how [J]. Br. Dent. J. **227**(4), 264–274 (Aug.2019)
60. Fontana, F., Maschera, E., Rocchietta, I., Simion, M.: Clinical classification of complications in guided bone regeneration procedures by means of a nonresorbable membrane [J]. Int J Periodontics Restorative Dent **31**(3), 265–273 (2011)
61. Ma, L., Zhang, L., Liu, Z., Wang, D., et al.: Application of e-PTFE Frontalis Suspension in the Treatment of Congenital Ptosis in Children [J]. Front. Surg. **9**, 904307 (2022)
62. Yan, F.H., Yuan, Z.Y.: The Challenges, Key Factors and Progress of Periodontal Regeneration Therapy [J]. Journal of Oral Science Research **39**(6), 473–478 (Jun.2023)
63. Taba, M., Jin, Q., et al.: Current concepts in periodontal bioengineering [J]. Orthod. Craniofac. Res. **8**(4), 292–302 (Nov.2005)
64. Cortellini, P., Tonetti, M.S.: Focus on intrabony defects: guided tissue regeneration [J]. Periodontol. **22**(2000), 104–132 (2000)
65. Hansen, E.J., Schou, S., Harder, F., Hjorting-Hansen, E.: Outcome of Implant Therapy Involving Localised Lateral Alveolar Ridge and/or Sinus Floor Augmentation: A Clinical and Radio-graphic Retrospective 1-year Study [J]. Eur. J. Oral Implantol. **4**(3), 257–267 (2011)
66. Wan, P.: A 5-year clinical observation on the application of non-resorbable membranes for bone augmentation in the aesthetic zone [J]. Chin J Oral Implantol **29**(5), 445–452 (2024)
67. Liu, J.W., Pan, Y.P.: Research progress of technique of ridge preservation after tooth extraction [J]. Chinese Journal of Practical Stomatology. **9**(8), 495–500 (Aug.2016)
68. Xu, G.C., Mou, L.Z., Ge, Z.L.: The application of tooth extraction site preservation technology in orthodontics [J]. Journal of Oral Science Research **31**(3), 310–312 (Mar.2015)
69. N. Soldatos, P. Stylianou, V. Koidou, et al. Limitations and options using resorbable versus nonresorbable membranes for successful guided bone regeneration [J]. Quintessence international.Feb.2017:131–147
70. KY Kim, YC Su, A J. Kucine, et al. Guided Bone Regeneration Using Barrier Membrane in Dental Applications [J]. ACS Biomaterials Science & Engineering.Aug.2023. Vol 9, Issue 10
71. Dimitriou, R., Mataliotakis, G., Calori, G.M., et al.: The role of barrier membranes for guided bone regeneration and restoration of large bone defects: current experimental and clinical evidence [J]. BMC Med. **10**, 81 (2012)
72. Zhao, Y., Yang, M., Shang, Y.N., et al.: In Vivo Study of Biodegradable Pure Magnesium Membrane-Guided Bone Regeneration [J]. J Orthop Res Ther **8**, 1304 (2023)
73. Xie, M.M., Zhao, B.D., Wang, W.Y., et al.: Effects of oral biofilm on guided bone regeneration in dental implant [J]. Journal of Clinical Rehabilitative Tissue Engineering Research. **14**(16), 2911–2915 (2010)
74. N Luigi; S Duaa, et al. Periodontal infrabony defects: Systematic review of healing by defect morphology following regenerative surgery [J]. Journal of clinical periodontology.2021, 1
75. ZF Zhu, TT Yang, QY Chen, et al. Concentrated growth factor and collagen as barrier materials in alveolar ridge preservation for posterior teeth: a prospective cohort study with one-year follow-up [J]. West China Journal of Stomatology

76. P Papi, B D Murro, M Tromba, et al. The Use of a Non-Absorbable Membrane as an Occlusive Barrier for Alveolar Ridge Preservation: A One Year Follow-Up Prospective Cohort Study [J]. Antibiotics 2020, 9,110.2024–06, 42(3):346–352
77. Zhang, X., Li, Y.P., Zhang, X.J., et al.: Guided bone regeneration using preformed titanium mesh combined with bioabsorbable membranes in aesthetic area [J]. Chinese Journal of Tissue Engineering Research. **24**(26), 4112–4117 (2020)
78. Solomon, S.-M., Sufaru, I.-G., Teslaru, S., et al.: Finding the Perfect Membrane: Current Knowledge on Barrier Membranes in Regenerative Procedures: A Descriptive Review [J]. Appl. Sci. **12**, 1042 (2022)
79. S-Li Bee, Z A A Hamid. Asymmetric resorbable-based dental barrier membrane for periodontal guided tissue regeneration and guided bone regeneration: A review [J]. Journal of Biomedical Materials Research Part B: Applied Biomaterials, 2022
80. Rajpal, J., Arora, A., Prasad, R., et al.: Membrane Guided Regeneration in Periodontal Tissues [J]. Journal of Membrane and Separation Technology **2**, 198–205 (2013)
81. Bhojak, A., Arora, S.A., Kalsi, R., et al.: Bioengineered membranes-past, present and future in tissue regeneration [J]. J. Dent. Res. **6**(S2), 2336–2355 (2022)
82. R Yotsova, S Peev, T Georgiev. Alveolar ridge preservation using dense polytetrafluoroethylene membrane. A Review Article [J]. Scripta Scientifica Medicinae Dentalis, 2021; 7(2):31–38
83. Kothari, S., Thonthula, V., Raiendran, V., et al.: Artificial Intelligence-Enabled CBCT Analysis: A Game-Changer for Dental Implant Optimization [J]. Acta Scientific Dental Sciences **9**(7), 15–17 (2025)
84. Yang, F., Weng, X., Miao, Y., Lei, P.: Deep learning approach for automatic segmentation of ulna and radius in dual-energy X-ray imaging [J]. Insights Imaging **12**, 191 (2021)
85. YX Zhong, HY Yu. Computer aided design and computer aided manufacturing of prefabricated personalized allografts in bone augmentation surgery [J]. International Journal of Stomatology, 2024–05, 51(3):319–325
86. Peng, K., Lin, Y.M., et al.: Development prospect of orthopedic rehabilitation medicine based on three-dimensional printing technology [J]. Chinese Journal of Tissue Engineering Research **25**(4), 632–637 (2021)
87. Li, J., Jin, F., Wang, R.F., et al.: Guided Bone Regeneration in a Periodontally Compromised Individual with Autogenous Tooth Bone Graft: A Radiomics Analysis [J]. J. Funct. Biomater. **14**, 220 (2023)
88. Takahashi T, Nozaki K, Gonda T, et al. Deep learning-based detection of dental prostheses and restorations [J].Sci Rep,2021,11(1):1960
89. Elgarba BM, Van Aelst S, Swaity A, et al. Deep learning-based segmentation of dental implants on cone-beam computed tomography images: A validation study [J].Dent, 2023, 137:104639
90. Huang, N., Liu, P., Yan, Y., et al.: Predicting the risk of dental implant loss using deep learning [J]. Clin Periodontol **49**(9), 872–883 (2022)
91. Zinaida, K.: Artificial Intelligence (AI) in Surgical Planning [J]. Cancer Surg **9**, 124 (2024)
92. Zhang, Z.H., Liu, Z.L., Gao, Z.Z., et al.: Selection and application of bone substitute materials for repair of bone defects [J]. Chinese Journal of Tissue Engineering Research **16**(52), 9836–9843 (2012)
93. Zhou, S.J., Jiang, W.X., You, J.: Repair materials for bone defects: present status, needs and future developments [J]. Chinese Journal of Tissue Engineering Research **22**(14), 2251–2258 (2018)
94. Y Lee, P Wadhwa, H Cai, et al. Micro-CT and Histomorphometric Study of Bone Regeneration Effect with Autogenous Tooth Biomaterial Enriched with Platelet-Rich Fibrin in an Animal Model [J]. SCANNING, 2021(6656791)

95. Wang, X., Shao, X., Dai, T., et al.: In vivo study of the efficacy, biosafety, and degradation of a zinc alloy osteosynthesis system [J]. Acta Biomater. **90**(1), 351–361 (2019)
96. Ding, J.Y., Wei, L., Guo, J.P.: Different bone grafts for repair of periodontal alveolar bone defects [J]. Chinese Journal of Tissue Engineering Research **16**(16), 3033–3036 (2012)

Bidirectional Target Bias APF-RRT* Algorithm for Indoor Path Planning of Epidemic-Prevention Robots

Rili Wu[1], Yuhai Zhong[1](✉), Xiru Wu[1,2](✉), Yi Lu[1], and Aoliang Xu[1]

[1] School of Electronic Engineering and Automation, Guilin University of Electronic of Electronic Technology, Guilin 541004, China
yuhaizhong523@mail.nwpu.edu.cn, xiruwu@guet.edu.cn

[2] Key Laboratory of Intelligence Integrated Automation, Guangxi Universities, Guilin 541004, China

Abstract. To address the challenges faced by epidemic-prevention robots operating in complex indoor multi-room environments with dense human presence, this work proposes a global path planning algorithm termed Bidirectional Target Bias APF-RRT* (BTB-APF-RRT*). The approach employs morphological closing operations from image processing to preprocess the environment map, thereby extracting inter-room connectivity boundaries and optimizing connected regions to reduce ineffective search spaces. By integrating the bidirectional RRT* framework, the algorithm significantly accelerates convergence, while the incorporation of a bidirectional target bias strategy and artificial potential field guides the expansion of random search trees, effectively mitigating randomness and blind exploration. Simulation results conducted in multi-room indoor scenarios with high human density demonstrate that, compared with existing state-of-the-art algorithms, the proposed method achieves notable improvements in terms of sampled nodes, planning time, and path length, thereby exhibiting superior convergence efficiency and path optimization performance.

Keywords: Epidemic Prevention Robot · Path Planning · Artificial Potential Field Method · RRT* Algorithm · Trajectory Optimization

1 Introduction

During the COVID-19 pandemic, to minimize person-to-person transmission, epidemic prevention robots have been deployed on the front lines across medical care, delivery, inspection, and household applications. These robots are upgraded versions of existing intelligent service robots, designed to effectively reduce human contact and minimize virus transmission risks [1]. Commonly deployed in medical care, delivery, inspection, and household settings during outbreaks, they perform functions such as temperature screening, mask detection, health code verification, and disinfection. They assist medical professionals in pandemic prevention efforts across outdoor public spaces like hospitals, schools, and communities. When deploying epidemic prevention robots for disinfection,

S. S. Ge et al. (Eds.): ICSR + BioMed 2025, LNAI 16435, pp. 80–94, 2026.
https://doi.org/10.1007/978-981-95-7538-1_8

medical support, and other tasks, path planning serves as a critical prerequisite for autonomous navigation in complex outdoor environments.

The RRT* algorithm in path planning has become a research hotspot due to its broad applicability, ease of implementation, and lack of requirement for constructing complex structures. However, owing to the randomness of sampling, the traditional RRT* algorithm also suffers from weaknesses such as poor goal-directedness, slow convergence time, and the generation of numerous redundant random nodes during the growth of the random search tree [2, 3]. To address these limitations of the RRT* algorithm, researchers worldwide have proposed numerous improvements [2, 4–9]. Ma et al. [4] proposed a simple and effective bidirectional random tree algorithm that alternately expands two search trees to enhance efficiency, though its performance remains constrained in complex environments. Tahirovic et al. [5] introduced the Rapid Random Vine (RRV) algorithm for efficient exploration, employing Principal Component Analysis (PCA) to determine local environment types. Liu et al. [6] proposed an improved GBB-RRT* algorithm. By employing a target-biased strategy to expand two random trees bidirectionally at each iteration, they accelerated convergence but failed to address the issue of excessive redundant points in the random trees. Karaman et al. [7] introduced an RRT* variant with progressive optimality. These represent significant derivative RRT* algorithms that have driven substantial progress.

The aforementioned studies have improved the RRT* algorithm through various approaches, achieving corresponding progress. However, they have not resolved issues such as excessive redundant points and overly convoluted paths. Furthermore, considering the application of epidemic prevention robots in complex indoor environments with numerous occupants, constraints such as confined spaces and restricted movement arise. To address these challenges, this paper proposes a path planning algorithm for epidemic prevention robots in indoor scenarios based on bidirectional target-biased APF-RRT*. An artificial potential field is constructed using target point and surrounding obstacle information to guide the RRT* algorithm toward more intelligent search. The random tree expansion process enables more efficient and rapid obstacle avoidance, effectively preventing local optima. Bidirectional pruning and reconnection strategies eliminate redundant path points and reduce path consumption. This method enhances the robot's adaptability to complex indoor environments with people, improves path planning safety and feasibility in real-world scenarios, and achieves faster convergence, providing more reliable path solutions for autonomous navigation. The main contributions of this paper are as follows:

(1) Preprocess the map using closed operations from image processing to extract the boundaries of connected regions between rooms, then optimize these connected regions to reduce the algorithm's ineffective search space.
(2) Introduce a probabilistic target bias mechanism during the random sampling phase. By adjusting the probability distribution of sampling points, the new node generation process gains directional targeting. Through probabilistic settings, target points are directly selected as candidate points, guiding the random tree to sample toward the target direction and reducing the probability of ineffective spatial exploration.
(3) The artificial potential field method is integrated with the bidirectional RRT* algorithm to construct a random search tree extension method based on the artificial

potential field. For the nearest node during random tree extension, two types of forces are simultaneously applied: the gravitational field generated by the target point and the repulsive field triggered by obstacles. The vector sum of these forces determines the gradient direction of the potential field, refining the optimal extension direction for new nodes.

(4) After obtaining an initial feasible path, a triangular pruning strategy is employed to eliminate redundant path segments. Geometric principles identify and remove redundant nodes from the path, achieving path optimization while ensuring safety.

2 Map Preprocessing

2.1 Extraction of Connected Boundaries in Map Regions Based on Image Closure Operations

This paper employs image closing operations to process two-dimensional environment maps. Image closing operations refer to the process where an image first undergoes dilation followed by erosion. This technique is characterized by its ability to fill gaps and holes within an image, thereby achieving the goal of extracting the connected boundaries of regions. Image closing is defined as:

$$A \cdot B = (A \oplus B) \ominus B \tag{1}$$

where $\cdot$ represents the closing operation, $\oplus$ represents the dilation operation, and $\ominus$ represents the erosion operation. A is the mapping image of obstacle space q_{obs} onto the grid map, and B is the structural operator for dilation and erosion operations. The closing operation can be expressed as applying dilation with B to A, followed by erosion with B on the result. The overall closing operation process is shown in Fig. 1, where the white areas represent the overall background, the gray areas represent obstacles, the green squares denote the structural operator, and the center origin is marked in orange.

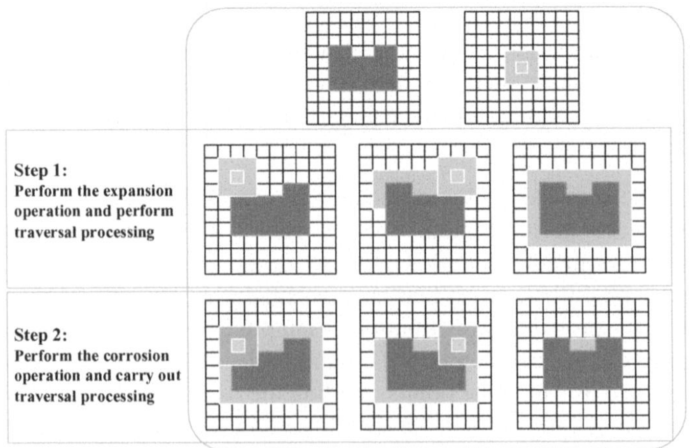

Fig. 1. Complete process of image closed-set operations.

The expansion operation process can be defined as:

$$A \oplus B = \{z|(B)_z \cap A \neq \emptyset\} \tag{2}$$

where $(B)_z$ denotes the translation of the structural operator B centered at z. The dilation operation enlarges the obstacle regions within the image, causing boundaries to expand outward and connecting previously disconnected areas.

The corrosion process can be defined as:

$$A \ominus B = \{z|(B)_z \subseteq A\} \tag{3}$$

where $(B)_z$ denotes the translation of the structural operator B centered at z. The erosion operation reduces the size of the obstacle region within the image, causing the boundary to contract inward.

Closing operations do not alter the external contours of obstacles. Their primary function is to fill cavities within obstacles and bridge gaps between adjacent obstacles. Based on the properties of the closing operation, when applying morphological closing to multi-room obstacle maps using identical structural operators, this closing effectively fills minute gaps in the connecting regions of adjacent rooms while strictly preserving the original obstacles' geometric shapes, dimensions, and spatial distribution characteristics. By performing a bitwise XOR operation between the closed obstacle map and the original obstacle map, the regionally connected boundary can be obtained, expressed by the formula:

$$C = (A \cdot B) xor\ A \tag{4}$$

where C denotes the connected boundary of the region in the map, and *xor* represents the exclusive-OR operation.

An illustrative example of the regional connectivity boundary extraction process is presented in Fig. 2. Specifically, Fig. 2(a) depicts the original map image of a single room. Figure 2(b) shows the dilation result of the original image, where the green areas represent the newly expanded regions. Subsequently, Fig. 2(c) illustrates the eroded map derived from Fig. 2(b), which effectively restores the connectivity between the room and the external space. Finally, Fig. 2(d) presents the outcome of the XOR operation between Fig. 2(a) and Fig. 2(c), from which the complete regional connectivity boundaries are successfully extracted.

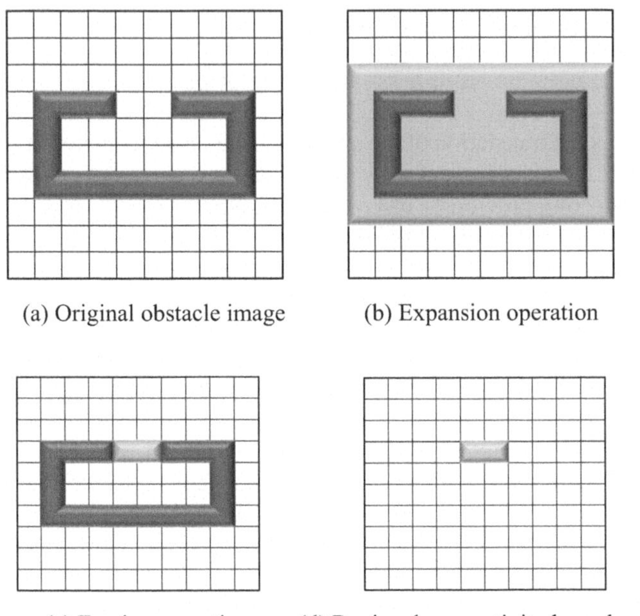

(a) Original obstacle image (b) Expansion operation

(c) Erosion operation (d) Regional connectivity boundary

Fig. 2. Regional connectivity boundary extraction process.

2.2 Map Connectivity Zone Optimization

Indoor complex environment maps typically contain multiple spatial regions, most of which are invalid spaces. These invalid spaces increase the difficulty of searching the algorithm's random tree. Building upon closed-form operations, a preprocessing method is proposed: redundant connected regions are treated as obstacles. The algorithm's structural framework remains unchanged. This approach reduces the algorithm's invalid search space and enhances its overall search efficiency.

After completing closed-form operations on the map, perform corresponding optimizations. When a spatial region satisfies any one of the following conditions, convert it into a black obstacle region to reduce the invalid search space of the random tree. The connected region boundaries within this spatial region will be converted into black obstacle regions.

Condition 1: The spatial region does not contain the start node or the target node internally, or there are no connected region boundaries within the region.

Condition 2: The spatial region contains neither the start node nor the goal node, and contains only one connected region boundary. It is determined that the algorithm's optimal path will not traverse this spatial region.

3 BTB-APF-RRT* Algorithm

3.1 BTB-APF-RRT* Algorithm Flowchart

The BTB-APF-RRT* algorithm constructs search trees rooted at the starting point and target point respectively, achieving rapid path convergence through a dual-tree search mechanism. The target bias strategy simultaneously constrains the generation of two sampling points in each iteration, guiding the two random trees to expand alternately. The distance between each sampling point and the nearest node in the random tree is computed. Collision detection filters candidate points satisfying collision-free constraints and optimal distance as valid expansion nodes. The artificial potential field method adjusts the position of newly expanded nodes for obstacle avoidance. Upon reaching the target point, a triangular pruning strategy generates the optimized path. The algorithmic steps are shown in Algorithm 1 (Table 1).

Table 1. Table captions should be placed above the tables.

Algorithm 1 BTB-APF-RRT* Algorithm				
Input: Starting point q_{start}, goal point q_{goal}, obstacles				
Output: Path				
1	Initialized the vertex set $V \leftarrow q_{start}$, the set of edges $E = \emptyset$			
2		**while** target point q_{goal} not found **do**		
3			Generate sampling points q_{rand} through a bidirectional target bias constraint strategy	
4			Traverse the vertex set V to find the nearest node $q_{nearset}$ to the sampling point q_{rand}	
5			Extend the fixed step size from $q_{nearset}$ to q_{rand} to generate a new node q_{new}	
6			By manually correcting the node position q_{new} based on the potential field, considering the target point q_{goal} and the obstacle q_{obs}, the corrected node $\dot{q}_{new}$ is obtained	
7			**if** the set of nearby points $q_{near} \neq \emptyset$ **then**	
8				Search for the set of neighboring points q_{near} for node $\dot{q}_{new}$ in the vertex set V
9			**else**	
10				Resume the search using a fixed radius r
11			**end if**	
12			Re-select the optimal parent node for node $\dot{q}_{new}$, then add $\dot{q}_{new}$ to the vertex set V	

(*continued*)

Table 1. *(continued)*

Algorithm 1 BTB-APF-RRT* Algorithm	
13	**end while**
14	Employing a triangular pruning strategy for path optimization
15	**Return** path
16	**end**

3.2 Bidirectional Target Bias Strategy

To optimize the path search efficiency of the algorithm, a bidirectional target bias expansion strategy is adopted. This strategy assigns differentiated weights to the sampling point and target point directions, ensuring that the expansion direction of new nodes is not solely guided by the sampling point but results from the collaborative influence of both the sampling point and target point. This strategy enables each expansion of the random tree to move closer to the target point, thereby enhancing the search efficiency of the algorithm.

The p_{bias} parameter is initialized to 0.1, and the random probability p is computed based on a uniform distribution. If $p < p_{bias}$, the target point is selected as the sampling location; otherwise, a random sampling point is generated within the search space. The target-biased sampling formula can be expressed as:

$$q_{rand} = \begin{cases} q_{goal} & (p < p_{bias}) \\ R & (p \geq p_{bias}) \end{cases} \quad (5)$$

where R denotes the random sampling function, p_{bias} represents the target bias probability, and p is the random probability value.

During the random sampling point generation process, the primary method for target-constrained sampling is as follows: Each randomly generated sampling point undergoes position evaluation to determine whether it is closer to the target point along the X-axis or Y-axis than the previous sampling point. If this condition is satisfied, the sampling is deemed successful; otherwise, sampling iterations continue until the constraint is met. It is worth noting that the path starting point is initialized as the first reference sampling point and is continuously updated throughout the subsequent process. A schematic illustration of the bidirectional target offset constraint extension is shown in Fig. 3.

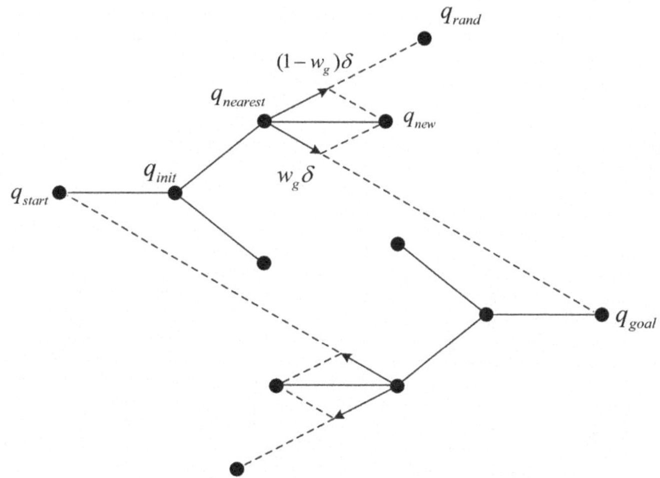

Fig. 3. Bidirectional target bias expansion intent.

The target bias strategy for new nodes can be expressed by the following formula:

$$q_{new} = q_{nearest} + \delta(w_g n_{goal} + (1 - w_g)n_{rand}) \tag{6}$$

$$n_{goal} = \frac{q_{goal} - q_{nearest}}{\|q_{goal} - q_{nearest}\|}, n_{rand} = \frac{q_{rand} - q_{nearest}}{\|q_{rand} - q_{nearest}\|} \tag{7}$$

where δ denotes the expansion step size, $q_{nearset}$ represents the nearest neighboring node to the sampling point, w_g denotes the directional weight toward the target point, n_{goal} denotes the unit direction vector toward the target point, n_{rand} denotes the unit direction vector of the sampling point.

3.3 Artificial Potential Field-Guided Dual Search Tree Extension Strategy

The bidirectional artificial potential field-guided expansion method constructs two search trees at the starting and ending points respectively. It employs a composite potential field model, combining the target's gravitational field with the obstacle's repulsive field, to guide node expansion. During each iteration, bidirectional sampling points are generated simultaneously. After expanding to produce new nodes via fixed-step increments, node positions are dynamically adjusted based on potential field gradients to avoid obstacles and approach the target. The schematic of bidirectional search tree expansion guided by artificial potential fields is shown in Fig. 4.

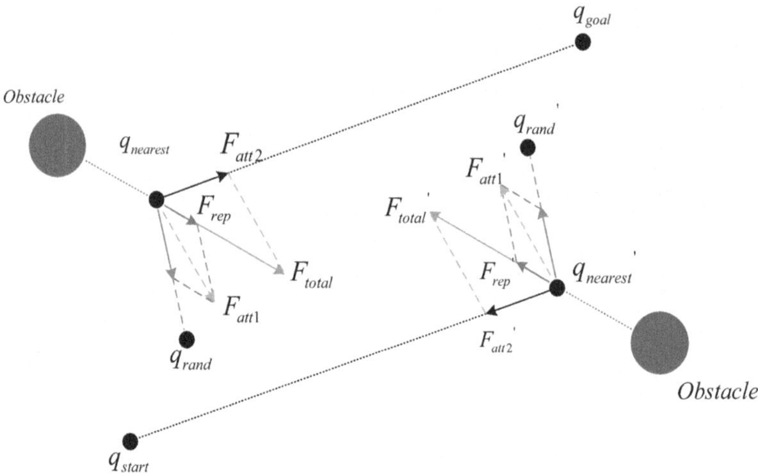

Fig.4. Artificial potential field-guided dual-tree expansion.

3.4 Triangular Pruning Optimization Strategy

After generating an initial path connecting the starting and ending points using an algorithm, a pruning optimization strategy based on the triangle inequality principle is employed. This strategy optimizes the connection relationships between nodes by eliminating redundant nodes in the path, thereby shortening the final path length. For any three consecutive nodes along the path, if the sum of the lengths of the two adjacent path segments exceeds the straight-line distance between the end nodes, the middle node is identified as redundant and removed, achieving path length reduction. The triangular inequality pruning optimization strategy is outlined below.

$$D(q_1, q_2) + D(q_2, q_3) \geq D(q_1, q_3) \tag{8}$$

where q_1, q_2, q_3 represent three nodes in the final path, and $D(q_i, q_j)$ denotes the distance between nodes q_i and q_j. After verifying that path connections satisfy this formula and selecting the shortest connection path for reconnection or pruning, the optimized path must not collide with obstacles.

The triangular inequality pruning diagram is shown in Fig. 5. Figure 5(a) depicts the initial path. As shown in Fig. 5(b), path nodes q_1 and q_3 avoid obstacles while skipping node q_2 for direct connection, reducing path consumption. Figure 5(c) presents the optimized path.

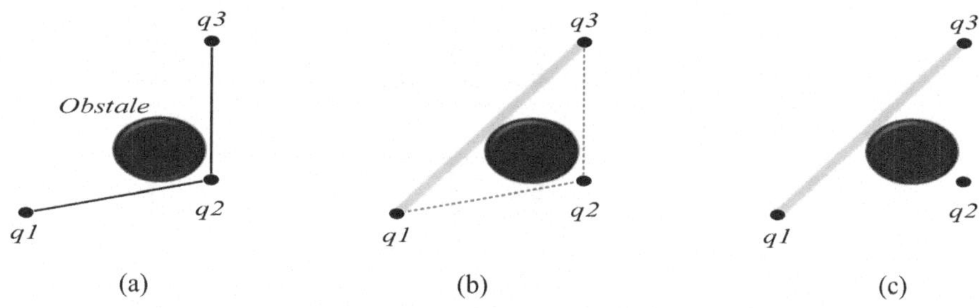

Fig.5. Triangle inequality pruning.

4 Simulation Results and Analysis

4.1 Map Construction and Simulation Parameter Configuration

Environment Map Settings. Three complex indoor scene maps were designed for simulation experiments. The indoor environment maps are shown in Fig. 6. The three environment maps in Fig. 6 are sized at 100 × 100. Map 1 simulates an environment transitioning from indoors to outdoors and then back into another indoor space. Map 2 simulates a multi-room indoor environment map, commonly found in hospitals or office buildings. Map 3 simulates a stairwell area within an indoor environment.

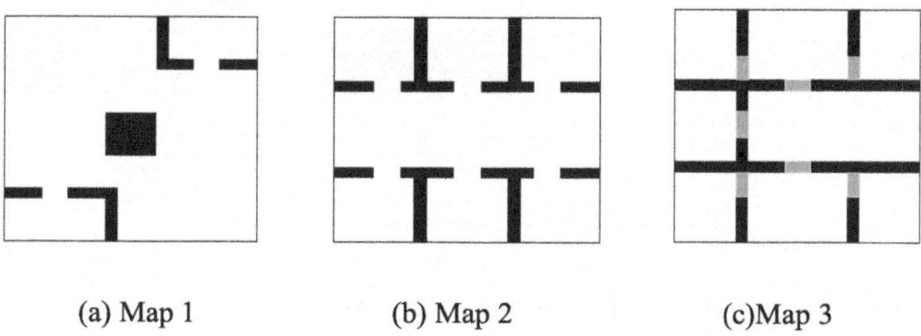

(a) Map 1 (b) Map 2 (c)Map 3

Fig.6. Simulated environment map.

Map Preprocessing. The purpose of preprocessing the map using closed operations is to extract the connected boundaries between indoor rooms. During the closed operation, a 20 × 20 square structure operator is employed, with the maximum extraction width for connected region boundaries set to 20. The map after closed operation preprocessing is shown in Fig. 7.

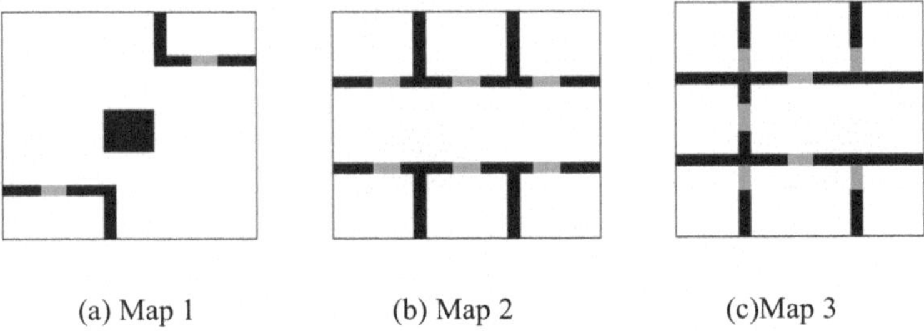

(a) Map 1 (b) Map 2 (c)Map 3

Fig.7. Closed-form processing results for map operations.

Figure 7 shows the connected region boundaries extracted after closed-set operations on the green areas. Map 1 extracted connected boundaries for 2 regions, Map 2 for 6 regions, and Map 3 for 7 regions. After extracting the connected region boundaries, the obstacle map optimized for spatial regions is shown in Fig. 8. All spatial regions in Map 1 fail to meet any optimization criteria, resulting in no changes compared to the initial map. Corresponding optimized regions in Maps 2 and 3 that satisfy the conditions are treated as black obstacles.

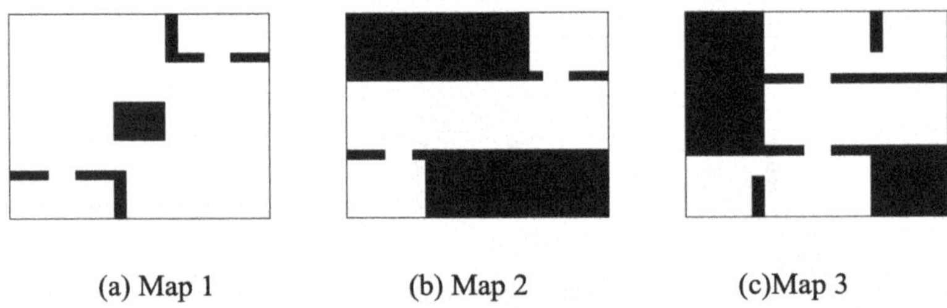

(a) Map 1 (b) Map 2 (c)Map 3

Fig.8. Connected region optimization map.

4.2 Algorithm Simulation Comparison and Analysis

The comparative simulation experiments of the proposed algorithm were conducted on three different maps (Map 1, Map 2, and Map 3) under two environmental conditions, namely with and without pedestrians, to emulate the complex indoor scenarios encountered by epidemic-prevention robots during real-world task execution.

One hundred path planning simulation experiments will be conducted with the APF-RRT*, BI-RRT* algorithms and BI-APF-RRT* algorithms in both pedestrian and non-pedestrian states, and the average values of the three data, namely path length, the number of path nodes and path planning time, will be compared. The green dot in the lower left corner of the map is the starting point, the red dot is the ending point, the black figure is the obstacle, the blue path is the random search tree starting from the starting point, the purple path is the random search tree starting from the ending point, the red line is the final path, and the green line is the path optimized by triangular pruning. The map uses oval-shaped obstacles to simulate pedestrians or pets, making the map more in line with the environment in which the epidemic prevention robots are actually performing their tasks.

Map 1 Simulation Experiment Comparative Analysis. As shown in Fig. 9, under both pedestrian-free and pedestrian-present scenarios on Map 1, the proposed algorithm consistently outperforms the comparison algorithms in terms of path length, number of nodes, and planning time. Table 2 indicates that compared to APF-RRT*, the path length is reduced by 4.8–9.7%, the number of nodes decreases by 37.6–43.3%, and time savings range from 62.2% to 67.3%. Compared to BI-RRT*, path length decreased by 12–13.1%, the number of nodes dropped by 40.3–43.8%, and time savings reached 41.8–43.1%. In comparison with BI-APF-RRT*, the reductions are 5.6–5.7% in path length, 4.3–6.6% in nodes, and 29.8–34.8% in planning time. The results demonstrate that the proposed algorithm achieves superior convergence efficiency and path simplicity.

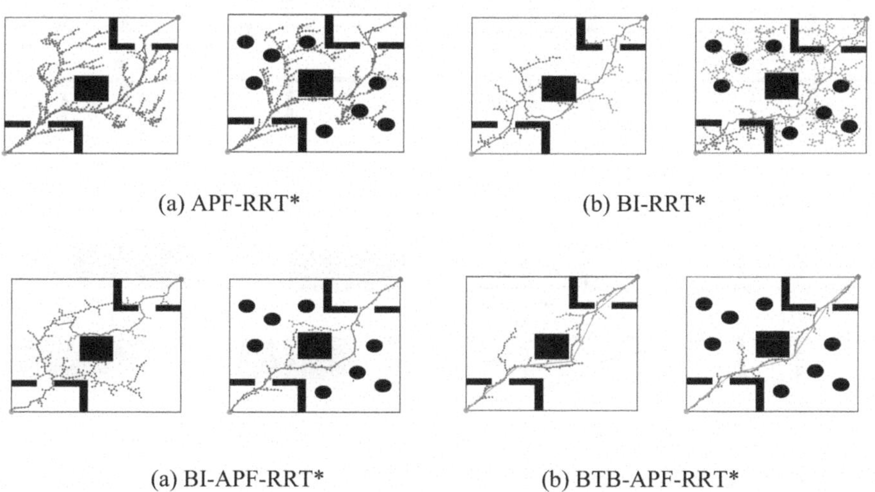

(a) APF-RRT* (b) BI-RRT*

(a) BI-APF-RRT* (b) BTB-APF-RRT*

Fig.9. Simulation results for map 1 (left: unmanned environment, right: manned environment).

Table 2. Comparison of average simulation results for map 1.

Algorithm	Path length (unmanned/manned)	Number of path nodes (unmanned/manned)	Planning time(unmanned/manned)
APF-RRT*	167.21/159.77	271/314	5.10/4.60
BI-RRT*	171.58/173.91	283/317	2.87/3.06
BI-APF-RRT*	160.00/161.35	181/186	2.38/2.67
BTB-APF-RRT*	**151.07/152.15**	**169/178**	**1.67/1.74**

Map 2 Simulation Experiment Comparative Analysis. As shown in Fig. 10, the algorithm proposed in this paper still maintains a significant advantage in complex multi-room environments. It can be seen from Table 3 that compared with APF-RRT*, the path length is reduced by 3.8–10.0%, the number of nodes is reduced by 38.6–47.3%, and the time is saved by 53.33–55.5%. Compared with BI-RRT*, the path length is reduced by 12.4–12.8%, the number of nodes is reduced by 13.3–29.1%, and the time is reduced by 51.8–58.8%. Compared with BI-APF-RRT*, the path length, the number of nodes and the time were reduced by 3.8–4.7%, 12.4–13.9% and 22.1–30.6% respectively. The algorithm performs outstandingly in redundant space suppression and path smoothing.

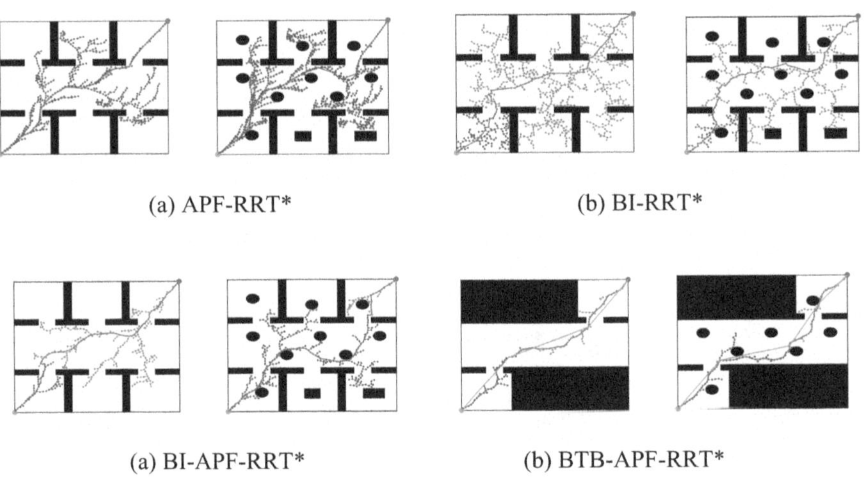

(a) APF-RRT* (b) BI-RRT*

(a) BI-APF-RRT* (b) BTB-APF-RRT*

Fig.10. Simulation results for map 2 (left: unmanned environment, right: manned environment).

Table 3. Comparison of average simulation results for map 2.

Algorithm	Path length (unmanned/manned)	Number of path nodes (unmanned/manned)	Planning time(unmanned/manned)
APF-RRT*	157.87/169.91	293/347	4.13/3.79
BI-RRT*	174.31/174.57	254/211	3.82/4.30
BI-APF-RRT*	157.93/160.53	209/203	2.36/2.55
BTB-APF-RRT*	**151.92/152.97**	**180/183**	**1.84/1.77**

Map 3 Simulation Experiment Comparative Analysis. As shown in Fig. 11, in a complex environment with staircase entrances, the algorithm proposed in this paper still performs optimally. It can be seen from Table 4 that compared with APF-RRT*, the

path length is reduced by 5.5–5.8%, the number of nodes is significantly reduced by 74.7–84.7%, and the time is saved by 81.95–89.2%. Compared with BI-RRT*, the path length is reduced by 14.1–14.6%, the number of nodes is reduced by 21.7–24.9%, and the time is reduced by 62.2–65.2%. Compared with BI-APF-RRT*, the path length, the number of nodes and the time were reduced by 3.4–4.8%, 8.1–17.5% and 49.4–56.3% respectively. The results show that the algorithm proposed in this paper is particularly suitable for scenarios with complex structures and many narrow channels.

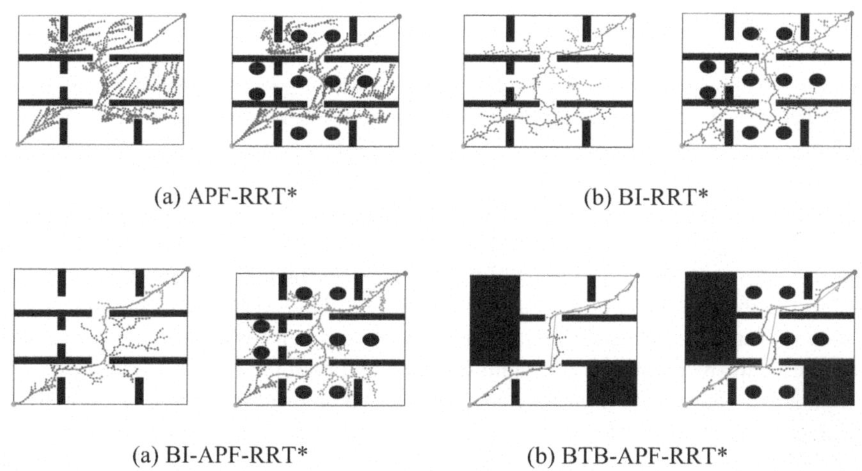

(a) APF-RRT* (b) BI-RRT*

(a) BI-APF-RRT* (b) BTB-APF-RRT*

Fig.11. Simulation results for map 3 (left: unmanned environment, right: manned environment).

Table 4. Comparison of average simulation results for map 3.

Algorithm	Path length (unmanned/manned)	Number of path nodes (unmanned/manned)	Planning time(unmanned/manned)
APF-RRT*	167.25/167.09	672/966	11.30/15.61
BI-RRT*	185.13/183.22	217/197	5.39/4.83
BI-APF-RRT*	163.50/165.43	206/161	4.67/3.32
BTB-APF-RRT*	**158.42/157.47**	**170/148**	**2.04/1.68**

Through simulation experiments comparing three different environments with and without pedestrians, the proposed algorithm demonstrates significant improvements in both path planning time and the number of path nodes. Path planning time is reduced by an average of approximately 40%–70%, indicating high real-time performance. Regarding the number of path nodes, an average reduction of about 13%–61% is achieved, resulting in more concise final paths with reduced complexity. Although the improvement in path consumption is relatively modest, it still demonstrates a certain degree of optimization.

Comprehensive analysis reveals that the proposed algorithm demonstrates superior planning efficiency and path quality across diverse indoor scenarios, with its advantages being particularly pronounced in complex and dynamic environments. Closed-form preprocessing effectively reduces redundant search areas, while bidirectional target bias and potential field guidance significantly enhance search directionality and convergence speed. By ensuring path quality while substantially improving computational efficiency and reducing path complexity, the algorithm possesses strong practical value.

5 Conclusion

This paper proposes an APF-RRT* global path planning algorithm for epidemic prevention robots operating in complex indoor multi-room environments with numerous occupants. It employs a bidirectional target bias strategy combined with an artificial potential field to guide the algorithm's random search tree expansion, thereby reducing its blindness and significantly shortening convergence time. A bidirectional objective bias strategy combined with a manual potential field guides the expansion of the algorithm's random search tree, reducing blindness and significantly shortening convergence time. Simulation results demonstrate that the proposed algorithm achieves superior path planning performance in complex indoor multi-room environments with people, showing notable improvements in both planning time and path node count. Future work will focus on addressing challenges such as planning lag caused by parameter staticization and reduced search efficiency due to delays from large-scale map preprocessing.

References

1. Ward, M., Li, X.D., Tian, K.G.: Novel coronavirus 2019, an emerging public health emergency. Transbound. Emerg. Dis. **67**(2), 469–470 (2020)
2. Qi, J., Yang, H., Sun, H.: MOD-RRT*: a sampling-based algorithm for robot path planning in dynamic environment. IEEE Trans. Industr. Electron. **68**(8), 7244–7251 (2020)
3. Wang, J., Chi, W., Li, C.: Neural RRT*: Learning-based optimal path planning. IEEE Trans. Autom. Sci. Eng. **17**(4), 1748–1758 (2020)
4. Ma, G., Duan, Y., Li, M.: A probability smoothing Bi-RRT path planning algorithm for indoor robot. Futur. Gener. Comput. Syst. **143**, 349–360 (2023)
5. Tahirovic, A., Ferizbegovic, M.: Rapidly-exploring random vines (RRV) for motion planning in configuration spaces with narrow passages. In: 2018 IEEE International Conference on Robotics and Automation (ICRA), pp. 7055–7062. IEEE (2018)
6. Liu, A.B., Yuan J.: Robot path planning based on goal biased bidirectional RRT* algorithm. Comput. Eng. Appl. **58**(6), 234–240 (2022)
7. Karaman, S., Frazzoli, E.: Sampling-based algorithms for optimal motion planning. Int. J. Robot. Res. **30**(7), 846–894 (2011)
8. Fan, J., Chen, X., Liang, X.: UAV trajectory planning based on bi-directional APF-RRT* algorithm with goal-biased. Expert Syst. Appl. **213**, 119–137 (2023)
9. Li, H.C., Liu, W.J., Yang, C.: An optimization-based path planning approach for autonomous vehicles using the DynEFWA-artificial potential field. IEEE Trans. Intell. Veh. **7**(2), 263–272 (2022)

Comprehensive Review on Bioceramic Bone Repair Scaffolds with TPMS Lattice Structure Based on Vat Photopolymerization

Zhisheng Liu[1,2], Yinghao Zhao[1,2], Haonan Zhang[1,2], Xiaohu Chen[1], Mengjie Wang[1], Chunliang Chen[1,2], Yanen Wang[1,2](✉), and Chi Zhang[1,2]

[1] School of Mechanical Engineering, Northwestern Polytechnical University, Xi'an, China
wangyanen@nwpu.edu.cn

[2] Bio-Additive Manufacturing University-Enterprise Joint Research Center of Shaanxi Province, Northwestern Polytechnical University, Xi'an 710072, China

Abstract. The TPMS structure exhibits excellent mechanical properties and pore connectivity, and can achieve a high porosity, making it highly prospective for applications in bone tissue engineering. Bioceramic photopolymerization can be used to prepare dense bone repair scaffolds with high precision, complex pore structures, and good biocompatibility. This paper systematically summarizes the current research on bioceramic bone repair scaffolds with TPMS lattice structure based on Vat Photopolymerization (VP) from the perspectives of structural design, material preparation, and manufacturing, and also discusses the factors that affect scaffold performance. Finally, a brief summary is provided, and possible future research directions in this field are proposed.

Keywords: TPMS Structure · Vat Photopolymerization · Bioceramic Scaffold · Ceramic Slurry

1 Introduction

A bone defect, whose circumferential loss exceeds 50% or is greater than 2 cm, is typically defined as a critical bone defect [1] If this critical threshold is exceeded, the bone remodeling process will be delayed or impaired, calling for bone scaffolds to replace the defective tissue [2–5]. Bone tissue engineering demands that suitable bone scaffolds should be provided with high porosity, good bioactivity, appropriate mechanical properties, and degradability [6–9], which poses challenges to materials, design and fabrication of bone scaffolds.

The current design methods for scaffolds primarily include: non-parametric design [10], image-based design [11], topology optimization [12], and triply periodic minimal surfaces (TPMS) [13]. Among these, TPMS structures have attracted increasing attention due to their combination of high porosity and favorable mechanical properties. TPMS are periodic structured surfaces with zero mean curvature, exhibiting the minimal surface area for a given boundary [14, 15].

S. S. Ge et al. (Eds.): ICSR + BioMed 2025, LNAI 16435, pp. 95–107, 2026.
https://doi.org/10.1007/978-981-95-7538-1_9

Bioactive ceramics exhibit excellent biocompatibility, osteoinductivity, and degradability [16–18], and are regarded as ideal materials for fabricating artificial bone scaffolds. Photopolymerization slurries are the most commonly used materials for ceramic scaffold fabrication, typically formulated as suspensions where ceramic powders are dispersed in a photosensitive premix. The properties of the slurry largely influence the fabrication and final performance of the scaffold, which is mainly reflected in three aspects: solid loading, viscosity, and stability [19].

VP shows significant advantages in printing complex structures (such as TPMS structures) because of its excellent printing precision and surface quality. This technology was first applied in the field of ceramic forming by Griffith et al. [20], establishing the process flow for ceramic VP: slurry preparation—printing—debinding and sintering. Therefore, it is necessary to summarize the relevant work on the influence of DLP parameters on scaffold properties, so as to provide a reference for future research (Fig. 1).

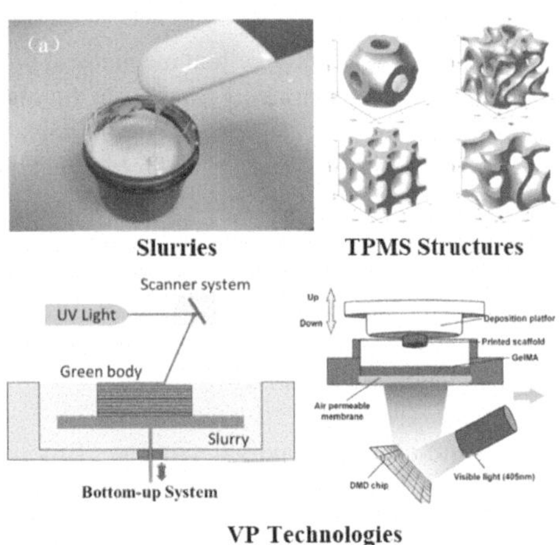

Fig. 1. Overview of this review. Reproduced with permission from [21]. CC BY 4.0. Reproduced with permission from [22]. CC BY 4.0.

In this review, we systematically summarized the current research advances of TPMS-structured bioceramic bone scaffolds based on VP from the perspectives of materials, design, and manufacturing, and also discussed the influencing factors of scaffold performance. Firstly, we introduced the types and design methods of current TPMS structures, and discussed the effects of design parameters on scaffold performance. Secondly, we described the requirements of scaffold performance for slurries. Additionally, classified by irradiation methods, we reviewed the research progress of current ceramic VP technologies, and discussed how to optimize scaffold performance by improving process parameters of DLP. Finally, a brief summary of this work was presented.

2 Design of TPMS Structures

The design of scaffolds has a big impact on their biological performance and mechanical properties. TPMS surfaces can be constructed using implicit functions, where key structural parameters (such as porosity, pore size, etc.) are clearly shown in these implicit function equations. By bringing in external functions or replacing parameters, various types of TPMS structures can be made while their surfaces are kept smooth. In this work, we explain the features and design methods of uniform, graded, hybrid, and multiscale TPMS structures.

The implicit function method utilizes the characteristic that TPMS surfaces have zero mean curvature everywhere. Geometric periodicity and symmetry further simplify the constraints; then, based on numerical methods, it generates triangular meshes that gradually approximate the theoretical shape of the surface. For generating TPMS structures used in bone scaffolds, the implicit function method is extensively used [23–27].

For an implicit surface $\phi(x, y, z) = 0$, its mean curvature H can be expressed as:

$$H = -\frac{1}{2}\nabla \cdot \mathbf{n} \tag{1}$$

where ∇ is the gradient operator and $\mathbf{n}$ is the unit normal vector, compute the divergence of the unit normal vector $\nabla \cdot \mathbf{n}$:

$$\nabla \cdot \mathbf{n} = \frac{1}{|\nabla\phi|^3}\begin{bmatrix} \left(\phi_{xx}|\nabla\phi|^2 - \phi_x\left(\phi_x\phi_{xx} + \phi_y\phi_{xy} + \phi_z\phi_{xz}\right)\right) \\ +\left(\phi_{yy}|\nabla\phi|^2 - \phi_y\left(\phi_x\phi_{xy} + \phi_y\phi_{yy} + \phi_z\phi_{yz}\right)\right) \\ +\left(\phi_{zz}|\nabla\phi|^2 - \phi_z\left(\phi_x\phi_{xz} + \phi_y\phi_{yz} + \phi_z\phi_{zz}\right)\right) \end{bmatrix} \tag{2}$$

where ϕ_x and ϕ_{xx} denote the first-order and second-order partial derivatives of $\phi(x, y, z)$ with respect to x, respectively, and ϕ_{xy} denotes the mixed partial derivative of $\phi(x, y, z)$ with respect to x and y(similarly for other variables). Introduce the Laplace operator Δ and the Hessian quadratic form:

$$\Delta\phi = \phi_{xx} + \phi_{yy} + \phi_{zz} \tag{3}$$

$$(\nabla\phi)^T\left(\nabla^2\phi\right)(\nabla\phi) = \left(\phi_x\ \phi_y\ \phi_z\right)\begin{pmatrix} \phi_{xx} & \phi_{xy} & \phi_{xz} \\ \phi_{xy} & \phi_{yy} & \phi_{yz} \\ \phi_{xz} & \phi_{yz} & \phi_{zz} \end{pmatrix}\begin{pmatrix} \phi_x \\ \phi_y \\ \phi_z \end{pmatrix} \tag{4}$$

Substituting Eqs. (3) and (4) into Eq. (2), we can obtain:

$$\nabla \cdot \mathbf{n} = \frac{1}{|\nabla\phi|^3}\left[\Delta\phi \cdot |\nabla\phi|^2 - (\nabla\phi)^T\left(\nabla^2\phi\right)(\nabla\phi)\right] \tag{5}$$

Substituting Eq. (5) into Eq. (1), the mean curvature of $\phi(x, y, z)$ is:

$$H = \frac{(\nabla\phi)^T(\nabla^2\phi)(\nabla\phi) - |\nabla\phi|^2\Delta\phi}{2|\nabla\phi|^3} \tag{6}$$

Set $H \equiv 0$. Obviously, without considering singular points ($|\nabla\phi| = 0$), $|\nabla\phi| > 0$ holds always, that is:

$$(\nabla\phi)^T(\nabla^2\phi)(\nabla\phi) = |\nabla\phi|^2\Delta\phi \tag{7}$$

The left-hand side of Eq. (7) represents the second-order rate of change of the surface $\phi(x, y, z) = 0$ along the normal direction, while the right-hand side denotes the overall bending strength of the surface in coordinate directions. All surfaces $\phi(x, y, z) = 0$ satisfying this equation are level surfaces with zero mean curvature. Using the level set method, we define a dynamic evolution function $\phi(x, y, z, t)$, and specify the evolution equation as:

$$\frac{\partial\phi}{\partial t} = -H \cdot |\nabla\phi| \tag{8}$$

For Eq. (8), when $H > 0$, the surface contracts along the normal direction; when $H < 0$, it expands along the normal direction. When the evolution reaches a steady state, $\frac{\partial\phi}{\partial t} = 0$ (i.e., $H = 0$), yielding the minimal surface satisfying Eq. (7). Introducing periodicity and symmetry constraints to construct the initial function, trigonometric functions are obviously a good choice. Discretize and solve it iteratively via numerical methods, and approximate the obtained surface with triangular patches to plot the STL model of the TPMS surface. In the expressions listed in Table 1, $\omega_i (i = x, y, z)$ is directly related to the period of the TPMS structure. C is a constant, and controlling its magnitude allows regulation of the porosity of the TPMS structure [28]. The TPMS surface divides the finite space within one period into two regions. Filling either region ($\phi(x, y, z) \geq 0$) or ($\phi(x, y, z) \leq 0$) with an isotropic material while leaving the other region empty yields the solid network of the TPMS structure. This can be determined by controlling $\phi(x, y, z) - C > 0$ or $\phi(x, y, z) - C \leq 0$ to define the region which will be filled with material. Correspondingly, offsetting the TPMS surface by a certain distance on both sides and filling the intermediate space with material results in the sheet network of the TPMS structure (Fig. 2). This means the thickness of the TPMS sheet network is uniform across the surface. Existing studies have shown that sheet networks perform better mechanical properties and a larger specific surface area than solid networks, which benefits the scaffold's support performance and cell adhesion and growth [13, 29].

3 Bioceramic Slurry for VP

Typically, ceramic slurry consists of ceramic powder and a photosensitive premix. The photosensitive premix contains resin monomers, prepolymers, and photoinitiators, and its photopolymerization process is shown in Fig. 3. Under UV light, the photoinitiator is excited to generate free radicals, triggering the opening of double bonds in the resin monomers and prepolymers, which then link end-to-end to form long chains. This ultimately results in the formation of a robust network that encapsulates the ceramic particles, creating a dense solid structure [31].

The performance of ceramic slurry is critical to the manufacture of ceramic bone scaffolds using the VP process. Its solid-loading is directly related to the sintering density and mechanical properties of the scaffold after sintering, while the bioceramic type

Table 1. TPMS Expressions

Unit type	equations
Gyroid	$\phi(x, y, z) = \sin(\omega_x x)\cos(\omega_y y) + \sin(\omega_y y)\cos(\omega_z z) + \sin(\omega_z z)\cos(\omega_x x) = C$
Primitive	$\phi(x, y, z) = \cos(\omega_x x) + \cos(\omega_y y) + \cos(\omega_z z) = C$
Diamond	$\phi(x, y, z) = \cos(\omega_x x)\cos(\omega_y y)\cos(\omega_z z) - \sin(\omega_x x)\sin(\omega_y y)\sin(\omega_z z) = C$
F-RD	$\phi(x, y, z) = 4\cos(\omega_x x)\cos(\omega_y y)\cos(\omega_z z) - \begin{bmatrix} \cos(2\omega_x x)\cos(2\omega_y y) \\ +\cos(2\omega_x x)\cos(2\omega_z z) \\ +\cos(2\omega_y y)\cos(2\omega_z z) \end{bmatrix} = C$

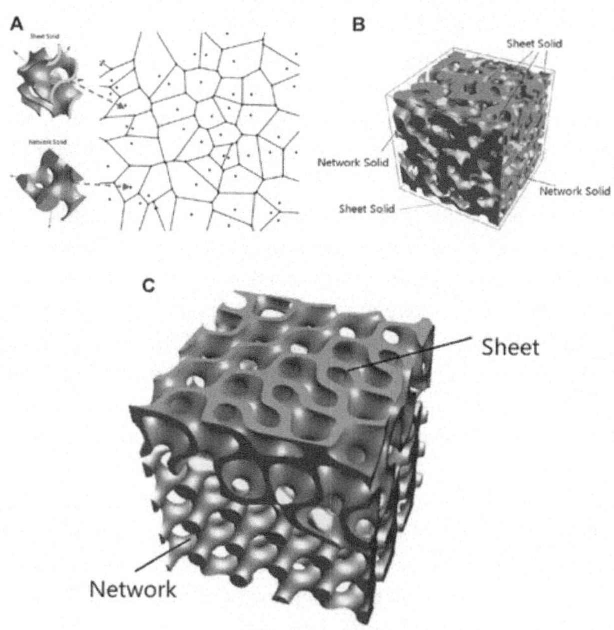

Fig. 2. Solid and sheet network. Reproduced with permission from ref [30]. CC BY 4.0.

directly determines the scaffold's biocompatibility [32]. Higher solid-loading results in less dimensional shrinkage, higher sintering density, and better mechanical properties [33]. However, as solid-loading increases, the viscosity of the slurry rises exponentially. Excessively high viscosity makes the slurry difficult to self-level, making printing unavailable. Additionally, the slurry must have good stability to prevent sintering defects caused by ceramic particle sedimentation during printing.

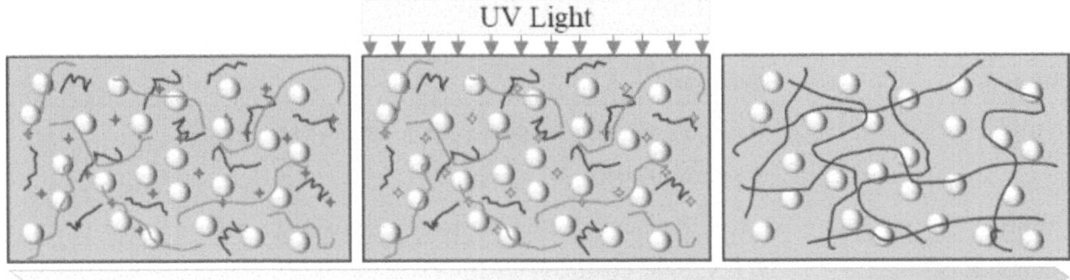

Fig. 3. Polymerization process of ceramic slurry.

Photopolymerizable slurries can be regarded as colloidal dispersions composed of fixed ceramic particles and freely flowing resin. Ceramic particles typically exhibit hydrophilicity, while resins are often hydrophobic. Modifying ceramic particles with dispersants can significantly enhance the affinity between ceramic particles and resin, enabling the modified ceramic particles to adsorb free-flowing resin molecules [34]. Smaller ceramic particles have a larger surface area, leading to the adsorption of more free resin molecules and thus reducing the fluidity of the slurry. Additionally, ceramic particles also adsorb to each other, and powders with smaller particle sizes are more prone to agglomeration, making uniform dispersion more difficult [32]. This implies that smaller particle sizes result in higher slurry viscosity and greater stability (Fig. 4) [35].

Due to the presence of hydroxyl groups, ceramic materials typically exhibit hydrophilic properties, while resin materials are generally hydrophobic, requiring the addition of dispersants to ensure uniform dispersion of ceramic particles in the premix [36] The van der Waals forces between ceramic particles can lead to agglomeration of ceramic powder, significantly increasing the viscosity of the slurry. This phenomenon is particularly noticeable in nanoscale ceramic particles, as the small particle size increases the surface area, aggravating the van der Waals forces between particles. With the help of dispersants, the surface of ceramic particles can be modified to be hydrophobic, introducing spatial repulsive forces between ceramic particles and reducing powder agglomeration [37]. Due to the high density of the solid component, ceramic particles will sediment in the slurry. With the addition of a dispersant, steric hindrance occurs on the surface of ceramic particles, inhibiting particle sedimentation and ensuring the stability of the slurry. Therefore, the addition of a dispersant is important for the preparation of high-solid-loading, low-viscosity ceramic slurries.

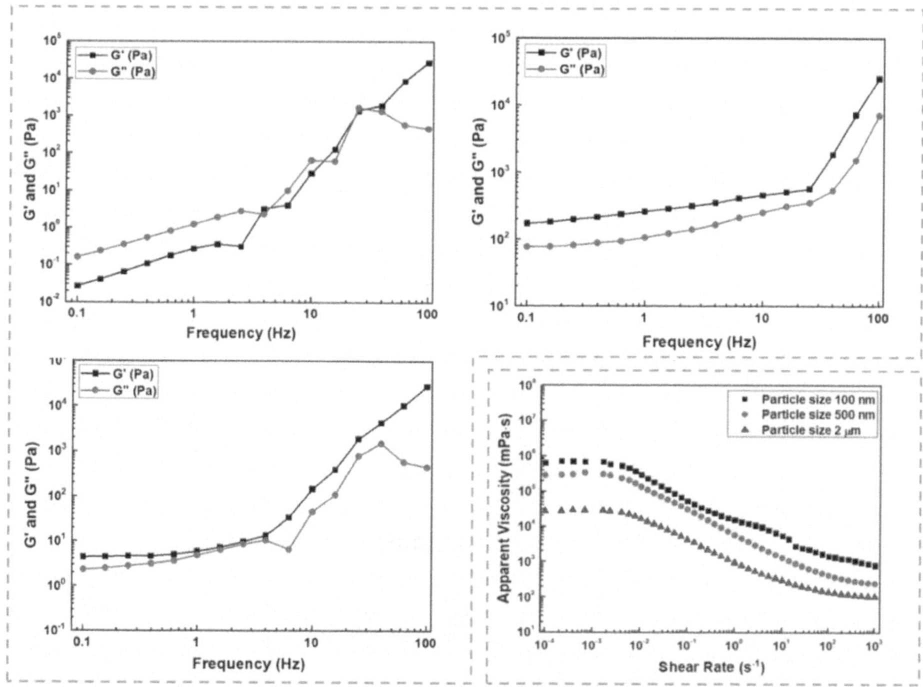

Fig. 4. The effect of particle size on slurry viscosity. Reproduced with permission from ref [38]. CC BY 4.0.

4 VP Technologies for Ceramic Printing

The development of VP technology has made it possible to manufacture high-precision ceramic bone scaffolds with complex pores. Due to its excellent printing resolution, VP technology is considered to be very advantageous when printing complex internal pores [39]. Figure 5a shows the overview of early attempts made for ceramic AM. Although VP has limited printing size, it still has significant advantages when printing bone scaffolds with complex and tiny pore structures [40]. Common VP techniques used in ceramic additive manufacturing can be categorized based on exposure methods into point-based polymerization, plane-based polymerization, layerless polymerization, and hybrid polymerization. Figure 5b illustrates the general process of ceramic VP printing using DLP as an example.

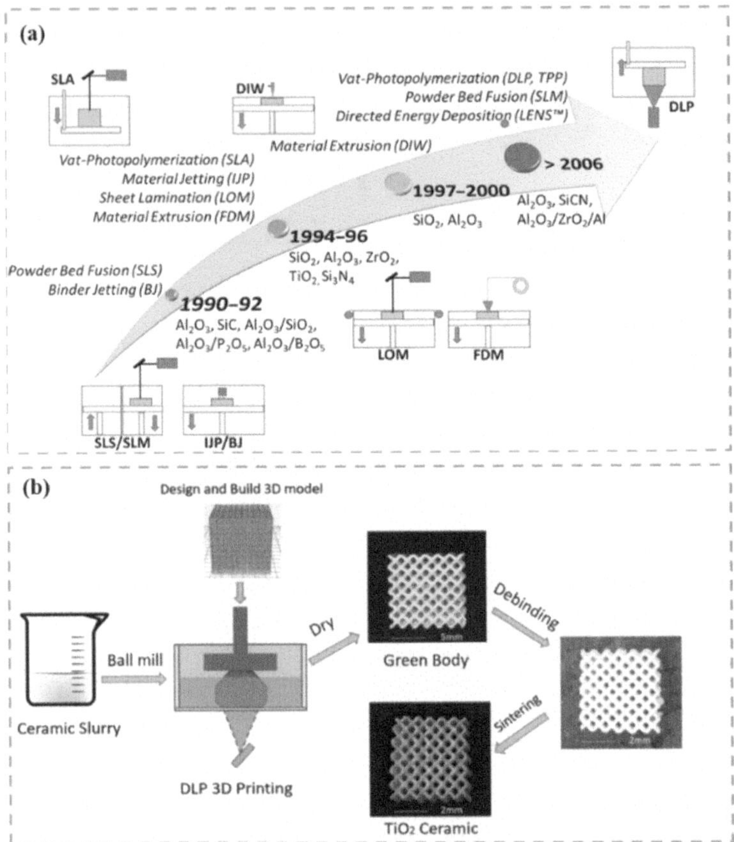

Fig. 5. (a) A overview of ceramic AM. Reproduced with permission from ref [41]. CC BY 4.0. (b) The general process of VP printing ceramic bone scaffolds. Reproduced with permission from ref [42]. CC BY 4.0.

4.1 SLA

SLA has two construction methods: bottom-up and top-down (Fig. 6a) [43]. Both construction methods follow the point-line-plane-volume construction process. The UV light is reflected onto the resin surface by a rotating scanning mirror, causing a point to cure quickly. The mirror deflects the light beam to scan the slurry surface along a set path, and the area swept by the light spot is cured. After scanning one layer, the platform moves by a layer thickness to scan the next layer, stacking layer by layer to form a solid. The difference is that the bottom-up system requires the slurry to impregnate the entire green body, which consumes a large amount of slurry. Due to the complex pores inside the scaffold and the high viscosity of the high-solid-loading slurry, it becomes more difficult to remove excessive slurry from the pores [44]. In comparison, the top-down system only needs to scrape a small amount of slurry with a scraper and spread it evenly on the building platform to print, which not only reduces slurry consumption but also makes it easier to remove excess slurry. Chen et al. [45] evaluated the cytotoxicity of SLA-printed HA scaffolds and proved that sintered HA scaffolds are cytotoxically safe. The above studies show that by optimizing the SLA printing process, it is possible to prepare ceramic bone scaffolds with excellent mechanical and biological properties. In addition, other studies have pointed out that the mechanical and biological properties of SLA 3D-printed ceramic scaffolds can be further optimized by using doped ceramic slurry [46].

4.2 DLP

Digital Light Processing (DLP) is the most widely used VP technology in ceramic additive manufacturing [19]. DLP uses a Digital Micromirror Device (DMD) to project a 2D image onto the surface of the slurry to solidify it, thereby forming a scaffold layer by layer. Similar to SLA, DLP can also be divided into bottom-up and top-down systems according to the construction direction, as shown in Fig. 6b. The precision of DLP printing is usually between 20 and 50 μm. Although the maximum printing size is limited by the projection size, it still has significant potential in the manufacture of ceramic bone scaffolds with complex micro-pores [35]. Due to the widespread application of DLP in the field of ceramic scaffold manufacturing, its process parameters and post-processing optimization have been extensively studied.

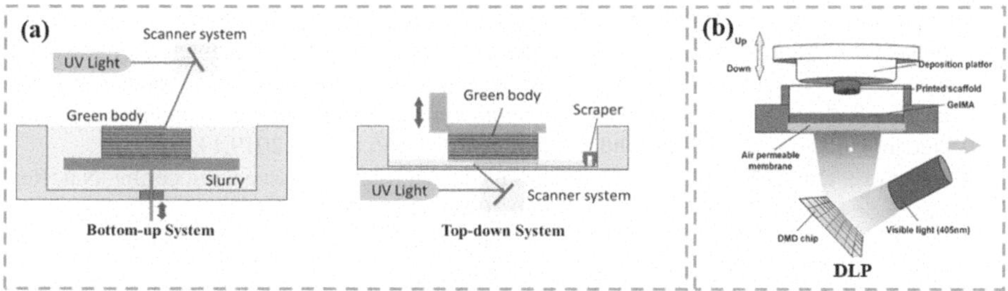

Fig. 6. (a) Two types of SLA. Left: bottom-up system. Right: top-dowm system. (b) Principles of DLP. Reproduced with permission from ref [22]. CC BY 4.0.

5 Conclusion and Outlook

The preparation of TPMS VP bioceramic scaffolds with excellent performance requires comprehensive consideration of design, materials, and manufacturing factors.

TPMS structures have evolved into various types. Surface generation strategies based on implicit functions are the most convenient and efficient, and are the most commonly used TPMS generation methods. Bioceramic slurries used for DLP should have high solid loading, high stability, and low viscosity, but these three characteristics are somewhat conflicting. VP technology has a inherent advantage in the field of ceramic bone scaffold manufacturing. The TPMS structure and VP technology are highly compatible. VP technology makes the manufacture of TPMS structures simple and fast, while the excellent pore connectivity inherent in TPMS makes it easy to remove excessive slurry after VP printing. At the same time, the excellent integrity of the TPMS structure eliminates the need for support during the printing process. As the most promising bone scaffold material, VP manufacturing technology for bioceramics is also becoming increasingly mature. In summary, VP-based TPMS bioceramic scaffolds are bone repair scaffolds with significant potential. Future research needs to focus on making their structural design, material formulation, and manufacturing process efficient and convenient. It is believed that these advances will promote their gradual transition from the laboratory to clinical use.

Acknowledgments. This work was supported by the National Key Research and Development Program of China (Grant No. 2022YFB3304000) and Key Program of the National Natural Science Foundation of China (Grant No. 52535008).

Disclosure of Interests. The authors have no disclosable conflicts of interest related to the content of this article.

References

1. Mauffrey, C., Barlow, B.T., Smith, W.: Management of Segmental Bone Defects. J. Am. Acad. Orthop. Surg. **23**, 143–153 (2015). https://doi.org/10.5435/JAAOS-D-14-00018R1
2. Vidal, L., Kampleitner, C., Brennan, M.Á., Hoornaert, A., Layrolle, P.: Reconstruction of large skeletal defects: current clinical therapeutic strategies and future directions using 3D printing. Front. Bioeng. Biotechnol. **8**, 61 (2020). https://doi.org/10.3389/fbioe.2020.00061
3. Mirkhalaf, M., Men, Y., Wang, R., No, Y., Zreiqat, H.: Personalized 3D printed bone scaffolds: a review. Acta Biomater. **156**, 110–124 (2023). https://doi.org/10.1016/j.actbio.2022.04.014
4. Bose, S., Sarkar, N.: Natural medicinal compounds in bone tissue engineering. Trends Biotechnol. **38**, 404–417 (2020). https://doi.org/10.1016/j.tibtech.2019.11.005
5. Koons, G.L., Diba, M., Mikos, A.G.: Materials design for bone-tissue engineering. Nat. Rev. Mater. **5**, 584–603 (2020). https://doi.org/10.1038/s41578-020-0204-2
6. Wang, C., et al.: 3D printing of bone tissue engineering scaffolds. Bioact. Mater. **5**, 82–91 (2020). https://doi.org/10.1016/j.bioactmat.2020.01.004
7. Bose, S., Roy, M., Bandyopadhyay, A.: Recent advances in bone tissue engineering scaffolds. Trends Biotechnol. **30**, 546–554 (2012). https://doi.org/10.1016/j.tibtech.2012.07.005
8. Schieker, M., Seitz, H., Drosse, I., Seitz, S., Mutschler, W.: Biomaterials as scaffold for bone tissue engineering. Eur. J. Trauma. **32**, 114–124 (2006). https://doi.org/10.1007/s00068-006-6047-8
9. Milovanović, J., Stojković, M., Trifunović, M., Vitković, N.: Review of bone scaffold design concepts and design methods. FU Mech. Eng. **21**, 151 (2023). https://doi.org/10.22190/FUME200328038M
10. Entezari, A., Swain, M.V., Gooding, J.J., Roohani, I., Li, Q.: A modular design strategy to integrate mechanotransduction concepts in scaffold-based bone tissue engineering. Acta Biomater. **118**, 100–112 (2020). https://doi.org/10.1016/j.actbio.2020.10.012
11. Guarino, V., Guaccio, A., Netti, P.A., Ambrosio, L.: Image processing and fractal box counting: user-assisted method for multi-scale porous scaffold characterization. J. Mater. Sci. Mater. Med. **21**, 3109–3118 (2010). https://doi.org/10.1007/s10856-010-4163-9
12. Liu, M., et al.: Topology optimization for reducing stress shielding in cancellous bone scaffold. Comput. Struct. **288**, 107132 (2023). https://doi.org/10.1016/j.compstruc.2023.107132

13. Kapfer, S.C., Hyde, S.T., Mecke, K., Arns, C.H., Schröder-Turk, G.E.: Minimal surface scaffold designs for tissue engineering. Biomaterials **32**, 6875–6882 (2011). https://doi.org/10.1016/j.biomaterials.2011.06.012
14. Feng, J., Fu, J., Shang, C., Lin, Z., Li, B.: Porous scaffold design by solid T-splines and triply periodic minimal surfaces. Comput. Methods Appl. Mech. Eng. **336**, 333–352 (2018). https://doi.org/10.1016/j.cma.2018.03.007
15. Li, J., Fan, H., Hua, L., Du, J., He, Y., Jin, Y.: Bone implants with triply periodic minimal surface architectures: design, fabrication, and biological performance. Bio-des. Manuf. **8**, 672–704 (2025). https://doi.org/10.1631/bdm.2400267
16. He, F., et al.: Preparation and characterization of iron/β-tricalcium phosphate bio-cermets for load-bearing bone substitutes. Ceram. Int. **43**, 8348–8355 (2017). https://doi.org/10.1016/j.ceramint.2017.03.173
17. Liu, M., Wang, Y., Zhang, H., Wei, Q., Liu, Z., Liu, X.: Influence of particle size distribution on hydroxyapatite slurry and scaffold properties fabricated using digital light processing. J. Manuf. Process. **131**, 401–411 (2024). https://doi.org/10.1016/j.jmapro.2024.09.036
18. Cho, Y.S., Yang, S., Choi, E., Kim, K.H., Gwak, S.-J.: Fabrication of a porous hydroxyapatite scaffold with enhanced human osteoblast-like cell response via digital light processing system and biomimetic mineralization. Ceram. Int. **47**, 35134–35143 (2021). https://doi.org/10.1016/j.ceramint.2021.09.056
19. Liu, M., Wang, Y., Liu, X., Wei, Q., Bao, C., Zhang, K.: Comprehensive review on fabricating bioactive ceramic bone scaffold using vat photopolymerization. ACS Biomater. Sci. Eng. **9**, 3032–3057 (2023). https://doi.org/10.1021/acsbiomaterials.3c00051
20. Griffith, M.L., Halloran, J.W.: Freeform fabrication of ceramics via stereolithography. J. Am. Ceram. Soc. **79**, 2601–2608 (1996). https://doi.org/10.1111/j.1151-2916.1996.tb09022.x
21. Wang, N., et al.: Preparation of high-stability ceramic slurry with gel behavior for stereolithography 3D printing. Materials. **16**, 2816 (2023). https://doi.org/10.3390/ma16072816
22. Li, H., et al.: Digital light processing (DLP)-based (bio)printing strategies for tissue modeling and regeneration. Aggregate **4**, e270 (2023). https://doi.org/10.1002/agt2.270
23. Bouakaz, I., et al.: 3D printed triply periodic minimal surfaces calcium phosphate bone substitute: the effect of porosity design on mechanical properties. Ceram. Int. **50**, 2623–2636 (2024). https://doi.org/10.1016/j.ceramint.2023.10.238
24. Li, Z., Chen, Z., Chen, X., Zhao, R.: Multi-objective optimization for designing porous scaffolds with controllable mechanics and permeability: a case study on triply periodic minimal surface scaffolds. Compos. Struct. **333**, 117923 (2024). https://doi.org/10.1016/j.compstruct.2024.117923
25. Zhang, J., et al.: Design of a biomimetic graded TPMS scaffold with quantitatively adjustable pore size. Mater. Des. **218**, 110665 (2022). https://doi.org/10.1016/j.matdes.2022.110665
26. Li, M., et al.: Bioadaptable bioactive glass-β-tricalcium phosphate scaffolds with TPMS-gyroid structure by stereolithography for bone regeneration. J. Mater. Sci. Technol. **155**, 54–65 (2023). https://doi.org/10.1016/j.jmst.2023.01.025
27. Song, K., Wang, Z., Lan, J., Ma, S.: Porous structure design and mechanical behavior analysis based on TPMS for customized root analogue implant. J. Mech. Behav. Biomed. Mater. **115**, 104222 (2021). https://doi.org/10.1016/j.jmbbm.2020.104222
28. El Khadiri, I., Abouelmajd, M., Zemzami, M., Hmina, N., Lagache, M., Belhouideg, S.: Comprehensive analysis of flow and heat transfer performance in triply periodic minimal surface (TPMS) heat exchangers based on Fischer-Koch S, PMY, FRD, and Gyroid structures. Int. Commun. Heat Mass Transfer **156**, 107617 (2024). https://doi.org/10.1016/j.icheatmasstransfer.2024.107617

29. Al-Ketan, O., Rowshan, R., Abu Al-Rub, R.K.: Topology-mechanical property relationship of 3D printed strut, skeletal, and sheet based periodic metallic cellular materials. Addit. Manuf. **19**, 167–183 (2018). https://doi.org/10.1016/j.addma.2017.12.006
30. Yang, N., Fan, S., Zhuang, J., Zhang, Y., Qian, Z.: Individual roles of network and sheet solids in architectured porous materials. Front. Phys. **10** (2022). https://doi.org/10.3389/fphy.2022.892525
31. Gao, X., Chen, J., Chen, X., Wang, W., Li, Z., He, R.: How to improve the curing ability during the vat photopolymerization 3D printing of non-oxide ceramics: a review. Materials **17**, 2626 (2024). https://doi.org/10.3390/ma17112626
32. Wang, W., Sun, J., Guo, B., Chen, X., Ananth, K.P., Bai, J.: Fabrication of piezoelectric nanoceramics via stereolithography of low viscous and non-aqueous suspensions. J. Eur. Ceram. Soc. **40**, 682–688 (2020). https://doi.org/10.1016/j.jeurceramsoc.2019.10.033
33. Dong, X., et al.: Mechanical and dielectric properties of Si_3N_4-SiO_2 ceramics prepared by digital light processing based 3D printing and oxidation sintering. Ceram. Int. **49**, 29699–29708 (2023). https://doi.org/10.1016/j.ceramint.2023.06.210
34. Sun, J., Binner, J., Bai, J.: Effect of surface treatment on the dispersion of nano zirconia particles in non-aqueous suspensions for stereolithography. J. Eur. Ceram. Soc. **39**, 1660–1667 (2019). https://doi.org/10.1016/j.jeurceramsoc.2018.10.024
35. Wu, Y., et al.: Optimized fabrication of DLP-based 3D printing calcium phosphate ceramics with high-precision and low-defect to induce calvarial defect regeneration. Mater. Des. **233**, 112230 (2023). https://doi.org/10.1016/j.matdes.2023.112230
36. Liu, M., et al.: Effects of dispersant concentration on the properties of hydroxyapatite slurry and scaffold fabricated by digital light processing. J. Manuf. Process. **109**, 460–470 (2024). https://doi.org/10.1016/j.jmapro.2023.12.040
37. Xu, X., Zhou, S., Wu, J., Zhang, C., Liu, X.: Inter-particle interactions of alumina powders in UV-curable suspensions for DLP stereolithography and its effect on rheology, solid loading, and self-leveling behavior. J. Eur. Ceram. Soc. **41**, 2763–2774 (2021). https://doi.org/10.1016/j.jeurceramsoc.2020.12.004
38. Ryu, K., Kim, J., Choi, J., Kim, U.: The 3D printing behavior of photocurable ceramic/polymer composite slurries prepared with different particle sizes. Nanomaterials **12**, 2631 (2022). https://doi.org/10.3390/nano12152631
39. Chen, Q., Zou, B., Lai, Q., Zhao, Y., Zhu, K.: Influence of irradiation parameters on the curing and interfacial tensile strength of HAP printed part fabricated by SLA-3D printing. J. Eur. Ceram. Soc. **42**, 6721–6732 (2022). https://doi.org/10.1016/j.jeurceramsoc.2022.07.019
40. Song, S., Park, M., Lee, J., Yun, J.: A study on the rheological and mechanical properties of photo-curable ceramic/polymer composites with different silane coupling agents for SLA 3D printing technology. Nanomaterials **8**, 93 (2018). https://doi.org/10.3390/nano8020093
41. Bose, S., et al.: 3D printing of ceramics: advantages, challenges, applications, and perspectives. J. Am. Ceram. Soc. **107**, 7879–7920 (2024). https://doi.org/10.1111/jace.20043
42. Abdelkader, M., Petrik, S., Nestler, D., Fijalkowski, M.: Ceramics 3D printing: a comprehensive overview and applications, with brief insights into industry and market. Ceramics **7**, 68–85 (2024). https://doi.org/10.3390/ceramics7010006
43. del-Mazo-Barbara, L., Ginebra, M.-P.: Rheological characterisation of ceramic inks for 3D direct ink writing: a review. J. Eur. Ceram. Soc. **41**, 18–33 (2021). https://doi.org/10.1016/j.jeurceramsoc.2021.08.031
44. Manapat, J.Z., Chen, Q., Ye, P., Advincula, R.C.: 3D Printing of polymer nanocomposites via stereolithography. Macro Mater. Eng. **302**, 1600553 (2017). https://doi.org/10.1002/mame.201600553

45. Chen, Q., et al.: A study on biosafety of HAP ceramic prepared by SLA-3D printing technology directly. J. Mech. Behav. Biomed. Mater. **98**, 327–335 (2019). https://doi.org/10.1016/j.jmbbm.2019.06.031
46. Dong, D., et al.: Enhanced mechanical properties and biological responses of SLA 3D printed biphasic calcium phosphate bioceramics by doping bioactive metal elements. J. Eur. Ceram. Soc. **43**, 4167–4178 (2023). https://doi.org/10.1016/j.jeurceramsoc.2023.03.007

Chemical Modification Strategies, Performance Optimization and Challenges of Conductive Hydrogels for Wearable Health Monitoring

Lijun Yang[1](✉), Tuanjie Chen[2], and Caijuan Li[3]

[1] Lanzhou No.9 Middle School, Lanzhou, Gansu 730050, People's Republic of China
yanglijun7309@163.com
[2] Lanzhou No. 63 Middle School, Lanzhou, Gansu 730060, People's Republic of China
[3] Lanzhou Institute of Technology, Lanzhou, Gansu 730050, People's Republic of China

Abstract. With the rapid advancement of flexible electronics technology, conductive hydrogels have gained recognition as an ideal candidate material for constructing next-generation wearable health monitoring devices, which are characterised by their outstanding electrical conductivity, mechanical flexibility, biocompatibility, and structural biomimetic properties. However, practical applications demand multi-dimensional performance requirements. Hydrogels must not only exhibit high electrical conductivity but also maintain exceptional mechanical properties, stable self-adhesion, and favourable environmental stability. Current materials still face performance bottlenecks. This paper systematically reviews recent advances in overcoming these limitations and enhancing hydrogel performance through chemical modification strategies. Regarding enhanced conductivity, targeted incorporation of conductive polymers (e.g., PEDOT:PSS), carbon nanomaterials (e.g., graphene, carbon nanotubes) and ionic liquids enables directional improvement of hydrogel conductivity. For mechanical property optimisation, strategies including dual-network structure design, nanocomposite modification, and microsphere reinforcement can significantly enhance the mechanical toughness and tensile properties of hydrogels. To impart reliable self-adhesive characteristics, designs based on the chemical principles of catechol and the bionic mechanism of dopamine can effectively fulfil this functional requirement. The application of these chemical modification strategies effectively advances the application potential of conductive hydrogels in cutting-edge fields such as wearable sensing, real-time health monitoring, and human–machine interaction.

Keywords: Chemical modification · Conductive hydrogel · Wearable devices

1 Introduction

With the rapid advancement of flexible electronics technology, wearable health monitoring devices are undergoing a revolutionary shift from rigid, cumbersome forms towards flexible, lightweight and comfortable designs [1, 2]. This transformation is facilitated by breakthroughs in new materials technology, particularly the emergence of flexible

S. S. Ge et al. (Eds.): ICSR + BioMed 2025, LNAI 16435, pp. 108–119, 2026.
https://doi.org/10.1007/978-981-95-7538-1_10

sensing materials with multifunctional integration capabilities [3]. Among numerous candidate materials, conductive hydrogels have garnered significant attention due to their unique properties [4, 5]. Not only do they exhibit excellent electrical conductivity, enabling efficient transmission of bioelectrical signals, but they also possess flexibility and elastic modulus similar to human tissue. This minimises mechanical mismatch at the skin interface, while their water-rich three-dimensional network structure confers outstanding biocompatibility and wear comfort. These properties position conductive hydrogels as an ideal material for constructing next-generation wearable health monitoring devices, demonstrating significant application potential for long-term, continuous, and non-invasive health monitoring [6–8].

However, numerous technical challenges must still be overcome before conductive hydrogels can be genuinely applied to wearable devices. Firstly, the electrical conductivity of intrinsic hydrogels is typically low (generally below 0.1 S/m), making it difficult to meet the signal-to-noise ratio requirements for bioelectrical signal acquisition [9, 10]. Secondly, conventional hydrogels exhibit poor mechanical properties and are prone to fracture, rendering them incapable of withstanding the repeated stretching and bending generated by human movement [11, 12]. Furthermore, unstable contact between the hydrogel and skin interface during dynamic use degrades signal quality, necessitating reliable self-adhesive properties in the material [13, 14]. Concurrently, hydrogels readily dehydrate and dry out in air while becoming excessively swollen in humid environments, both factors compromising their long-term stability.

To realise its immense potential in practical applications, an ideal conductive hydrogel must integrate multiple key performance metrics [15]. Regarding electrical properties, conductivity typically requires values exceeding 1 S/m to ensure low-impedance transmission and high-fidelity acquisition of electrophysiological signals [16]. In terms of mechanical properties, the material should combine high extensibility (elongation at break $> 500\%$) with high toughness to accommodate complex deformations and repeated stresses during human movement [17]. Furthermore, it must possess sufficient self-adhesive strength to ensure a stable, comfortable interface connection with the skin, effectively suppressing motion artefacts. Environmental stability is another critical factor, as hydrogels must resist dehydration and swelling under fluctuating temperature and humidity conditions while maintaining long-term mechanical and electrical performance reliability [18]. It is precisely these stringent and multifaceted performance requirements that make the precise regulation and multifunctional balancing of hydrogel properties through chemical modification strategies a core challenge and key research focus.

Currently, researchers are progressively addressing these challenges through various innovative chemical modification strategies [19, 20]. For instance, the conductivity of hydrogels has been enhanced by incorporating conductive polymers and carbon nanomaterials [21]. The mechanical properties of hydrogels can be strengthened through dual-network structures and nanocomposite techniques [22]. The adhesion properties at the hydrogel-skin interface can be improved by employing biomimetic adhesion mechanisms [23]. Environmental stability can be achieved by incorporating moisturising agents and self-healing components [24]. These advances have significantly propelled the application of conductive hydrogels in wearable health monitoring, which provides a solid foundation for the development of next-generation flexible medical devices.

2 Chemical Strategies for Enhancing Electrical Conductivity

Strategies for enhancing the conductivity of hydrogels primarily revolve around introducing conductive fillers or ionic conductors. Conductive polymers such as poly(3,4-ethylenedioxythiophene):poly(styrenesulfonate) (PEDOT:PSS) are widely employed due to their high electrical conductivity and favourable processability [25]. For instance, Zhang et al. [26] successfully prepared flexible, stretchable, and conductive PVA/PEDOT:PSS composite hydrogels by infiltrating the conductive agent PEDOT:PSS polymer chains into the PVA network. The conductivity of this hydrogel increased from 4.5×10^{-3} S/m to 0.36 S/m, enabling its application in flexible electronic skin and sensitive strain sensors (Fig. 1a).

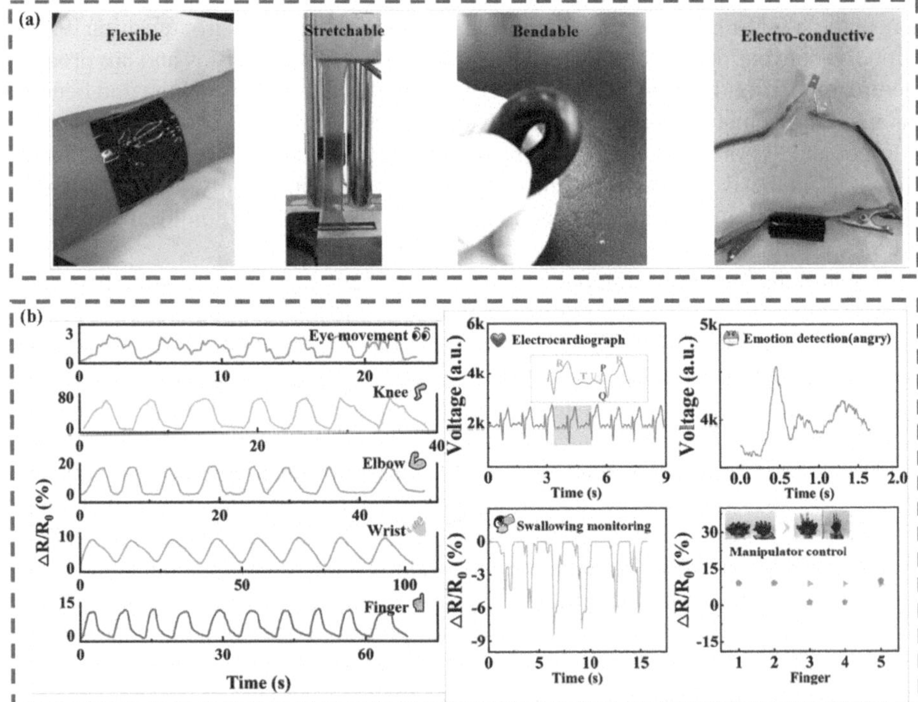

Fig. 1 (a) Stretchability, bendability and conductivity of the SIPN-PVA/PEDOT:PSS hydrogel. Reproduced with permission from [26]. Copyright 2019, CC BY-NC-ND. (b) LTGH hydrogel for motion sensing and physiological electrodes. Reproduced with permission from [27]. Copyright 2025, Wiley

Carbon nanomaterials such as graphene and carbon nanotubes (CNTs) are incorporated into hydrogel networks via covalent functionalisation (e.g., amide bond grafting) or non-covalent modifications (e.g., π-π stacking). Their high specific surface area and intrinsic conductivity not only enhance electrical conductivity but also improve mechanical properties. Wang et al. [27] synthesised a cost-effective lignin-tannin nanosphere graphene-doped hydrogel (LTGH) by dispersing graphene within a hydrogel matrix via self-assembly of sodium lignosulphonate and tannic acid nanospheres. The LTGH hydrogel achieved an electrical conductivity of 28 S/m, demonstrating broad application potential in wearable electronics, continuous human activity monitoring and human–machine interaction (Fig. 1b).

Ionic liquids (ILs) such as [EMIM][Cl] and [BMIM][Cl], serving as novel conductive media, can replace the aqueous dispersion phase to produce ion-conductive hydrogels resistant to drying, whilst simultaneously offering high ionic conductivity and thermal stability. Liu et al. [28] developed a polyvinyl alcohol (PVA) ionic conductive hydrogel by introducing the ionic liquid EMImAc, which exhibits exceptional anti-freezing and moisture-retention properties. This hydrogel maintains remarkable flexibility and high conductivity (2.98 S/m) across a broad temperature range from − 50 °C to 95°C. The multimodal sensor constructed with this material demonstrates high sensitivity and rapid response to pressure, strain, and temperature variations, providing an innovative strategy for developing stable and durable flexible electronic devices (Fig. 2).

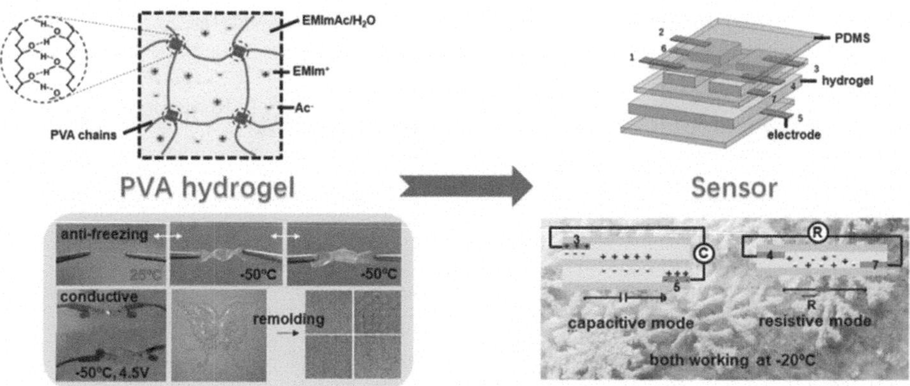

Fig. 2 Schematic diagram of PVA/EMImAc antifreeze conductive hydrogel and its integration in capacitance/resistance dual-mode sensor. Reproduced with permission from [28]. Copyright 2021, American Chemical Society

3 Chemical Strategies for Enhancing Mechanical Properties

The core of enhancing hydrogel mechanical properties lies in establishing efficient energy dissipation mechanisms. The dual-network (DN) strategy employs interpenetrating rigid primary networks (e.g., polyacrylamide) and flexible secondary networks (e.g., sodium alginate), utilising sacrificial bond cleavage to dissipate energy. This significantly enhances the hydrogel's fracture energy and extensibility.

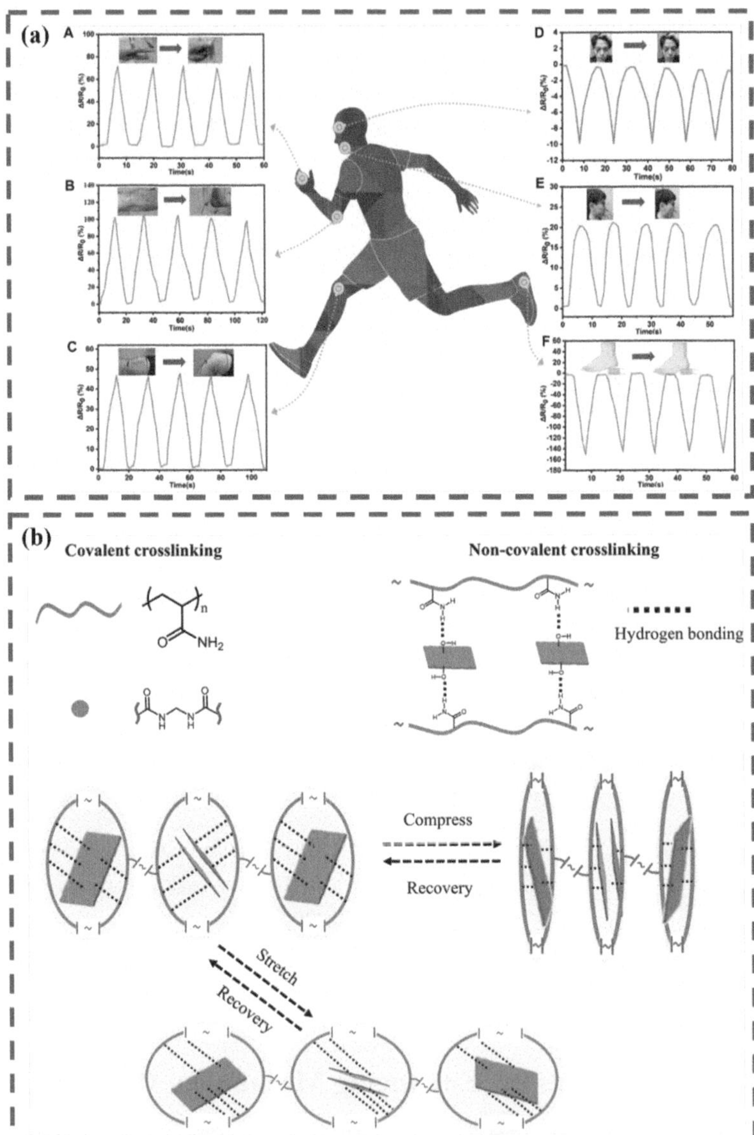

Fig. 3 (a) Strain sensor based on $ADN_{1.5}$ hydrogel for real-time monitoring of human movement. Reproduced with permission from [29]. Copyright 2022, CC BY. (b) A dual network containing multiple loops held by the NiCoAl LDH nanosheet-PAM complexation (structure extracted from the shadow area in the above), the mechanically induced change of the composite hydrogel from a microscopic point of view, as well as alignment of the nanosheets upon loading and recovery. Reproduced with permission from [30]. Copyright 2022, Wiley

Chen et al. [29] developed an ADN hydrogel by constructing a dual-network structure of calcium alginate and polyzwitterions, which simultaneously achieves exceptional mechanical properties (1375% tensile strain), conductivity (0.25 S/m), self-healing capability, and high transparency (92.2%). This material demonstrates outstanding performance as a flexible wearable strain sensor, accurately monitoring large human joint movements, plantar pressure, and localized muscle activities, thereby providing an innovative solution for health monitoring and human–machine interaction applications (Fig. 3a).

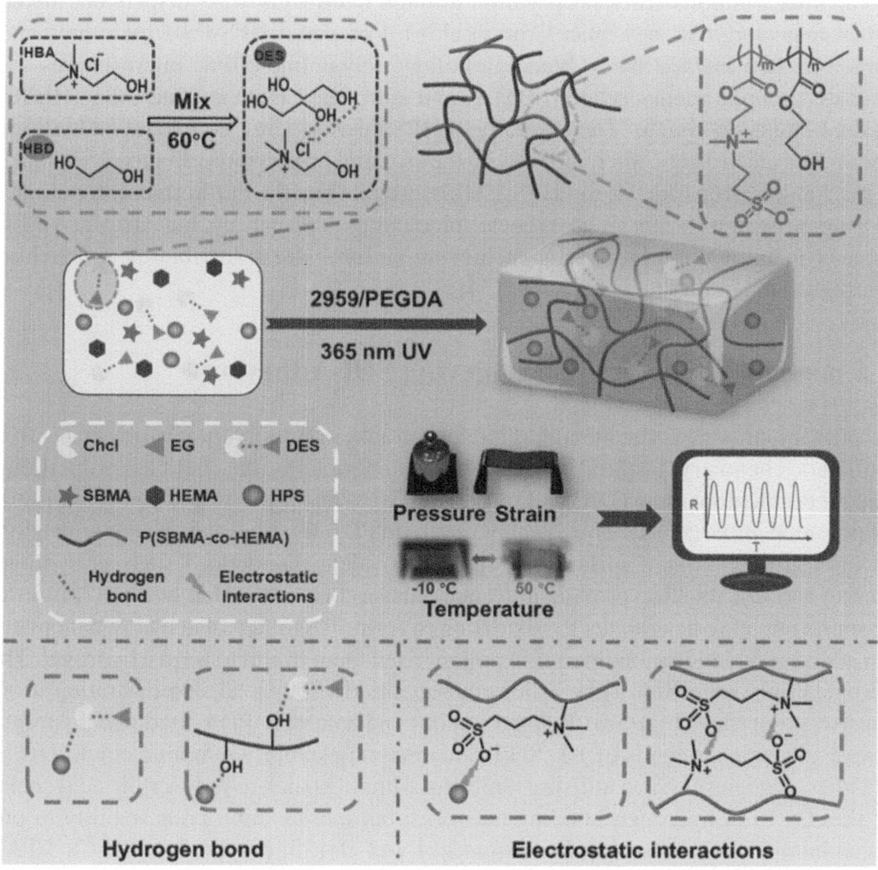

Fig. 4 Scheme of the preparation application and formation mechanism of HPS-PSH gels containing HEMA, SBMA, HPS microspheres, and DES. Reproduced with permission from [33]. Copyright 2025, ACS Publications

The nano-composite (NC) strategy employs nanoparticles (such as clay nanosheets and cellulose nanocrystals) as physical crosslinking points, achieving multiple energy dissipation pathways through reversible hydrogen bonds or ionic bonds to produce highly resilient hydrogels [31]. Chen et al. [30] developed a highly efficient mechanically reinforced composite hydrogel by incorporating nickel–cobalt layered double hydroxide (LDH) nanosheets into a polyacrylamide (PAM) hydrogel network crosslinked with bisacrylamide (BisA). This hydrogel exhibits high deformability (elongation > 1100%) and achieves a 100% hysteresis ratio within just one minute during large-scale stretching. This is attributable to the dynamic interactions of the nanoplate reinforcement acting as sacrificial non-covalent bonds, which perform multiple roles within the synergistic functional groups of the composite hydrogel (Fig. 3b).

Additionally, the microsphere reinforcement strategy involves dispersing elastic microspheres (such as polyurethane microspheres) within the hydrogel matrix [32]. This approach inhibits crack propagation through interfacial stress dispersion, thereby further enhancing tear resistance. Yan et al. [33] prepared HPS-PSH hydrogels via a simple one-step method by co-blending hollow polyaniline (HPS) microspheres with sulfonated betaine methacrylate (SBMA) and sulfonated methacrylate ester (HEMA) in a dual-emulsion system. The elasticity of HPS microspheres, coupled with hydrogen bonding and electrostatic interactions with the crosslinked network, effectively enhanced the mechanical properties of the HPS-PSH hydrogel (Fig. 4). Furthermore, topological slip ring structures (such as host–guest interactions between cyclodextrin and PEG) enable crosslinking point migration, achieving uniform stress distribution and yielding ultra-high extensibility and toughness [34].

4 Chemical Strategies for Achieving Self-Adhesion

The primary strategy for achieving reliable self-adhesion in hydrogels originates from biomimetic chemistry. Inspired by mussel adhesion proteins, the chemical properties of catechol enable dopamine (DA) and its derivatives to undergo oxidative polymerisation into poly-dopamine (PDA). The catechol groups in PDA form covalent bonds with amino and thiol groups on skin surfaces, while non-covalent interactions such as hydrogen bonding and π-π stacking provide universal adhesion [35, 36]. Han et al. [37] inserted dopamine into clay nanoplates for oxidation to form PDA-intercalated clay nanoplates, then added acrylamide monomers and polymerised them in situ to form a hydrogel. This hydrogel firmly adhered to a glass slide and supported a 500g load, demonstrating strong adhesive properties (Fig. 5a). Related studies indicate that PDA-modified hydrogels achieve adhesion strengths of 10–30 kPa, maintaining stability in humid conditions.

Other strategies involve utilising ionic cross-linking (such as polyacrylic acid chelating skin Ca^{2+}) or hydrogen-bonding networks, but these exhibit poor stability in prolonged humid conditions [40]. For instance, Lv et al. [38] prepared an SL-Ca^{2+}/PAM hydrogel by co-mixing sodium lignosulphonate (SL), acrylamide (AM), and anhydrous calcium chloride ($CaCl_2$). This hydrogel exhibits outstanding adhesive properties (48.5 kPa), high ionic conductivity (0.72 S/m), favourable tensile characteristics (elongation at break 1153%) and high toughness (758 kJ/m^3), positioning it as a flexible sensing material with broad application prospects (Fig. 5b).

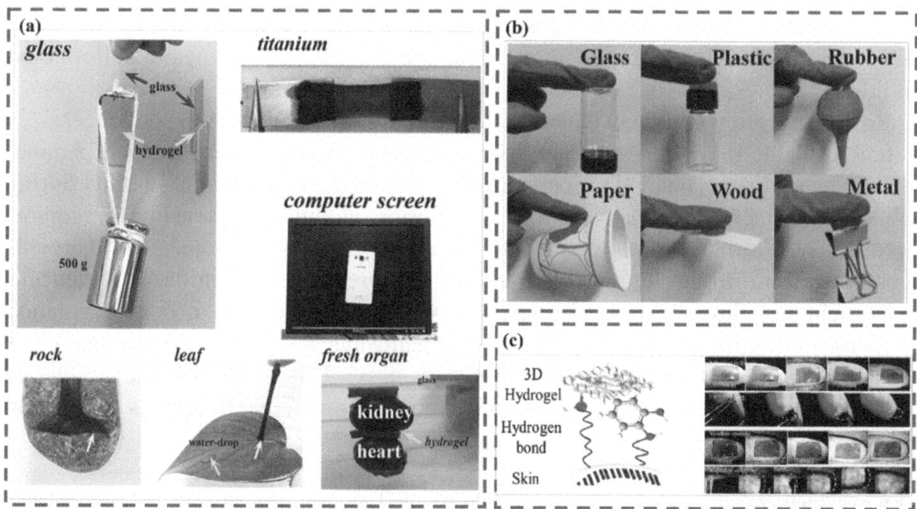

Fig. 5 (a) Adhesive property of the PDA-clay-PAM hydrogel. Reproduced with permission from [37]. Copyright 2017, ACS Publications. (b) Adhesiveness of the SL-Ca^{2+}/PAM hydrogel. Reproduced with permission from [38]. Copyright 2023, CC-BY-NC-ND 4.0. (c) The adhesion of DOPA@DNG to skin. Reproduced with permission from [39]. Copyright 2021, CC BY-NC 3.0

In recent years, synergistic interactions between dopamine and nanomaterials such as graphene have been developed [41]. These not only enhance adhesion but also confer antibacterial and conductive properties upon hydrogels. Sun et al. [39] successfully developed a bilayer hydrogel patch based on dopamine/zinc oxide nanoparticle doping (DOPA@DNG), where the dense upper layer effectively retards water evaporation (maintaining > 50% water retention after 3 days) while the lower layer combines ultra-high stretchability (1600%), self-healing capability, and tissue adhesion. This bilayer gel with synergistically optimized moisturizing, adhesive, and mechanical properties provides a novel solution for wearable devices and electronic skin applications (Fig. 5c). Regarding interface compatibility optimisation, biomimetic adhesion techniques such as dopamine modification enable stable, low-irritation bonding between hydrogels and skin surfaces. This effectively suppresses motion artefact interference, ensuring the accuracy of health monitoring data.

5 Conclusion

As the core functional materials for wearable health monitoring devices, the performance optimization of conductive hydrogels relies on multidisciplinary chemical modification strategies. To enhance conductivity, the targeted incorporation of conductive fillers (such as PEDOT:PSS, carbon nanomaterials and ionic liquids) significantly improves charge transport efficiency within the hydrogel. In terms of mechanical performance regulation, strategies including double-network structures, nanocomposite modifications, and microsphere reinforcement can establish efficient energy dissipation mechanisms, thereby markedly enhancing the tensile toughness and structural stability of hydrogels to meet the service requirements of wearable devices under dynamic deformation conditions.

However, current conductive hydrogel development still faces core challenges.

It is difficult to achieve a synergistic balance of multiple performance parameters (conductivity, mechanical properties, adhesion), and environmental stability during long-term service (such as dehydration, temperature and humidity sensitivity) requires improvement. Furthermore, low-cost, large-scale fabrication techniques for hydrogels remain immature. In the future, it is expected that breakthroughs in these bottlenecks can be achieved through in-depth exploration of dynamic chemical bond regulation mechanisms, multifunctional integrated design pathways, and intelligent response characteristics (such as pH and temperature responsiveness). This is anticipated to accelerate the practical implementation and industrialisation of conductive hydrogels in the field of flexible electronics.

Acknowledgements. This research was funded by the Lanzhou Municipal Education Science '14th Five-Year Plan' Project (LZ[2024]GH0074).

Disclosure of Interests. The authors have no competing interests to declare that are relevant to the content of this article.

References

1. Ali, S.M., Noghanian, S., Khan, Z.U., Alzahrani, S., Alharbi, S., Alhartomi, M., Alsulami, R.: Wearable and flexible sensor devices: recent advances in designs, fabrication methods, and applications. Sensors **25**, 1377 (2025). https://doi.org/10.3390/s25051377
2. Ali, A., Ashfaq, M., Qureshi, A., Muzammil, U., Shaukat, H., Ali, S., Altabey, W.A., Noori, M., Kouritem, S.A.: Smart detecting and versatile wearable electrical sensing mediums for healthcare. Sensors **23**, 6586 (2023). https://doi.org/10.3390/s23146586
3. Molahalli, V., Soman, G., Sharma, A., Bijapur, K., Chattham, N., Pai, R.K., Alodhayb, A., Hegde, G.: Flexing the future: strategic insights into wearable sensor development. ChemNanoMat **11**, e202500063 (2025). https://doi.org/10.1002/cnma.202500063
4. Chen, Z., Xu, C., Chen, X., Huang, J., Guo, Z.: Advances in electrically conductive hydrogels: performance and applications. Small Methods **9**, 2401156 (2025). https://doi.org/10.1002/smtd.202401156
5. Huang, B., Wang, Q., Li, W., Kong, D.: Stretchable and body conformable electronics for emerging wearable therapies. Interdisc. Med. **3**, e20240064 (2025). https://doi.org/10.1002/INMD.20240064
6. Li, J., Ding, Q., Wang, H., Wu, Z., Gui, X., Li, C., Hu, N., Tao, K., Wu, J.: Engineering smart composite hydrogels for wearable disease monitoring. Nano-Micro Lett. **15**, 105 (2023). https://doi.org/10.1007/s40820-023-01079-5
7. Chen, Z., Chen, Y., Hedenqvist, M.S., Chen, C., Cai, C., Li, H., Liu, H., Fu, J.: Multifunctional conductive hydrogels and their applications as smart wearable devices. J. Mater. Chem. B. **9**, 2561–2583 (2021). https://doi.org/10.1039/D0TB02929G
8. Omidian, H., Chowdhury, S.D.: High-performing conductive hydrogels for wearable applications. Gels. **9**, 549 (2023). https://doi.org/10.3390/gels9070549
9. Wang, Z., Wei, H., Huang, Y., Wei, Y., Chen, J.: Naturally sourced hydrogels: emerging fundamental materials for next-generation healthcare sensing. Chem. Soc. Rev. **52**, 2992–3034 (2023). https://doi.org/10.1039/D2CS00813K

10. Kayser, L.V., Lipomi, D.J.: Stretchable conductive polymers and composites based on PEDOT and PEDOT:PSS. Adv. Mater. **31**, 1806133 (2019). https://doi.org/10.1002/adma.201806133
11. Wu, W., Chang, J., He, Y., Guo, Z., Wang, S., Mao, J.: Phytic acid-based super antifreeze multifunctional conductive hydrogel for human motion monitoring and energy harvesting devices. Sustain. Mater. Technol. **42**, e01126 (2024). https://doi.org/10.1016/j.susmat.2024.e01126
12. Fang, Y., Bai, Z., Xu, W., Xiong, X., Wei, J., Hu, Q., Wang, H., Cui, J.: Mechanical design principles of conductive gels applied for flexible electronics. Adv. Funct. Mater. **35**, 2416398 (2025). https://doi.org/10.1002/adfm.202416398
13. Ullah, A., Kim, D.Y., Lim, S.I., Lim, H.-R.: Hydrogel-based biointerfaces: recent advances, challenges, and future directions in human-machine integration. Gels. **11**, 232 (2025). https://doi.org/10.3390/gels11040232
14. Shao, C., Meng, L., Cui, C., Yang, J.: An integrated self-healable and robust conductive hydrogel for dynamically self-adhesive and highly conformable electronic skin. J. Mater. Chem. C. **7**, 15208–15218 (2019). https://doi.org/10.1039/C9TC05467G
15. Li, Y., Cheng, Q., Deng, Z., Zhang, T., Luo, M., Huang, X., Wang, Y., Wang, W., Zhao, X.: Recent progress of anti-freezing, anti-drying, and anti-swelling conductive hydrogels and their applications. Polymers **16**, 971 (2024). https://doi.org/10.3390/polym16070971
16. Liu, D., Huyan, C., Wang, Z., Guo, Z., Zhang, X., Torun, H., Mulvihill, D., Xu, B.B., Chen, F.: Conductive polymer based hydrogels and their application in wearable sensors: a review. Mater. Horiz. **10**, 2800–2823 (2023). https://doi.org/10.1039/D3MH00056G
17. Harris, K.D., Elias, A.L., Chung, H.-J.: Flexible electronics under strain: a review of mechanical characterization and durability enhancement strategies. J. Mater. Sci. **51**, 2771–2805 (2016). https://doi.org/10.1007/s10853-015-9643-3
18. Lei, K., Chen, M., Guo, P., Fang, J., Zhang, J., Liu, X., Wang, W., Li, Y., Hu, Z., Ma, Y., Jiang, H., Cui, J., Li, J.: Environmentally adaptive polymer hydrogels: maintaining wet-soft features in extreme conditions. Adv. Funct. Mater. **33**, 2303511 (2023). https://doi.org/10.1002/adfm.202303511
19. Xu, J., Tsai, Y.-L., Hsu, S.: Design strategies of conductive hydrogel for biomedical applications. Molecules **25**, 5296 (2020). https://doi.org/10.3390/molecules25225296
20. Wang, S., Duan, S., Yang, T., He, Z., Xia, Z., Zhao, Y.: A self-powered strain sensor utilizing hydrogel-nanosheet composites, Zn foil, and silver-coated nylon. Sens. Actuat. A **364**, 114824 (2023). https://doi.org/10.1016/j.sna.2023.114824
21. Tomczykowa, M., Plonska-Brzezinska, M.: Conducting polymers, hydrogels and their composites: preparation, properties and bioapplications. Polymers **11**, 350 (2019). https://doi.org/10.3390/polym11020350
22. Ning, X., Huang, J., A,Y., Yuan, N., Chen, C., Lin, D.: Research advances in mechanical properties and applications of dual network hydrogels. IJMS **23**, 15757 (2022). https://doi.org/10.3390/ijms232415757
23. Pei, X., Wang, J., Cong, Y., Fu, J.: Recent progress in polymer hydrogel bioadhesives. J. Polym. Sci. **59**, 1312–1337 (2021). https://doi.org/10.1002/pol.20210249
24. Wang, Y., Yao, A., Dou, B., Huang, C., Yang, L., Liang, J., Lan, J., Lin, S.: Self-healing, environmentally stable and adhesive hydrogel sensor with conductive cellulose nanocrystals for motion monitoring and character recognition. Carbohyd. Polym. **332**, 121932 (2024). https://doi.org/10.1016/j.carbpol.2024.121932
25. Shi, H., Liu, C., Jiang, Q., Xu, J.: Effective approaches to improve the electrical conductivity of PEDOT:PSS: a review. Adv. Elect. Mater. **1**, 1500017 (2015). https://doi.org/10.1002/aelm.201500017

26. Zhang, Y.-F., Guo, M.-M., Zhang, Y., Tang, C.Y., Jiang, C., Dong, Y., Law, W.-C., Du, F.-P.: Flexible, stretchable and conductive PVA/PEDOT:PSS composite hydrogels prepared by SIPN strategy. Polym. Testing **81**, 106213 (2020). https://doi.org/10.1016/j.polymertesting.2019.106213
27. Wang, Y., Li, Y., Zhang, Y., You, L., Song, Y., Li, T., Fang, Z., Gui, A., Li, Y., Liao, L., Yang, R.: Graphene-doped hydrogels with enhanced conductivity and stretchability for all-weather wearable devices. Adv. Func. Mater. **35**, 2425014 (2025). https://doi.org/10.1002/adfm.202425014
28. Liu, Y., Wang, W., Gu, K., Yao, J., Shao, Z., Chen, X.: Poly(vinyl alcohol) hydrogels with integrated toughness, conductivity, and freezing tolerance based on ionic liquid/water binary solvent systems. ACS Appl. Mater. Interfaces **13**, 29008–29020 (2021). https://doi.org/10.1021/acsami.1c09006
29. Chen, K., Liu, M., Wang, F., Hu, Y., Liu, P., Li, C., Du, Q., Yu, Y., Xiao, X., Feng, Q.: Highly transparent, self-healing, and self-adhesive double network hydrogel for wearable sensors. Front. Bioeng. Biotechnol. 10, (2022). https://doi.org/10.3389/fbioe.2022.846401.
30. Chen, F., Huang, Z., Li, T., Xiao, T., Wang, S., Bai, G., Sun, H., Zhu, S., Yang, W., Lu, H., Wei, C.: Highly deformable and durable hydrogels through synergy of covalent crosslinks and nanosheet-reinforced dynamic interactions toward flexible sensor. Adv. Mat. Technol. **8**, 2200745 (2023). https://doi.org/10.1002/admt.202200745
31. Afolabi, O.A., Ndou, N.: Synergy of hybrid fillers for emerging composite and nanocomposite materials—A review. Polymers **16**, 1907 (2024). https://doi.org/10.3390/polym16131907
32. Guo, T., Luo, L., Wang, L., Zhang, F., Liu, Y., Leng, J.: Smart polymer microspheres: preparation, microstructures, stimuli-responsive properties, and applications. ACS Nano **19**, 18003–18036 (2025). https://doi.org/10.1021/acsnano.5c00998
33. Yan, K., Gong, M., Xu, Q., Zhang, C., Zong, Y., Sun, X., Xue, R.: Hollow polyaniline microspheres encapsulated in eutectogels for multimodal flexible sensors toward human health monitoring. ACS Appl. Polym. Mater. **7**, 3054–3066 (2025). https://doi.org/10.1021/acsapm.4c03746
34. Du, R., Bao, T., Kong, D., Zhang, Q., Jia, X.: Cyclodextrins-based polyrotaxanes: from functional polymers to applications in electronics and energy storage materials. ChemPlusChem **89**, e202300706 (2024). https://doi.org/10.1002/cplu.202300706
35. Guo, Q., Chen, J., Wang, J., Zeng, H., Yu, J.: Recent progress in synthesis and application of mussel-inspired adhesives. Nanoscale **12**, 1307–1324 (2020). https://doi.org/10.1039/C9NR09780E
36. Chen, J., Han, L., Liu, J., Zeng, H.: Mussel-inspired adhesive hydrogels: chemistry and biomedical applications†. Chin. J. Chem. **41**, 3729–3738 (2023). https://doi.org/10.1002/cjoc.202300423
37. Han, L., Lu, X., Liu, K., Wang, K., Fang, L., Weng, L.-T., Zhang, H., Tang, Y., Ren, F., Zhao, C., Sun, G., Liang, R., Li, Z.: Mussel-inspired adhesive and tough hydrogel based on nanoclay confined dopamine polymerization. ACS Nano **11**, 2561–2574 (2017). https://doi.org/10.1021/acsnano.6b05318
38. Lv, H., Zong, S., Li, T., Zhao, Q., Xu, Z., Duan, J.: Room temperature Ca^{2+} -initiated free radical polymerization for the preparation of conductive, adhesive, anti-freezing and UV-blocking hydrogels for monitoring human movement. ACS Omega **8**, 9434–9444 (2023). https://doi.org/10.1021/acsomega.2c08097
39. Sun, F., Li, R., Jin, F., Zhang, H., Zhang, J., Wang, T., Feng, Z.-Q.: Dopamine/zinc oxide doped poly(N-hydroxyethyl acrylamide)/agar dual network hydrogel with super self-healing, antibacterial and tissue adhesion functions designed for transdermal patch. J. Mater. Chem. B. **9**, 5492–5502 (2021). https://doi.org/10.1039/D1TB00822F

40. Wang, Y., Shen, Z., Wang, H., Song, Z., Yu, D., Li, G., Liu, X., Liu, W.: Progress in research on metal ion crosslinking alginate-based gels. Gels. **11**, 16 (2024). https://doi.org/10.3390/gels11010016
41. Suhito, I.R., Angeline, N., Kim, T.-H.: Nanomaterial-modified hybrid platforms for precise electrochemical detection of dopamine. BioChip J. **13**, 20–29 (2019). https://doi.org/10.1007/s13206-019-3106-x

Evaluation of UAV Crash Risk for Low-Altitude Biothreat Sample Transport Using Fuzzy Bayesian Networks

Yichuan Yang[1,2], Peng Hu[1,2](✉), Weiwei Yu[3], Xiang Zou[1,2], Yi Ai[4], and Guangyuan Zhang[5]

[1] Low-Altitude Traffic Intelligent Control Key Laboratory of Sichuan Province, Chengdu, China
hupengbaby@163.com

[2] Intelligent Management and Control of Low-Altitude Traffic Key Laboratory of Sichuan Province, Chengdu, China

[3] Northwestern Polytechnical University, Xi'an, China

[4] Civil Aviation Flight, University of China, Deyang, China

[5] School of Transportation and Logistics, Southwest Jiaotong University, Chengdu, China

Abstract. In the era when drone technology is highly advanced, it is necessary to address the safety issues arising from UAV crashes under current conditions. This paper first employs a fuzzy Bayesian network to identify the key factors contributing to UAV crashes. Subsequently, relevant experts in the civil aviation field are invited to provide fuzzy linguistic evaluations of each risk factor, from which the prior probabilities of root nodes are obtained. The prior probabilities of non-root nodes are derived using a judgment matrix. Then, a Bayesian network model for UAV crash risk is constructed using GeNIe software, followed by single-factor analysis, as well as forward and backward reasoning to determine the critical factors influencing UAV crashes. Finally, an Event Sequence Diagram (ESD) is used to analyze the consequences of UAV crashes, providing provides ideas for UAV crash risk assessment and post-accident consequence control methods.

Keywords: Low-altitude economy · Fuzzy Bayesian network · GeNIe · Event sequence diagram · Risk assessment

1 Introduction

With the widespread application of unmanned aerial vehicles (UAVs) in urban low-altitude public airspace, the field of UAV logistics has become an important direction for development in China, significantly improving the efficiency of goods transportation and industrial inspection. Biological sample drone transportation is an emerging field in the development of drone logistics. It combines drone technology with the requirements of biomedical transportation, significantly improving the efficiency of transporting biological samples and meeting the urgent delivery needs of medical and research institutions for samples. However, the rapid development of the UAV industry is accompanied by

S. S. Ge et al. (Eds.): ICSR + BioMed 2025, LNAI 16435, pp. 120–130, 2026.
https://doi.org/10.1007/978-981-95-7538-1_11

numerous safety issues. Therefore, it is necessary to assess UAV safety risk factors to provide a theoretical basis and technical support for the scientific management of UAVs in China. Traditional risk assessment research has mainly focused on the safety of UAV flights, employing mathematical models and scientific calculation methods to analyze the potential consequences and impacts of accidents. The probabilistic safety assessment method based on Bayesian Networks (BN) can effectively integrate various types of information and intuitively display the dependency or independence relationships among variables, thereby supporting system safety assessment and decision-making.

In recent years, domestic and international researchers have focused on improving the accuracy.

of risk assessment and the efficiency of risk management using various methods. In 2018, Plioutsias [1] applied System-Theoretic Process Analysis (STPA) to develop a set of safety requirements for small UAV systems, revealing differences in how various UAV models meet safety requirements through comparisons with popular models. In 2019, Allouch [2] combined STPA with Bayesian Network algorithms to build a probabilistic risk model, employing a qualitative and quantitative approach to calculate accident probabilities. In 2020, Xin [3] developed a model focusing on low-altitude UAV airspace risk in urban environments, highlighting that increased altitude can significantly reduce third-party risk, providing important safety guidance for urban UAV logistics. In 2020, Han Peng [4] extracted operational risk factors for logistics UAVs and used a Bayesian Network to assess UAV failure risks. In 2022, Hong [5] proposed a new method for risk assessment of UAVs in warehouse operations, considering the system's specific operating environment. In 2023, Li [6] identified the main risk factors affecting UAV logistics through real collision case studies and literature review, and then constructed a Bayesian Network using an Interpretive Structural Model (ISM) to pinpoint key and sensitive factors leading to UAV collisions. In 2024, Geng [7] constructed a fuzzy Bayesian Network model to identify and evaluate critical risk factors for low-altitude UAV operations. In the same year, Liu [8] identified risk factors in the transportation of biological samples via UAVs from five dimensions—human, machine, environment, management, and hazard—and built a Bayesian Network to determine the primary causes of UAV transport risks. In 2025, Tian [9] addressed parameter uncertainties in UAV component failure distributions by using Bayesian theory to adjust the failure distribution parameters of basic events, ultimately establishing a comprehensive UAV safety assessment and decision analysis process.

The above-mentioned research on UAV risks has achieved certain results; however, most studies have only focused on identifying key risk factors, with relatively few addressing the risk evolution and consequence assessment of the entire UAV operation process. Therefore, this paper targets the operational system of UAVs in complex low-altitude environments and integrates a fuzzy Bayesian Network with an Event Sequence Diagram to construct a UAV crash risk assessment model. This model is used to analyze the main factors influencing UAV crash risk, evaluate the consequences of UAV crashes, and formulate UAV crash risk control strategies, thereby providing a scientific basis for the development of specific UAV safety prevention and control measures in the future.

2 Analysis of UAV Operational System Risk Assessment Indicators

Considering the complexity of the UAV operational system, this paper draws on the *Specific Operations Risk Assessment – V2.5* issued by the European Union Aviation Safety Agency (EASA), China's *Civil Unmanned Aircraft Operational Safety Management Regulations*, and relevant research literature on UAV hazard assessment. Based on these sources, the risk impact factors related to personnel, UAV facilities and equipment, and the planning environment are summarized. Taking into account the safety requirements for low-altitude UAV operations and combining them with practical experience, the specific risk categories and key influencing risk factors selected are shown in Table 1 below.

Table 1. UAV operational system risk factors and related descriptions

Risk category	Risk factors
Human factors	Pilot skill level
	Supervisor competency
	Pilot fatigue
UAV-related facilities and equipment	Communication facilities
	Monitoring facilities
	Power system
	Power supply system
	Navigation facilities
UAV operational environment	UAV density
	Meteorological conditions
	Terrain environment
	Electromagnetic environment

3 UAV Crash Risk Assessment Methods

3.1 Theory of Bayesian Networks

The Bayesian Network combines propagation logic with Bayes' theorem from probability theory. By constructing a directed acyclic graph (DAG) within a network framework, it describes the dependencies among variables and consists of nodes, directed edges, arcs, and conditional probability tables (CPTs). The conditional probability for each node includes all possible combinations of its parent nodes. Once the initial probability values of the nodes are obtained, the joint probability distribution of all nodes can be determined. The formula for the joint probability distribution is as follows:

$$P(x_1, \ldots, x_n) = \prod_{i=i}^{n} P(x_1 | R(x_i)) \tag{1}$$

$P(x_1, ..., x_n)$ represents the occurrence probability of a mutually exclusive and collectively exhaustive combination of events, and $R(x_i)$ denotes the set of its parent nodes.

3.2 The Event Sequence Diagram

The Event Sequence Diagram (ESD) is a graphical tool used to describe the causal chain of accidents or adverse events in a system. It illustrates the logical sequence of a series of possible events through logic gates and symbols, providing an intuitive representation of the evolution process of different accident outcomes. A standard ESD mainly consists of initial events, condition/state transitions, intermediate events, end states, and connecting arrows. In this study, the ESD model is used to analyze the scenario events occurring during a UAV crash, and is combined with the UAV crash risk Bayesian Network to form a complete UAV crash consequence BN model, thereby providing a solid foundation for subsequent UAV crash risk assessment.

3.3 Calculation of Node Probabilities in Risk Assessment

After establishing the risk assessment indicators for the UAV operational system, in order to accurately evaluate UAV safety during operation, it is necessary to determine the UAV risk assessment levels and their corresponding fuzzy linguistic terms, and to obtain fuzzy prior probabilities based on expert experience. In this study, triangular membership functions are used to describe the fuzzy possibility of each node. The fuzzy piecewise function $u(x)$ is shown as follows:

$$u(x) = \begin{cases} 0, x < l \\ \dfrac{x-l}{m-l}, l \le x \le m \\ \dfrac{n-x}{n-m}, m \le x \le n \\ 0, x > n \end{cases} \tag{2}$$

In the formula, l, m, n and represent the three parameters of the triangular fuzzy number.

The probability of occurrence of risk factors is divided into four levels: low impact, moderate impact, high impact, and very high impact. The risk assessment levels and the corresponding fuzzy linguistic evaluation criteria are described in Table 2 below.

Table 2. Fuzzy linguistic terms and corresponding triangular fuzzy numbers

Number	Fuzzy linguistic terms	Triangular fuzzy numbers
1	Low Impact	(0, 0.2, 0.4)
2	Moderate Impact	(0.2, 0.4, 0.6)
3	High Impact	(0.4, 0.6, 0.8)
4	Very High Impact	(0.6, 0.8, 1.0)

In this UAV crash risk assessment, five experts were invited to perform fuzzy evaluations of the risk indicators. To ensure the professionalism of the questionnaire results, all five experts are from civil aviation universities or other relevant civil aviation organizations, hold at least intermediate professional titles, and possess a high level of familiarity with the civil aviation field, enabling them to assess the prior probabilities of the root nodes in the Bayesian Network. Since the experts differ in experience, research level, and background, corresponding weights are assigned to different categories of experts based on their professional titles. The relationship between expert weights and professional titles is shown in Table 3 below.

Table 3. Classification of expert authority coefficients

Expert professional titles	Authority coefficients
Senior	0.5
Associate senior	0.3
Intermediate	0.2

By combining the fuzzy linguistic ratings and their corresponding authority coefficients, the experts' authority coefficients are normalized to calculate the prior probabilities of the root nodes. Let e_j be the authority coefficient of the j-th expert, and s_{ij} be the fuzzy linguistic rating for the *j*-th risk factor. Then, the weighted average of the fuzzy number $\overline{W}_i$ for the i-th risk factor can be expressed as:

$$\overline{W}_i = \frac{e_j * s_{ij}}{\sum_{j=1}^{n} e_j} \tag{3}$$

After obtaining the fuzzy weighted average through the above calculation, it is necessary to convert this value into a crisp value for subsequent risk analysis. At the same time, to reduce information loss and more intuitively display the relative magnitude of risk factors, this model adopts the area scoring method. The steps of the area scoring method are as follows:

Step 1: take the maximum value among all fuzzy numbers as the ideal optimal fuzzy number $\tilde{A}^*$:

$$\tilde{A}^* = (\max l_i, \max m_i, \max u_i) \tag{4}$$

In this study, (0.6, 0.8, 1.0) is taken as the ideal optimal fuzzy number.

Step 2: Calculate the area difference between each object and the ideal fuzzy number. In this study, the weighted distance method is used to compute the area difference, as expressed by the following formula:

$$D_i = \frac{1}{6}(|l_i - \max l_i| + 4|m_i - \max m_i| + |u_i - \max u_i|) \tag{5}$$

Step 3: Normalize the calculated scores, which is computed using the following formula:

$$S_i = 1 - \frac{D_i}{D_{max}} \tag{6}$$

4 UAV Crash Risk Assessment Based on Fuzzy Bayesian Networks

4.1 UAV Crash Risk Assessment

4.1.1 Construction of the UAV Crash Bayesian Network

Based on the UAV "Human–Machine–Environment" risk indicator system established in Table 1, a UAV crash risk Bayesian Network (BN) model is constructed according to the intrinsic causal relationships among the various risk sources. To facilitate the determination of conditional probabilities for the nodes, several state nodes are added to the original risk indicator system to represent direct factors leading to a UAV crash, thereby illustrating the immediate causes of UAV crashes. The newly added intermediate state nodes are "Deviation from Normal Path," "Control Failure," "Power Loss," and "Collision Occurrence." These additional nodes do not affect the final risk assessment results. Combining expert experience and actual influencing factors, the constructed UAV risk BN is shown in Fig. 1.

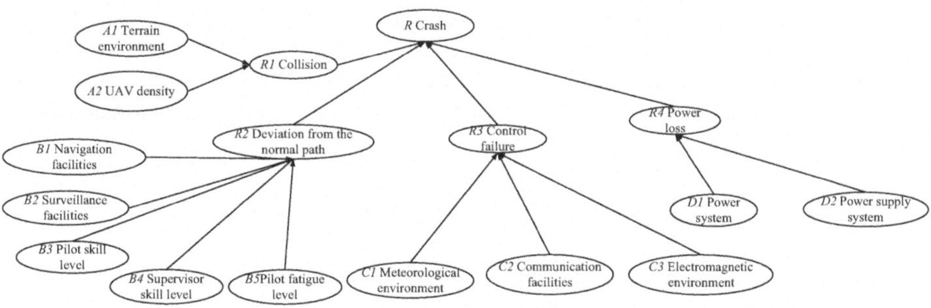

Fig. 1. Bayesian network model of UAV crash risk

4.1.2 Calculation of Node Probabilities

When calculating the probabilities of root nodes in the BN, the expert evaluation scores are combined with the fuzzy scoring formulas. After normalizing the expert weights, weighted calculations and defuzzification are performed. The final weighted triangular fuzzy means for all root nodes are shown in Table 4 below.

Table 4. Triangular fuzzy weighted means of risk root nodes

Node	Triangular fuzzy weighted mean	Node	Triangular fuzzy weighted mean
A1	(0.31, 0.51, 0.71)	B5	(0.57, 0.77, 0.97)
A2	(0.48, 0.68, 0.88)	C1	(0.54, 0.74, 0.94)
B1	(0.43, 0.63, 0.83)	C2	(0.47, 0.67, 0.87)
B2	(0.02, 0.22, 0.42)	C3	(0.46, 0.66, 0.86)
B3	(0.49, 0.69, 0.89)	D1	(0.54, 0.74, 0.94)
B4	(0.06, 0.26, 0.46)	D2	(0.30, 0.50, 0.70)

By substituting the above weighted fuzzy numbers into the defuzzification formulas (4)–(6), the prior probabilities of the root nodes are obtained, as shown in Table 5 below.

Table 5. Prior Probabilities of Risk Root Nodes

Node	Prior probability		Prior probability
A1	0.50	B5	0.94
A2	0.78	C1	0.90
B1	0.71	C2	0.77
B2	0	C3	0.75
B3	0.80	D1	0.90
B4	0.06	D2	0.48

For calculating the conditional probabilities of non-root nodes in the network, a judgment matrix is first constructed, with the elements of the matrix representing all child nodes. The square root method is then used to compute and normalize the relative weights, which serve as the conditional probabilities for the non-root nodes. Taking the top node "UAV Crash" as an example, the calculation of its conditional probabilities is shown in Table 6 below.

Table 6. UAV crash risk judgment matrix table

	R1	R2	R3	R4	Relative weight
R1	1	4	3	2	0.5878
R2	0.25	1	0.5	0.333	0.0279
R3	0.333	2	1	0.5	0.105
R4	0.5	3	2	1	0.2792

4.1.3 FBN Analysis

After calculating the prior and conditional probabilities for each risk factor, all parameters are imported into GeNIe 5 software to construct a fuzzy Bayesian Network model for UAV crash risk. The probabilities of each node are shown in Fig. 2. For root nodes, "YES" indicates the degree of influence on their parent nodes, while for non-root nodes, "YES" represents their prior probability of occurrence.

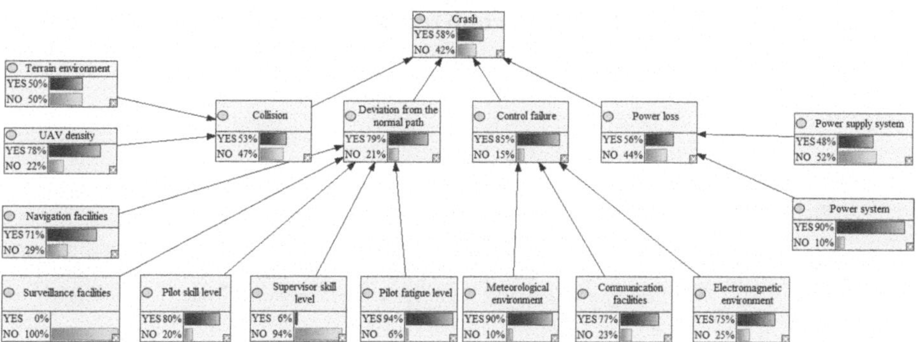

Fig. 2. Bayesian network model of UAV crash risk

Using GeNIe software for backward reasoning, the significant influencing factors when a UAV crash occurs can be intuitively observed. By setting the probability of a UAV crash to 100%, a reverse inference analysis is performed, and the resulting posterior probabilities are shown in Fig. 3.

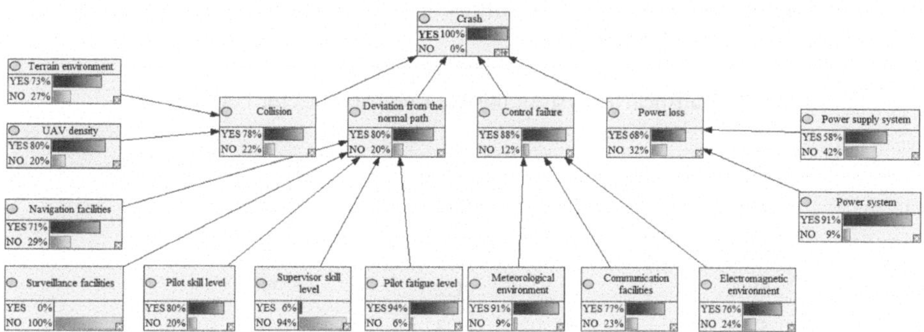

Fig. 3. Backward reasoning results of UAV crash risk posterior probabilities

The results of the backward inference indicate that when a UAV crash occurs, the risk probabilities for pilot fatigue (94%), meteorological conditions (91%), and the power system (91%) are relatively high. This suggests that changes or failures in these factors significantly increase the likelihood of a UAV crash.

4.2 UAV Crash Risk Management and Decision Analysis

As discussed in Sect. 4.1, multiple factors may contribute to a UAV crash. To identify which factors have the greatest impact on the probability of a UAV crash when a specific risk factor is absent, this study sets the "YES" probability of each root node in the Bayesian Network to 0 sequentially and performs forward reasoning, calculating the posterior probability of a UAV crash under each condition. The posterior probabilities under these scenarios are then compared with the prior probability of a crash to determine which factor most significantly reduces crash risk when it does not occur. The forward reasoning result for the node "Terrain Environment" with a probability set to 0 is shown in Fig. 4.

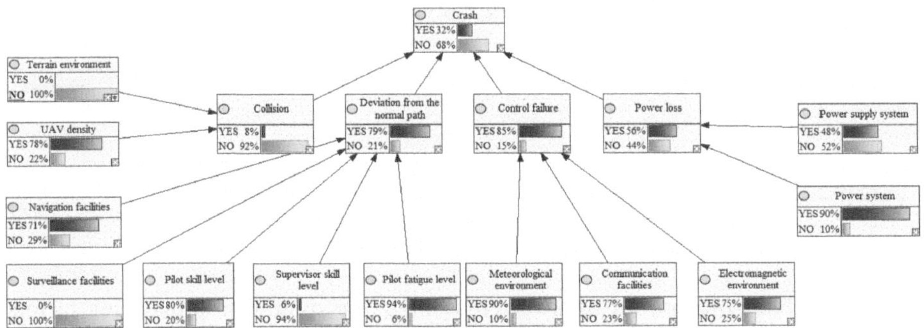

Fig. 4. Forward reasoning result for the "terrain environment" factor

Similarly, the "YES" value of each remaining single node is sequentially set to 0 for forward reasoning. The posterior probabilities of UAV crash risk under these conditions are summarized in Table 7 below.

Table 7. Statistical analysis of posterior probabilities for UAV crashes

Node	Posterior probability	Node	Posterior probability
A1	32%	B5	57%
A2	53%	C1	52%
B1	58%	C2	57%
B2	58%	C3	56%
B3	57%	D1	53%
B4	52%	D2	47%

From Table 7, it can be seen that when risk factor A1 (Terrain Environment) is inactive, the probability of a UAV crash decreases the most. Therefore, terrain factors should be given special consideration during UAV flight operations.

4.3 UAV Crash Consequence Control Based on Event Sequence Diagrams

The consequences of a UAV crash depend on the environment in which the crash occurs. If the UAV crashes in a densely populated area, it may cause casualties; if the crash occurs in a major transportation hub, it could lead to traffic disruptions or even trigger traffic accidents. Based on the various scenario combinations during a UAV crash and considering three dimensions—casualties, ground facility damage, and traffic disruption—an ESD model is constructed. The ESD model for a UAV crash is shown in Fig. 5.

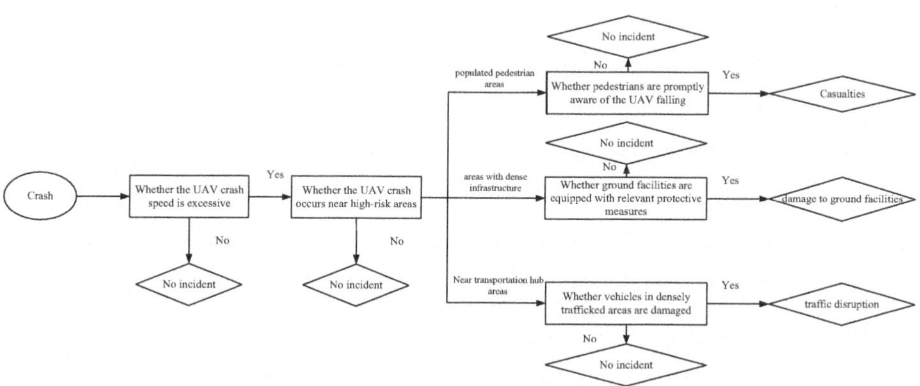

Fig. 5. ESD diagram of UAV crash incidents

From the ESD model constructed in Fig. 5, it can be seen that the hazardous events caused by a UAV crash are associated with multiple unsafe factors; no single factor directly causes the hazardous event. By analyzing the various stages of accidents resulting from UAV crashes, the following risk consequence control measures are proposed:

1. To prevent the UAV from descending too quickly during a crash, it is recommended to equip UAVs with emergency parachutes.
2. UAV flight routes should, as much as possible, avoid high-risk or sensitive areas.
3. Pedestrians should actively cultivate safety awareness and remain vigilant when UAVs are operating nearby.
4. For the protection of ground facilities, decisions on installing protective equipment should consider practical investment costs.
5. To maintain traffic order, it is recommended to deploy personnel in densely trafficked areas to manage traffic and supervise UAV operations.

5 Summary

1. This study constructs a fuzzy Bayesian Network (FBN) model to identify the key factors influencing UAV crashes. Regarding UAV collisions, UAV density is the critical factor; for deviation from the normal flight path, pilot fatigue is the most influential factor; in terms of control failures, meteorological conditions are the main influencing factor; and for power loss, the UAV power system is the primary factor.

2. Based on FBN backward reasoning, pilot fatigue (94%), meteorological conditions (91%), and the power system (91%) are identified as the key factors leading to UAV crashes. Furthermore, node influence analysis indicates that terrain environment is a critical factor in reducing UAV crash risk.
3. By analyzing the risk evolution following UAV crash incidents, an ESD model is constructed, and preventive measures are proposed to mitigate the occurrence of hazardous events during the evolution of such accidents.

References

1. Plioutsias, A., Karanikas, N., Chatzimichailidou, M.: Hazard analysis and safety requirements for small drone operations: to what extent do popular drones embed safety. Risk Anal. **38**, 562–584 (2018)
2. Allouch, A., Koubâa, A., Khalgui, M., et al.: Qualitative and quantitative risk analysis and safety assessment of unmanned aerial vehicles missions over the internet. IEEE Access **7**, 53392–53410 (2019)
3. Xinhui, R., Cheng, C.: Model of third-party risk index for unmanned aerial vehicle delivery in urban environment. Sustainability **12**, 8318 (2020)
4. Han, P., Wang, M., Zhao, Y.: Failure risk assessment of logistics UAV based on Bayesian network. China Saf. Sci. Technol. **16**(11), 178–183 (2020)
5. Honghong, Z., Xusheng, G., Ying, L., et al.: Risk assessment framework for low-altitude UAV traffic management. J. Intell. Fuzzy Syst. **42**(3), 2775–2792 (2022)
6. Li, H., Nie, F.: Collision Risk Assessment of Logistics UAVs Based on Bayesian Network. Sci. Technol. Eng. **23**(15), 6700–6706 (2023)
7. Geng, Z., Chen, J.: Risk assessment of low-altitude unmanned aerial vehicle operationbased on fuzzy Bayesian network. China Saf. Sci. J. **34**(08), 53–60 (2024). https://doi.org/10.16265/j.cnki.issn1003-3033.2024.08.1295
8. Liu, Q., Shen, T.: Risk assessment of biological sample transport by UAVsbased on Bayesian networks. China Saf. Sci. J. **35**(01), 16–24 (2025). https://doi.org/10.16265/j.cnki.issn1003-3033.2025.01.0441
9. Tian, Y., Rao, H., Xiao, N.: Safety assessment and decision analysis of UAV considering uncertainty. J. Civil Aviation Univ. China **43**(01), 83–88+96 (2025)

Deep Motion Physics Model for Parkinson's Motion Deficit Classification

Ajay Kishore Ponnada[1], Hongsheng He[2], and Fujian Yan[3](✉)

[1] Wichita State University, Wichita, KS 67260, USA
[2] University of Alabama, Tuscaloosa, AL 35487, USA
[3] Truman State University, Kirksville, MO 63501, USA
fujian.yan@wichita.edu

Abstract. Parkinson's Disease (PD) manifests through a variety of motor impairments that significantly impact patients' quality of life. Accurate motion data analysis enables earlier diagnosis and treatment planning. Recent advancements leverage Inertial Measurement Unit (IMU) sensors to non-invasively capture time-series data during activity, supporting motion deficit assessment in PD. This study presents QUaternion + AI-based Deficit Detection (QUAID), a deep learning-based framework designed to classify motion deficits in PD patients using IMU data. QUAID introduces a novel integration of quaternion kinematics and physical constraints using a physics-guided quaternion estimator for orientation estimation, followed by motion classification through a Bayesian-inspired classification network that quantifies predictive uncertainty. Comparative analysis shows that QUAID outperforms the Robust IMU-based Attitude Neural Network in orientation estimation accuracy, reducing the quaternion angular loss in orientation estimation from 0.0373 to 0.0083. On the classification task, QUAID achieves 97% accuracy while providing well-calibrated, uncertainty-aware predictions that enhance clinical interpretability.

Keywords: Parkinson's Disease · Motion Deficit Classification · Physics-Informed Neural Network · Bayesian Neural Network · Inertial Measurement Unit

1 Introduction

Parkinson's Disease (PD) is a progressive neurodegenerative disorder with motor and non-motor symptoms, significantly impacting quality of life [6]. With a growing aging population, there is increasing demand for early, non-invasive, and robust monitoring systems. Wearable technologies, especially Inertial Measurement Units (IMUs), enable continuous motion capture outside clinical settings, motivating further research into intelligent motion analysis [10].

While deep learning has advanced PD detection, most models rely on statistical correlations and overlook the biomechanics of human motion, leading

S. S. Ge et al. (Eds.): ICSR + BioMed 2025, LNAI 16435, pp. 131–140, 2026.
https://doi.org/10.1007/978-981-95-7538-1_12

to overfitting, poor generalization, and physically implausible outputs. Neural Networks (NNs) have outperformed classical models across modalities [4,14], with some two-stage architectures reporting accuracies above 99% on constrained datasets [9]. However, these high results often stem from over-optimized models on controlled data, lacking robustness in noisy, variable, and clinically ambiguous scenarios. Moreover, more models produce deterministic predictions without quantifying uncertainty, a drawback in clinical applications where decision confidence is critical. To address these challenges, we incorporate physics-based constraints and uncertainty-aware reasoning, aiming for models that are not only accurate but also reliable, interpretable, and generalizable to out-of-distribution motion patterns.

Modeling human motion from IMU data requires learning temporal dependencies across time steps to capture both short-term dynamics and long-term transitions. This motivates the use of time-series models such as Recurrent Neural Networks (RNNs), Temporal Convolutional Networks (TCNs), and Transformer-based models [12]. Although Transformers excel in vision and NLP tasks, their high data requirements and computational cost limit their applicability in real-time or low-data clinical scenarios [5]. TCNs offer efficiency and parallelization but are stateless, making them less suited for long-range dependencies [1]. In contrast, Gated Recurrent Units (GRUs), a variant of RNNs, strike a balance between complexity and temporal awareness, making them well-suited for limited clinical datasets where subtle motion deficits unfold over time.

In this paper, we propose QUaternion + AI-based Deficit Detection (QUAID), a framework for motion deficit classification in PD. QUAID estimates body segment orientations using quaternion kinematics, followed by probabilistic classification of motion windows. A Physics-Guided Quaternion Estimator (PGQE) enforces bio-mechanical consistency through quaternion normalization and kinematic constraints, producing physically plausible orientation estimates. These outputs, combined with raw IMU data, are passed into a Bayesian-Inspired Classification Network (BICN) for uncertainty aware classification. Unlike prior work focused on lower-limb gait [7,11], our approach targets upper-body dynamics using five IMUs placed on the upper/lower arms and chest. Data from structured daily living tasks is segmented into sliding windows for analysis through the hybrid pipeline. To improve generalization under limited data, QUAID applies jittering, scaling, and time warping for augmentation and uses cross-subject validation to ensure robustness. This research contributes to the field by:

1. Developing a Physics-Guided Quaternion Estimator that incorporates quaternion kinematics to ensure bio-mechanically valid motion representation.
2. Designing a Bayesian-Inspired Classification Network that enables uncertainty-aware motion deficit detection, enhancing reliability and interpretability in clinical decision-making.

2 Quaternion + AI-Based Deficit Detection

The QUAID architecture, illustrated in Fig. 1, follows a modular pipeline designed for interpretable motion analysis. Raw accelerometer and gyroscope signals from wearable IMU sensors are segmented into overlapping windows, processed by the PGQE to predict orientation trajectories as unit quaternions, and concatenated with IMU inputs. This representation undergoes data augmentation before being passed to the BICN, which classify motion deficits and quantifies predictive uncertainty to support clinical decision-making.

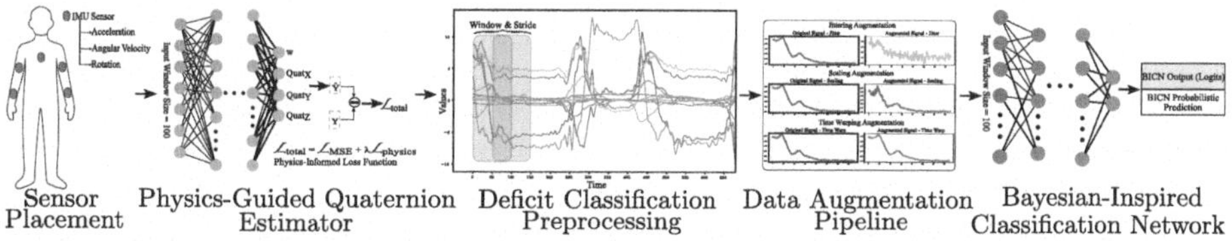

Fig. 1. Overview of the QUAID architecture for motion deficit detection using IMU sensor data.

2.1 Physics-Guided Orientation Estimation

We designed the PGQE to predict rotational orientation from IMU data while maintaining physical plausibility. The model processes time-series data using a GRU-based architecture as shown in Fig. 2, outputting unit quaternions:

$$\hat{\mathbf{q}}_{1:\mathrm{T}} = \mathcal{F}_{\mathrm{GRU}}(\mathbf{X}_{\mathrm{IMU}}; \theta) \tag{1}$$

where $\mathbf{X}_{\mathrm{IMU}} \in \mathbb{R}^{\mathrm{T}\times\mathrm{d}}$ with $\mathrm{d} = 6$, and $\hat{\mathbf{q}}_{1:\mathrm{T}} \in \mathbb{R}^{\mathrm{T}\times 4}$.

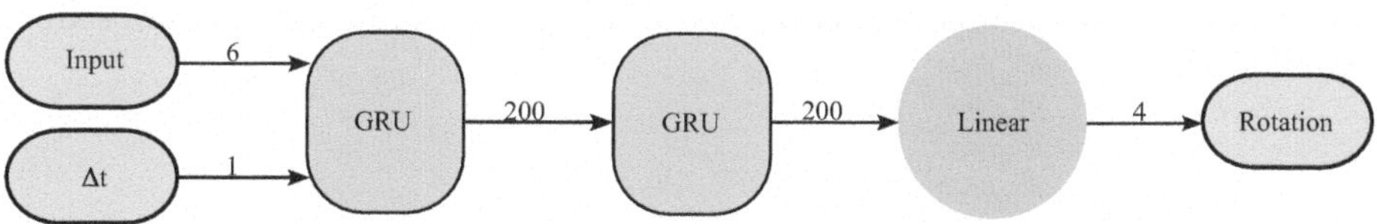

Fig. 2. Architecture of PGQE for quaternion prediction. The model takes six IMU sensor features along with time-step value. The inputs are processed sequentially using two stacked GRU layers, each with 200 hidden units, to capture temporal dependencies. The final output is a 4-dimensional quaternion representing the predicted orientation at the last time step, ensuring continuous rotational representation.

To ensure biomechanical validity, we embed physical constraints into the loss function:

$$\mathcal{L}_{\mathrm{total}} = \mathcal{L}_{\mathrm{data}} + \lambda_1 \mathcal{L}_{\mathrm{quat-norm}} + \lambda_2 \mathcal{L}_{\mathrm{kinematic}} + \lambda_3 \mathcal{L}_{\mathrm{smoothness}} + \lambda_4 \mathcal{L}_{\mathrm{physics-quat}} \tag{2}$$

where $\mathcal{L}_{\text{data}}$ is the standard Mean Squared Error (MSE) with ground-truth quaternions and the other terms enforce quaternion validity, motion smoothness, and kinematic consistency. Scalars $\lambda_{1:4}$ balance data fidelity and physical realism.

Each loss component contributes to a different aspect of the model's physical awareness. The quaternion normalization loss:

$$\mathcal{L}_{\text{quat-norm}} = \sum(||q_{\text{pred}}||^2 - 1)^2 \tag{3}$$

enforces the unit quaternion constraint, where the norm of a valid quaternion representing rotation must equal 1. This ensures that all predicted quaternions lie on the 4D unit hypersphere, preserving valid orientation representation. The kinematic constraint loss penalizes discrepancies between the predicted rotational displacement and the angular motion inferred from the gyroscope:

$$\mathcal{L}_{\text{kinematic}} = MSE(\theta_{\text{pred}}, \theta_{\text{gyro}}) \tag{4}$$

where θ_{pred} is the angle of rotation derived from the predicted quaternion, and θ_{gyro} is the total angular displacement computed by integrating the norm of angular velocity over time, i.e., $\theta_{\text{gyro}} = \int ||\omega(t)||dt$. This constraint ensures consistency between the model's predicted orientation change and the motion observed by the gyroscope. The smoothness loss encourages continuity in angular velocity, minimizing abrupt variations across time steps:

$$\mathcal{L}_{\text{smoothness}} = \frac{1}{T-1} \sum_{t=1}^{T-1} ||\omega_{\text{t+1}} - \omega_{\text{t}}||^2 \tag{5}$$

minimizes abrupt changes in angular velocity between consecutive time steps to ensure physically realistic motion transitions. Finally, the physics-based quaternion evolution constraint models orientation propagation using a first-order kinematic update:

$$q_{\text{pred}} = q_{\text{t}} + \frac{1}{2} q_{\text{t}} \otimes \omega_{\text{t}} \cdot dt, \tag{6}$$

$$\mathcal{L}_{\text{phyiscs-quat}} = \sum_{t=1}^{T} ||q_{\text{true}}^{(t)} - q_{\text{pred}}^{(t)}||^2. \tag{7}$$

This enforces that the predicted quaternion for the next time step ($q_{\text{pred}}^{\text{t+1}}$) evolves according to the physics-based model derived from angular velocity and the time difference (dt).

2.2 Motion Deficit Classification with Uncertainty Awareness

Quaternions generated by the PGQE are concatenated with IMU data:

$$\mathrm{X_{BICN}} = [\mathrm{X_{IMU}}||\hat{\mathrm{q}}_{1:\mathrm{T}}] \tag{8}$$

which is then segmented into motion windows for classification.The BICN maps this fused input to generate a predictive distribution:

$$\hat{\mathrm{y}}_{1:\mathrm{T}} = \mathcal{G}_{\mathrm{Bayes}}(\mathrm{X_{BICN}}; \phi) \tag{9}$$

where $\mathcal{G}_{\mathrm{Bayes}}(\cdot)$ is a Bayesian classification function parameterized by variational weights ϕ. This formulation enables the network to model uncertainty in its predictions by learning distributions over weights, rather than fixed point estimates.

To implement this probabilistic framework, the BICN employs variational inference through a DenseVariational layer. Each weight is drawn from a learned posterior distribution:

$$q(w) = \mathcal{N}(\mu = t_1, \sigma = \mathrm{softplus}(t_2)) \tag{10}$$

where t_1 and t_2 are trainable parameters, and the softplus ensures positive variance. The prior probability $p(w)$ is modeled as a normal distribution with trainable mean and fixed unit variance, i.e., $p(w) = \mathcal{N}(\mu = t, \sigma = 1)$, where the mean μ is a trainable parameter initialized using a VariableLayer. The variational loss combines data likelihood and regularization via KL divergence:

$$\mathcal{L} = \mathrm{E}_{q(w)}[-\mathrm{log}p(y|x, w)] + \beta \cdot KL(q(w)||p(w)) \tag{11}$$

where $\beta = \frac{1}{n}$ scales the divergence by the number of training samples.

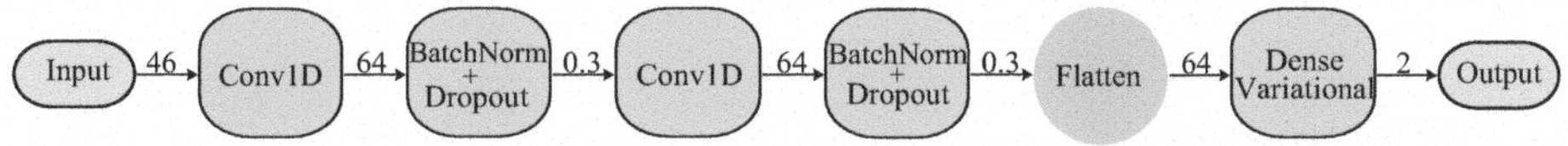

Fig. 3. Architecture of the BICN for motion deficit classification. The model takes as input a feature vector of size 246 derived from IMU sensor data and quaternion features. The input is processed through two sequential Conv1D layers, each with 64 filters, followed by Batch Normalization and a Dropout layer with a rate of 0.3 to improve generalization. After flattening the feature maps, a Dense Variational layer produces the probabilistic output, enabling uncertainty estimation alongside classification.

A final deterministic dense layer maps the learned features to class logits, which are optimized using sparse categorical cross-entropy. The full BICN architecture is illustrated in Fig. 3.

2.3 Data Augmentation Strategy and Training

To address data scarcity in clinical motion analysis, a structured data augmentation strategy was applied to IMU time-series data to enhance training diversity while preserving biomechanical plausibility. The process involves three transformations on accelerometer and gyroscope time-series data: jittering, scaling, and time warping. Jittering introduces zero-mean Gaussian noise across all channels to simulate real-world measurement fluctuations and sensor drift, $\mathbf{X}_{\text{aug}} = \mathbf{X} + \mathcal{N}(0, \sigma^2)$. Scaling simulates variability in motion amplitude across subjects by multiplying the signal with a factor sampled from a normal distribution centered at 1.0, formulated as $\mathbf{X}_{\text{aug}} = \mathbf{X} \cdot \mathcal{N}(1.0, \sigma^2)$. Time warping introduces temporal variation by stretching or compressing activity segments through interpolation, $x_{\text{warped}} = \text{interp}(x_{\text{orig}}, \text{new\_steps})$, where new_steps modifies the time indices to simulate altered motion speed. Signals are then truncated or zero-padded to ensure window consistency. To address class imbalance, synthetic data was generated and combined with real samples to exclusively train the BICN. This biomechanically consistent augmentation strategy improved the model's robustness and uncertainty-aware classification, thereby reinforcing its clinical reliability. Both models were trained using an implementation strategy optimizing for convergence, generalization, and compatibility of the proposed physics and probabilistic structures. All models were implemented using PyTorch (PGQE) and TensorFlow (BICN) to enable modular integration of physics-based loss constraints and variational inference. Input sequences were divided into overlapping windows of length m and stride n, and each window was used to estimate orientation at the final time step using an autoregressive structure. Both PGQE and BICN were trained using the Adam optimizer with an initial learning rate of 0.001, and training was guided by early stopping and learning rate scheduling based on validation performance. Hyperparameters were tuned empirically using cross-subject validation to support generalization across different movement patterns.

3 Experiments

To evaluate QUAID, we designed experiments that reflect real-world variability in PD motion data. The analysis targeted two tasks: predicting physically valid orientations from IMU signals and classifying motion deficits with high reliability. Cross-subject validation ensured training and testing on separate individuals. Beyond accuracy, we emphasized uncertainty awareness, physical plausibility, and model behavior benchmarking against a physics-agnostic baseline to demonstrate the value of embedding domain knowledge.

3.1 Dataset and Preprocessing Strategy

The dataset comprised twelve individuals, six diagnosed with PD and six healthy controls performing a upper-body tasks designed to mimic daily activities. IMU sensors were placed at five anatomical locations recording synchronized tri-axial accelerometer and gyroscope signals. The raw sensor streams were synchronized and aligned by timestamp, ensuring consistent temporal correspondence across all modalities. All signals were normalized to zero mean and unit variance per channel to stabilize learning. Data was segmented into overlapping windows of 100 time steps with a stride of 50 increasing training instances while preserving temporal continuity. Each window served as an independent sample across all sensor placements.

3.2 PGQE: Orientation Accuracy and Physical Plausibility

Orientation estimation was evaluated using Mean Absolute Error (MAE), Root Mean Squared Error (RMSE) and, Quaternion Angular Error (QAE):

$$e_{\alpha}(t_{\mathrm{k}}) = 2 \cdot \arccos(|\langle \mathbf{q}(t_{\mathrm{k}}), \hat{\mathbf{q}}(t_{\mathrm{m}}) \rangle|) \tag{12}$$

where $\mathbf{q}(t_{\mathrm{k}})$ and $\hat{\mathbf{q}}(t_{\mathrm{k}})$ denote the ground-truth and predicted unit quaternions at time step $\mathrm{t_k}$, respectively. QAE quantifies rotational discrepancy between $\mathbf{q}(t_{\mathrm{k}})$ and $\hat{\mathbf{q}}(t_{\mathrm{k}})$, accounting for quaternion double-covering.

Table 1. Quaternion Prediction Performance Comparison

Model	Loss (Convergence)	MAE	RMSE
RIANN [13]	0.0373	0.14	0.19
This Paper	0.0083	0.11	0.16

Table 1 shows that PGQE outperformed the RIANN baseline, reducing reconstruction loss by 0.029, MAE by 0.03, and RMSE by 0.03despite using the same GRU-based architecture. These gains stem from physics-informed constraints guiding the model toward more realistic rotational dynamics without added complexity.

In addition to numerical metrics, visual inspection of the predicted orientation trajectories confirmed the qualitative advantage of PGQE. Unlike RIANN, which produced abrupt transitions and non-unit quaternion anomalies, PGQE generated smooth, bio-mechanically valid trajectories across diverse movement segments. Predicted quaternions from PGQE aligned closely with ground truth across time, as shown in Fig. 4, while preserving unit norm constraints and suppressing erratic drift commonly observed in unconstrained models. These improvements are especially relevant in clinical biomechanics, where rotational smoothness and interpretability support downstream tasks such as rehabilitation analysis.

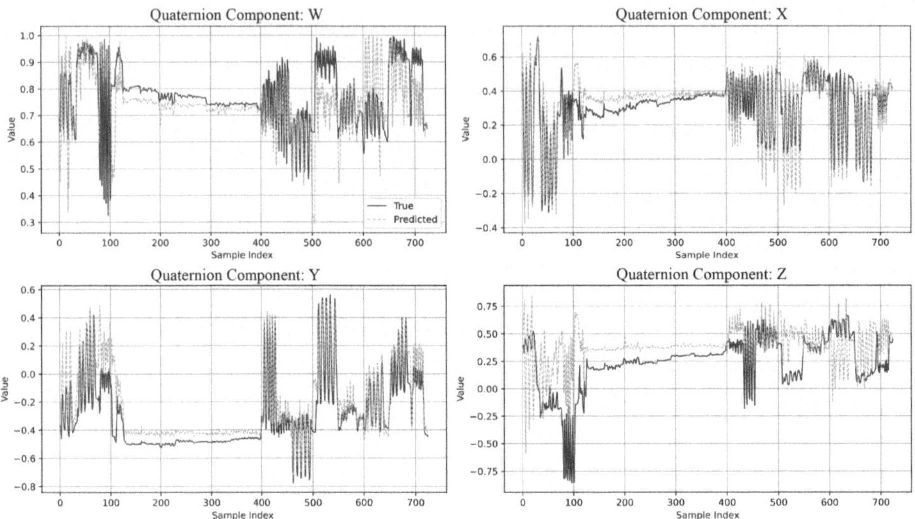

Fig. 4. Comparison between true and predicted quaternion components over sample indices. Each subplot displays one component of the quaternion, scalar (w) and vector parts (x, y, z), with true values and predicted values plotted together.

3.3 BICN: Uncertainty-Aware Motion Deficit Classification

BICN performance was evaluated using Accuracy, Precision, Recall, and F1-Score, along with reliability and calibration metrics critical to uncertainty-aware systems. The motion deficit class (label 0) achieved a precision of 0.97, recall of 0.96, and F1-score of 0.97, while the no motion deficit class (label 1) attained a precision of 0.96, recall of 0.98, and F1-score of 0.97. Macro and weighted averages also aligned at 0.97, indicating balanced classification across both classes. In addition, BICN produced well-calibrated probability estimates, with a Brier Score [2] of 3.25×10^{-2} and a Log Loss of 5.18×10^{-1}, reflecting high-quality confidence scoring. Agreement-based metrics such as Cohen's Kappa [3] at 0.934 and Matthews Correlation Coefficient (MCC) [8] at 0.935 further supported the classifier's robustness under class imbalance and motion ambiguity.

We conducted an ablation experiment by training BICN with and without quaternion inputs. The inclusion of quaternions led to a 3.1% improvement in classification accuracy and a 3.2% increase in F1-score. A paired t-test on per-sample correctness confirmed this improvement as statistically significant ($t = 5.08, p = 4.78 \times 10^{-7}$), validating the integration of PGQE output as an informative feature source.

Table 2. ROC AUC and Predictive Uncertainty Metrics Across Models

Model	ROC AUC	Mean Predictive Std. Dev.
BICN (With Orientation)	0.983	0.061
BICN (No Orientation)	0.972	0.058
FNN (No Orientation) [9]	0.923	N/A
SVM (No Orientation) [7]	0.994	N/A

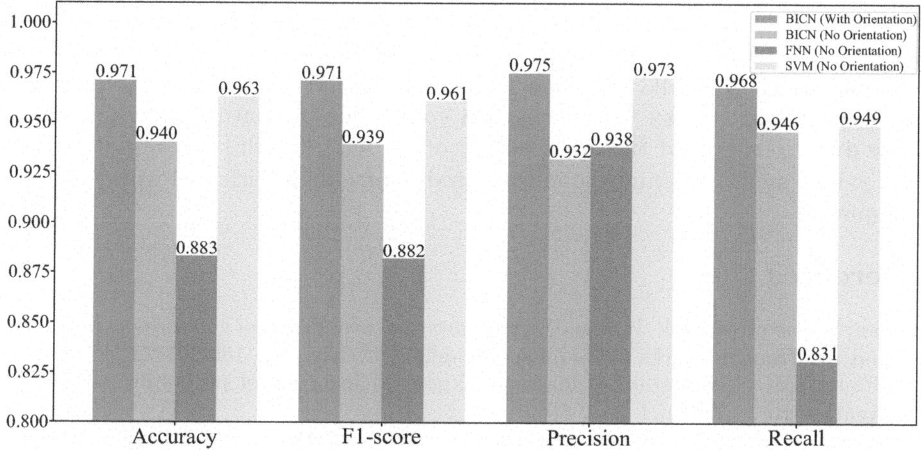

Fig. 5. Comparison of model performance across multiple evaluation metrics for motion deficit classification in Parkinson's Disease patients using the QUAID framework.

Compared with conventional classifiers, Support Vector Machine (SVM) achieved a competitive accuracy but lacked probabilistic outputs, as reflected in its absence from the Brier Score and Log Loss metrics in Fig. 5. A fully connected neural network (FNN) underperformed, underscoring the importance of temporal modeling. Table 2 highlights BICN's superior ROC AUC and calibrated uncertainty estimates, a key feature for clinical deployment.

Qualitative analysis showed BICN assigned moderate confidence to ambiguous transitions and high confidence to clear patterns such as tremors or consistent healthy motion. This behavior, driven by variational inference and probabilistic sampling, allows BICN to capture epistemic uncertainty and flag ambiguous predictions. These confidence scores provide clinicians with additional insight, helping prioritize manual review or clinical intervention. The low Brier Score and Log Loss values further confirm the calibration quality and clinical value of this uncertainty-aware classification design. These uncertainty estimates generated by BICN help clinicians identify cases where the model's prediction may be less reliable, guiding attention to samples that needed more in-depth evaluation or supplementary diagnostics. This capability supports improved workflow and patient care by enabling better prioritization and resource management in clinical decision-making.

4 Conclusion

In this paper, we proposed QUAID, which integrates a PGQE for orientation estimation with a BICN for motion deficit detection. Designed for IMU-based analysis in PD, the system achieved 97% classification accuracy while providing uncertainty estimates to support clinical decision-making. Although evaluated on a small cohort and limited to IMU signals, this work establishes a foundation for future studies with larger and more diverse populations. Incorporating additional modalities such as EMG or video capture could further enhance robustness, and longitudinal studies will strengthen confidence in continuous clinical use. These directions extend the applicability of QUAID, which by design leverages physics-informed constraints to ensure predictions align with real-world motion dynamics.

References

1. Bai, S., Zico Kolter, J., Koltun, V.: An empirical evaluation of generic convolutional and recurrent networks for sequence modeling. ArXiv, abs/1803.01271 (2018)
2. Brier, G.W.: Verification of forecasts expressed in terms of probability. Monthly Weather Rev., **78**(1), 1–3 (1950)
3. Cohen, J.: A coefficient of agreement for nominal scales. Educ. Psychol. Measur. **20**(1), 37–46 (1960)
4. Govindu, A., Palwe, S.: Early detection of Parkinson's disease using machine learning. Procedia Comput. Sci. **218**, 249–261 (2023)
5. Grassi, S.: Examining the limitations and challenges of using transformers for time series forecasting. Preprint available at ResearchGate (2024)
6. Joseph Jankovic and Eng King Tan: Parkinson's disease: etiopathogenesis and treatment. J. Neurol. Neurosurg. Psych. **91**(8), 795–808 (2020)
7. Li, A., Li, C.: Detecting Parkinson's disease through gait measures using machine learning. Diagnostics **12**(10), 2404 (2022)
8. Matthews, B.W.: Comparison of the predicted and observed secondary structure of t4 phage lysozyme. Biochimica et Biophysica Acta (BBA) - Protein Structure **405**(2), 442–451 (1975)
9. Pedrero-Sánchez, J.F., Belda-Lois, J.M., Serra-Añó, P., Mollà-Casanova, S., López-Pascual, J.: Classification of Parkinson's disease stages with a two-stage deep neural network. Front. Aging Neuroscience **15**, 1152917 (2023)
10. Pfister, F.M.J., et al.: High-resolution motor state detection in Parkinson's disease using convolutional neural networks. Sci. Rep. **10**(1), 5860 (2020)
11. Tsakanikas, V., et al.: Evaluating gait impairment in Parkinson's disease from instrumented insole and IMU sensor data. Sensors **23**(8), 3902 (2023)
12. Wang, J., Chen, Y., Hao, S., Peng, X., Lisha, H.: Deep learning for sensor-based activity recognition: a survey. Pattern Recogn. Lett. **119**, 3–11 (2019)
13. Weber, D., Gühmann, C., Seel, T.: Riann – a robust neural network outperforms attitude estimation filters. AI **2**(3), 444–463 (2021)
14. Yan, F., Gong, J., Zhang, Q., He, H.: Learning motion primitives for the quantification and diagnosis of mobility deficits. IEEE Trans. Biomed. Eng. **71**(12), 3339–3349 (2024)

Development of Physiological Temperature Responsive Shape Memory Polymer for Bone Tissue Engineering

Xiaolu Zheng[1], Yanqing Yang[2], Junchen Zhou[1], Xun Yuan[1], Xian Cheng[2], and Wei Zhu[1](✉)

[1] HNU College of Mechanical and Vehicle Engineering, Hunan University, Changsha, China
zhuwei@hnu.edu.cn

[2] Xiangya Stomatological Hospital and Xiangya School of Stomatology, Central South University, Changsha, China

Abstract. Large and irregular bone defects remain a major clinical challenge, as critical-sized defects cannot heal through the body's intrinsic regenerative capacity and typically require bone grafting. Irregularly shaped defects further increase surgical complexity and the risk of secondary damage. In this study, a temperature-responsive shape memory polymer poly(lactide-co-caprolactone) (PLCL) with a transition temperature close to physiological conditions was synthesized via ring-opening copolymerization of L-LA and ε-CL monomers at an optimized reaction temperature of 150 °C. PLCL scaffolds were successfully fabricated by selective laser sintering (SLS) 3D printing and exhibited shape fixation and recovery rates both exceeding 90% at 37 °C, enabling precise conformity to the edges of irregular bone defects. The scaffolds also demonstrated mechanical properties matching those of cancellous bone, with a tensile modulus of 138.23 ± 13.02 MPa and a tensile strength of 5.43 ± 0.71 MPa. These results suggest that SLS-printed PLCL scaffolds provide a promising strategy for repairing large, irregular bone defects.

Keywords: 4D Printing · Shape Memory Polymer · Poly(lactide-co-caprolactone) · Bone Tissue Engineering

1 Introduction

Large and irregular bone defects caused by trauma, osteosarcoma, and other diseases can severely impair or even abolish the intrinsic self-healing capacity of bone tissue. Repairing such defects remains a major clinical challenge, often necessitating bone transplantation using autologous, allogeneic, or artificial grafts. The irregular geometry of these defects increases surgical complexity and the risk of secondary injury. Although autologous and allogeneic bone grafts are currently considered the gold standard for the treatment, their clinical application is limited by restricted availability and potential adverse effects, including donor-site infection and immune rejection [1]. Consequently, artificial bone substitutes with wide availability and good biocompatibility have emerged as a research hotspot.

S. S. Ge et al. (Eds.): ICSR + BioMed 2025, LNAI 16435, pp. 141–150, 2026.
https://doi.org/10.1007/978-981-95-7538-1_13

Shape memory polymers (SMPs) have demonstrated broad potential in various biomedical applications, such as vascular stents and bone tissue engineering, due to their shape memory effect (SME) [2, 3]. Medical devices fabricated from shape memory polymers (SMPs) can be delivered in a collapsed or folded state via minimally invasive surgery and subsequently recover their intended shape at the target site. Currently, injectable temperature-responsive hydrogels represent a promising strategy for bone defect repair. Delivered in a liquid state to fill the defect site and undergo sol–gel transition upon temperature stimulation, enabling close adhesion to the irregular defect margins. However, their limited mechanical strength restricts their use in critical-sized, load-bearing bone defects [4]. In contrast, SMPs combine excellent biocompatibility and biodegradability with mechanical properties closer to those of native bone [1], providing essential early-stage support and sustained biomechanical stimulation to promote bone regeneration [5].

Despite these advantages, SMPs face several challenges in bone repair. Polylactide (PLA) and polycaprolactone (PCL), both FDA-approved SMPs [6]. have shape transition temperatures well above physiological temperature [7, 8], preventing shape recovery under normal body conditions and necessitating additional thermal stimulation in clinical applications. High transition temperatures also pose a risk of thermal damage to surrounding cells during recovery [9]. Polylactide-co-caprolactone (PLCL), synthesized via ring-opening copolymerization of L-LA and ε-CL, offers tunable transition temperatures and mechanical properties, making it a promising SMP for bone repair. Traditional fabrication methods often struggle to produce scaffolds with complex porous architectures. Selective laser sintering (SLS), a layer-by-layer additive manufacturing technique (Fig. 1a), enables the production of parts with arbitrary geometries, independent of structural complexity, and is well suited for fabricating scaffolds with intricate internal architectures [10].

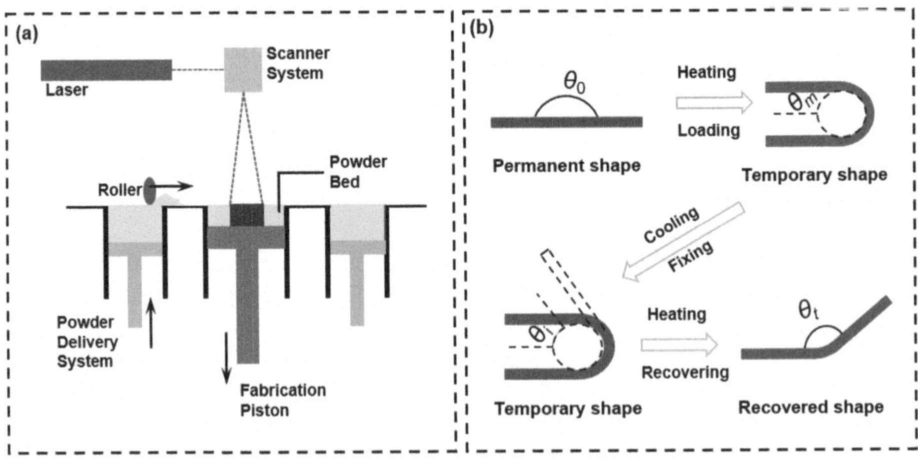

Fig. 1. (a) Schematic diagrams of SLS process, and (b) shape recovery cycle of PLCL.

In this study, SLS-based 4D printing was employed to fabricate a PLCL-based shape memory bone scaffold with physiological temperature responsiveness and mechanical properties compatible with natural bone. The copolymer transition temperature was first tuned by controlling the reaction conditions to enable shape recovery under physiological conditions. SLS printing parameters were then optimized to ensure mechanical performance matching that of natural bone. Finally, the shape fixation and recovery rates (R_f and R_r) of the PLCL specimens were quantitatively evaluated, and the scaffold's conformity to the edges of an irregular bone defect model at physiological temperature was qualitatively assessed.

2 Materials and Methods

2.1 Materials

L-lactide (L-LA, $\geq$ 99.5% purity, water content $\leq$ 0.4%) was supplied from Daigang Biomaterials Co., Ltd. (Jinan, China). ε-caprolactone (ε-CL, $\geq$ 99% purity), Dichloromethane (DCM, $\geq$ 99.5% purity), and polyvinyl alcohol (PVA) were obtained from Aladdin Biochemical Technology Co., Ltd. (Shanghai, China). Stannous octoate ($\geq$ 95% purity) was supplied by Shanghai Adamas Reagent Co., Ltd. (Shanghai, China). Anhydrous ethanol (analytical grade) was obtained from Innochem Technology Co., Ltd. (Beijing, China)

2.2 Methods

Synthesis of random PLCL copolymers: L-LA was placed in a flask and subjected to three vacuum–nitrogen purge cycles (10 min each) using a Schlenk line to remove air and water. ε-CL was then added at a molar ratio of L-LA to ε-CL of 75:25. The flask was heated in an oil bath until the monomers were completely melted. Stannous octoate was added as a catalyst at a monomer to catalyst molar ratio of 2000:1, and the reaction was carried out under a nitrogen atmosphere for 24 h. The crude product was dissolved in DCM and precipitated with anhydrous ethanol to remove unreacted monomers and residual catalyst. The purified copolymer was collected by filtration and dried in a vacuum oven at 40 °C to constant weight to obtain the final product.

PLCL powder preparation: PLCL powder was prepared using an oil-in-water (O/W) emulsion solvent evaporation method. Briefly, a 0.25 g/mL PLCL solution in DCM was added to a 0.01 g/mL aqueous solution of PVA. The mixture was emulsified at 9000 r/s for 10 min to form a primary emulsion, which was then stirred continuously until DCM was completely evaporated. The resulting solid particles were collected, washed repeatedly with deionized water to remove residual PVA, and freeze-dried. The dried powder was sieved, and particles with a size of 30–100 μm were collected for subsequent experiments.

1H NMR: 1H NMR spectra were recorded on a Bruker Ascend 400 spectrometer operating at 600 MHz using 5 mm outer-diameter sample tubes at room temperature. Deuterated chloroform ($CDCl_3$) was used as the solvent, with tetramethylsilane (TMS) serving as the internal standard.

Differential scanning calorimetry (DSC): DSC was conducted using a TA DSC-25 calorimeter under a nitrogen atmosphere. The PLCL samples were subjected to the following thermal cycle: heating from – 20 °C to 180 °C at a rate of 10 °C/min, cooling back to – 20 °C at 10 °C/min, reheating to 180 °C at 10 °C/min, and finally cooling to room temperature at 10 °C/min.

Orthogonal experimental design for printing parameter optimization: The sintering quality of parts fabricated via SLS is strongly dependent on the laser energy density. The volume energy density (ED) is defined as

$$ED = \frac{P \cdot SC}{v \cdot s \cdot h} \tag{1}$$

where P is the laser power, SC is the count of scans, v is the scan speed, s is the hatching distance, and h is the powder layer thickness (set to 0.1 mm)

To efficiently investigate the impact of multiple process parameters on printing performance and to determine the optimal parameter combination, a three-factor, three-level orthogonal experiment was implemented using IBM SPSS Statistics (version 31.0.0). The factor levels used in this study are summarized in Table 1.

Table 1. Orthogonal experimental design for optimizing printing process parameters.

No.	A:Laser power(W)	B:Scan speed(mm/s)	C:Hatching distance(mm)
1	2.8(A_1)	600(B_1)	0.05(C_1)
2	2.8(A_1)	900(B_2)	0.1(C_3)
3	2.8(A_1)	1200(B_3)	0.08(C_2)
4	4.2(A_2)	600(B_1)	0.08(C_2)
5	4.2(A_2)	900(B_2)	0.05(C_1)
6	4.2(A_2)	1200(B_3)	0.1(C_3)
7	5.6(A_3)	600(B_1)	0.1(C_3)
8	5.6(A_3)	900(B_2)	0.08(C_2)
9	5.6(A_3)	1200(B_3)	0.05(C_1)

Mechanical testing: The tensile properties of 5B specimens (ISO 527-2) were measured using a SHIMADZU AGS-X universal testing machine (5 kN capacity) at 25 °C and a crosshead speed of 2 mm/min.

Shape memory effect: Specimens (40 × 8 × 1 mm) was subjected to a deformation-fixation-recovery cycle, which included deformation at deformation temperature (T_d) in hot water, fixation in ice water, and recovery at T_d, with both ends constrained. The shape fixation (R_f) and recovery (R_r) ratios were calculated according to Eqs. (2) and (3).

$$R_f = \frac{\theta_0 - \theta_i}{\theta_0 - \theta_m} \times 100\% \tag{2}$$

$$R_r = \frac{\theta_t - \theta_i}{\theta_0 - \theta_i} \times 100\% \quad (3)$$

here, θ_0 represents the initial angle (set to 180°), θ_m denotes the deformation angle applied by the external force (set to 0°), θ_i refers to the angle of the temporary shape, and θ_t corresponds to the angle of the specimen after recovery for t seconds.

3 Results and Discussion

3.1 Copolymer Composition

As shown in Fig. 2a, the methine proton peaks of the L-LA monomer appeared at $\delta = 5.0 - 5.5$ ppm, while the ε- and α-methylene peaks of ε-CL were observed at $\delta = 4.0 - 4.5$ ppm, confirming the successful copolymerization of PLCL at various reaction temperatures. The copolymer composition was determined from the ratio of the integrated area of the L-LA methine peak to the average of the ε- and α-methylene peaks of ε-CL [11]. The reaction temperature significantly influenced the copolymer composition. Higher reaction temperatures produced copolymers with compositions closer to the feed ratio. At temperatures below 140 °C, the low reactivity of ε-CL led to incomplete incorporation into the polymer chains and poor control of the copolymerization process, resulting in an actual L-LA content higher than the feed ratio [12]. When the reaction temperature reached 140 °C or higher, the reactivities of the two monomers became comparable, yielding a copolymer composition closer to the feed ratio. Beyond 150 °C, further increases in temperature had little effect, and the PLCL composition stabilized at approximately 80:20.

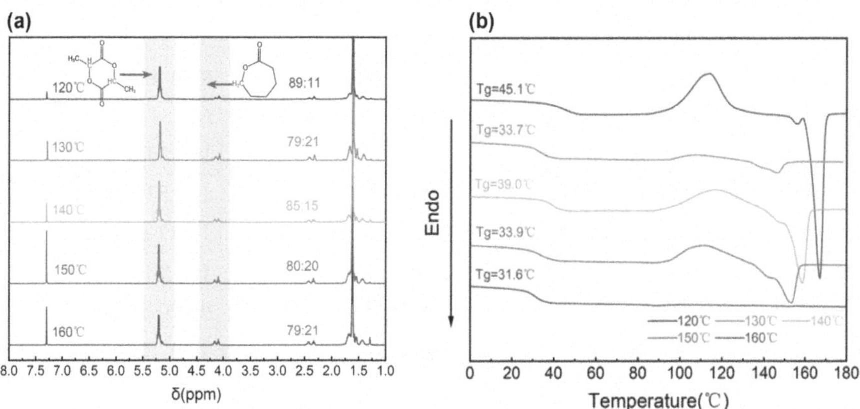

Fig. 2. (a) 1H NMR spectrum of PLCL synthesized at different reaction temperatures; (b) second heating scan curves of PLCL synthesized at different reaction temperatures.

3.2 Thermal Properties

The DSC second heating curves of PLCL copolymers are shown in Fig. 2b. As the reaction temperature increased, the glass transition temperature (T_g) gradually decreased due to the higher incorporation of ε-CL segments into the polymer chains [13]. The temperature dropped from 45.1 °C at 120 °C to 31.6 °C at 160 °C. Simultaneously, the melting temperature (T_m) also decreased with increasing ε-CL content. When the copolymer composition (L-LA: ε-CL) approached 80:20, T_g fell below a physiological temperature (37°C). Notably, at a reaction temperature of 160°C, no melting peak was observed in the DSC curve, indicating that PLCL became an amorphous polymer. This phenomenon is attributed to transesterification between L-LA and ε-CL during high-temperature ring-opening copolymerization [14]. Such a side reaction prevents the formation of sufficiently regular chain segments by both monomers, hindering their ability to fold and form crystalline structures, and thereby markedly reducing the crystallinity of PLCL [15]. Therefore, to obtain PLCL copolymers capable of shape recovery under physiological conditions, the polymerization should be carried out at 150°C.

3.3 Mechanical Properties

The results of the orthogonal experiments are summarized in Table 2. When the volume energy density (*ED*) was too low (No. 2, No. 3, and No. 6), the laser energy was insufficient to fully melt the powder, resulting in poor particle bonding and a loose structure. Consequently, elongation at break and tensile strength were significantly lower, and at $ED = 0.29$, the material failed to form. Owing to the ε-CL segments in the polymer chain, SLS-printed PLCL exhibited excellent toughness, with elongation at break reaching a maximum of 125.53 ± 7.72% (Fig. 3d), nearly comparable to that of pure PCL.

Table 2. Orthogonal experiment results.

No.	ED (J/mm^3)	Elastic modulus (MPa)	Tensile strength (MPa)	Elongation at break (%)
1	0.93	74.77 ± 37.89	3.54 ± 0.20	59.72 ± 8.36
2	0.31	40.06 ± 42.85	1.29 ± 0.88	8.83 ± 2.72
3	0.29	/	/	/
4	0.88	105.06 ± 25.60	3.50 ± 0.21	110.33 ± 22.23
5	0.93	93.66 ± 10.51	3.31 ± 0.07	125.53 ± 7.72
6	0.35	88.58 ± 19.74	2.73 ± 0.09	19.47 ± 6.32
7	0.93	77.12 ± 24.57	3.19 ± 0.07	105.90 ± 13.17
8	0.78	89.64 ± 18.40	3.28 ± 0.12	92.20 ± 6.85
9	0.93	79.54 ± 12.2	3.10 ± 0.1	96.47 ± 16.02
10	1.40	138.23 ± 13.02	5.43 ± 0.71	81.77 ± 25.67

To further optimize the SLS process, a range analysis of the orthogonal experimental results was conducted to identify the primary and secondary factors affecting the elastic modulus and to determine the optimal parameter combination. As shown in Fig. 3c, the influence of factors on the elastic modulus followed the order: laser power > scanning speed > hatching distance, with laser power exerting the most significant effect. Analysis of factor averages indicated that the optimal parameters for achieving the highest elastic modulus are $A_2B_1C_1$, corresponding to a laser power of 4.2 W, a scanning speed of 600 mm/s, and a hatching distance of 0.05 mm. The mechanical properties of specimens printed under these conditions (No. 10, Table 2) are presented in Fig. 3c–d, showing an elastic modulus of 138.23 ± 13.02 MPa and a tensile strength of 5.43 ± 0.71 MPa, closely matching those properties of distal femoral cancellous bone [16]. These results demonstrate that SLS-printed PLCL can potentially be used to fabricate bone scaffolds with mechanical properties comparable to cancellous bone.

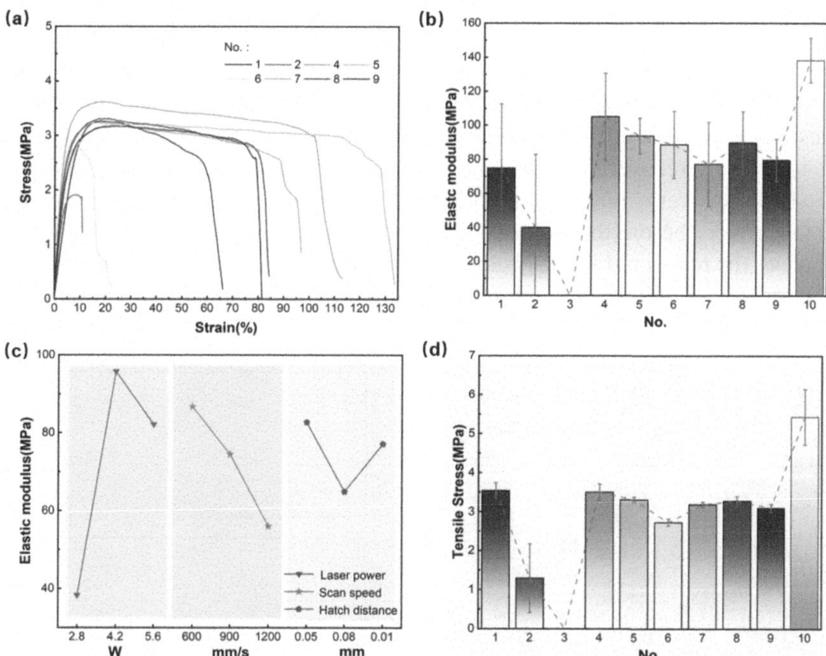

Fig. 3. (a) Stress-strain curves of PLCL parts, (b) Elastic modulus of PLCL parts under different process combinations, (c) Main effects plot of factors on elastic modulus, (d) Tensile strength of PLCL parts under different process combinations.

3.4 Shape Memory Effect of PLCL

The shape memory effect of PLCL originates from its molecular architecture, which consists of a fixation phase and a reversible phase. The reversible phase comprises the amorphous L-LA and ε-CL segments, whereas the stationary phase is formed by LA crystalline domains and physical cross-links resulting from chain entanglement [17]. When the temperature exceeds the transition temperature (T_{trans}), the amorphous segments of PLCL transform from a glassy to a rubbery state, significantly enhancing molecular chain mobility. Under an external force, the chains rearrange, leading to deformation of the permanent shape. Upon cooling below T_{trans}, chain mobility decreases sharply, fixing the temporary shape and creating a dynamic potential well within the molecular network. When the material is reheated above T_{trans}, the molecular chains are reactivated and spontaneously return to a thermodynamically stable state through thermal motion, thereby completing the shape recovery process [18].

Figure 4a–c illustrates the shape memory process of PLCL at deformation temperatures of 32°C, 37°C, and 42°C, with the corresponding R_f and R_r values summarized in Fig. 4d. Both R_f and R_r increased with rising T_d. Owing to the broad glass transition range of PLCL, shape recovery at 32°C involved only partial activation of the amorphous chains, resulting in a lower recovery rate of 68.6 ± 5.8%. At 37°C, however, both R_f and R_r exceeded 90%, reaching 93.5 ± 4.3% and 92.3 ± 0.7%, respectively. At a T_d of 42°C, R_r further increased. These results demonstrate that 4D-printed PLCL with an 80:20 copolymer composition and a T_g of 33.9 °C achieved efficient shape recovery at physiological temperature, exhibiting excellent shape memory performance. Figure 4e–f further illustrated the shape recovery of PLCL samples with different structural designs at physiological temperature. The sample with a negative Poisson's ratio almost completely recovered its original shape. The bone scaffold also underwent successful shape recovery; however, its thick walls delayed heat conduction, preventing complete recovery before the water cooled, and thus resulting in a lower recovery rate. Nonetheless, the recovered scaffold closely conformed to the edges of the irregular bone defect, demonstrating its adaptability and potential for biomedical applications.

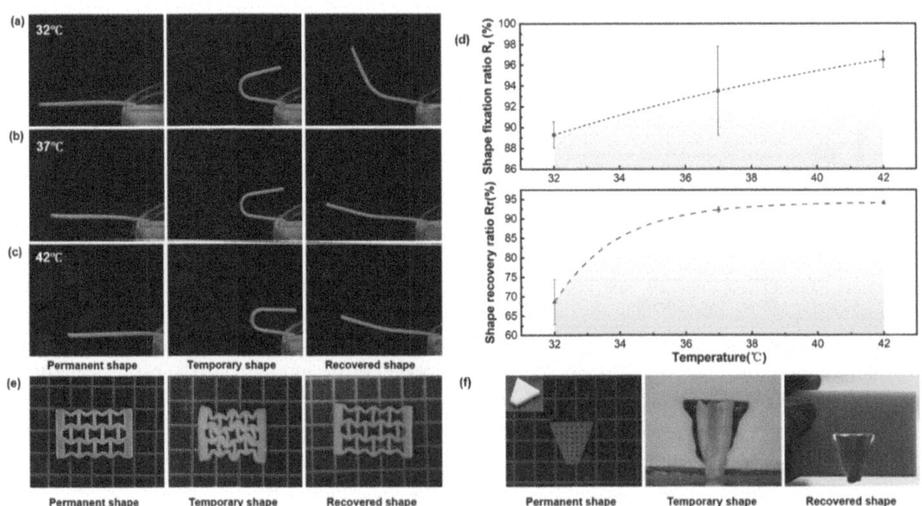

Fig. 4. Shape memory process of PLCL at different T_d (a) 32 °C (b) 37 °C (c) 42 °C (d) R_f and R_r of PLA/PCL40 at different T_d; Shape memory process at 37 °C (e) negative Poisson's ratio (NPR) structure (f) Bone scaffold matching in irregular bone defect model.

4 Conclusions and Outlooks

In this study, a temperature-responsive shape memory polymer was synthesized via ring-opening copolymerization of L-LA and ε-CL. The resulting PLCL copolymer, with an L-LA: ε-CL composition of 80:20 and a T_g of 33.9°C, was prepared at a reaction temperature of 150°C. This T_{trans} is close to physiological temperature, allowing the polymer to recover its shape under body temperature conditions. The optimal SLS printing parameters for PLCL were determined as 4.2 W laser power, 600 mm/s scanning speed, and 0.05 mm hatching distance. Under these conditions, the PLCL scaffolds exhibited mechanical properties of 138.23 ± 13.02 MPa and 5.43 ± 0.71 MPa, comparable to those of natural cancellous bone. Additionally, at physiological temperature (37 °C), the PLCL samples exhibited R_f and R_r exceeding 90%. The SLS-printed PLCL bone scaffold could effectively unfold under physiological conditions and conform closely to the edges of irregular bone defects, fulfilling the functional requirements for repairing large, irregular bone defects.

While this study demonstrated the feasibility of 4D-printed PLCL bone scaffolds for intelligent bone repair under physiological temperature, further investigation is required. This work focuses mainly on the material itself, whose properties remain limited. Optimizing scaffold structure to enhance compressibility is essential for minimally invasive implantation and efficient *in vivo* deployment.

References

1. Yuan, X., Zhu, W., Yang, Z., et al.: Recent advances in 3D printing of smart scaffolds for bone tissue engineering and regeneration. Adv. Mater. **36**(34), 2403641 (2024)
2. Chen, G.-Q., Patel, M.K.: Plastics derived from biological sources: present and future: a technical and environmental review. Chem. Rev. **112**(4), 2082–2099 (2012)
3. Saini, P., Arora, M., Kumar, M.N.V.R.: Poly(lactic acid) blends in biomedical applications. Adv. Drug Deliv. Rev. **107**, 47–59 (2016)
4. Zhao, W., Yue, C., Liu, L., et al.: Research progress of shape memory polymer and 4D printing in biomedical application. Adv. Healthc. Mater. **12**(16), 2201975 (2023)
5. Bao, M., Lou, X., Zhou, Q., et al.: Electrospun biomimetic fibrous scaffold from shape memory polymer of PDLLA-co-TMC for bone tissue engineering. ACS Appl. Mater. Interfaces **6**(4), 2611–2621 (2014)
6. Cao, Y., Jiang, J., Jiang, Y., et al.: Biodegradable highly porous interconnected poly(ε-caprolactone)/poly(L-lactide-co-ε-caprolactone) scaffolds by supercritical foaming for small-diameter vascular tissue engineering. Polym. Adv. Technol. **33**(1), 440–451 (2021)
7. Senatov, F.S., Niaza, K.V., Zadorozhnyy, M.Y., et al.: Mechanical properties and shape memory effect of 3D-printed PLA-based porous scaffolds. J. Mech. Behav. Biomed. Mater. **57**, 139–148 (2016)
8. Zhang, F., Zhang, Z., Liu, Y., et al.: Thermosetting epoxy reinforced shape memory composite microfiber membranes: fabrication, structure and properties. Comp. Part A: Appl. Sci. Manuf. **76**, 54–61 (2015)
9. Paunovic, N., Meyer, D., Krivitsky, A., et al.: 4D printing of biodegradable elastomers with tailorable thermal response at physiological temperature. J. Control. Release **361**, 417–426 (2023)
10. Tan, K.H., Chua, C.K., Leong, K.F., et al.: Scaffold development using selective laser sintering of polyetheretherketone-hydroxyapatite biocomposite blends. Biomaterials **24**(18), 3115–3123 (2003)
11. Kwon, I.K., Kidoaki, S., Matsuda, T.: Electrospun nano- to microfiber fabrics made of biodegradable copolyesters: structural characteristics, mechanical properties and cell adhesion potential. Biomaterials **26**(18), 3929–3939 (2005)
12. Fernández, J., Etxeberria, A., Sarasua, J.-R.: Synthesis, structure and properties of poly(L-lactide-co–caprolactone) statistical copolymers. J. Mech. Behav. Biomed. Mater. **9**, 100–112 (2012)

13. Hashimoto, K., Kurokawa, N., Hotta, A.: Controlling the switching temperature of biodegradable shape memory polymers composed of stereocomplex polylactide/poly (-lactide-co-ε-caprolactone) blends. Polymer **233**, 124190 (2021)
14. Lipik, V.T., Widjaja, L.K., Liow, S.S., et al.: Effects of transesterification and degradation on properties and structure of polycaprolactone–polylactide copolymers. Polym. Degrad. Stab. **95**(12), 2596–2602 (2010)
15. Zhang, M., Chang, Z., Wang, X., et al.: Synthesis of Poly(l-lactide-co-epsilon-caprolactone) Copolymer: structure, Toughness, and Elasticity. Polymers (Basel) **13**(8), 1270(2021).
16. An, Y.H., Draughn, R.A.: Mechanical Testing of Bone and the Bone-Implant Interface. CRC Press, Boca Raton (2000)
17. Fernández, J., Meaurio, E., Chaos, A., et al.: Synthesis and characterization of poly (l-lactide/ε-caprolactone) statistical copolymers with well resolved chain microstructures. Polymer **54**(11), 2621–2631 (2013)
18. Xie, T.: Recent advances in polymer shape memory. Polymer **52**(22), 4985–5000 (2011)

Employing Soft Robotic Systems to Replicate the Kinematics and Biomedical Properties of Upper Limb Joints

Muhsina Muneer[1], Sarah Arif[1], and John-John Cabibihan[2](✉)

[1] Department of Electrical Engineering, Qatar University, Doha, Qatar
[2] Department of Mechanical Engineering, Qatar University, Doha, Qatar
john.cabibihan@qu.edu.qa

Abstract. Soft robots with biological features have revolutionized their applications. The orientation and position of the upper limb joints can be emulated by carefully engineered soft materials. Due to their versatility and adaptability, these materials can imitate complex joint kinematics such as flexion and extension. The upper limb joints' mobility permits human beings to perform basic and advanced tasks. There exists a lack of comprehensive studies that replicate the exact upper limb joint movements for use in different applications. This paper provides an overview of the recent breakthroughs in soft robots that clone the design and kinematics of the human upper limb joints. Studies have shown that it is possible to successfully achieve some degree of similarity between the proposed model and upper limb joints. Nevertheless, soft robotics is still an emerging field that requires more research on robust and biocompatible materials to be fully integrated for commercialization.

Keywords: soft robots · kinematics · biomechanics · bioengineering · upper limb joints · soft actuators

1 Introduction

The flexibility, safety and versatility of soft materials make them ideal for bioinspired technologies. Soft robotics has gained maximum traction in the field of medicine. As a matter of fact, these were first researched with the intent to miniaturize robots for medical applications, and have continued to emerge ever since [1].

Soft robots are recommended over traditional, rigid robots in many rehabilitation applications due to their lower complexity and cost-effectiveness [2]. These robots perform tasks using tension and compression and their integration with biological joints and more Degrees of Freedom (DOFs) allows greater comfort, mobility and flexibility [3, 4]. Wearable soft devices exhibit higher torque than the physiological capabilities of a subject [5]. Furthermore, soft robots are inherently safe, as their material characteristics are inspired by skin and muscle tissues [6]. The human skin above joints consists of several creases and folds to permit stretching and shrinking of the skin upon movement [7].

S. S. Ge et al. (Eds.): ICSR + BioMed 2025, LNAI 16435, pp. 151–168, 2026.
https://doi.org/10.1007/978-981-95-7538-1_14

Therefore, it is essential to consider both rotation and stretch motions when designing a human joint-inspired soft robot.

The wrist, hand, elbow, and shoulder make up the most mobile component of the body [8]. The high DOFs offered by the upper limb joints make them ideal for enabling movements across different planes. These joints play a vital role in fulfilling basic and complicated tasks. A human arm is capable of performing complex movements such as grasping, lifting, twisting, touching the back of the head and so on [9]. Precise manipulation and motor control are required for these motions to take place. Thus, successful replication of the upper limb joints for both assistive and standalone devices can achieve dexterity.

This review paper aims to highlight the recent literature on the design and biomechanical properties of soft robotic systems that can replicate upper limb joints. Although previous papers have reviewed studies on wearable soft robotics devices for the upper limb, to the best of our knowledge, there has not been a review that focuses explicitly on joint replication. This paper bridges the gap between the biomimicry of soft robotics and the upper limb joints. In this context, biomimicry refers to the replication of the movements of the human upper limb joints with respect to assistive, i.e., for patients and industry workers, as well as standalone devices, i.e., joint-inspired gripper. Section 2 presents the methodology used to extract the selected papers for this review. Sections 3–6 cover the design of finger, wrist, elbow and shoulder joints, respectively. Finally, Sect. 7 provides the conclusion and future directions.

2 Methodology

This section discusses the selection criteria with keywords and the inclusion criteria. The thorough literature search utilized scientific databases including IEEE Xplore, ScienceDirect, ProQuest, PubMed, Springer and Google Scholar. Initially, 50 papers were collected with keywords like "soft robots" OR "soft exoskeleton" AND "shoulder joints" OR "elbow joints" OR "wrist" OR "finger" AND "rehabilitation". The search was constrained to papers published from 2019 to ensure the latest and most advanced technologies are included.

Papers were selected based on their quality, relevance, and specific exclusion and inclusion criteria. All papers were filtered to English, the last six years (2019–June 2025), and peer-reviewed articles. The inclusion criteria covered papers that: (1) only discuss soft exoskeletons for upper limb joints, (2) are relevant to the subject matter with a focus on the design of the system, and (3) provide experimental results. Finally, after removing duplicates and passing through the inclusion criteria, a set of 25 papers was included in the study, as shown in Fig. 1.

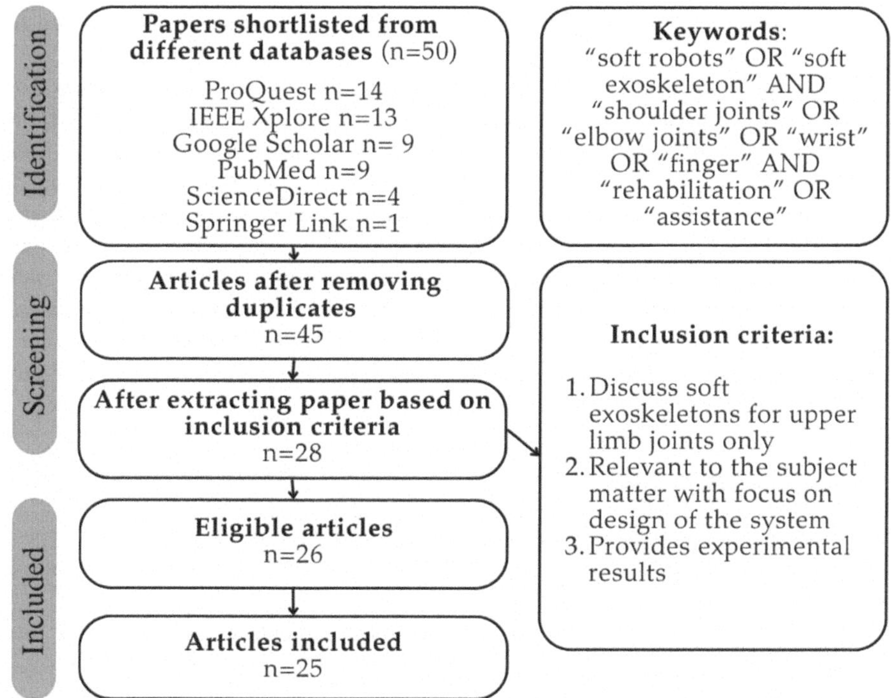

Fig. 1. PRISMA flowchart to illustrate the methodology for this review paper.

3 Soft Finger Replication

The anatomy of a finger is comprised of three phalanges: distal, middle and proximal. The finger joints, from top to bottom, are known as Distal Interphalangeal (DIP), Proximal Interphalangeal (PIP) and Metacarpophalangeal (MCP) joints, respectively. It must be noted that many studies classify an arc-shaped gripper as a finger-inspired soft robot. However, this review only considers literature that replicates the design and motion of an actual human finger. The Range of Motion (ROM) of a finger is influenced by many characteristics such as length of the finger, age, gender and genetics [7].

3.1 Design

Janghorban et al. [7] designed the DIP and PIP joints with Ecoflex-30 and used Moldstar-30 for the three distal, middle and proximal phalange links. To prevent the links from bending, plexiglass was incorporated to act as a limitation layer. The soft pneumatic bending joint actuators consist of an upper part, the chamber, made of silicone, whereas the lower part is an inextensible layer attached to the chamber. The pressure in the chamber and inclusion of fiber that enables linear extension allows the nonhomogeneous structure to bend like a finger. This paper solely mimicked the behaviour of the human finger without further designing for wearability. Similar to this study but with a wearable feature, Jeong et al. [6] produced detachable pneumatic soft actuators in the form of a stretchable glove. Enclosed fasteners were attached to the actuator and sewn on the dorsal area of the glove's fingers.

A pneumatic, 3D printed 11-DOF anthropomorphic female hand developed from 21 rigid-flexible integrated soft finger actuators was proposed [10]. With a printing time of approximately 5 h, this hand provides customized architecture design for faster assembly of fingers and base skeleton as compared to other 3D-printed soft hands. Following the same biomechanical properties, Li et al. [11] integrated biotensegrity and thin McKibben muscles to replicate a human hand. Based on the finger anatomy, three authors constructed three phalanges using 4-bar tensegrity with strings and sticks embedded in the MCP, PIP and DIP joints. The thin McKibben muscles, manipulated by pneumatic valves, inflate and deflate. This triggers a flexion and extension motion in the fingers. To control the speed at which the fingers open and close, a flow rate control valve can be added to the side of the muscle.

3.2 Results and Discussion

Table 1 contains the summary of the materials utilized, type of actuators used, type of control method, and performance of the soft robot.

Table 1. Summary of soft robots for finger replication.

Materials used	Actuation type	Control strategy	Performance	Refs.
Silicone (Ecoflex-30, Moldstar-30)	Pneumatic	Pneumatic	Highly accurate and reliable DIP/PIP ratio error less than 5% at 30kPa DIP and PIP ratio errors are 8.6% and 0.7% respectively at 25kPa	[7]
Mold: ABS Silicone (Dragon Skin 30)	Pneumatic	Pneumatic	Highly accurate with efficient force transfer	[6]
Agilus 30, Vero series, Agilus30-Vero digital materials	Pneumatic	Sequential pneumatic	Highly accurate $< 10\%$ flexion angle error	[10]
McKibben artificial muscles (Actuator) Elastic strings and wooden sticks (Structure)	Pneumatic (McKibben muscles)	Pneumatic (Solenoid valves + Microcontroller – (NUCLEO-F411RE)	High success rate for lighter objects (40g–130g) 26% horizontal compression 30% compression of finger thickness	[11]

The bending deformation is inversely proportional to the offset distances, and the bending angle increases with a decrease in torque [6]. Based on the results of [7], the DIP and PIP angles varied the most at pressures between 10 and 30 kPa. For [6], a pressure of 90 kPa results in an extension rate of 112%. The vast differences in the pressure required come from the usage of different materials, sizes and weights. It is also worth noting that [7] used Polylactic Acid (PLA), whereas [6] used Acrylonitrile Butadiene Styrene (ABS) to 3D print their respective moulds, but neither explicitly stated their reasoning for the choice of filament. However, both studies successfully achieved the motion and design of a finger. On one hand, the 138 g hand developed by [10] could only hold below 50 g of weight but has the potential to withstand vertical hammer impact without any damage. On the other hand, the complex biotensigrity structure of [11] can hold 130 g, but the lower coefficient factor of the material posed difficulties even with 40 g.

4 Soft Actuators for Wrist Joints

The natural ROM of a wrist includes flexion, extension, ulnar and radial deviations, pronation and supination, as shown in Fig. 2. The design of wrist replication must take these movements and positions into account [12]. Based on the literature review, however, most papers do not discuss pronation and supination movements. Unlike finger-inspired soft robots, the majority of wrist-based soft actuators are wearables that focus on replication in terms of kinematics, rather than shape.

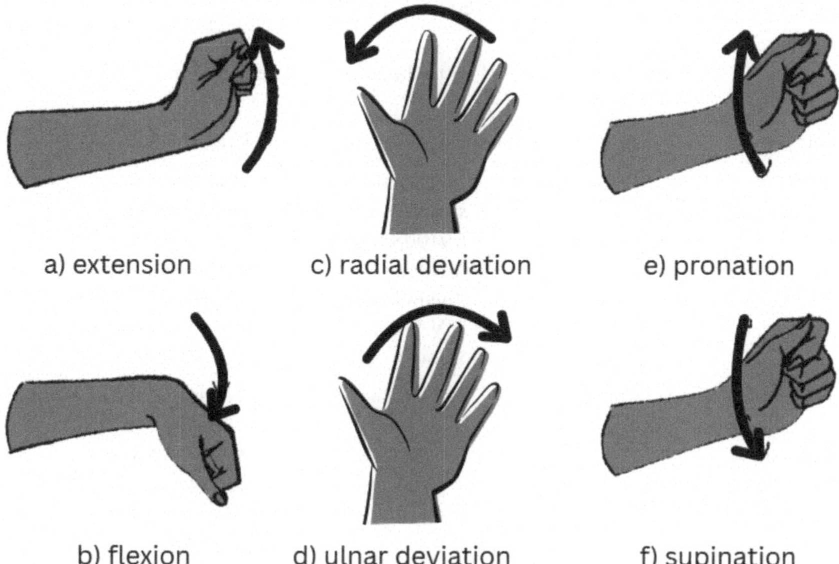

Fig. 2. Human wrist movements a) extension b) flexion c) radial deviation d) ulnar deviation e) pronation f) supination.

4.1 Design

The use of soft actuators for wrist rehabilitation has been widely studied in recent times. This usually comes in the form of a wearable sleeve or glove to assist the motion of the wrist. Thus, the design should be lightweight and adjustable, and the actuator's geometry must align with the wrist anatomy for ease and comfort [12]. Thermoplastic polyurethane (TPU) was a commonly selected material to design the actuators due to its cost-effectiveness, elasticity, high resistance to air permeability, and robustness to mirror natural wrist motion [12–14]. RTV silicone rubber, fabric pneumatic artificial muscles and ethylene-vinyl acetate copolymer were also chosen for soft wrist actuators [14–17].

Although wrist-inspired soft actuators are mostly employed for rehabilitation, they have also been adapted for gripping applications. Chen et al. and Hu et al. [18, 19] designed a 3-DOF wrist-inspired soft gripper from Ecoflex-0200 and E360 liquid silicone, respectively. It is worth highlighting that these studies considered and attained the pronation and supination motions. A traditional three-finger gripper was used by [18], while [19] utilized a particle jamming joint to pick-and-place objects. The rotation angle was found to increase with the actuation frequency and decrease with increased jamming pressure. Both grippers achieved the wrist-like bending and twisting motions and can bear loads.

4.2 Results and Discussion

A summary of the materials utilized, type of actuators used, type of control method, and performance of the soft robot is presented in Table 2.

Table 2. Summary of soft robots for wrist replication.

Materials used	Actuation type	Control strategy	Performance	Refs.
Thermoplastic Polyurethane (TPU) sheets	Pneumatic	Industrial control system (Arduino + L9100S motor driver) Pneumatic control (6V Solenoid valves)	High control precision and repeatability Produced highest torque of 0.25 N·m at 0°, 0.19 Nm at 45°, 0.1 Nm at 90°	[12]
TPU-based X60 (Shore hardness 60A) Ninjaflex (Shore hardness 60A) Polyester sleeves	Pneumatic	Pneumatic	Reduced muscle activation, ROM: 81.6% of wrist contraction 94.1% of wrist expansion 85.5% ulnar deviation 71.1 weighted contraction	[13]

(*continued*)

Table 2. (*continued*)

Materials used	Actuation type	Control strategy	Performance	Refs.
Polyurethane rubber (PMC™-724, Smooth-on) Silicon rubber (RTV-4234-T4, Xiameter®, Dow Corning)	Pneumatic	PD Controller	ROM: One-actuator mode—Flexion up to 45° and extension up to 7° Two-actuator mode—Both flexion and extension up to 45° Output Torque: One-actuator mode—5.46 Nm at 0° Two-actuator mode—4.69 Nm (flexion), 4.80 Nm (extension) at 0°	[14]
Ethylene Vinyl Acetate (Actuators) Fabric anchors and Spandex layers	Pneumatic	Cascaded control system + Arduino Mega microcontroller	High repeatability, ROM: 31° of wrist contraction 30° of wrist expansion 22° ulnar deviation 33° radial deviation Torque: 58% of max. Torque of healthy wrist (0.76Nm)	[15]
RTV Silicone rubber (XIAMETER® RTV-4234-T4)	Pneumatic	PD flow-based controller	Angular errors ranged from 0.37 to 7.3	[16]
Silicone-coated ripstop nylon fabric	Pneumatic	Closed-loop antagonistic feedback control system	ROM: 44.5° ± 7.5° of wrist contraction 38.7° ± 5.2° of wrist expansion 26.8° ± 3.4° ulnar deviation 16.0° ± 3.3° radial deviation Torque: Peak torque of 3.3 Nm at 103 kPa	[17]

(*continued*)

Table 2. (*continued*)

Materials used	Actuation type	Control strategy	Performance	Refs.
Silicone (Ecoflex-0020 liquid silicone) Kevlar fibres	Pneumatic	Pressure	ROM: 54° bending angle and 23° twisting angles at 50 kPa with deviation within 2.5%	[18]
SRBPAs (Soft-Ring-Reinforced Bellows-Type Pneumatic Actuators) Liquid silicone rubber (E630) TPU	Pneumatic	Pressure	At − 70 kPa actuation pressure: Rotation around x-axis: 55.4° Rotation around y-axis: 59.3° Twisting around z-axis: 19.4° Output Force/Torque: At − 70 kPa, Force (x-axis): 29.6 N Force (y-axis): 36 N Torque (z-axis): 2.2 Nm	[19]

The 2-DOF motion of the wrist joint, i.e., flexion, extension, ulnar and radial deviations were achieved by all of the reviewed studies [12, 13, 15, 17–19] apart from [14, 16], which only satisfied flexion and extension movements and did not consider ulnar/radial deviation. In terms of statistics, the soft robot wrist brace produced 58% of the maximum torque of the wrist in ulnar/radial deviation [15]. In comparison, the soft robotic wrist sleeve by [13] could reach the ROM of up to 81.6% and 71.1% of the subject's original wrist ROM with just the sleeve and with the added weight of lifting a 375 ml filled water bottle. Future soft-wrist studies need to consider pronation and supination motions and enhance their design to effectively support ulnar/radial deviation.

5 Soft Exoskeletons for Shoulder Joints

Shoulders are vital for the movement of the upper limb. Injuries to the spinal cord or due to stroke and intense use of arms for industrial work could cause damage to the mobility of the arms. Soft exoskeletons utilizing fabrics, or even soft materials like silicone, help with rehabilitation. Additionally, such systems can assist with heavy-weightlifting activities, reducing the amount of load exerted on vital joints [20]. In this section, the materials used, actuation mechanisms, and control strategies utilized for soft exosuits for shoulder joints are discussed.

5.1 Design

5.1.1 Materials and Actuation Mechanisms

Soft shoulder exoskeletons are mostly made with textiles and soft materials like shape memory alloys. This example of an exoskeleton for the shoulder actuator was designed with a single layer material consisting of TPU and coated nylon with inbuilt bending angles. This actuation unit can be mounted on the body with neoprene straps and adjustable Velcro-based belts [21]. Pneumatic actuators are popular for their lightweight, ease of use, and flexibility. A design with such an actuator with two components of fabric spine and fabric inflation with TPU and nylon sheets, along with neoprene sleeves, was also explored [22].

5.1.2 Control Strategy

A kinematics-based controller was proposed to actively modify the threshold and control a pneumatic actuator for a shoulder exoskeleton. This ensures the best performance even with repeated work of the exoskeleton with arms raised overhead. Moreover, it identifies the user's intentions and moves accordingly with high precision, excellent classification and reduced calibration for ease of use [20]. According to the design by Campioni et al. [21], a simple control box with two normally closed solenoid valves, two pumps, a microcontroller, and some electronics enables actuator control as shown in Fig. 3.

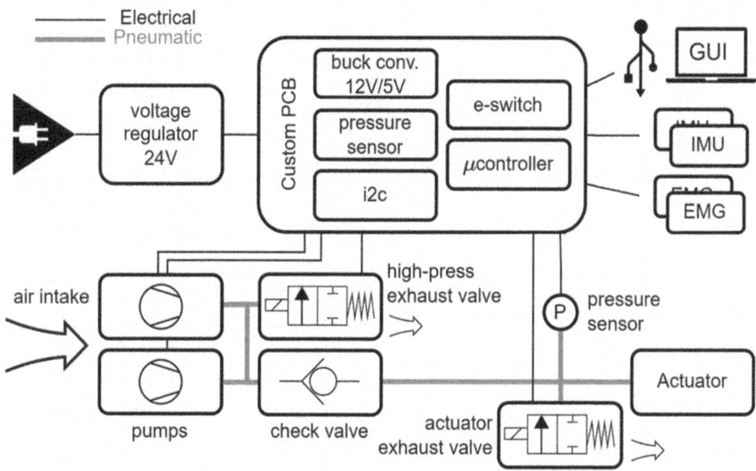

Fig. 3. Block diagram of control box operating the control loop by providing air to the soft actuator. The graphical User Interface (GUI) is used to set and display the pressure along with the data from other sensors. Reproduced from [21], © 2025 IEEE, licensed under CC BY 4.0.

5.2 Results and Discussion

An overview of the materials used, type of actuation, type of control method, and performance of the soft robot is presented in Table 3.

Table 3. Summary of soft robots for shoulder replication.

Materials used	Actuation type	Control strategy	Performance	Refs.
Textile	Pneumatic	Kinematics and EMG	Accuracy Kinematics controller: Experiment 1: 99.7% Experiment 2: 98.7% EMG controller: Experiment 1: 95.6% Experiment 2: 57.4%	[20]
TPU-coated nylon, neoprene	Pneumatic	Manual	Max torque: ~ 8 Nm at 90° and 76 kPa Reduction in muscle activation: Anterior deltoid: up to 41% reduction during flexion Middle deltoid: up to 46% reduction during abduction	[21]
Nylon sheets coated with TPU TPU based filament Neoprene (sleeve) C16:C25	Pneumatic	Pressure	ROM: Full bending at 10kPa while unloaded Peak torque: D1: 10.24 Nm D2: 11.15 Nm D3: 15.54 Nm Reduction in muscle activity: Lateral deltoid: 65% (abduction), ↓66% (adduction) Anterior deltoid: 45% (forward flexion) Pectoralis major: 33% (horizontal flexion) Posterior deltoid: 12% (horizontal extension)	[22]

The most significant results from the above-mentioned experiments are discussed below. The kinematics-based controller by Zhou et al. [20] shows a high accuracy of 99.7% and 98.7% at two different experiment settings. Additionally, the participants preferred the kinematic controller. In addition, it was observed that the controller was able to adjust the offset velocity with each experiment, with the offset velocity reduced by 19°/s by the final experiment, resulting in a quick reaction.

The results obtained from the soft inflatable exoskeleton by Campioni et al. [21] demonstrate a significant reduction in muscle activity to around 50% and 60% during contraction and expansion, respectively, while carrying weights. Moreover, the systems had a significant improvement in a patient's motion dynamics of the shoulder joint. In the case of soft exosuits for shoulder assistance, a reduction of muscle activity by 66% for extension and 65% for contraction of the lateral deltoid was observed. Furthermore, the exosuit can produce a torque of 11.15 Nm and 4.44 Nm at the resting position and arms at shoulder level, respectively [22].

6 Soft Robotic Systems for Elbow Joints

Soft exoskeleton for the elbow is used in multiple applications such as rehabilitation and assistance for patients with stroke, neuromuscular injuries, weak upper limbs or even athletes like baseball players [23–26]. The main advantage of using light-weight soft exoskeletons for athletes is the ease of use and mobility, enabling regular rehab sessions [27]. The development of elbow assistive soft robots includes multiple segments such as the materials utilized, types of soft actuators, and control systems employed in the suit, as examined in the following section.

6.1 Design

6.1.1 Material Design

Soft materials like Lycra fabrics, Velcro straps, flexible plastic sheet, silicone, along with Polyethylene Terephthalate (PET), nylon and neoprene are used to develop soft elbow sleeves for exoskeleton [23–26, 28, 29]. XIAMETER ® RTV-4234-T4 silicone, coupled with neoprene and nylon-infused micro-fiber, was used for a soft exosuit due to its flexible and durable nature, improving comfort and usability [28].

6.1.2 Soft Actuation Techniques

Shape memory alloy-based actuators were used in soft elbow exoskeleton (e.g. So-bee-SMA) designed by Xie et al. [30]. This design utilized SMA springs which are beneficial for their extreme stretchability, strain and self-sufficiency. Cable-driven actuation was also commonly used to actuate soft exosuits. Bowden cables are utilized for actuation coupled with brushless motors [26].

However, most soft exoskeleton designs use pneumatic muscle actuators (pMA) due to their ability to replicate effortless motion, low weight, comfort and safety [27]. Sridhar et al. [28] proposed an elbow exoskeleton to minimize the overexertion on muscles using a pneumatic actuator. Additionally, a single actuator ensures highly accurate movements and minimal stress on muscles, along with deviation of torque from the plane. Irshaidat et al. [23] combined three pMAs for muscle contraction and expansion as it can generate the required force for actuating muscles. These actuators are controlled by air pumped by the MATRIX3/3 750 series solenoid valve. This system maintains minimal energy consumption with position control.

6.1.3 Control Systems

Control systems are essential to maintain stability and manage dynamic, non-linear systems. Model Reference Adaptive Control (MRAC) is used for enhanced tracking of the given reference [23]. Xiloyannis et al. [26] earlier designed a controller for smooth motion of the arm with minimal effort and torque applied. They used a torque loop to counterbalance the gravitational forces and a velocity loop to achieve smooth movements. The torque loop develops a controlled back drivability by monitoring the torque characteristic that changes with position. Whereas the velocity loop uses collocated admittance control by closing the loop at the motor instead of the joint while stabilizing the transmission non-linearity in real time via tracking the velocity output from the torque loop. Wu et al. [25] suggest Admittance Backstepping Sliding Mode Control with Neural Network compensation (ABSMCNN), a block diagram in Fig. 4, as the most efficient control strategy for elbow assistive soft robots. This control method combines admittance control, backstepping sliding mode control, neural network compensation, and sEMG-based force approximation to facilitate four different training modes for patients.

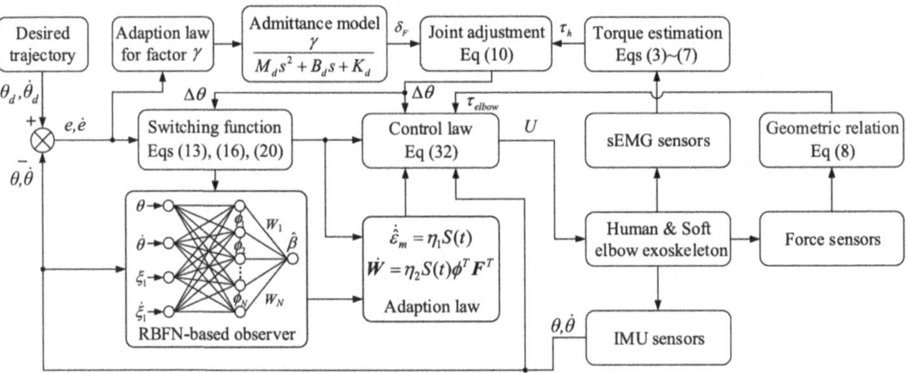

Fig. 4. Overall block diagram of ABSMCNN control strategy. Reproduced from [25], © 2023 IEEE, licensed under CC BY 4.0.

6.2 Results and Discussion

Table 4 contains the recap of the different materials used, type of actuation, control methods and performance metrics of the soft robots.

Table 4. Summary of soft robots for elbow replication.

Materials used	Actuation type	Control strategy	Performance	Refs.
McKibben artificial muscles (Actuator) Polyethylene terephthalate sleeve	Pneumatic	Model Reference Adaptive	ROM: Up to 150°	[23]

(continued)

Table 4. (*continued*)

Materials used	Actuation type	Control strategy	Performance	Refs.
Soft-fabric sleeve	Cable-driven	N/A	Elbow flexion range: 10° to 90° Torque Output: 4.01 Nm with 2.5 kg load 8.31 Nm with 5 kg load Torque R^2: 0.8879, RMSE: 0.9335 Nm sEMG power reduction: 30.2% with 2.5 kg load 51.2% with 5 kg load Angle R^2: 0.9412, RMSE: 4.601°	[24]
Velcro straps (wearable suit)	Cable-driven	Adaptive Cooperative Multi-Mode Control	RMSE: 3.18° Peak Error (PE): 5.68° Active Cooperation Level (ACL): High admittance: 4.51°/Nm Middle admittance: 6.63°/Nm Low admittance: 10.99°/Nm	[25]

(*continued*)

Table 4. *(continued)*

Materials used	Actuation type	Control strategy	Performance	Refs.
Soft-fabric sleeve EVA foam, 3D polyamide, ballistic nylon, PE sponge	Cable-driven	Collocated admittance control PID controller	Accuracy (r^2): Unpowered: 0.91 ± 0.02 Powered: 0.80 ± 0.06 Biceps effort reduction: 64.8 ± 7.66%, $p = 5 \times 10^{-15}$ Biological torque reduction: − 59.20 ± 5.58%, $p = 9 \times 10^{-14}$ Significant reduction: $p = 8 \times 10^{-5}$ Smoothness (SPARC index): Unpowered: − 1.76 ± 0.10 Powered: − 1.82 ± 0.14 3.4% drop, $p = 2 \times 10^{-13}$	[26]
Braided polypropylene threaded mesh Lightweight plastic wearable sleeve	Pneumatic	Pressure modulation	Reduction in muscle activation: Triceps: 40% in passive mode, 30% in active mode Biceps: 60% in passive mode, 50% in active mode All reductions statistically significant ($p < 0.05$)	[27]

(continued)

Table 4. (*continued*)

Materials used	Actuation type	Control strategy	Performance	Refs.
XIAMETER® RTV-4234-T4 silicone Onyx (micro carbon fiber-filled nylon)	Pneumatic	Manual	Maximum torque: 4.39 Nm at 21 PSI Reduction in muscle activation: Task 1 (Static lifting): Biceps = 22.36%, Triceps = 18.19% Task 2 (Assembly with basic tools): Biceps = 14.41%, Triceps = 11.37% Task 3 (Assembly with power tools): Biceps = 10.21%, Triceps = 5.22%	[28]
Tin-cure silicone rubber (Smooth-On Mold Max 20, Shore A 20) [Elbow] Polyethylene heat-shrinking tubes, silicone rubber strips (Ecoflex 00–20) [Shoulder] PLA and ABS plates, TPU layers, polyester mesh	Pneumatic	Model-based	ROM: 112.2° (Elbow), 122.5° (Shoulder) Output Torque: 12.5 N/0.6 Nm at 100 kPa (Elbow), 49.5 N/5.5 Nm at 100 kPa (Shoulder)	[29]
NiTi alloy (springs) Antagonistic muscle	Shape memory alloy	Pulse width modulation	Achieved ROM: 0–80° 66.7% of normal ROM obtained	[30]

The controller design presented by Xiloyannis et al. [26] showed a reduction in muscle strain of 64.8 ± 7.66% with reduced biological torque and arm strain after prolonged work; however, the motion smoothness and precision were compromised. Apart from this, the MRAC controller design showed significant precision when following the rehabilitation protocol but with slight deviation since air pressure is always present in the system [23].

Wu et al. [25] establish that the proposed control strategy ABMSCNN has the highest precision for position control with 26.05% error reduction for trajectory tracking with NN compensation. This study shows that disabled subjects can perform the training tasks with ease. In addition, the exosuit designed by Sridhar et al. [28] showed 24.18% and 19.24% reduction in activation of biceps and triceps, respectively, when lifting different weights from 3lbs to 10 lbs. Moreover, the actuator demonstrates quick reaction with 0.22s to inflate at 25 PSI, highlighting its efficiency.

7 Conclusion and Future Directions

To conclude, this review paper discusses the frontline soft robots that mimic upper limb joints. The state-of-the-art soft robots made for fingers, wrists, elbows, and shoulders were discussed with detailed examination of their design, actuator and control systems, and crucial results. Unlike rigid robotic systems, soft systems are light-weight, flexible, adjustable and comfortable to use. Soft materials such as silicon, TPU, neoprene, and fabric straps are used to ensure durability and adaptability for effortless integration with the human body. Soft robotic systems have proved to improve and quicken the recovery of patients. Advanced control systems used have ensured natural movements mimicking the human body. However, there are many challenges to over-come in order to ensure a complete, stable and optimal operation of soft robots. Most soft robotic wearables reviewed were in the preliminary stage, only being tested for simple tasks. Future research can focus on testing the system on complex rehab routines and tasks, enabling full-scale implementation of these systems. Additionally, a refined structure and actuator modules with lightweight components may be added to ensure accessibility and portability of these robots to assist users even in the absence of a professional physiotherapist.

Acknowledgments. This work was supported by Qatar Research, Development and Innovation (QRDI) under Grant AICC06-0515-240005. The statements made herein are solely the responsibility of the authors.

References

1. Russo, M., et al.: Continuum robots: an overview. Adv. Intell. Syst. **5**(5) (2023). https://doi.org/10.1002/aisy.202200367
2. Davarzani, S., Ahmadi-Pajouh, M.A., Ghafarirad, H.: Design of sensing system for experimental modeling of soft actuator applied for finger rehabilitation. Robotica **40**(7), 2091–2111 (2022). https://doi.org/10.1017/s0263574721001533
3. Arif, S., Muneer, M.: Sustainable development and disintegration of soft robots: an overview. Procedia Comput. Sci. **265**, 499–506 (2025). https://doi.org/10.1016/j.procs.2025.07.210
4. Zhang, Y., Lu, M: A review of recent advancements in soft and flexible robots for medical applications. Int. J. Med. Robot. **16**(3) (2020). https://doi.org/10.1002/rcs.2096
5. Proietti, T., et al.: Sensing and control of a multi-joint soft wearable robot for upper-limb assistance and rehabilitation. IEEE Robot. Autom. Lett. **6**(2), 2381–2388 (2021). https://doi.org/10.1109/lra.2021.3061061
6. Jeong, H., Wang, W.D.: Self-adaptive detachable pneumatic soft actuators using uniformly distributed temporary-bonding-fasteners for wearable applications. Sens. Actuators Phys. **349**, 114083 (2023). https://doi.org/10.1016/j.sna.2022.114083
7. Janghorban, A., Dehghani, R.: Design and motion analysis of a bio-inspired soft robotic finger based on multi-sectional soft reinforced actuator. J. Intell. Robot. Syst. **104**(4) (2022). https://doi.org/10.1007/s10846-022-01579-3

8. Ning, Y., Wang, H., Liu, Y., Wang, Q., Rong, Y., Niu, J.: Design and analysis of a compatible exoskeleton rehabilitation robot system based on upper limb movement mechanism. Med. Biol. Eng. Comput. **62**(3), 883–899 (2024). https://doi.org/10.1007/s11517-023-02974-0
9. Yan, H., et al.: Configuration design of an upper limb rehabilitation robot with a generalized shoulder joint. Appl. Sci. **11**(5), 2080 (2021). https://doi.org/10.3390/app11052080
10. Zhang, N., Ge, L., Xu, H., Zhu, X., Gu, G.: 3D printed, modularized rigid-flexible integrated soft finger actuators for anthropomorphic hands. Sens. Actuators Phys. **312**, 112090 (2020). https://doi.org/10.1016/j.sna.2020.112090
11. Li, W.-Y., Nabae, H., Endo, G., Suzumori, K.: New soft robot hand configuration with combined biotensegrity and thin artificial muscle. IEEE Robot. Autom. Lett. **5**(3), 4345–4351 (2020). https://doi.org/10.1109/lra.2020.2983668
12. Gharibkhanian, A., Yousefi-Koma, A., Zareinejad, M., Barahimi, A., Bagha, P.A.A., Sobhani, P.: Design, fabrication and control of a soft robotic wrist sleeve for wrist rehabilitation. In: 2024 12th RSI International Conference on Robotics and Mechatronics (ICRoM), Tehran, Iran, Islamic Republic of: IEEE, pp. 107–112 (2024). https://doi.org/10.1109/icrom64545.2024.10903527
13. Ang, B.W.K., Yeow, C.-H.: Design and characterization of a 3D printed soft robotic wrist sleeve with 2 DoF for stroke rehabilitation. In: 2019 2nd IEEE International Conference on Soft Robotics (RoboSoft), Seoul, Korea (South), pp. 577–582. IEEE, USA (2019). https://doi.org/10.1109/robosoft.2019.8722771
14. Singh, I., et al.: Development of soft pneumatic actuator based wrist exoskeleton for assistive motion. In: 2023 IEEE/ASME International Conference on Advanced Intelligent Mechatronics (AIM), Seattle, WA, USA, pp. 359–366. IEEE, USA (2023). https://doi.org/10.1109/aim46323.2023.10196235
15. Liu, S., et al.: A compact soft robotic wrist brace with origami actuators. Front. Robot. AI **8** (2021). https://doi.org/10.3389/frobt.2021.614623
16. Ridremont, T., et al.: Soft robotic bilateral rehabilitation system for hand and wrist joints. Machines **12**(5), 288 (2024). https://doi.org/10.3390/machines12050288
17. Schäffer, K., Ozkan-Aydin, Y., Coad, M.M.: Soft wrist exosuit actuated by fabric pneumatic artificial muscles. IEEE Trans. Med. Robot. Bionics **6**(2), 718–732 (2024). https://doi.org/10.1109/tmrb.2024.3385795
18. Chen, G., Lin, T., Ding, S., Chen, S., Ji, A., Lodewijks, G.: Design and test of an active pneumatic soft wrist for soft grippers. Actuators **11**(11), 311 (2022). https://doi.org/10.3390/act11110311
19. Hu, T., Lu, X., Yi, J., Wang, Y., Xu, D.: Biomimetic soft robotic wrist with 3-DOF motion and stiffness tunability based on ring-reinforced pneumatic actuators and a particle jamming joint. Sci. China Technol. Sci. **67**(3), 774–790 (2024). https://doi.org/10.1007/s11431-023-2579-8
20. Zhou, Y.M., Hohimer, C., Proietti, T., O'Neill, C.T., Walsh, C.J.: Kinematics-based control of an inflatable soft wearable robot for assisting the shoulder of industrial workers. IEEE Robot. Autom. Lett. **6**(2), 2155–2162 (2021). https://doi.org/10.1109/lra.2021.3061365
21. Campioni, L., et al.: Preliminary evaluation of a soft wearable robot for shoulder movement assistance. IEEE Trans. Med. Robot. Bionics **7**(1), 315–324 (2025). https://doi.org/10.1109/tmrb.2025.3527708
22. Natividad, R.F., Miller-Jackson, T., Chen-Hua, R.Y.: A 2-DOF shoulder exosuit driven by modular, pneumatic, fabric actuators. IEEE Trans. Med. Robot. Bionics **3**(1), 166–178 (2021). https://doi.org/10.1109/tmrb.2020.3044115
23. Irshaidat, M., Soufian, M., Al-Ibadi, A., Nefti-Meziani, S.: A novel elbow pneumatic muscle actuator for exoskeleton arm in post-stroke rehabilitation. In: 2019 2nd IEEE International Conference on Soft Robotics (RoboSoft), Seoul, Korea (South), pp. 630–635. IEEE, USA (2019). https://doi.org/10.1109/robosoft.2019.8722813

24. Shao, Z., Xi, W., Wu, Q.: Design and transmission modeling of a soft elbow exosuit using double artificial tendon system. Proc. Inst. Mech. Eng. Part C J. Mech. Eng. Sci. **237**(7), 1728–1740 (2023). https://doi.org/10.1177/09544062221129824
25. Wu, Q., Wang, Z., Chen, Y.: SEMG-based adaptive cooperative multi-mode control of a soft elbow exoskeleton using neural network compensation. IEEE Trans. Neural Syst. Rehabil. Eng. **31**, 3384–3396 (2023). https://doi.org/10.1109/tnsre.2023.3306201
26. Xiloyannis, M., Chiaradia, D., Frisoli, A., Masia, L.: Physiological and kinematic effects of a soft exosuit on arm movements. J. NeuroEng. Rehabil. **16**(1) (2019). https://doi.org/10.1186/s12984-019-0495-y
27. Khan, M.U.A., Ajmal, H.M.S., Hassan, H.A., Azam, A., Malik, E.: A soft robotic sleeve for physiotherapy: improving elbow rehabilitation in baseball pitchers. Physiother. Res. Int. **30**(1) (2025). https://doi.org/10.1002/pri.70025
28. Sridhar, E.P., Erel, V., Nasirian, A., Wijesundara, M.B.J., Rahman, M.: Design, development, and evaluation of a pneumatically actuated soft wearable robotic elbow exoskeleton for reducing muscle activity and perceived workload. J. Rehabil. Assist. Technol. Eng. **12** (2025). https://doi.org/10.1177/20556683251347517
29. Zhang, H., Naquila, G., Bae, J., Wu, Z., Hingwe, A., Deshpande, A.: Novel bio-inspired soft actuators for upper-limb exoskeletons: design, fabrication and feasibility study. Front. Robot. AI **11** (2024). https://doi.org/10.3389/frobt.2024.1451231
30. Xie, Q., et al.: Design of a soft bionic elbow exoskeleton based on shape memory alloy spring actuators. Mech. Sci. **14**(1), 159–170 (2023). https://doi.org/10.5194/ms-14-159-2023

Eye Movement Recognition and Gaze Point Prediction with Webcam

Jiawei Shen[1], Ruoyu Wang[2], Weiwei Yu[1](✉), and Gautam Srivastava[1,2]

[1] School of Mechanical Engineering, Northwestern Polytechnical University, Xi'an, China
yuweiwei@nwpu.edu.cn

[2] Department of Mathematics and Computer Science, Brandon University, Brandon, MB, Canada

Abstract. With the advancement of human-computer interaction, virtual reality, and related fields, gaze prediction, as a core technology, has been widely applied in various scenarios. Traditional gaze prediction methods mostly rely on expensive hardware devices such as infrared cameras, which limits their practical applications. To address this issue, this paper proposes a low-cost gaze prediction method based on a regular camera. By integrating multi-modal feature fusion of head pose and eye features, along with a lightweight multi-layer perceptron (MLP) model, we achieve a balance between high accuracy and real-time performance without relying on additional hardware. Experimental results demonstrate that the proposed method can achieve a gaze prediction accuracy of 3.95° using a regular laptop camera and only contains 7.73 million parameters.These experiments verify the effectiveness and feasibility of the proposed method on low-cost devices, providing a new solution for gaze prediction in practical applications.

Keywords: Low-cost · Feature extraction · Gaze estimation

1 Introduction

Gaze point prediction, as a crucial research direction in fields such as human–computer interaction, driver monitoring, and virtual reality, has received extensive attention in recent years. Traditional gaze point prediction methods mostly rely on high-precision cameras, infrared light sources, and other special-purpose hardware devices. Although they can provide high accuracy, the hardware costs are high, and the usage environment is limited, making it difficult to be widely promoted in daily applications [1]. Currently, some emerging methods have tried to break through the hardware limitations, but they still have deficiencies in accuracy and stability.

Conducting gaze point prediction research under the condition of relying solely on the built-in webcam of a laptop computer without any additional hardware support is extremely challenging. On the one hand, the limited resolution and frame rate of the webcam result in poor-quality collected images. On the other hand, without the assistance of additional light sources, the system is highly vulnerable to factors such as illumination changes, head pose offsets, and occlusions. In this situation, how to achieve

S. S. Ge et al. (Eds.): ICSR + BioMed 2025, LNAI 16435, pp. 169–180, 2026.
https://doi.org/10.1007/978-981-95-7538-1_15

high precision prediction while ensuring the real time performance of the system has become a problem that urgently needs to be solved.

To address the abovementioned problems, this paper proposes a low-cost gaze point prediction method based on an ordinary webcam. This method integrates head pose information and eye specific details features, and realizes high precision gaze point prediction by means of multi modal feature fusion technology and lightweight neural network modeling.

Meanwhile, a personalized calibration mechanism is designed to effectively alleviate the prediction instability caused by individual differences. The output layer weights of the model are fine-tuned using 5–10 s of user-specific gaze data to ensure personalized adjustments, thereby enhancing the model's prediction stability and accuracy. In addition, the proposed system can not only output the gaze point but also extract and analyze eye related features in real-time, providing strong support for subsequent multi-scene extended applications.

2 Review of Related Work

With the rapid development of artificial intelligence (AI) and computer vision technologies, eye movement recognition and gaze prediction techniques have become increasingly prominent in numerous scenarios, such as human-computer interaction, driver monitoring, and medical rehabilitation. Gaze prediction technology has undergone multi-stage evolution from geometric models to deep learning methods. Although existing studies have made progress in accuracy and real-time performance, obvious limitations remain, which are detailed as follows.

2.1 Eye Feature Extraction Methods

In addition to gaze point prediction, eye feature extraction plays a crucial role in improving the accuracy and robustness of gaze estimation systems. Eye feature extraction techniques focus on detecting and analyzing specific details of the eye region, such as the pupil, eyelids, iris, and sclera. These features are essential for accurate gaze tracking, as they provide valuable information that can be used to estimate the direction of gaze more reliably.

Earlier methods in eye feature extraction typically relied on geometric models to locate key eye features, often combined with infrared lighting or high-resolution cameras. However, the advent of computer vision techniques and deep learning has enabled more robust methods that rely on regular cameras. Modern approaches often use deep learning-based models to automatically extract these eye features from images, eliminating the need for complex manual feature selection. Convolutional Neural Networks (CNNs) have become a popular choice for automatic feature extraction due to their ability to learn hierarchical features directly from raw pixel data [2]. These networks can effectively detect pupil center positions, eyelid shapes, and eye openness, even under challenging conditions such as varying lighting or partial occlusions.

However, challenges remain in real-time extraction and maintaining high accuracy in the face of variable lighting conditions, low-resolution input, or when users' faces are not perfectly aligned with the camera. Additionally, the generalization of deep learning models across diverse populations, including individuals with different eye shapes, skin tones, or glasses, continues to be a subject of ongoing research.

2.2 Gaze Point Prediction Methods

2.2.1 Geometric Model-Based Methods

Early research on gaze prediction focused on geometric modeling, calculating gaze points by analyzing the positional relationship between the pupil center and corneal reflections. Such methods typically require the combination of infrared light sources and high-resolution cameras, enabling extremely high accuracy in controlled environments. However, they exhibit strong dependence on hardware: not only do they demand dedicated imaging devices and fixed experimental conditions (resulting in high costs), but they also struggle to be promoted in daily scenarios. For instance, systems based on the Pupil Center Corneal Reflection (PCCR) technology [3] require precise deployment of light sources and cameras around the user's eyes to ensure accurate gaze estimation. With the popularization of ordinary cameras, the academic community has gradually explored appearance-based gaze estimation methods, directly estimating the user's gaze direction or gaze coordinates using image information. This type of method has broken through the bottleneck of hardware dependence to a certain extent and gradually become a mainstream research direction in the field.

2.2.2 Appearance Feature-Based Methods

Appearance feature-based gaze prediction methods usually first extract appearance features (e.g., eye contour, pupil position, and eyelid shape), and then construct gaze regression models using traditional machine learning methods such as Support Vector Machines (SVM) and Random Forests. Compared with geometric model methods, their hardware requirements are significantly reduced; some studies can run on ordinary cameras, effectively lowering the application threshold. For example, the literature [4] proposes a full-face appearance-based gaze estimation method. By using full-face images instead of only eye features, this method enhances the model's sensitivity to head pose and expression changes, improving its generalization ability in practical scenarios. However, such methods are highly sensitive to lighting changes and head pose deviations, with limited generalization ability—when the usage environment fluctuates, the prediction accuracy decreases significantly.

2.2.3 Deep Learning-Based Methods

In recent years, deep learning has brought breakthroughs to gaze prediction. Early deep learning methods centered on Convolutional Neural Networks (CNNs): high-level features of eye regions or full-face images are extracted via convolutional layers, and then end-to-end gaze coordinate regression is completed using fully connected layers [5–7]. Subsequent researchers found that binocular images contain symmetric structural information, thus proposing binocular input-based gaze prediction models. These models reduce the uncertainty caused by pose changes by leveraging binocular symmetry, effectively improving prediction accuracy in complex scenarios.

Beyond single-modal input, multi-modal fusion methods have become a current research hotspot. Researchers have gradually explored combining head pose information with eye region image features to construct multi-modal feature vector input models [8], but such methods are still limited to image-based end-to-end modeling. Meanwhile, lightweight network structures have become a new research focus due to their ability to adapt to real-time prediction requirements of resource-constrained devices. Some studies have also introduced personalized calibration strategies: by fine-tuning the model with a small amount of user calibration data, the problem of prediction instability caused by individual differences is alleviated.

Recent studies have also explored the fusion of eye features with other body landmarks, such as facial keypoints, to further improve accuracy. For example, combining head pose information with eye detail features has been shown to enhance gaze prediction models' robustness, especially in dynamic and real-world scenarios [9]. The integration of eye feature extraction with gaze prediction models provides a more comprehensive solution, allowing systems to better handle factors like eye movement, eyelid occlusion, and facial expression changes. However, the challenge remains to extract these features with high precision and in real-time, particularly when dealing with low-quality or noisy input images from webcam.

Although existing methods continue to expand in accuracy and application scope, three core limitations remain: first, geometric model methods rely too heavily on hardware to be popularized under low-cost conditions; second, appearance-based methods reduce hardware thresholds but suffer from poor environmental adaptability and insufficient stability; third, although deep learning methods can handle complex environments, most of these studies still require additional hardware support, and their exploration of the "high accuracy-lightweight" balance is insufficient—for example, some lightweight models reduce the parameter scale by 40% while suffering an accuracy loss of over 8%. Overall, how to balance the accuracy and real-time performance of gaze prediction under the condition of relying only on the built-in camera of a laptop remains an unsolved problem in the field.

Based on the above analysis, this study takes ordinary cameras as the hardware foundation, combines head pose and eye detail features, and improves prediction accuracy through multi-modal fusion and lightweight modeling, aiming to explore a low-cost and scalable gaze prediction solution. The main contributions of this paper are summarized as follows:

(i) It verifies the feasibility of gaze prediction using only the built-in webcam of a laptop, providing support for the application of low-cost devices;
(ii) It constructs a unified framework of "gaze point output-eye feature extraction" enriching the functional value of gaze prediction technology and laying a foundation for multi-scenario expansion.

3 Proposed Methods

3.1 Overall Framwork

This paper proposes a low-cost gaze prediction method that relies exclusively on the built-in camera of a laptop, providing a cost-effective solution for gaze estimation without requiring additional hardware. As illustrated in Fig. 1.

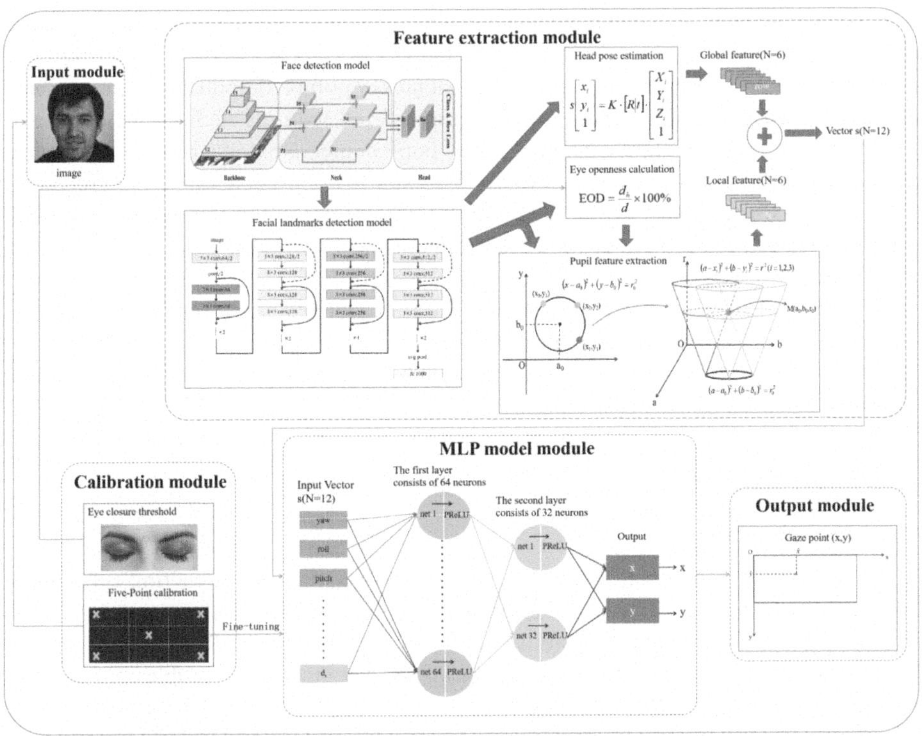

Fig. 1. Overall framework design for eye feature extraction and gaze estimation.

The overall framework of the system is composed of five core modules: an input module, a feature extraction module, a Multi-Layer Perceptron (MLP) model module, an output module, and a calibration module. The input module handles the real-time video stream captured by the laptop's camera, serving as the foundation for the entire system. The feature extraction module is responsible for identifying and processing the relevant facial and eye features that are crucial for accurate gaze prediction. It includes face detection, facial landmarks detection, head pose estimation, eye openness calculation, pupil feature extraction, and multi-modal feature fusion. Each of these components works in tandem to isolate key features such as the head orientation and eye details, which are essential for understanding the user's gaze direction. Once these features are extracted, they are passed to the MLP model module, where a lightweight neural network is used to predict the gaze point coordinates on the screen, based on the combined global (head pose) and local (eye features) information. The output module then presents the predicted gaze point, providing a visual representation of where the user is looking. Finally, the calibration module fine-tunes the model using a small set of personalized gaze data, ensuring that the predictions are accurate and stable for individual users. This modular design enables the system to be flexible, efficient, and easily adaptable to different environments and users.

The input of the system is the real-time video stream captured by the laptop's built-in camera, and its workflow is as follows: First, a face detection algorithm is used to locate the face region, and then facial landmarks detection is applied to obtain the precise coordinates of eye-related landmarks. Subsequently, head pose estimation is completed based on the spatial positional relationship of facial key points (outputting pitch, yaw, and roll angles), while simultaneously extracting eye detail features such as eye openness, pupil diameter, and the relative position of the pupil center. Next, the head pose features and eye detail features are subjected to multi-modal fusion to generate a feature vector with a unified dimension. Finally, this feature vector is input into the lightweight MLP regression model, which outputs the 2D coordinates (x, y) of the gaze point on the screen and eye state features.

By virtue of lightweight modeling and multi-modal feature complementarity, this framework achieves a balance between real-time performance and prediction accuracy under the hardware condition of an ordinary camera, meeting the application requirements of daily scenarios.

3.2 Feature Extraction

3.2.1 Face Detection

Face detection is a fundamental task in computer vision, directly impacting subsequent tasks such as facial keypoint localization and eye state recognition. To meet the low-cost hardware requirements, this study adopts the lightweight SCRFD [10] (Selective Refinement for Face Detection) model. By employing depthwise separable convolutions and channel pruning, SCRFD effectively balances accuracy and speed, making it suitable for ordinary laptop webcams. With a resolution of 640 × 480, SCRFD achieves 30 FPS with an accuracy of 94.2%, effectively supporting the subsequent facial landmarks detection task.

3.2.2 Facial Landmarks Detection

Facial landmarks detection plays a crucial role in gaze point prediction, as it directly influences the accuracy of head pose estimation and eye feature extraction. To balance detection accuracy and computational overhead, this study uses the ResNet-18 [11] model for landmarks detection. ResNet-18, through residual connections, mitigates the vanishing gradient problem in deep networks, maintaining strong feature extraction capabilities and high localization accuracy in low-resource environments. The model achieves 3.12% Normalized Mean Error (NME) on the GazeCapture dataset and processes 640 × 480 video streams at 28 FPS.

3.2.3 Head Pose Estimation

Head pose estimation is a key component in gaze estimation, as it affects the accuracy of gaze direction prediction. This study uses the EPnP [12] (Efficient Perspective-n-Point) algorithm, which calculates head pose angles using 68 facial landmarks and 3D coordinates of a standard face model. Known for its computational efficiency and accuracy, the EPnP algorithm is particularly suitable for real-time head pose estimation, fulfilling the requirements for real-time applications on low-resource devices.

3.2.4 Eye Feature Extraction

Eye Detail Feature Extraction is crucial for accurate gaze point estimation, especially in cases of large head movement or occlusion, where relying solely on head pose estimation may not precisely capture the gaze focus. Accurately extracting eye details, such as pupil center and pupil diameter, can further enhance the accuracy and robustness of gaze point prediction.

In the feature extraction process, we first crop the eye regions based on the face detection and facial landmarks data. Then, image processing techniques are applied to extract pupil center and diameter, as well as compute the eye openness. The cropped eye images undergo preprocessing and edge detection, followed by Hough Circle detection to fit the pupil features, including the pupil center and diameter, as shown in Fig. 2.

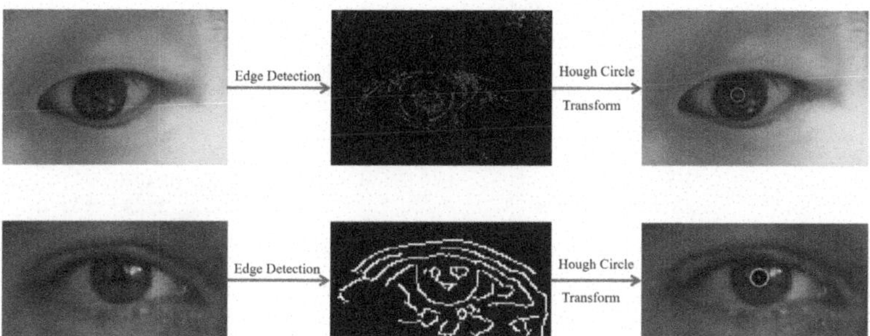

Fig. 2. Steps for extracting pupil center and diameter from cropped eye region images.

To provide accurate input features for the gaze prediction model, we fuse the extracted head pose features and eye details. The head pose features consist of three pose angles (yaw, roll, pitch) and the head's translation vector(t), totaling 6 dimensions. The eye features include the pupil center position (left pupil(x_l,y_l) and right pupil(x_r,y_r)) 、left pupil diameter (d_l) and right pupil diameter (d_r), accounting for 6 dimensions. Finally, these features are normalized and concatenated into a 12-dimensional feature vector as follow (s), which is used as input to the regression model.

$$s = (yaw, roll, pitch, t, x_l, y_l, d_l, x_r, y_r, d_r) \quad (1)$$

3.3 Gaze Point Prediction Based on MLP-G

To address the limitations of resolution and frame rate in ordinary webcams, this paper employs a lightweight Multi-Layer Perceptron for gaze estimation (MLP-G) [13] model, as shown in Fig. 3. The model consists of three fully connected layers, with 12-dimensional fused features as input and gaze point coordinates as output. The fused features include head pose and eye-related characteristics, such as pupil position and eye openness. The hidden layers use the PReLU (Parametric ReLU) activation function, which helps prevent vanishing gradients and improves model training efficiency. The output layer performs linear regression, predicting the 2D gaze coordinates on the screen.

The MLP-G model is designed with a compact architecture, making it computationally efficient while maintaining good prediction accuracy. This lightweight design allows it to perform real-time inference on standard hardware, such as a laptop webcam, without requiring specialized equipment. The simplicity of the MLP structure enables fast training and inference, making it ideal for applications where both speed and accuracy are critical. The model's ability to balance computational efficiency and high performance in real-time scenarios is one of its key advantages.

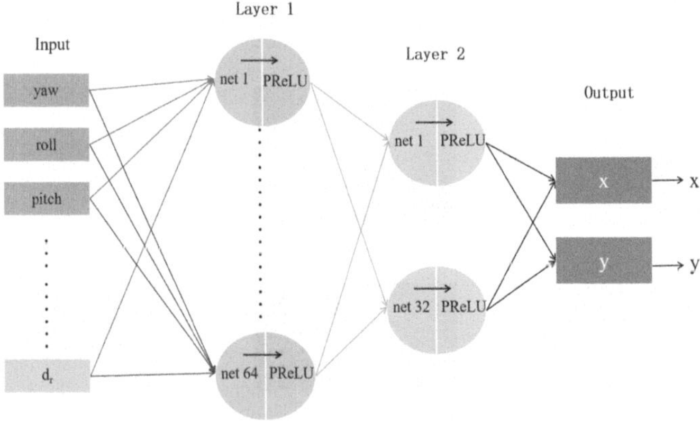

Fig. 3. The MLP-G model structure.

4 Experiment

4.1 Experiment Setup

4.1.1 Training and Evaluation Datasets

The GazeCapture dataset is used in this study, which is collected by participants using the front-facing camera of a device. The dataset includes participants from various age groups and ethnicities, ensuring high realism and naturalness. The subset used in this paper consists of 174,536 samples from 1,200 subjects. 80% of the data (139,629 samples) is used for training, while the remaining 20% (34,907 samples) is used for evaluation to validate the model's performance.

4.1.2 Training Process

All models are trained using the PyTorch framework on NVIDIA GeForce GTX 1650 to accelerate the training process and ensure efficient performance on large-scale datasets. In this study, we train an MLP model using MSE loss as the baseline loss function, with the Adam optimizer and a learning rate of 0.001.

To improve training effectiveness and stability, we use the EarlyStopping callback (which halts training early when the validation loss stops improving) and ReduceLROn-Plateau callback (which reduces the learning rate when validation loss does not improve). The training parameters are set as follows:

Batch Size: 500
Epochs: Up to 100 epochs
Learning Rate: 0.001
Weight Decay: 0.5.

The model is trained on the training set, and the validation set error is monitored during training. Early stopping and learning rate decay are employed to ensure that the model converges within a reasonable time and avoid overfitting. At the end of each epoch, we evaluate MAE and MSE on the validation set to monitor the model's performance.

4.2 Experimental Results and Comparison

During the training process, both the training loss and validation loss gradually decreased, indicating that the model was continuously optimizing. The loss and error curves (MSE and MAE) for the training process are shown in Fig. 4. After 60 epochs, the model stabilized at a lower error level and was able to predict the gaze points in real-time.

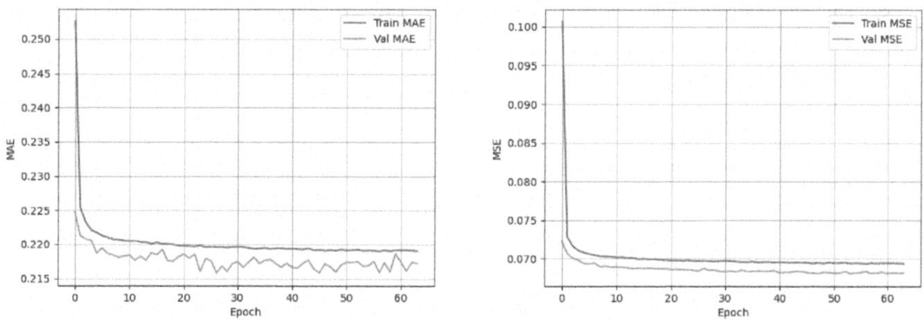

Fig. 4. Curve of MAE and MSE variation with Epochs during MLP model training.

Left Chart shows the MAE curve, which intuitively reflects the average deviation between the predicted gaze points and the ground truth gaze points on the screen coordinates. After training completion, the MAEon the validation set converged to approximately 0.217, and the trend of the curves on the training and validation sets remained consistent. There were no significant fluctuations or increases in error on the validation set, indicating that the model did not overfit, and the convergence was stable.

Right Chart shows the MSE curve. MSE decreased rapidly in the early stages of training, eventually stabilizing around 0.067. The square root of the MSE yields the RMSE (Root Mean Square Error), which was approximately 0.26 at the end of training.

Additionally, we conducted comparison experiments by adjusting the number of hidden layers and neurons in the MLP model to explore the effect of model structure on the training results. The comparison results are shown in Table 1.

Table 1. Comparison of training results of MLP models with different structural parameters.

Number of layers	Number of neurons	MAE
2	(64,32)	0.217
2	(96,48)	0.219
3	(64,32,16)	0.221
3	(128,64,32)	0.224
4	(128,64,32,16)	0.229

According to the comparison results, when the number of hidden layers was 4, the MAEsignificantly increased, indicating that the model had overfitted. The excess parameters caused the model to learn more noise, which increased the prediction error. When the number of hidden layers was 3, there was still some overfitting. However, when the number of hidden layers was reduced to 2, there was little difference in the MAE between the two sets of neurons. We believe that the error mainly comes from the cascading errors in the feature extraction method, which causes the final feature values to be inaccurate, affecting the data quality and resulting in prediction errors.

To verify the balance between real-time performance and accuracy of thc proposed method, we compared it with several existing deep learning-based gaze point prediction methods, using the GazeCapture dataset. The comparison experiment focused on evaluating two aspects:

(i) Accuracy: We used angular error as the evaluation metric to assess the model's prediction accuracy in different devices and scenarios. Smaller errors indicate better model performance. Angular error is a commonly used metric for gaze direction estimation.
(ii) Real-time Performance: We evaluated the model's response speed by the model size.

The comparison results are shown in Table 2.

Table 2. Comparison of accuracy and model size with other deep learning models.

Method	Angular error	Model size
MLP-G	3.95°	7.73M

(*continued*)

Table 2. *(continued)*

Method	Angular error	Model size
ResNet-50 [14]	4.11°	25.5M
GazeTR-Conv [14]	4.21°	11.2M

Our proposed method achieves a good balance between accuracy and real-time performance, making it especially suitable for deployment in low-cost devices and practical application scenarios.

4.3 Experimental Discussion

Through comparisons with other deep learning models, the experimental results demonstrate that the proposed low-cost gaze point prediction method excels in both accuracy and real-time performance, particularly under the constraints of an ordinary laptop webcam and low-resource environments. The method not only meets the real-time performance requirements but also achieves comparable accuracy to existing methods, highlighting its great potential for practical applications.

The key advantage of the proposed method lies in its ability to balance real-time performance with accuracy, which is achieved through the fusion of head pose and eye feature information. By leveraging both global (head pose) and local (eye features) data, the model improves gaze prediction accuracy while maintaining computational efficiency. The lightweight MLP model further contributes to the system's success by minimizing computational complexity, making it suitable for use on low-cost devices without sacrificing performance.

However. One notable issue is the sensitivity to lighting conditions, which can affect the accuracy of pupil detection, especially in low-light or high-contrast environments. The limitation point to areas for improvement, such as enhancing lighting adaptability to increase the system's versatility.

5 Conclusion

This study proposes a low-cost gaze point prediction method based on a standard webcam, combining multimodal fusion of head pose and eye features, and employing a lightweight MLP-G model to successfully balance accuracy and real-time performance. The experimental results show that, without relying on infrared lighting and high-end equipment, the proposed method achieves an accuracy of 3.95° with only 7.73M parameters, demonstrating excellent real-time inference capabilities suitable for low-cost devices.

Although the method performs well in terms of both accuracy and real-time performance, it is still affected by lighting variations and large head pose changes. Future research could explore improvements in lighting adaptability, optimization for mobile devices, and personalized calibration mechanisms. Additionally, innovations in deep learning architectures and the expansion of cross-scenario applications will be important directions for future work.

Acknowledgements. This study was supported by National Natural Science Foundation of China (Grant No.62376220),and National Foreign Expert Program (Grant No.H20251040).

References

1. Wang, X., Zhao, S., Mao, X., et al.: DGRGaze: a difference-guided gaze estimation framework based on 6D rotation matrix representation. In: 2025 IEEE International Conference on Image Processing (ICIP), pp. 1894–1899. IEEE, USA (2025)
2. Ruiz-Beltrán, C.A., Romero-Garcés, A., González-García, M., et al.: FPGA-Based CNN for eye detection in an Iris recognition at a distance system. Electronics **12**(22), 4713 (2023)
3. Zhang, C., Chi, J.N., Zhang, Z.H., et al.: Gaze estimation in a gaze tracking system. Sci. China Inf. Sci. **54**(11), 2295–2306 (2011)
4. Zhang, X., Sugano, Y., Fritz, M., et al.: It's written all over your face: Full-face appearance-based gaze estimation. In: Proceedings of the IEEE Conference on Computer Vision and Pattern Recognition Workshops, pp. 51–60 (2017)
5. Vidhya, V., Resende, F.D.: Real-time gaze estimation using webcam-based cnn models for human-computer interactions. Computers **14**(2), 57 (2025)
6. Karmi, R., Rahmany, I., Khlifa, N.: Gaze estimation using convolutional neural networks. SIViP **18**(1), 389–398 (2024)
7. Aunsri, N., Rattarom, S.: Novel eye-based features for head pose-free gaze estimation with web camera: New model and low-cost device. Ain Shams Eng. J. **13**(5), 101731 (2022)
8. Bao, Y., Cheng, Y., Liu, Y., et al.: Adaptive feature fusion network for gaze tracking in mobile tablets. In: 2020 25th International Conference on Pattern Recognition (ICPR), pp. 9936–9943. IEEE, USA (2021)
9. Zhu, C.: For higher accuracy: 3D eye movement gaze depth estimation method based on Mix-TCN. J. Phys. Conf. Ser. **2646**(1) 012044 (2023)
10. Chi, C., Zhang, S., Xing, J., et al.: Selective refinement network for high performance face detection. In: Proceedings of the AAAI Conference on Artificial Intelligence, vol. 33, no. 01, pp. 8231–8238 (2019)
11. Xu, W., Fu, Y. L., Zhu, D.: ResNet and its application to medical image processing: research progress and challenges. Comput. Methods Prog. Biomed. **240**, 107660 (2023)
12. Wang, B., Bai, A., Ma, F., et al.: A 3D object localization method based on EPNP and dual-view images. In: 2024 IEEE 7th Advanced Information Technology, Electronic and Automation Control Conference (IAEAC) , vol. 7, pp. 1349–1353. IEEE, USA (2024)
13. Wu, Z., Zhang, D., Wu, Y., et al.: An efficient and high-precision 3D gaze estimation method based on MLP. Comput. Eng. Sci. **45**(11), 1982 (2023)
14. Cheng, Y., Lu, F.: Gaze estimation using transformer. In: 2022 26th International Conference on Pattern Recognition (ICPR), pp. 3341–3347. IEEE, USA (2022)

Evaluation of LVA Treatment Efficacy for Secondary Lymphedema of the Limbs in Middle and Advanced Stages Using the LYMQOL Score

Zhongyu Jia[1], Gaofeng Liang[1], Zonghai Jia[1], and Chi Zhang[2,3](✉)

[1] Norinco General Hospital, Xi'an 710065, China
[2] Department of Industry Engineering, School of Mechanical Engineering, Northwestern Poly-Technical University, Xi'an 710072, China
lgflgf4488@163.com
[3] Bio-Additive Manufacturing University-Enterprise Joint Research Center of Shaanxi Province, Northwestern Polytechnical University, Xi'an 710072, China

Abstract.
Objective To investigate the therapeutic efficacy and surgical experience of lymphaticovenular anastomosis (LVA) in treating secondary lymphedema of the limbs at the intermediate and advanced stages. Methods: From May 2022 to August 2025, 42 patients with moderate-to-severe secondary lymphedema of the extremities underwent LVA to reconstruct limb lymphatic function. Combined with postoperative compression therapy, this aimed to alleviate limb edema and reduce complications. Patients underwent regular postoperative follow-up with limb circumference and volume measurements. Surgical efficacy was assessed using the LYMQOL score across four dimensions: function, appearance, symptoms, and emotional well-being. Results: Among the 42 patients, 16 involved the upper limbs and 26 involved the lower limbs. ISL staging: Stage II: 34 cases; Stage III: 8 cases. At the 1-year postoperative follow-up, limb volume decreased in 15 patients compared to preoperative measurements: 8 upper limbs (50.0%) and 9 lower limbs (26.9%), with a higher reduction rate in upper limbs. At 1 year postoperatively, the LYMQOL scores for appearance and symptoms decreased in upper limbs compared to preoperative levels, while only the symptom dimension improved in lower limbs. Overall quality of life scores improved in both upper and lower limb groups postoperatively. Conclusion: Although LVA shows limited efficacy in reducing limb volume for treating mid-to-late stage secondary lymphedema in the extremities, it effectively improves patients' subjective perceptions. For patients with high surgical risk and minimal cosmetic concerns, LVA represents a viable surgical option.

Keywords: Lymphovenous anastomosis · Mid-to-late stage lymphedema · LYMQOL score

S. S. Ge et al. (Eds.): ICSR + BioMed 2025, LNAI 16435, pp. 181–191, 2026.
https://doi.org/10.1007/978-981-95-7538-1_16

1 Introduction

Secondary lymphedema is a pathological condition caused by damage to lymph nodes or lymphatic vessels in the limbs due to factors such as tumor surgery, radiation therapy for tumors, infection, or trauma. This damage obstructs lymphatic fluid return, leading to stasis in the interstitial spaces [1]. With the rising incidence of malignant tumors in China, cancer treatment has become the primary cause of secondary lymphedema [2]. Early-stage lymphedema primarily manifests as edema, while advanced stages may involve tissue fibrosis, fat deposition, and recurrent infections. Lymphatic Vascular Access (LVA) surgery, favored for its minimal invasiveness and rapid postoperative recovery, is widely adopted as a treatment modality for lymphedema [3]. LVA is indicated for early-stage lymphedema, but its suitability for advanced-stage patients remains controversial. Due to the difficulty in identifying functional lymphatic vessels in patients with advanced lymphedema [4], some scholars consider advanced lymphedema a relative contraindication for LVA surgery [5]. With advances in lymphedema research and increased diagnostic tools, it has become feasible to identify functional lymphatic vessels and perform LVA surgery in patients with advanced lymphedema [6]. However, reports on the efficacy of LVA for treating advanced lymphedema remain scarce. This study reviewed the application of LVA technology in the treatment of patients with secondary lymphedema of the extremities in our department since 2022, evaluated the postoperative LYMQOL score of the patients, and assessed the surgical efficacy from multiple dimensions such as function, appearance, symptoms, emotion, and quality of life. It was found that the overall quality of life of the patients improved. The report is as follows.

2 Materials and Methods

2.1 General Information

This group consisted of 42 patients: 41 females and 1 male, aged 45–83 years with a mean age of 62 years. Sixteen cases involved the upper extremity, all following radical mastectomy with concurrent radiotherapy. Twenty-six cases involved the lower extremity, including 1 case after trauma surgery and the remainder after gynecological tumor surgery. The duration from symptom onset to surgical intervention ranged from 6 months to 20 years, with a mean of 5.1 ± 4.9 years. According to ISL staging [7]: Stage I: 0 cases Stage II: 34 cases Stage III: 8 cases All patients initially underwent LVA surgery.

2.2 Limb Measurement

Limb circumference measurements must be taken upon patient admission and during postoperative follow-up. Upper limb measurement points: - Level of the olecranon process - 5 cm above/below the olecranon process - 10 cm above/below the olecranon process - 15 cm above/below the olecranon process Lower limb measurement points: Mid-patella level, 5 cm above/below mid-patella, 10 cm above/below mid-patella, 15 cm above/below mid-patella, 20 cm above/below mid-patella. (see Fig. 1) Calculate limb volume based on limb circumference. The calculation method involves approximating the limb segment between each measurement point as a cylinder. Calculate the cylinder volume using the top and bottom circumferences. The total limb volume approximates the sum of the volumes of each segmental cylinder. The calculation formula is:

$$V = \sum_{n=1}^{n} \frac{H(C_n^2 + C_n C_{n+1} + C_{n+1}^2)}{12pi} \tag{1}$$

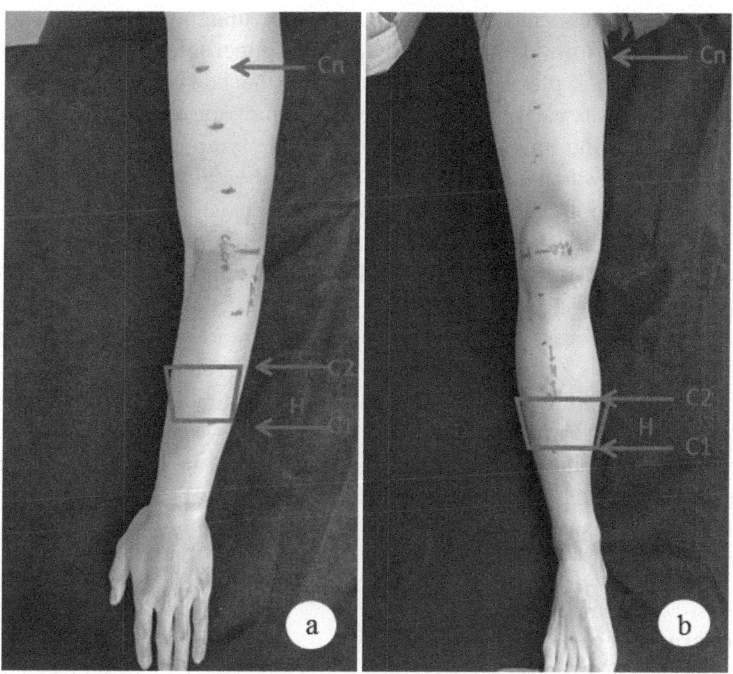

Fig. 1. Measurement points on the upper and lower limbs. (a) Schematic diagram of upper limb circumference measurement. (b) Schematic diagram of lower limb circumference measurement. Estimate limb volume by calculating the sum of the volumes of each cylinder. $C_{(1-n)}$ represents the limb circumference (cylinder edge length), and H represents the distance between adjacent limb circumferences (cylinder height).

2.3 Lymphedema Score

Based on the Lymphatic Edema Quality of Life (LYMQOL) score published in 2010 [8], questionnaire assessments were conducted at preoperative and 1-year postoperative follow-up. Scoring was divided into upper limb and lower limb questionnaires. The questionnaire assessed four dimensions: function, appearance, symptoms, and emotional well-being. Each item was rated on a scale from "never" to "very often" (1 to 4), with lower scores indicating less impact of edema on daily life. The final question of the questionnaire assesses overall quality of life based on the patient's subjective perception, scored from 0 to 10 ranging from "poor" to "good." A higher score indicates a better quality of life. The upper limb questionnaire comprised 21 questions: 3 functional questions (12 points), 5 appearance questions (20 points), 6 symptom questions (24 points), 6 emotional questions (24 points), and the overall quality of life score. The lower limb questionnaire comprised 22 questions: 3 functional questions (12 points), 6 appearance questions (24 points), 5 symptom questions (20 points), 6 emotional questions (24 points), and the overall quality of life score.

2.4 Surgical Procedure

All patients undergo preoperative magnetic resonance imaging to assess subcutaneous fat distribution in the limb and ultrasound mapping of superficial veins. The procedure is performed under brachial plexus block or spinal anesthesia. Following successful anesthesia, ICG imaging was used to mark superficial lymphatic vessels. A tourniquet was applied proximally to the limb. Based on preoperative lymphatic vessel localization, a 2–4 cm skin incision was made, dissecting through the epidermis and dermis. Under microscopic visualization, superficial lymphatic vessels and subcutaneous veins were identified within the subdermal fat layer. Intraoperative ICG imaging aided in lymphatic vessel localization. Perform end-to-end or sleeve anastomosis between the distal lymphatic vessel and proximal vein (lymphatic vessel diameter is smaller than the vein). For multiple lymphatic vessels, use the "octopus" anastomosis technique. If performing end-to-side anastomosis between lymphatic vessels and veins, ligate the vein distal to the anastomosis. After completion, assess anastomotic patency via ICG imaging, noting any lymphatic washout or venous backflow.

Postoperative continuous compression therapy with elastic bandages. Wound dressing change on the second postoperative day. Sutures removed at 2 weeks postoperatively. Switch to compression sleeves or compression pants for compression therapy at 4 weeks postoperatively.

2.5 Postoperative Follow-Up

All 42 cases in this group were followed up, with each patient receiving at least one year of follow-up. Follow-up methods included regular outpatient visits, telephone follow-ups, and WeChat follow-ups. Pressure therapy was discontinued one day prior to follow-up. Follow-up assessments included: limb appearance, limb circumference measurement (for limb volume calculation), and LYMQOL score documentation. Surgical efficacy was evaluated at the one-year postoperative milestone.

2.6 Statistical Analysis

For changes in quality of life and volume, a paired t-test was used to examine preoperative and postoperative effects. $P < 0.05$ was considered statistically significant.

3 Result

Surgery was performed on 44 limbs across 42 patients. An average of 8.7 ± 0.8 lymphatic-venous anastomoses were performed per upper limb, and 8.8 ± 1.0 per lower limb. All upper limb lymphedema patients achieved primary wound healing. No complications such as wound infection, fat liquefaction, or lymphatic fistulae occurred. Five subcutaneous fluid collections developed at five sites in two lower limb lymphedema patients. These sites healed secondarily after suture removal without requiring re-suturing. General patient conditions are summarized in Table 1.

Table 1. General patient conditions

	Upper limb	Lower limbs
	N = 16	N = 26
Affected limb Unilateral	16	24
Bilateral	0	2
Onset Time	5.0 ± 5.4	5.1 ± 4.6
Stage		
I	0	0
II	18	24
III	2	4

3.1 Limb Volume

Among the 42 patients, 15 experienced a reduction in limb volume postoperatively, yielding a limb volume improvement rate of 35.7%. Among 16 upper limb lymphedema patients, 8 showed decreased limb volume at 1 year postoperatively compared to preoperative measurements, yielding a limb volume improvement rate of 50.0%. Among 26 lower limb lymphedema patients, 7 showed decreased limb volume at 1 year postoperatively compared to preoperative measurements, yielding a limb volume improvement rate of 26.9%. The improvement rate for upper limbs was significantly higher than that for lower limbs ($P < 0.01$). The mean limb volume decreased from 2519.8 ± 324.9 mL to 2276.6 ± 324.4 mL in the upper limbs and from 6368.1 ± 1764.9 mL to 6063.5 ± 1522.7 mL in the lower limbs (see Table 2).

3.2 Limb Score

The LYMQOL score for the upper limb decreased from 29.7 ± 2.9 preoperatively to 26.6 ± 2.7 ($P < 0.01$). However, analysis of efficacy across different dimensions revealed statistically significant reductions only in the appearance and symptoms dimensions. The patients' overall quality of life (QOL) score increased from 5.6 ± 1.0 to 6.5 ± 1.0

postoperatively. However, two patients (12.5%) experienced a decrease in their overall QOL score and considered the surgery ineffective (see Table 3).

Lower limb LYMQOL scores decreased from 34.1 ± 2.9 preoperatively to 32.6 ± 2.7 ($P < 0.01$). Analysis of efficacy across different dimensions revealed only the symptom dimension showed a statistically significant decrease. The patients' overall quality of life (QOL) score increased from 6.0 ± 1.2 to 6.7 ± 1.0 postoperatively. Among these, 5 patients (19.2%) experienced a decrease in their overall QOL score, reporting that the surgery was ineffective (see Table 4).

Typical cases are shown in Figs. 2 and 3.

Table 2. Comparison of limb volume in the affected extremity before and after surgery

	Improvement Cases at 1 Year Post-Surgery	Preoperative (average volume in ML)	1 year post-surgery (average volume in mL)	P-value
Upper limb (N = 16)	8(50.0%)	2519.8 ± 324.9	2276.6 ± 324.4	<0.01
Lower limbs (N = 26)	7(26.9%)	6368.1 ± 1764.9	6063.5 ± 1522.7	<0.01
P-value	<0.01			

Table 3. Comparison of LYMQOL and overall quality of life in patients with upper limb lymphedema before surgery and one year postoperatively

Upper limb	LYMQOL				Overall Quality of Life Score
	Function (12)	Appearance (20)	Symptoms (24)	Emotion (24)	
Preoperative	5.6 ± 2.8	9.4 ± 4.5	10.9 ± 2.4	8.3 ± 2.4	5.6 ± 1.0
1 year after surgery	5.3 ± 2.7	8.2 ± 3.2	9.4 ± 1.4	7.7 ± 1.6	6.5 ± 1.0
P-value	0.96	< 0.01	< 0.01	0.33	< 0.01

Table 4. Comparison of LYMQOL and overall quality of life in patients with lower limb lymphedema before surgery and one year postoperatively

Lower limb	LYMQOL				Overall Quality of Life Score
	Function (12)	Appearance (20)	Symptoms (24)	Emotion (24)	
Preoperative	5.9 ± 2.4	10.4 ± 4.3	9.9 ± 2.1	8.1 ± 2.2	6.0 ± 1.2
1 year after surgery	5.7 ± 2.1	9.9 ± 3.9	8.6 ± 1.6	8.1 ± 1.8	6.7 ± 1.0

(*continued*)

Table 4. *(continued)*

Lower limb	LYMQOL				Overall Quality of Life Score
	Function (12)	Appearance (20)	Symptoms (24)	Emotion (24)	
P-value	0.63	0.54	< 0.01	0.86	< 0.01

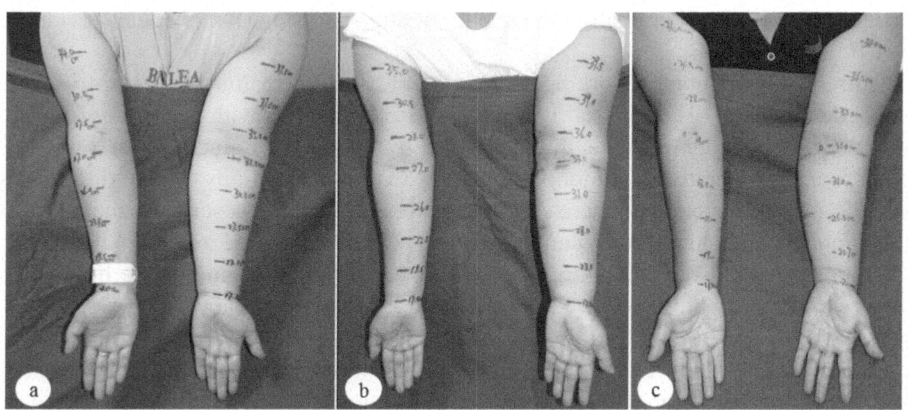

Fig. 2. 46-year-old female, 4 years post-left breast cancer surgery, with 3-year history of left upper limb swelling. (a) Preoperative bilateral upper limb appearance. (b) 6-month postoperative bilateral upper limb appearance, with 0.7% increase in affected limb volume. (c) 1-year postoperative bilateral upper limb appearance, with 8.7% reduction in affected limb volume.

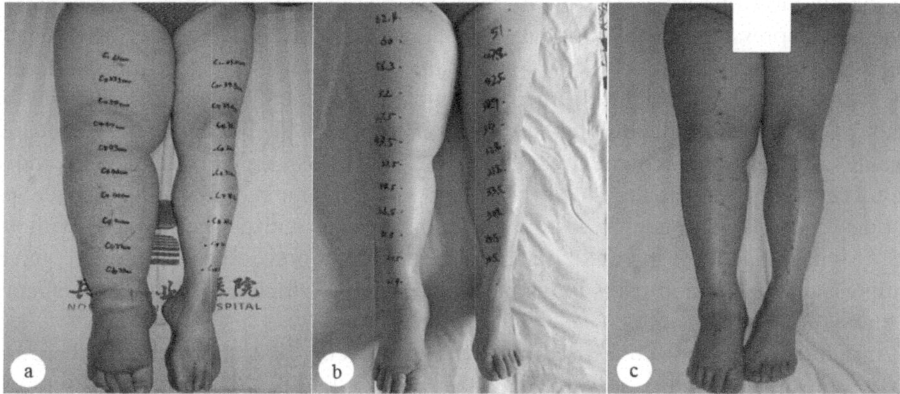

Fig. 3. 71-year-old female, 10 years post-hysterectomy for endometrial cancer, 8 years of right lower limb swelling. (a) Preoperative bilateral lower limb appearance. (b) Bilateral lower limb appearance 6 months post-surgery. (c)Bilateral lower limb appearance 1 year post-surgery, with 10.8% reduction in affected limb volume.

4 Discussion

LVA was first reported by O'Brien in 1977 for the treatment of secondary lymphedema [8]. Numerous articles have documented favorable outcomes in lymphedema patients treated with LVA [2, 9, 10]. It is generally accepted that LVA is primarily effective for early-stage lymphedema. For patients with advanced lymphedema, where functional lymphatic vessels are difficult to identify, LVA is not considered suitable. With advances in microsurgery, the American Society of Plastic Surgeons, based on evidence-based medicine, recognizes that LVA yields better outcomes for patients with early-stage lymphedema. However, LVA remains effective for treating late-stage lymphedema (evidence level 1C) [11].

Currently, few studies report the application of LVA for treating moderate-to-severe lymphedema. Cha [12] described LVA surgery in 42 patients with moderate-to-severe lower limb lymphedema, achieving an average limb volume reduction rate of 15.5% at one year postoperatively. Among 22 patients with bilateral limb volume differences exceeding 20%, this number decreased to 7 postoperatively; however, the exact number of patients experiencing limb volume reduction was not specified in the article. Onoda [13] reported on 28 patients with moderate-to-severe lymphedema in the limbs who underwent LVA combined with comprehensive decongestive therapy. At 6 months postoperatively, 25 patients showed limb volume reduction, with an average volume reduction rate of 13.7%. Hara [14] reported follow-up results at an average of 8.6 months after LVA surgery in 42 patients with moderate-to-severe lower limb lymphedema. The average limb circumference decreased from 221.7 cm preoperatively to 215.9 cm postoperatively. This study included 42 cases of secondary lymphedema in the limbs. Although the average limb volume decreased postoperatively compared to preoperatively, only 34% (15/42) of cases showed a reduction in limb volume. The upper limbs showed a significantly higher reduction rate than the lower limbs, which is lower than the efficacy rates reported in most literature. Possible reasons may be related to postoperative rehabilitation and compression therapy. Compression therapy after LVA treatment is also crucial. Since lymphatic pressure is typically lower than venous pressure [15], compression therapy can increase lymphatic pressure and promote lymphatic drainage. Simultaneously, compression therapy reduces lymph production, alleviates the burden on the lymphatic system, enhances short-term treatment outcomes, and plays a crucial role in maintaining long-term therapeutic effects. However, compression therapy requires full patient cooperation. Many patients undergo postoperative compression with elastic bandages without professional guidance or even external assistance. Furthermore, obtaining properly fitted compression sleeves and pants in China is challenging, which impedes improvements in limb volume post-surgery.

In addition to the objective assessment indicator of changes in limb volume, there are many scores that can objectively evaluate the patient's feelings. The LYMQOL score is specifically designed for patients with limb lymphedema, evaluating treatment outcomes across four dimensions: function, appearance, symptoms, and emotional well-being. Additionally, the final overall quality of life score indirectly reflects patients' subjective satisfaction with treatment. For patients with both upper and lower limb lymphedema, significant improvements in the symptom dimension were observed post-surgery, aligning with patients' commonly reported experiences of "feeling lighter" and "no longer feeling swollen." The LYMQOL score is specifically designed for patients with limb lymphedema, evaluating treatment outcomes across four dimensions: function, appearance, symptoms, and emotional well-being. Additionally, the final overall quality of life score indirectly reflects patients' subjective satisfaction with treatment. For patients with both upper and lower limb lymphedema, significant improvements in the symptoms dimension were observed post-surgery, aligning with patients' frequently reported experiences of "feeling lighter" and "no longer feeling swollen." Cha [12] also noted in the article that 70% of patients experienced improvement in heaviness postoperatively. Patients with upper limb lymphedema also showed improvements in the appearance dimension, which correlates with the higher rate of limb volume reduction after upper limb surgery, indicating superior treatment outcomes for upper limb lymphedema compared to lower limb cases [2, 16]. Despite symptom improvement, functional dimension improvements were not statistically significant, potentially due to patients still needing to wear compression garments postoperatively, which may impact activities of daily living. The overall improvement in quality of life scores indicates that most patients were satisfied with the surgery. However, it remains important to note that if the primary goal is to reduce limb volume, LVA should be chosen with caution. In this case, most patients whose quality of life scores decreased considered the surgery ineffective due to insufficient limb volume reduction. For such patients, liposuction, which offers better limb contouring effects, is recommended to improve limb volume.

Vascularized lymph node transfer (VLNT) is also effective for moderate-to-severe lymphedema. However, compared to VLNT, lymphatic vein anastomosis (LVA) offers advantages such as minimal surgical trauma, faster postoperative recovery, and fewer surgical complications. It is particularly suitable for older patients with poor general health and multiple underlying conditions. Furthermore, the procedure is confined to the affected limb, avoiding damage to lymph nodes in other areas. Literature reports indicate that complications associated with LVA surgery are primarily limited to hypertrophic scarring at the surgical incision site [17]. In this case series, two patients experienced secondary wound healing. Due to the small size of the surgical incision, re-suturing was generally unnecessary. The procedure is safe and well-tolerated by patients.

LVA presents greater surgical challenges in advanced-stage patients due to poor lymphatic vessel quality, with preoperative ICG unable to locate high-quality lymphatics. Preoperative preparation requires magnetic resonance lymphography (MRL) and high-frequency ultrasound-assisted lymphatic vessel localization. During surgery, we observed significantly higher-quality lymphatic vessels at the wrist and ankle joints compared to other sites, consistent with literature reporting superior lymphatic vessel quality near joints [18]. Therefore, when designing preoperative incisions, if ICG fails to clearly identify linear lymphatic vessels, incisions near joints may facilitate easier detection of viable lymphatic vessels.

This case series still has several limitations. The majority of secondary lymphedema cases in patients were triggered by tumor surgery, while other causes such as trauma or infection-related lymphedema were less common. For patients with bilateral lower limb lymphedema, the possibility of primary lymphedema could not be completely ruled out in this cohort. The follow-up period for this cohort was relatively short, as all patients had resumed preoperative levels of activity and work within one year postoperatively. However, continued follow-up is necessary to monitor for potential recurrence of edema.

5 Conclusion

LVA offers limited improvement in limb volume for treating secondary lymphedema in the limbs at the middle to advanced stages. However, it enhances patients' subjective well-being. For patients with high surgical risk and minimal cosmetic concerns, LVA presents a viable surgical option. Nevertheless, LVA must be combined with postoperative compression therapy to achieve optimal therapeutic outcomes. Long-term efficacy remains to be further evaluated.

References

1. Grada, A.A., Phillips, T.J.: Lymphedema: pathophysiology and clinical manifestations. J. Am. Acad. Dermatol. **77**(6), 1009–1020 (2017). https://doi.org/10.1016/j.jaad.2017.03.022
2. Chang, D.W., Suami, H., Skoracki, R.: A prospective analysis of 100 consecutive lymphovenous bypass cases for treatment of extremity lymphedema. Plast. Reconstr. Surg. **132**(5), 1305–1314 (2013). https://doi.org/10.1097/PRS.0b013e3182a4d626
3. Schaverien, M.V., Coroneos, C.J.: Surgical treatment of lymphedema. Plast. Reconstr. Surg. **144**, 738–758 (2019). https://doi.org/10.1097/PRS.0000000000005993
4. Campisi, C., Eretta, C., Pertile, D., et al.: Microsurgery for treatment of peripheral lymphedema: long-term outcome and future perspectives. Microsurgery **27**, 333–338 (2007). https://doi.org/10.1002/micr.20346
5. Yang, J.C., Wu, S.C., Chiang, M.H., et al.: Intraoperative identification and definition of "functional" lymphatic collecting vessels for supermicrosurgical lymphatico-venous anastomosis in treating lymphedema patients. J. Surg. Oncol. **117**(5), 994–1000 (2018). https://doi.org/10.1002/jso.25014
6. Executive Committee of the International Society of Lymphology.: The diagnosis and treatment of peripheral Lymphedema: 2016 consensus document of the international society of lymphology. Lymphology **49**(4), 170–184 (2016)
7. Keeley, V., Crooks, S., Locke, J., et al.: A quality of life measure for limb lymphoedema (LYMQOL). J Lymphoedema. **5**, 26–37 (2010)
8. O'Brien, B.M., Sykes, P., Threlfall, G.N., Browning, F.S.: Microlymphaticovenous anastomoses for obstructive lymphedema. Plast. Reconstr. Surg. **60**(2), 197–211 (1977). https://doi.org/10.1097/00006534-197708000-00006
9. Mihara, M., Hara, H., Tange, S., et al.: Multisite Lymphaticovenular bypass using super microsurgery technique for lymphedema management in lower lymphedema cases. Plast. Reconstr. Surg. **138**(1), 262–272 (2016). https://doi.org/10.1097/PRS.0000000000002254
10. Seki, Y., Yamamoto, T., Yoshimatsu, H., et al.: The superior-edge-of-the-knee incision method in lymphaticovenular anastomosis for lower extremity Lymphedema. Plast. Reconstr. Surg. **136**(5), 665e–675e (2015). https://doi.org/10.1097/PRS.0000000000001715
11. Garza, R.M., Wong, D., Chang, D.W.: Optimizing outcomes in lymphedema reconstruction. Plast. Reconstr. Surg. **152**(6), 1131e–1142e (2023). https://doi.org/10.1097/PRS.0000000000010965
12. Cha, H.G., Oh, T.M., Cho, M.J., et al.: Changing the paradigm: lymphovenous anastomosis in advanced stage lower extremity lymphedema. Plast. Reconstr. Surg. **147**(1), 199–207 (2021). https://doi.org/10.1097/PRS.0000000000007507

13. Onoda, S., Nishimon, K.: The utility of surgical and conservative combination therapy for advanced stage lymphedema. J. Vasc. Surg. Venous Lymphat. Disord. **9**(1), 234–241 (2021). https://doi.org/10.1016/j.jvsv.2020.05.007
14. Hara, H., Mihara, M.: Lymphaticovenous anastomosis for advanced-stage lower limb lymphedema. Microsurgery **41**(2), 140–145 (2021). https://doi.org/10.1002/micr.30689
15. Krylov, V.S., Milanov, N.O., Abalmasov, K.G., et al.: Reconstructive microsurgery in treatment of lymphoedema in extremities. Int. Angiol. **4**(2), 171–175 (1985)
16. Qiu, S.S., Pruimboom, T., Cornelissen, A.J.M., et al.: Outcomes following lymphaticovenous anastomosis (LVA) for 100 cases of lymphedema: results over 24-months follow-up. Breast Cancer Res. Treat. **184**(1), 173–183 (2020). https://doi.org/10.1007/s10549-020-05839-4
17. Cornelissen, A.J.M., Kool, M., Lopez Penha, T.R., et al.: Lymphatico-venous anastomosis as treatment for breast cancer-related lymphedema: a prospective study on quality of life. Breast Cancer Res. Treat. **163**(2), 281–286 (2017). https://doi.org/10.1007/s10549-017-4180-1
18. Suzuki, Y., Sakuma, H., Yamazaki, S.: Comparison of patency rates of lymphaticovenous anastomoses at different sites for lower extremity lymphedema. J. Vasc. Surg. Venous Lymphat. Disord. **7**(2), 222–227 (2019). https://doi.org/10.1016/j.jvsv.2018.10.022

FES in Motor Function Reconstruction for Spinal Cord Injury: A Review

Hao Zeng(✉) and Yaoxing Hu

Department of Indurstry and Engineering, School of Mechanical Engineering, Northwestern Polytechnical University, Xi'an, Shaanxi 710072, People's Republic of China
haozeng@mail.nwpu.edu.cn

Abstract. Spinal cord injury (SCI) leads to motor, sensory and other functional disorders in patients, making it crucial to find effective methods for motor function recovery. As an emerging technology, functional electrical stimulation (FES) improves motor function by activating damaged neural pathways to promote muscle contraction. This paper reviews its research progress, including: in terms of mechanism, it uses low-frequency pulse current to activate α motor neurons to trigger muscle contraction, requiring the integrity of the lower motor neuron pathway; there are various technical types such as transcutaneous, implantable, wireless wearable ones, each with its own advantages and disadvantages; in application, it can restore grasping and other movements in the upper limbs and assist standing and walking in the lower limbs, but existing systems mostly rely on mechanical assistance, having portability and cost issues; current challenges include electrode performance, parameter optimization, muscle fatigue, etc.; future research hotspots focus on the combination with BCI, VR/AR, the development of new electrodes and intelligent systems to achieve more precise and efficient neural function reconstruction.

Keywords: Spinal cord injury · Functional electrical stimulation (FES) · Motor function reconstruction

1 Introduction

Spinal cord injury (SCI) represents a severe form of central nervous system trauma typically resulting from causes such as traffic accidents, occupational injuries, violent trauma, or underlying spinal pathologies [1]. This condition induces dysfunction in motor, sensory, and autonomic systems below the level of the lesion. SCI imposes profound physiological and psychological distress on affected individuals, concurrently generating substantial burdens for families and society. Consequently, the exploration of effective strategies to promote the recovery of motor function in SCI patients remains a major research focus within the fields of neuroscience and rehabilitation medicine.

Current therapeutic interventions for SCI encompass surgical management, pharmacological treatment, and rehabilitative approaches [2]. However, these conventional modalities rarely achieve complete restoration of motor function to pre-injury levels. Functional electrical stimulation (FES) is an emerging therapeutic technique that

S. S. Ge et al. (Eds.): ICSR + BioMed 2025, LNAI 16435, pp. 192–203, 2026.
https://doi.org/10.1007/978-981-95-7538-1_17

employs externally administered electrical currents to activate lesioned neural pathways in SCI patients. By eliciting action potentials within preserved neural circuits distal to the injury site, FES evokes controlled muscle contractions, thereby facilitating functional movement and enhancing motor recovery [3]. In recent years, significant advancements have been made in applying FES for motor function restoration in SCI [4], offering renewed hope for patient rehabilitation. Hence, a comprehensive review of research progress in FES-mediated motor function reconstruction holds significant clinical implications for improving SCI management.

2 The Mechanism and Technology Development of FES

Functional Electrical Stimulation (FES), a specialized form of Neuromuscular Electrical Stimulation (NMES) [5], shares fundamental physiological mechanisms with its parent modality. Both techniques utilize low-frequency pulsed currents (typically ranging from 20 to 100 Hz) to depolarize the axonal membranes of α-motor neurons innervating the target musculature. This depolarization triggers action potentials that propagate along the motor axons. Upon reaching the neuromuscular junction, these potentials are transmitted to the muscle fibers, resulting in controlled muscle contraction (as schematically illustrated in Fig. 1).The efficacy of the elicited neuromuscular response is critically determined by specific electrical stimulation parameters, including stimulation frequency, intensity, pulse width, and waveform. Strategic manipulation of these parameters enables selective recruitment of distinct populations of nerve fibers and muscle fiber types. This selective recruitment capability underlies the potential of FES/NMES to generate targeted motor functions.

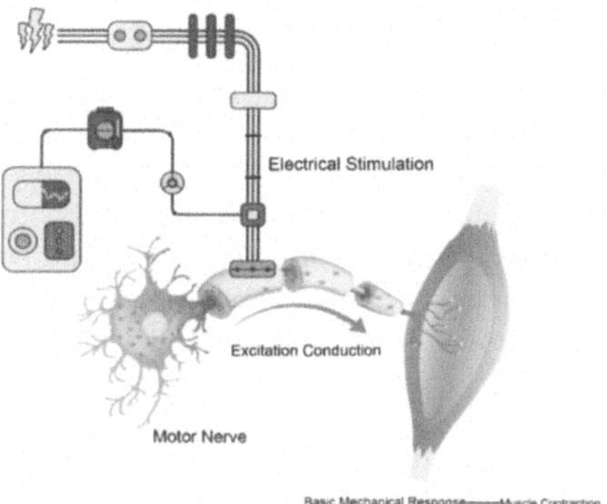

Fig. 1. Fundamental principles of FES

However, the clinical application of Functional Electrical Stimulation (FES) is contingent upon a critical anatomical prerequisite [6]: the axonal pathways from spinal cord ventral horn motor neurons to the target muscles, including the neuromuscular junctions, must retain structural and functional integrity. This integrity within the lower motor neuron pathway is imperative for translating electrical stimuli into functional movements.

Given this intact neural substrate, FES can dynamically drive coordinated contractions of specific muscle groups in real-time, thereby enabling targeted goal-oriented actions such as hand grasp [7] or ankle dorsiflexion during the gait cycle [8].

FES technology has evolved significantly, resulting in several distinct classes primarily categorized by principle and application: transcutaneous FES [9], implanted FES [10], closed-loop FES [11], multimodal integration approaches [12] and wireless wearable FES [13], as shown in Fig. 2.

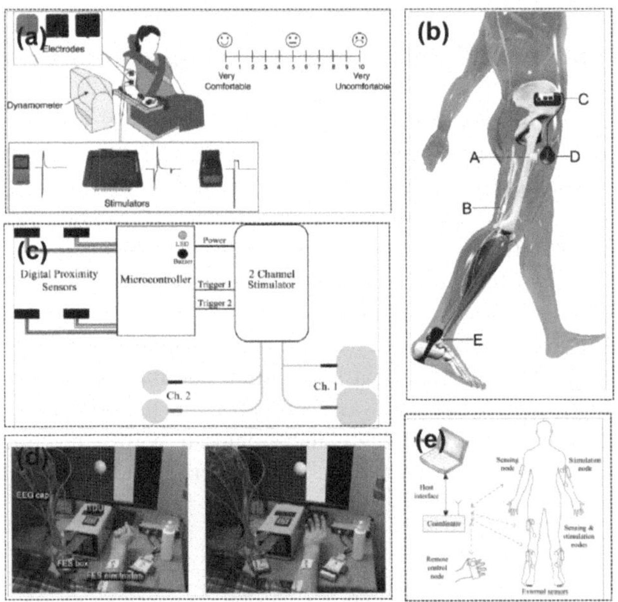

Fig. 2. (a) Transcutaneous FES. Reproduced with permission from [9]. Copyright 2024, The Author(s); CC BY4.0. (b) implanted FES. Reproduced with permission from [10]. Copyright 2019, The Author(s); CC BY4.0. (c) closed-loop FES. Reproduced with permission from [11]. Copyright 2019, CC BY 4.0. (d) multimodal integration approaches. Reproduced with permission from [12]. Copyright 2022 Remsik, van Kan, Gloe, Gjini, Williams, Nair, Caldera, Williams and Prabhakaran; CC BY 4.0. (e) wireless wearable FES. Reproduced with permission from [13]. Copyright 2012, Jovičić et al.; licensee BioMed Central Ltd; CC BY 4.0.

Transcutaneous FES delivers current non-invasively via surface electrodes, offering flexibility in stimulating diverse muscle groups [14]. However, stimulation efficacy is limited by cutaneous impedance, restricting achievable neural activation intensity. Prolonged application frequently induces cutaneous discomfort.

Implanted FES requires surgical electrode placement for direct stimulation of nerves or deep musculature [15]. It provides superior stimulation precision and stability. Nevertheless, this approach entails inherent surgical risks, necessitates long-term device maintenance, and incurs substantial costs [16].

Wireless Wearable FES incorporates flexible electronics for lightweight, integrated designs [17]. Key limitations include finite battery longevity and susceptibility to motion artifact interference, necessitating further optimization of materials and signal processing algorithms.

Closed-loop FES utilizes real-time feedback (e.g., electromyographic (EMG) signals, force sensors) to dynamically adjust stimulation parameters, establishing an adaptive control system [18]. This approach optimizes training by adapting to muscle state, making it especially valuable for complex motor function restoration. Challenges involve complex control algorithms, dependency on extensive clinical datasets, and higher equipment costs.

Multimodal Integration combines FES with complementary neuromodulation techniques. For instance, Brain-Computer Interface (BCI)-FES systems offer potential for complete SCI patients [19]; Transcranial Magnetic Stimulation (TMS) combined with FES can enhance movement synchronization [20]; Optogenetics integrated with FES [21], while still in the preclinical research stage, represents a novel direction for precise neural modulation.

Selection of the optimal FES modality requires comprehensive consideration of the patient's injury level, functional goals, economic constraints, and therapeutic expectations.

3 Applications of FES

3.1 Upper Limb Motor Function Reconstruction

Upper limb dysfunction following spinal cord injury (SCI) critically impairs patient independence by compromising essential activities of daily living (ADLs). Functional electrical stimulation (FES) plays a pivotal role in restoring upper extremity motor function in this population. Through targeted stimulation of specific muscle groups, FES facilitates elbow flexion/extension and wrist articulation when optimized stimulation parameters are applied. This intervention effectively restores fundamental movements (e.g., grasp and release) and enhances manual dexterity.

Seminal work by Freeman et al. [22] (early 2000s) pioneered the integration of FES with robotic technology for upper limb rehabilitation in paralysis. However, the substantial spatial requirements of the complex mechanical assembly substantially compromised system portability.

Addressing control limitations, Dalla Gasperina et al. [23] proposed a hybrid FES-robotic cooperative control framework for upper limb rehabilitation (Fig. 3). This system implemented a synergistic controller to optimally distribute torque generation between the robotic actuator and FES-activated musculature. This approach successfully achieved precise trajectory tracking through integrated robotic and FES actuation.Clinically, Tefertiller et al. [24] evaluated non-invasive spinal electrical stimulation combined with rehabilitation for chronic tetraplegia. These outcomes demonstrate significant improvement in arm and hand function with electrical stimulation, absent serious treatment-related adverse events, providing empirical evidence for optimizing FES parameter configuration during rehabilitation training.

Concurrently, advancements in distal upper limb rehabilitation have emerged. Usman et al. [25] developed a high-density electrode array FES system to enhance selective muscle recruitment during hand rehabilitation. Their system incorporated an automated calibration algorithm, utilizing prior knowledge from manual stimulation to determine optimal electrode configurations and stimulation parameters for individuated finger control. However, owing to current technological constraints, this implementation achieves isolated finger grasp but lacks control capabilities for proximal upper limb segments.

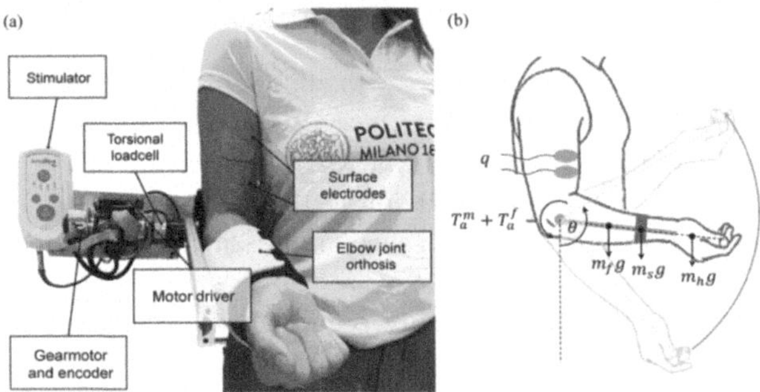

Fig. 3. Hybrid system integrating FES with robotic assistance. Reproduced with permission from [23]. Copyright 2024, CC BY 4.0.

3.2 Lower Limb Motor Function Reconstruction

Lower limb dysfunction following spinal cord injury (SCI) profoundly compromises patients' quality of life and capacity for independent living. Functional Electrical Stimulation (FES) is a therapeutic modality that utilizes controlled electrical currents to stimulate neuromuscular tissues, eliciting muscle contractions to substitute or correct impaired limb functions. During gait restoration protocols, FES systems can be programmed to deliver timed low-frequency pulsed stimuli based on the physiological gait sequence – a complex pattern involving coordinated activation across multiple lower limb joints and muscle groups [26]. This neuromodulation strategy aims to mimic natural ambulation patterns. By facilitating multi-joint movements through coordinated multi-muscle stimulation, this approach promotes more effective motor functional recovery.

Integrating FES with cycle ergometer training enables electrically induced lower limb muscle contractions to drive the pedaling motion [27]. This combined approach effectively enhances lower extremity muscle strength while simultaneously improving locomotor function and coordination. Research into the application of FES-assisted cycle ergometry for SCI rehabilitation is expanding. Watanabe et al. [28] developed an integrated FES and pedal-powered wheelchair system for lower limb rehabilitation. While capable of providing effective lower limb exercise assistance, this system lacked integration of the patient's volitional motor intent and real-time movement state into its control paradigm. This limitation resulted in insufficient guidance for active patient participation, constraining both personalization and interactivity during training. Addressing these shortcomings, Chen et al. [29] proposed a novel control strategy for lower limb rehabilitation robots by integrating FES with impedance control (Fig. 4). This strategy not only significantly increased active patient engagement but also markedly enhanced training efficiency. This approach provides a valuable framework for designing control strategies for lower limb rehabilitation robotics. Beyond FES-robotic integration, Farris et al. [30] developed a powered lower limb orthosis aimed at ambulation assistance for SCI patients. The orthosis successfully enabled repetitive gait patterns, demonstrating joint trajectories comparable to unimpaired gait. The study also highlighted the device's merits in lightweight, modular design while identifying future requirements for sensor-based automated gait phase transition capabilities.

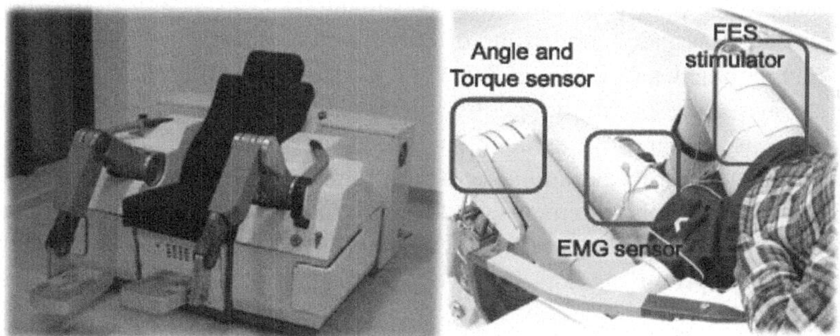

Fig. 4. The prototype of iLeg lower limb rehabilitation robot. Reproduced with permission from [29]. Copyright 2014, Chen et al.; licensee Springer; CC BY 4.0.

Most existing FES-based lower limb rehabilitation systems rely on mechanically assistive structures (e.g., wheelchair frames, robotic exoskeletons, orthotic braces). This dependence inherently results in cumbersome designs with poor portability. Consequently, substantial challenges remain for the clinical adoption and widespread implementation of such FES-assisted lower limb rehabilitation platforms.

4 Current Challenges

The clinical efficacy of Functional Electrical Stimulation (FES) systems remains constrained by significant challenges pertaining to core component performance, parameter optimization, and tissue response dynamics [31].

Electrode performance fundamentally dictates stimulation precision and therapeutic stability. Electrode-related issues constitute a primary bottleneck limiting overall system efficacy in current clinical practice. Dynamic instability of the electrode-tissue interface impedance predisposes to unintended fluctuations in stimulation intensity [32]. This phenomenon inherently compromises temporal consistency of therapeutic outcomes and hinders the standardization of treatment protocols. Furthermore, surface electrodes are prone to displacement during patient movement, resulting in misalignment of the stimulation target away from the intended muscle groups and consequent failure to effectively recruit the requisite motor units [33]. Im Conversely planted electrodes present biocompatibility concerns [34].Their long-term presence risks inducing localized inflammatory tissue responses. Collectively, these issues contribute to reduced electrode longevity and significantly diminished patient comfort and compliance.

Parameter Optimization Complexity: Achieving precise, individualized control of FES stimulation parameters represents a core prerequisite for personalized therapy [35].

However, the inherent complexity of parameter optimization substantially impedes clinical translation. FES parameters require continuous, patient-specific adjustment based on individual physiological characteristics to simultaneously ensure therapeutic safety and maximize efficacy [36]. A critical barrier is the current absence of standardized, objective methodologies for precise parameter optimization and quantitative outcome assessment in clinical settings.

Muscle Fatigue and Adaptation: Prolonged FES application induces muscle fatigue under sustained electrical stimulation [37]. Key manifestations include diminished muscle force production and degraded motor coordination, directly attenuating the effectiveness of functional motor restoration [38]. Concurrently, muscle tissue undergoes adaptive changes in response to repetitive electrical stimuli. This neuroplastic adaptation manifests as a progressive reduction in muscle activation efficiency under identical stimulation parameters, necessitating frequent parameter adjustments to maintain desired therapeutic effects. This requirement complicates clinical management and increases the risk of muscle over-activation or under-activation due to suboptimal parameter modulation, further compromising both the safety profile and the sustained efficacy of FES interventions.

5 Research Foci and Future Directions for FES

The integration of Functional Electrical Stimulation (FES) with other advanced technologies represents a pivotal strategy for expanding its therapeutic scope and enhancing rehabilitation efficacy. The convergence of FES with Brain-Computer Interface (BCI) technology exhibits particular innovation [39]. This synergistic interaction enables more naturalistic and precise motor control, affording SCI patients movement experiences approximating physiological normality. Empirical evidence supports the feasibility of this integrated paradigm. For instance, research teams have developed FES-BCI integrated systems demonstrating successful volitional modulation of FES devices via decoded brain signals, effectively ameliorating motor dysfunction in both upper and lower extremities [40].

Beyond BCI, the integration of FES with Virtual Reality (VR) or Augmented Reality (AR) technologies offers distinct advantages [41]. VR/AR platforms generate immersive rehabilitation environments, simulating functional tasks within ecologically valid contexts to significantly enhance patient engagement and motivation [42]. Concurrently, FES systems can dynamically adjust stimulation parameters based on real-time kinematic feedback derived from the virtual scenario, establishing a closed-loop "perception-feedback-modulation" training paradigm. This integration thereby optimizes the specificity and effectiveness of therapeuticizes the specificity and effectiveness of therapeutic interventions.

Within robotic-assisted rehabilitation, FES coupling with exoskeletons manifests diverse cooperative modalities, yielding highly efficient assistive solutions for SCI [43]. Consider the integration of exoskeletal robotics with FES [44]: The exoskeleton provides stable mechanical support and precise joint trajectory guidance, while FES synchronously elicits active contractions within targeted musculature. This complementary hybrid actuation model (passive mechanical assistance + active neuromuscular force generation) simultaneously reduces locomotor burden and enhances muscle strength and coordination through active contraction training.

Addressing limitations of conventional electrodes—such as inadequate conductivity, suboptimal biocompatibility, and propensity for local tissue complications—researchers are pursuing multi-faceted approaches. Innovations include bio-based hydrogel electrodes exhibiting superior conductivity, excellent biocompatibility, and mechanical compliance [45]. These conformal interfaces maintain secure skin contact, minimizing motion-induced interfacial impedance fluctuations. Alternative strategies employ Micro-Electro-Mechanical Systems (MEMS) technology to fabricate miniaturized, high-precision implantable microelectrode arrays [46]. By reducing electrode dimensions and optimizing array configurations, these systems achieve precise stimulation of target neural or muscular substrates, concurrently minimizing surgical invasiveness and enhancing stimulation accuracy and clinical safety.

The rapid advancement of intelligent algorithms is a key driver propelling FES towards personalized and precision rehabilitation. Researchers leverage artificial intelligence (AI) [47] and machine learning (ML) [48] to develop intelligent stimulation parameter modulation systems. These systems autonomously optimize stimulation parameters based on real-time physiological state and kinematic feedback, thereby enhancing therapeutic precision and efficacy. Such intelligent systems facilitate fully personalized, adaptive rehabilitation protocols, maximizing therapeutic outcomes and patient comfort.

6 Conclusion

Functional Electrical Stimulation (FES) demonstrates considerable translational promise for motor function restoration in individuals with spinal cord injury (SCI), primarily through targeted neuromuscular pathway activation to facilitate limb movement. Diverse FES modalities offer adaptable solutions for heterogeneous patient needs, with documented efficacy in restoring critical functions including upper limb grasping and ambulatory capacity. However, persistent challenges—including electrode performance instability, difficulties in achieving personalized parameter optimization, and muscle fatigue/adaptation dynamic—currently constrain widespread clinical adoption and limit therapeutic optimization.

Future research necessitates dedicated focus on interdisciplinary integration. Advancing the synergistic integration of FES with emergent technologies such as Brain-Computer Interfaces (BCI) and Virtual/Augmented Reality (VR/AR) is paramount. Concurrently, development priorities must encompass novel electrode materials with enhanced biocompatibility and intelligent, adaptive closed-loop systems. These innovations are essential to realize next-generation FES platforms capable of precise neural interfacing and truly personalized rehabilitation paradigms, ultimately translating into sustained functional recovery and enhanced independence in activities of daily living (ADL) for the SCI population.

Acknowledgments. No specific acknowledgments are required for this work.

Disclosure of Interests. The authors have no competing interests to declare that are relevant to the content of this article.

References

1. Zhang, D., Ren, Y., Gui, K., Jia, J., Xu, W.: Cooperative control for a hybrid rehabilitation system combining functional electrical stimulation and robotic exoskeleton. Front. Neurosci. **11**, (2017). https://doi.org/10.3389/fnins.2017.00725
2. Rehabilitative therapies after spinal cord injury. J. Neurotrauma. https://doi.org/10.1089/neu.2006.23.560. Last accessed 17 Sept 2025
3. Donaldson, N., Perkins, T., Fitzwater, R., Wood, D.E., Middleton, F.: FES cycling may promote recovery of leg function after incomplete spinal cord injury. Spinal Cord. **38**, 680–682 (2000). https://doi.org/10.1038/sj.sc.3101072
4. Functional electrical stimulation therapy for restoration of motor function after spinal cord injury and stroke: a review. BioMed. Eng. OnLine, https://doi.org/10.1186/s12938-020-00773-4. Last accessed 17 Sept 2025
5. Millis, D., Levine, D.: Canine Rehabilitation and Physical Therapy. Elsevier Health Sciences (2013)
6. Frontiers | Electrical stimulation for the treatment of spinal cord injuries: A review of the cellular and molecular mechanisms that drive functional improvements. https://doi.org/10.3389/fncel.2023.1095259/full. Last accessed 17 Sept 2025
7. Restoration of reaching and grasping movements through brain-controlled muscle stimulation in a person with tetraplegia: a proof-of-concept demonstration—The Lancet. https://www.thelancet.com/journals/lancet/article/PIIS0140-6736(17)30601-3/abstract?rss=yes=. Last accessed 17 Sept 2025
8. Zhang, L., et al.: Micro-nano hybrid-structured conductive film with ultrawide range pressure-sensitivity and bioelectrical acquirability for ubiquitous wearable applications. Appl. Mater. Today **20**, 100651 (2020). https://doi.org/10.1016/j.apmt.2020.100651
9. Marquez-Chin, M., Saadatnia, Z., Sun, Y.-C., Naguib, H.E., Popovic, M.R.: A dry polymer nanocomposite transcutaneous electrode for functional electrical stimulation. Biomed. Eng. OnLine. **23**, 10 (2024). https://doi.org/10.1186/s12938-024-01200-8
10. Berenpas, F., Weerdesteyn, V., Geurts, A.C., van Alfen, N.: Long-term use of implanted peroneal functional electrical stimulation for stroke-affected gait: the effects on muscle and motor nerve. J. NeuroEngineering Rehabil. **16**, 86 (2019). https://doi.org/10.1186/s12984-019-0556-2
11. Hodkin, E.F., et al.: Automated FES for upper limb rehabilitation following stroke and spinal cord injury. IEEE Trans. Neural Syst. Rehabil. Eng. **26**, 1067–1074 (2018). https://doi.org/10.1109/TNSRE.2018.2816238
12. Remsik, A.B., van Kan, P.L.E., Gloe, S., Gjini, K., Williams, L., Nair, V., Caldera, K., Williams, J.C., Prabhakaran, V.: BCI-FES with multimodal feedback for motor recovery poststroke. Front. Hum. Neurosci. **16**, (2022). https://doi.org/10.3389/fnhum.2022.725715
13. Jovičić, N.S., Saranovac, L.V., Popović, D.B.: Wireless distributed functional electrical stimulation system. J. NeuroEngineering Rehabil. **9**, 54 (2012). https://doi.org/10.1186/1743-0003-9-54
14. Chaikho, L., Clark, E., Raison, M.: Transcutaneous functional electrical stimulation controlled by a system of sensors for the lower limbs: a systematic review. Sensors. **22**, 9812 (2022). https://doi.org/10.3390/s22249812
15. Pellot-Cestero, J.E., et al.: Implanted electrodes for functional electrical stimulation to restore upper and lower extremity function: history and future directions. Neurosurgery **93**, 965 (2023). https://doi.org/10.1227/neu.0000000000002561
16. Popović, D.B.: Advances in functional electrical stimulation (FES). J. Electromyogr. Kinesiol. **24**, 795–802 (2014). https://doi.org/10.1016/j.jelekin.2014.09.008

17. Wang, H.-P., Guo, A.-W., Bi, Z.-Y., Zhou, Y.-X., Wang, Z.-G., Lu, X.-Y.: A novel distributed functional electrical stimulation and assessment system for hand movements using wearable technology. In: 2016 IEEE Biomedical Circuits and Systems Conference (BioCAS), pp. 74–77 (2016). https://doi.org/10.1109/BioCAS.2016.7833728
18. Real-time closed-loop functional electrical stimulation control of muscle activation with evoked electromyography feedback for spinal cord injured patients. Int. J. Neural Syst. https://doi.org/10.1142/S0129065717500630. Last accessed 17 Sept 2025
19. Müller-Putz, G., Leeb, R., Tangermann, M., Höhne, J., Kübler, A., Cincotti, F., Mattia, D., Rupp, R., Müller, K.-R., Millán, J. del R.: Towards noninvasive hybrid brain–computer interfaces: framework, practice, clinical application, and beyond. Proc. IEEE. **103**, 926–943 (2015). https://doi.org/10.1109/JPROC.2015.2411333
20. Salazar, A.P., Cimolin, V., Schifino, G.P., Rech, K.D., Marchese, R.R., Pagnussat, A.S.: Bicephalic transcranial direct current stimulation combined with functional electrical stimulation for upper-limb stroke rehabilitation: a double-blind randomized controlled trial. Ann. Phys. Rehabil. Med. **63**, 4–11 (2020). https://doi.org/10.1016/j.rehab.2019.05.004
21. Herrera-Arcos, G., Song, H., Yeon, S.H., Ghenand, O., Gutierrez-Arango, S., Sinha, S., Herr, H.: Closed-loop optogenetic neuromodulation enables high-fidelity fatigue-resistant muscle control. Sci. Robot. **9**, eadi8995 (2024). https://doi.org/10.1126/scirobotics.adi8995
22. Freeman, C.T., Hughes, A.-M., Burridge, J.H., Chappell, P.H., Lewin, P.L., Rogers, E.: A robotic workstation for stroke rehabilitation of the upper extremity using FES. Med. Eng. Phys. **31**, 364–373 (2009). https://doi.org/10.1016/j.medengphy.2008.05.008
23. Dalla Gasperina, S., Ferrari, F., Gandolla, M., Pedrocchi, A., Ambrosini, E.: Hybrid cooperative control of functional electrical stimulation and robot assistance for upper extremity rehabilitation. IEEE Trans. Biomed. Eng. **71**, 2642–2650 (2024). https://doi.org/10.1109/TBME.2024.3384939
24. Tefertiller, C., Trumbower, R., Morse, L., van Nes, I., Kalsi-Ryan, S., Purcell, M., Janssen, T., Krassioukov, A., Zhao, K., Guest, J., Marino, R., Murray, L., Wecht, J., Rieger, M., Pradarelli, J., Suggitt, J., Turner, A., Gelenitis, K., D'Amico, J., Moritz, C., Field-Fote, E.: Transcutaneous spinal cord stimulation (ARC-EX Therapy) is safe and effective at improving upper extremity function following spinal cord injury (P7-11.001). Neurology. **102**, 5309 (2024). https://doi.org/10.1212/WNL.0000000000205724
25. Usman, H., Zhou, Y., Metcalfe, B., Zhang, D.: A functional electrical stimulation system of high-density electrodes with auto-calibration for optimal selectivity. IEEE Sens. J. **20**, 8833–8843 (2020). https://doi.org/10.1109/JSEN.2020.2983004
26. Kralj, A.R., Bajd, T., Munih, M., Turk, R.: FES gait restoration and balance control in spinal cordinjured patients. In: Allum, J.H.J., Allum-Mecklenburg, D.J., Harris, F.P., and Probst, R. (eds.) Progress in Brain Research, Chap. 34, pp. 387–396. Elsevier (1993). https://doi.org/10.1016/S0079-6123(08)62298-0
27. Ambrosini, E., Ferrante, S., Ferrigno, G., Molteni, F., Pedrocchi, A.: Cycling induced by electrical stimulation improves muscle activation and symmetry during pedaling in hemiparetic patients. IEEE Trans. Neural Syst. Rehabil. Eng. **20**, 320–330 (2012). https://doi.org/10.1109/TNSRE.2012.2191574
28. Watanabe, T., Tadano, T.: Experimental tests of a prototype of IMU-based closed-loop fuzzy control system for mobile FES cycling with Pedaling wheelchair. IEICE Trans. Inf. E101-D, 1906–1914 (2018). https://doi.org/10.1587/transinf.2017EDP7299
29. Chen, Y., Hu, J., Peng, L., Hou, Z.: The FES-assisted control for a lower limb rehabilitation robot: simulation and experiment. Robot. Biomim. **1**, 2 (2014). https://doi.org/10.1186/s40638-014-0002-7
30. Farris, R.J., Quintero, H.A., Goldfarb, M.: Preliminary evaluation of a powered lower limb orthosis to aid walking in paraplegic individuals. IEEE Trans. Neural Syst. Rehabil. Eng. **19**, 652–659 (2011). https://doi.org/10.1109/TNSRE.2011.2163083

31. Denervated Muscles in Humans: Limitations and Problems of Currently Used Functional Electrical Stimulation Training Protocols – Kern—2002—Artificial Organs—Wiley Online Library. https://doi.org/10.1046/j.1525-1594.2002.06933.x. Last accessed 17 Sept 2025
32. Malešević, N.M., et al.: A multi-pad electrode based functional electrical stimulation system for restoration of grasp. J. NeuroEngineering Rehabil. **9**, 66 (2012). https://doi.org/10.1186/1743-0003-9-66
33. Yang, S., et al.: Stretchable surface electromyography electrode array patch for tendon location and muscle injury prevention. Nat. Commun. **14**, 6494 (2023). https://doi.org/10.1038/s41467-023-42149-x
34. Plenk, H., Jr.: The role of materials biocompatibility for functional electrical stimulation applications. Artif. Organs **35**, 237–241 (2011). https://doi.org/10.1111/j.1525-1594.2011.01221.x
35. Gil-Castillo, J., Herrera-Valenzuela, D., Torricelli, D., Gil-Agudo, Á., Opisso, E., Vidal, J., Font-Llagunes, J.M., del-Ama, A.J., Moreno, J.C.: A new modular neuroprosthesis suitable for hybrid FES-robot applications and tailored assistance. J. NeuroEng. Rehabil. **21**, 153 (2024). https://doi.org/10.1186/s12984-024-01450-6
36. Co, K., Begon, M., Bailly, F., Moissenet, F.: Optimal control driven functional electrical stimulation: A scoping review. http://arxiv.org/abs/2508.02899 (2025). https://doi.org/10.48550/arXiv.2508.02899
37. Thrasher, A., Graham, G.M., Popovic, M.R.: Reducing muscle fatigue due to functional electrical stimulation using random modulation of stimulation parameters. Artif. Organs **29**, 453–458 (2005). https://doi.org/10.1111/j.1525-1594.2005.29076.x
38. Sheng, Z., Iyer, A., Sun, Z., Kim, K., Sharma, N.: A hybrid knee exoskeleton using real-time ultrasound-based muscle fatigue assessment. IEEEASME Trans. Mechatron. **27**, 1854–1862 (2022). https://doi.org/10.1109/TMECH.2022.3171086
39. Brain computer interface training with motor imagery and functional electrical stimulation for patients with severe upper limb paresis after stroke: a randomized controlled pilot trial. J. NeuroEng. Rehabil. https://doi.org/10.1186/s12984-024-01304-1. Last accessed 2025
40. Brain-computer interface controlled functional electrical stimulation: evaluation with healthy subjects and spinal cord injury patients | IEEE J. Mag. | IEEE Xplore. https://ieeexplore.ieee.org/abstract/document/9764729. Last accessed 17 Sept 2025
41. Voinescu, A., Sui, J., Stanton Fraser, D.: Virtual reality in neurorehabilitation: an umbrella review of meta-analyses. J. Clin. Med. **10**, 1478 (2021). https://doi.org/10.3390/jcm10071478
42. Virtual/Augmented Reality for Rehabilitation Applications Using Electromyography as Control/Biofeedback: Systematic Literature Review. https://www.mdpi.com/2079-9292/11/14/2271. Last accessed 17 Sept 2025
43. Bersch, I., Alberty, M., Fridén, J.: Robot-assisted training with functional electrical stimulation enhances lower extremity function after spinal cord injury. Artif. Organs **46**, 2009–2014 (2022). https://doi.org/10.1111/aor.14386
44. del-Ama, A.J., Gil-Agudo, Á., Pons, J.L., Moreno, J.C.: Hybrid FES-robot cooperative control of ambulatory gait rehabilitation exoskeleton. J. NeuroEng. Rehabil. **11**, 27 (2014). https://doi.org/10.1186/1743-0003-11-27
45. Chen, J.X.M., et al.: Conductive bio-based hydrogel for wearable electrodes via direct ink writing on skin. Adv. Funct. Mater. **34**, 2403721 (2024). https://doi.org/10.1002/adfm.202403721
46. Xu, Q., et al.: An efficient MEMS microelectrode array with reliable interelectrode insulation processes for in vivo neural recording. Small **21**, 2407950 (2025). https://doi.org/10.1002/smll.202407950
47. Jafari, E., Metani, A., Moreau, B., Nollot, R., Feppon, N., Vergnes-Blanquer, L., Di Marco, J., Popović Maneski, L.: AI-Powered FES-Walking for gait rehabilitation after stroke. In: IFFESS 2024 International Conference 1st 3rd September 2024 Bath U.K. (2024)

48. Kostov, A., Andrews, B.J., Popovic, D.B., Stein, R.B., Armstrong, W.W.: Machine learning in control of functional electrical stimulation systems for locomotion. IEEE Trans. Biomed. Eng. **42**, 541–551 (1995). https://doi.org/10.1109/10.387193

Innovations in Electrical Materials for Flexible Sensors: From Metals, Hydrogels to Carbon-Based Materials and Polymer Conductors

Caijuan Li[1(✉)] and Hongxue Xu[2]

[1] Lanzhou Institute of Technology, Lanzhou, Gansu 730050, People's Republic of China
licaijuan0931@163.com

[2] Lanzhou Bowen College of Science and Technology, Lanzhou, Gansu 730101, People's Republic of China

Abstract. This paper reviews the recent research progress on key sensing materials for flexible sensors. Particular attention is given to four major categories of materials: metals, hydrogels, carbon-based materials, and conductive polymers. The design strategies, performance characteristics, and application prospects of these materials are systematically analyzed. Metal materials, through dimensional reduction and liquid metal technologies, simultaneously achieve high electrical conductivity and good flexibility. Hydrogels exhibit excellent biocompatibility and diverse conductive mechanisms, enabling broad applications in biosignal monitoring. Carbon-based materials and conductive polymers offer a favorable balance between performance and processability, supporting low-cost and large-scale manufacturing of flexible electronic devices. Despite their respective advantages, these materials generally suffer from limitations such as poor stability, low durability and relatively high cost. Looking ahead, future research is anticipated to emphasise multi-material composites, intelligent structural design and green manufacturing processes, thereby advancing the practical application of these materials in medical monitoring and human-machine interaction.

Keywords: Flexible sensors · Electrical materials · Functional materials

1 Introduction

With the rapid development of fields like consumer electronics, intelligent healthcare, and human-computer interaction, flexible electronics has increasingly attracted attention from researchers [1]. However, most traditional sensors are rigid components, which are hard to fit complex curved surfaces and difficult to monitor dynamic deformations [2]. Flexible sensors, relying on their excellent stretchability, flexibility, and portability, can achieve accurate real-time monitoring of human physiological signals, environmental parameters [3, 4]. They have shown great application potential in many forefront areas, including wearable devices, bionic robots, and smart skin. As the core component of flexible sensors, sensitive materials directly determine their electrical properties, mechanical flexibility, and biocompatibility [5–7]. Therefore, designing and preparing high-performance sensitive materials is the key to advancing the development of flexible sensor technology.

S. S. Ge et al. (Eds.): ICSR + BioMed 2025, LNAI 16435, pp. 204–214, 2026.
https://doi.org/10.1007/978-981-95-7538-1_18

In recent years, sensitive materials for flexible sensors have been extensively studied, which makes the performance of various new-type materials has been constantly improved [8–10]. From metal materials that were widely used in the early stage, to hydrogel materials with biocompatibility, and then to carbon-based materials with excellent performance and polymer conductors with high processability, these new materials have overcome technical bottlenecks in different application areas [11–14]. Comprehensively summarizing the research progress of various flexible sensor materials, and comparing their performance advantages and limitations, is of great theoretical and practical significance for clarifying the future direction of material research and development and promoting the further development of flexible sensor technology.

This paper provides a comprehensive review of the advances in flexible sensors based on metals, hydrogels, carbon-based materials, and polymer conductors. First, it elaborates on the technical principles by which each type of material achieves the integration of flexibility and electrical performance, analyzes their performance advantages and disadvantages, introduces their typical applications, and summarizes their design philosophies and performance boundaries. Finally, it presents prospects and discussions on the future development trends of electrical materials for flexible sensors, aiming to provide valuable references for researchers in related fields.

2 Metal Materials

As traditional conductive materials, metals have consistently held a pivotal position in the field of flexible sensors due to their outstanding electrical conductivity, providing a solid foundation for constructing high-performance flexible conductors [11–13]. To overcome the inherent rigidity limitations of metals, researchers have developed two core strategies: dimensional reduction and intrinsic flexibility enhancement [15–18]. One is to prepare nanoscale metallic structures such as silver nanowires through low-dimensionalization, using their high aspect ratio to maintain the integrity of the conductive network under tensile stress [19, 20]. Shuai et al. [21] fabricated a highly sensitive flexible capacitive pressure sensor with microstructures by using PVDF films coated with AgNWs as the dielectric layer and PDMS substrates as the top electrode. This sensor exhibits high sensitivity (2.94 kPa^{-1}), low detection limit (<3 Pa), fast response time (<50 ms), and excellent flexibility, making it suitable for electronic skin and wearable medical monitors (Fig. 1a). The second is to employ intrinsic flexibility strategies (liquid metals), leveraging their fluidic properties to impart outstanding stretchability to materials [22, 23]. Tao et al. [24] fabricated a resistive flexible sensor using gallium-based liquid metal (eutectic gallium-indium alloy, EGaIn) and polydimethylsiloxane (PDMS). This sensor exhibits flexibility, high plasticity, and excellent conductivity, offering broad application prospects in wearable sensing and human-machine interaction (Fig. 1b). These innovative strategies successfully reconcile high conductivity with stretchability in metallic materials, propelling metal-based flexible sensors toward ultra-high sensitivity and enabling widespread adoption in fields like stretchable electronics. However, metallic materials still face challenges such as performance degradation due to fatigue fracture and the high cost of precious metals, which to some extent limit their large-scale practical implementation [25, 26].

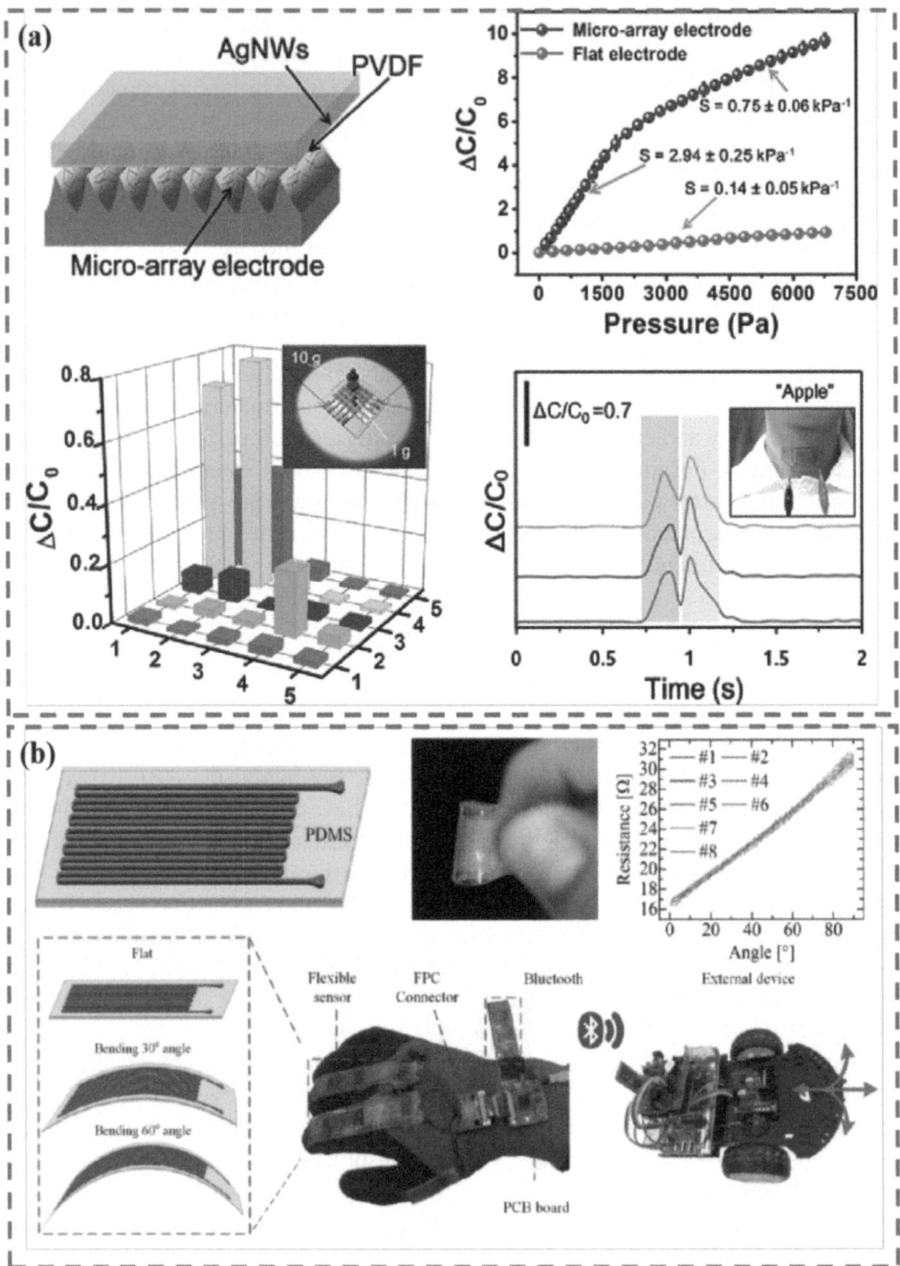

Fig. 1. (a)Highly Sensitive Flexible Pressure Sensor Based on Silver Nanowires-Embedded Polydimethylsiloxane Electrode with Microarray Structure. Reproduced with permission from [21]. Copyright 2017, ACS Publications. (b) Preparation, performance research and application of the liquid metal flexible sensor. Reproduced with permission from [24]. Copyright 2022, CC BY.

3 Hydrogel Materials

Hydrogel materials form three-dimensional network structures through physical or chemical crosslinking, exhibiting high stretchability and excellent biocompatibility [27, 28]. They have become a research focus in the field of flexible sensors, particularly for biocompatibility and structural innovation [29, 30].

Regarding the construction of conductive properties, hydrogels primarily achieve efficient conductivity through two approaches [31–33]. One is through the introduction of electrolyte media such as salt solutions or ionic liquids, forming conductive behavior dominated by ion migration, i.e., ionic conduction. Lv et al. [34] developed a chitin-based polyelectrolyte double-network hydrogel (CAA) by polymerizing acrylamide, acrylic acid, and chitin in a ternary molten salt system. Through the synergistic effect of dynamic metal coordination bonds and hydrogen bonds, the hydrogel successfully integrates outstanding mechanical properties with high ionic conductivity, enabling its use as a sensor for sensitively detecting various human joint movements (Fig. 2a) The second approach involves incorporating conductive nanomaterials, such as conductive polymers, carbon nanotubes, graphene, or metal nanowires—to establish continuous electronic transport pathways within the hydrogel network, achieving electronic conduction. Yuan et al. [35] prepared a PVA/PEG/TA-MXene-Na/Li (PPM-NL) composite nanogel using a hybrid matrix of polyvinyl alcohol (PVA) and polyethylene glycol (PEG), tannic acid (TA), modified MXene, lithium chloride (LiCl), and sodium chloride (NaCl). This hydrogel exhibits excellent flexibility (400% of elongation at break), electrical conductivity (8.1 S/m), high sensitivity (G = 1.12), and rapid response time (only 60 ms), providing inspiration for research on wearable flexible sensors and humanoid robots (Fig. 2b).

Based on its flexibly adjustable conductive mechanism, the hydrogel exhibits multifaceted functional advantages. It not only possesses low modulus and high elasticity similar to biological tissues but also features excellent optical transparency and surface modifiability. Responsive, self-healing, or adhesive properties can be further introduced through functional molecular grafting or composite modification [36, 37]. These combined advantages make hydrogels ideal materials for wearable electronics and bio-integrated devices [38]. They are now widely used for real-time monitoring of high-precision human physiological signals and multimodal sensing (pressure, temperature, humidity, etc.) in bionic electronic skins, driving breakthroughs in soft robotics and human-machine interaction [39]. However, hydrogels still suffer from inherent drawbacks such as susceptibility to water loss affecting stability and insufficient mechanical strength leading to structural damage [40]. There is an urgent need to enhance their comprehensive performance through material modification and structural design.

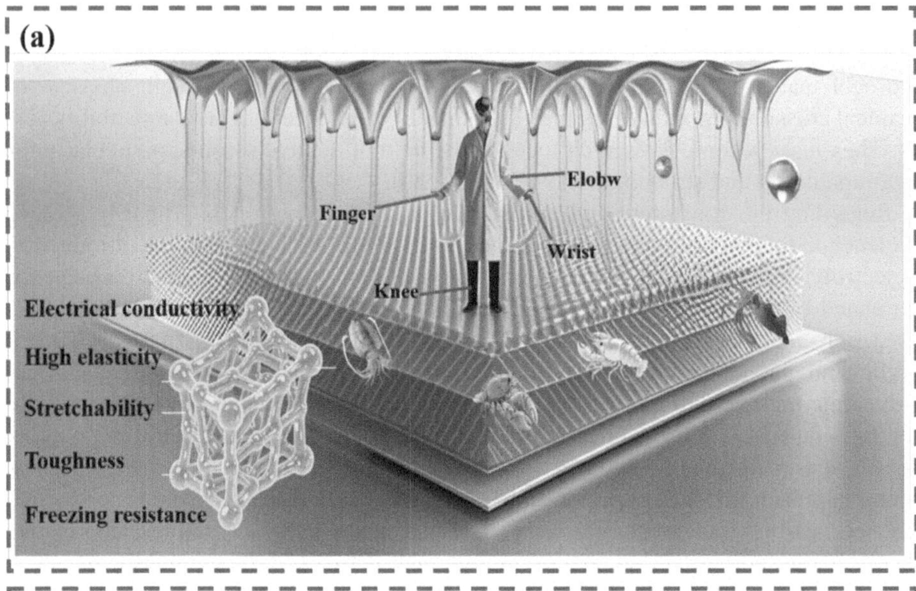

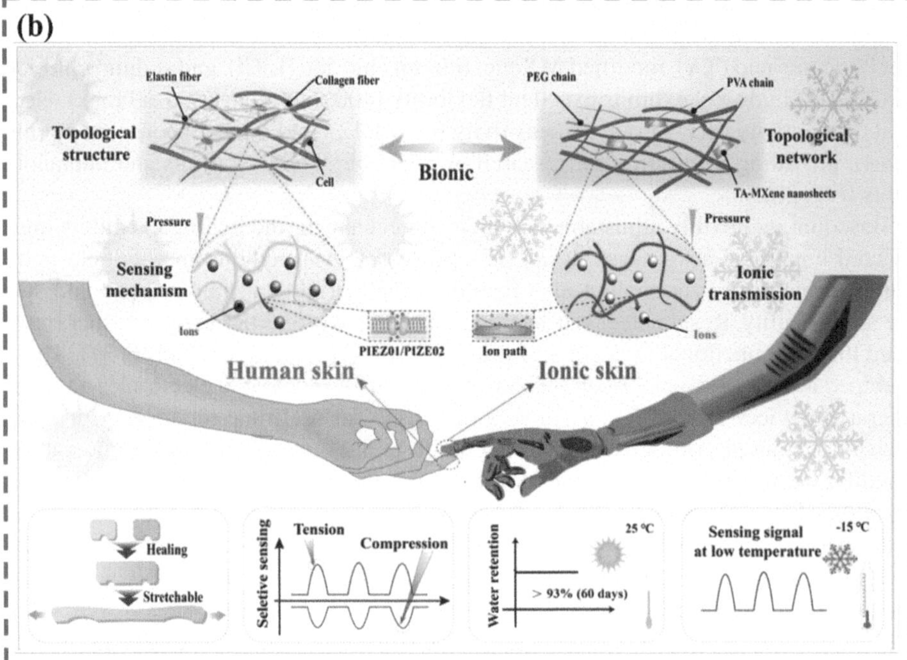

Fig. 2. (a) Polyelectrolyte-Chitin Double-Network Hydrogel (CAA) with Synergistically Achieved High Conductivity and Elasticity for Wearable Sensors. Reproduced with permission from [34]. Copyright 2025, CC BY. (b)The schematic diagram of ionic flexible sensor-ionic skin. Reproduced with permission from [35]. Copyright 2023, Wiley.

4 Carbon Materials and Conductive Polymers

Carbon materials and conductive polymers effectively combine high performance with excellent processability in the field of flexible sensors due to their unique properties [41].

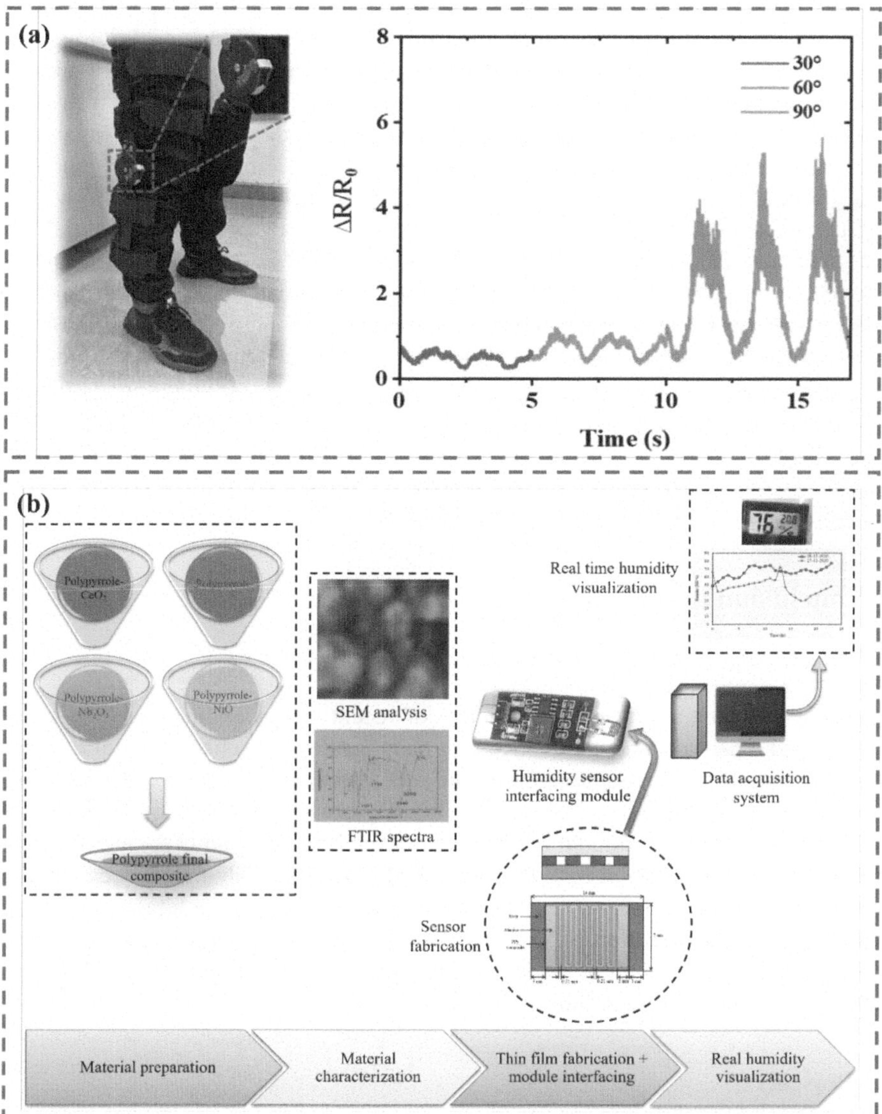

Fig. 3. (a) A MWCNT/Ecoflex-based sensor for monitoring exoskeleton motion across different bending angles. Reproduced with permission from [42]. Copyright 2025, CC BY. (b) A resistive humidity sensor based on PPy composite material. Reproduced with permission from [43]. Copyright 2021, CC BY.

Carbon materials (such as graphene and carbon nanotubes, CNTs) not only provide outstanding mechanical strength and electrical properties but also significantly widen their application scope through various macro-structural assembly strategies like films, fibers, and aerogels [44–46]. For instance, Guo et al. [42] developed a highly sensitive and stretchable strain sensor based on multi-walled carbon nanotubes and Ecoflex. By balancing sensitivity with stretchability, this sensor successfully enables real-time monitoring of human finger and knee joint movements, as well as exoskeleton device motions, providing a novel solution for enhancing exoskeleton performance and joint healthcare technology (Fig. 3a). Conductive polymers, exemplified by polypyrrole (PPy), are highly favored for their excellent process adaptability and flexible tuning capabilities. More importantly, they enable the preparation of high-performance flexible conductive layers through various low-cost fabrication routes. Hussain et al. [43] successfully developed a resistive humidity sensor based on a synthesized PPy composite material. This sensor demonstrates excellent performance within the 30% to 90% relative humidity range, exhibiting high stability and repeatability, with broad application prospects in fields such as tissue engineering, industrial automation, and agriculture (Fig. 3b).

In applications, carbon materials demonstrate significant potential in multifunctional integrated sensors and transparent electrodes, while conductive polymers are particularly suited for cost-sensitive scenarios like printed electronics [47]. However, both material classes still face distinct technical barriers: the first is that carbon materials often suffer performance degradation during macro-assembly, while conductive polymers struggle with issues like insufficient electrochemical stability.

5 Conclusion and Prospect

5.1 Conclusion

This paper provides a systematic overview of recent advances in metals, hydrogels, carbon-based materials, and conductive polymers for flexible sensors. Metal materials, leveraging dimensional reduction and liquid metal strategies, achieve a desirable integration of high conductivity and stretchability. Hydrogels, owing to their outstanding biocompatibility and multimodal conductive mechanisms, play an irreplaceable role in biosignal monitoring. Carbon-based materials and conductive polymers successfully balance functional performance with processability, paving the way for large-scale fabrication of flexible electronic devices. Despite these advances, these materials still encounter common challenges, including inadequate stability, limited mechanical durability, and relatively high cost, which constrain their broader practical applications.

5.2 Prospect

The future development of electrical functional materials for flexible sensors will increasingly focus on multi-material composites and intelligent structural design. These approaches aim to enhance conductivity, flexibility and environmental adaptability in an integrated manner.

Key research directions include the development of intelligent adaptive materials with self-healing, stimulus-responsive or biodegradable properties. Furthermore, artificial intelligence technologies are also expected to play an important role in assisting material design and optimization, thereby accelerating the rapid development of high-performance materials. Another promising direction is the construction of self-powered flexible sensing systems based on environmental energy harvesting, which can reduce reliance on traditional power sources. In addition, the integration of green degradable materials with low-energy printing electronic processes will be crucial for achieving sustainable manufacturing.

Closer collaboration among industry, academia and research institutions should also be encouraged to accelerate the large-scale application of material innovations in healthcare, intelligent robotics and wearable devices. Flexible sensors are poised to achieve breakthroughs in performance, intelligence and environmental compatibility through these endeavours, ultimately driving their widespread practical deployment.

Acknowledgments. This study was funded by 2024 Gansu Provincial Higher Education Institution Faculty In-novation Fund Project (grant number 2024A-194).

The authors have no competing interests to declare that are relevant to the content of this article.

References

1. Wu, C.K., Cheng, C.-T., Uwate, Y., Chen, G., Mumtaz, S., Tsang, K.F.: State-of-the-art and research opportunities for next-generation consumer electronics. IEEE Trans. Consum. Electron. **69**, 937–948 (2023). https://doi.org/10.1109/TCE.2022.3232478
2. Wang, H., Zhou, D., Cao, J.: Development of a skin-like tactile sensor array for curved surface. IEEE Sens. J. **14**, 55–61 (2014). https://doi.org/10.1109/JSEN.2013.2279394
3. Xu, K., Lu, Y., Takei, K.: Multifunctional skin-inspired flexible sensor systems for wearable electronics. Adv. Mater. Technol. **4**, 1800628 (2019). https://doi.org/10.1002/admt.201800628
4. Wang, X., Liu, Z., Zhang, T.: Flexible sensing electronics for wearable/attachable health monitoring. Small **13**, 1602790 (2017). https://doi.org/10.1002/smll.201602790
5. Wang, B., Zhou, S., Jiang, S., Qin, S., Gao, B.: Personalized medical devices connect monitoring and assistance: emerging wearable soft robotics. Anal. Chem. **95**, 8395–8410 (2023). https://doi.org/10.1021/acs.analchem.3c00950
6. Yang, J., Zhou, J., Tao, G., Alrashoud, M., Mutib, K.N.A., Al-Hammadi, M.: Wearable 3.0: from smart clothing to wearable affective robot. IEEE Netw. **33**, 8–14 (2019). https://doi.org/10.1109/MNET.001.1900059
7. Yang, J.C., Mun, J., Kwon, S.Y., Park, S., Bao, Z., Park, S.: Electronic skin: recent progress and future prospects for skin-attachable devices for health monitoring, robotics, and prosthetics. Adv. Mater. **31**, 1904765 (2019). https://doi.org/10.1002/adma.201904765
8. Rim, Y.S., Bae, S., Chen, H., De Marco, N., Yang, Y.: Recent progress in materials and devices toward printable and flexible sensors. Adv. Mater. **28**, 4415–4440 (2016). https://doi.org/10.1002/adma.201505118
9. Li, W., et al.: Recent advances in multiresponsive flexible sensors towards E-skin: a delicate design for versatile sensing. Small **18**, 2103734 (2022). https://doi.org/10.1002/smll.202103734

10. Liu, E., Cai, Z., Ye, Y., Zhou, M., Liao, H., Yi, Y.: An overview of flexible sensors: development, application, and challenges. Sensors **23**, 817 (2023). https://doi.org/10.3390/s23020817
11. Angione, M.D., et al.: Carbon based materials for electronic bio-sensing. Mater. Today **14**, 424–433 (2011). https://doi.org/10.1016/S1369-7021(11)70187-0
12. Nambiar, S., Yeow, J.T.W.: Conductive polymer-based sensors for biomedical applications. Biosens. Bioelectron. **26**, 1825–1832 (2011). https://doi.org/10.1016/j.bios.2010.09.046
13. Dhanjai Sinha, A., Kalambate, P.K., Mugo, S.M., Kamau, P., Chen, J., Jain, R.: Polymer hydrogel interfaces in electrochemical sensing strategies: a review. TrAC Trends Anal. Chem. **118**, 488–501 (2019). https://doi.org/10.1016/j.trac.2019.06.014
14. Pennella, M.A., Shokes, J.E., Cosper, N.J., Scott, R.A., Giedroc, D.P.: Structural elements of metal selectivity in metal sensor proteins. Proc. Natl. Acad. Sci. U.S.A. **100**, 3713–3718 (2003). https://doi.org/10.1073/pnas.0636943100
15. Zhu, Y., Song, E., Zhou, J., You, Z.: Optimal dimensionality reduction of sensor data in multisensor estimation fusion. IEEE Trans. Signal Process. **53**, 1631–1639 (2005). https://doi.org/10.1109/TSP.2005.845429
16. Rassam, M.A., Zainal, A., Maarof, M.A.: An adaptive and efficient dimension reduction model for multivariate wireless sensor networks applications. Appl. Soft Comput. **13**, 1978–1996 (2013). https://doi.org/10.1016/j.asoc.2012.11.041
17. Zhao, Z., Liu, K., Liu, Y., Guo, Y., Liu, Y.: Intrinsically flexible displays: key materials and devices (2022)
18. Xu, K., Lu, Y., Takei, K.: Flexible hybrid sensor systems with feedback functions. Adv. Funct. Mater. **31**, 2007436 (2021). https://doi.org/10.1002/adfm.202007436
19. Li, B.L., et al.: Low-dimensional transition metal dichalcogenide nanostructures based sensors. Adv. Funct. Mater. **26**, 7034–7056 (2016). https://doi.org/10.1002/adfm.201602136
20. Vaseashta, A., Dimova-Malinovska, D.: Nanostructured and nanoscale devices, sensors and detectors. Sci. Technol. Adv. Mater. **6**, 312–318 (2005). https://doi.org/10.1016/j.stam.2005.02.018
21. Shuai, X., et al.: Highly sensitive flexible pressure sensor based on silver nanowires-embedded polydimethylsiloxane electrode with microarray structure. ACS Appl. Mater. Interfaces **9**, 26314–26324 (2017). https://doi.org/10.1021/acsami.7b05753
22. Duan, S., Wu, J., Xia, J., Lei, W.: Innovation strategy selection facilitates high-performance flexible piezoelectric sensors. Sensors **20**, 2820 (2020). https://doi.org/10.3390/s20102820
23. Jang, H., Lee, J., Beak, C., Biswas, S., Lee, S., Kim, H.: Flexible neuromorphic electronics for wearable near-sensor and in-sensor computing systems. Adv. Mater. **37**, 2416073 (2025). https://doi.org/10.1002/adma.202416073
24. Tao, Y., Han, F., Shi, C., Yang, R., Chen, Y., Ren, Y.: Liquid metal-based flexible and wearable sensor for functional human–machine interface. Micromachines **13**, 1429 (2022). https://doi.org/10.3390/mi13091429
25. Ahmed, S., Schumacher, T., Thostenson, E.T., McConnell, J.: Performance evaluation of a carbon nanotube sensor for fatigue crack monitoring of metal structures. Sensors **20**, 4383 (2020). https://doi.org/10.3390/s20164383
26. Jia, L., Wu, S., Yuan, R., Xiang, T., Zhou, S.: Biomimetic microstructured antifatigue fracture hydrogel sensor for human motion detection with enhanced sensing sensitivity. ACS Appl. Mater. Interfaces **14**, 27371–27382 (2022). https://doi.org/10.1021/acsami.2c04614
27. Sun, X., Agate, S., Salem, K.S., Lucia, L., Pal, L.: Hydrogel-based sensor networks: compositions, properties, and applications—a review. ACS Appl. Bio Mater. **4**, 140–162 (2021). https://doi.org/10.1021/acsabm.0c01011
28. Hui, Y., et al.: Three-dimensional printing of soft hydrogel electronics. Nat Electron. **5**, 893–903 (2022). https://doi.org/10.1038/s41928-022-00887-8

29. Shen, P., et al.: Three-dimensional/two-dimensional photonic crystal hydrogels for biosensing. J. Mater. Chem. C. **9**, 5840–5857 (2021). https://doi.org/10.1039/D1TC00830G
30. Wu, J., et al.: Three-dimensional-structured boron- and nitrogen-doped graphene hydrogel enabling high-sensitivity NO_2 detection at room temperature. ACS Sens. **4**, 1889–1898 (2019). https://doi.org/10.1021/acssensors.9b00769
31. Zhu, T., et al.: Recent advances in conductive hydrogels: classifications, properties, and applications. Chem. Soc. Rev. **52**, 473–509 (2023). https://doi.org/10.1039/D2CS00173J
32. Zhou, Y., et al.: Highly stretchable, elastic, and ionic conductive hydrogel for artificial soft electronics. Adv. Funct. Mater. **29**, 1806220 (2019). https://doi.org/10.1002/adfm.201806220
33. Chen, J., Liu, F., Abdiryim, T., Liu, X.: An overview of conductive composite hydrogels for flexible electronic devices. Adv. Compos. Hybrid Mater. **7**, 35 (2024). https://doi.org/10.1007/s42114-024-00841-6
34. Lv, Y., Huang, H., Wu, G., Qian, Y.: Construction of chitin-based composite hydrogel via $AlCl_3/ZnCl_2/H_2O$ ternary molten salt system and its flexible sensing performance. Gels **11**, 501 (2025). https://doi.org/10.3390/gels11070501
35. Yuan, S., et al.: A multifunctional and selective ionic flexible sensor with high environmental suitability for tactile perception. Adv. Func. Mater. **34**, 2309626 (2024). https://doi.org/10.1002/adfm.202309626
36. Xiao, Q., et al.: Interfacial modification of hydrogel composite membranes for protein adsorption with cavitands as nano molecular containers. Sep. Purif. Technol. **339**, 126438 (2024). https://doi.org/10.1016/j.seppur.2024.126438
37. Peeva, P.D., Pieper, T., Ulbricht, M.: Tuning the ultrafiltration properties of anti-fouling thin-layer hydrogel polyethersulfone composite membranes by suited crosslinker monomers and photo-grafting conditions. J. Membr. Sci. **362**, 560–568 (2010). https://doi.org/10.1016/j.memsci.2010.07.016
38. Oh, J.Y., Lee, Y., Lee, T.: Skin-mountable functional electronic materials for bio-integrated devices. Adv. Healthcare Mater. **13**, 2303797 (2024). https://doi.org/10.1002/adhm.202303797
39. Schara, S., Blau, R., Church, D.C., Pokorski, J.K., Lipomi, D.J.: Polymer chemistry for haptics, soft robotics, and human-machine interfaces. Adv Funct Mater. **31**, 2008375 (2021). https://doi.org/10.1002/adfm.202008375
40. De France, K.J., Xu, F., Hoare, T.: Structured macroporous hydrogels: progress, challenges, and opportunities. Adv. Healthcare Mater. **7**, 1700927 (2018). https://doi.org/10.1002/adhm.201700927
41. Ates, M., Sarac, A.S.: Conducting polymer coated carbon surfaces and biosensor applications. Prog. Org. Coat. **66**, 337–358 (2009). https://doi.org/10.1016/j.porgcoat.2009.08.014
42. Guo, Z., Hu, X., Chen, Y., Ma, Y., Zhao, F., Guo, S.: Soft, stretchable, high-sensitivity, multi-walled carbon nanotube-based strain sensor for joint healthcare. Nanomaterials **15**, 332 (2025). https://doi.org/10.3390/nano15050332
43. Hussain, M., et al.: Design and fabrication of a fast response resistive-type humidity sensor using polypyrrole (ppy) polymer thin film structures. Polymers **13**, 3019 (2021). https://doi.org/10.3390/polym13183019
44. Zhu, W.-B., et al.: High-performance fiber-film hybrid-structured wearable strain sensor from a highly robust and conductive carbonized bamboo aerogel. ACS Appl. Bio Mater. **3**, 8748–8756 (2020). https://doi.org/10.1021/acsabm.0c01128
45. Hu, P., et al.: Multifunctional aramid nanofiber/carbon nanotube hybrid aerogel films. ACS Nano **14**, 688–697 (2020). https://doi.org/10.1021/acsnano.9b07459

46. Afroze, J.D., Tong, L., Abden, M.J., Chen, Y.: Multifunctional hierarchical graphene-carbon fiber hybrid aerogels for strain sensing and energy storage. Adv. Compos. Hybrid Mater. **6**, 18 (2023). https://doi.org/10.1007/s42114-022-00594-0
47. Howard, E.L., Österholm, A.M., Shen, D.E., Panchumarti, L.P., Pinheiro, C., Reynolds, J.R.: Cost-effective, flexible, and colorful dynamic displays: removing underlying conducting layers from polymer-based electrochromic devices. ACS Appl. Mater. Interfaces **13**, 16732–16743 (2021). https://doi.org/10.1021/acsami.1c00463

Neuro-symbolic Model for Motion Deficit Detection in Parkinson's Disease Patients

Sai Leela Harika Thota[1], Hongsheng He[2], and Fujian Yan[3](✉)

[1] Wichita State University, Wichita, KS 67260, USA
[2] University of Alabama, Tuscaloosa, AL 35487, USA
[3] Truman State University, Kirksville, MO 63501, USA
fujian.yan@wichita.edu

Abstract. Parkinson's Disease (PD) is a progressive neurodegenerative disorder affecting millions globally, characterized by motor symptoms such as rigidity, tremor, bradykinesia and postural instability. While deep learning has shown promise in detecting motion deficit in PD, its black-box nature and reliance on large, homogeneous datasets limit clinical interpretability and generalizability. To address this, we propose a Neuro-Symbolic Motion Deficit Detection (NSMDD) framework that combines data-driven learning with symbolic reasoning to detect motion deficit in PD patients. The study uses real-world IMU data from nine structured motor tasks, extracting 810 time-series features and seven motion-based indicators such as standard deviation, range of motion, angular velocity magnitude, root mean square, dominant frequency, jerk, and sway magnitude to represent key motor symptoms. Symbolic knowledge encoded in first-order logic (FOL) generated interpretable motion deficit labels, integrated with neural features in the NSMDD model. The framework achieved 92% accuracy on a hold-out patient set, showing strong generalization. In contrast, CNN and SVM baselines, though effective on validation data, dropped significantly on the hold-out set, with 34% and 31% performance gaps, respectively. These results highlight the advantage of embedding clinically grounded symbolic knowledge for robust and interpretable motion deficit detection in PD.

Keywords: Neuro-Symbolic Model · Parkinson's Disease · MDS-UPDRS Part - III · Knowledge Extraction

1 Introduction

Parkinson's disease (PD) hallmark motor impairments includes rigidity (RG), tremor (TR), bradykinesia (BK), and postural instability (PI), commonly evaluated using Part III of the Movement Disorder Society-Unified Parkinson's Disease Rating Scale (MDS-UPDRS) [3]. However, MDS-UPDRS is subjective, time-consuming, and requires expert evaluation [8]. In recent years, deep learning models havehave shown substantial promise in human activity recognition

S. S. Ge et al. (Eds.): ICSR + BioMed 2025, LNAI 16435, pp. 215–224, 2026.
https://doi.org/10.1007/978-981-95-7538-1_19

and neurological disorder detection [12]. While these models are highly effective at capturing complex temporal patterns from raw sensor data and have been widely applied in Parkinson's disease (PD) research to identify motor impairments, their limited interpretability remains a critical barrier to clinical adoption [13,14]. To address this, we developed a Neuro-Symbolic Motion Deficit Detection (NSMDD) model that integrates the data driven methods with symbolic knowledge to detect motion deficits in PD patients. The model processes multivariate IMU sensor data using a neural network to learn temporal movement patterns, while a symbolic layer applies first-order logic (FOL) rules derived from clinically aligned, data-driven thresholds. These rules model four core PD motor symptoms such as RG, TR, BK, and PI enabling the system to produce interpretable, symptom-aware predictions consistent with expert scoring standards like the MDS-UPDRS. This paper propose the following contributions:

1. Designed a neuro-symbolic model (NSMDD) to detect motion deficits in Parkinson's disease patients, emphasizing interpretability and clinical relevance.
2. Integration of clinically aligned knowledge into the learning pipeline through first-order logic (FOL) rules that encode symptom-specific movement patterns. These rules enable transparent decision-making by grounding the model's outputs in expert-defined indicators of motor impairment.

2 Neuro-symbolic Motion Deficit Detection (NSMDD)

The proposed NSMDD is illustrated in Fig. 1. It uses kinematic data from five IMUs recorded during three activities of daily living (ADLs), capturing 810 features segmented via a sliding window. Seven motion-based indicators such as standard deviation (SD), range of motion (ROM), magnitude of angular velocity (AV), dominant frequency (DF), root mean square (RMS), jerk (J), and sway magnitude (SM) are appended, yielding 817 features per segment. A neural module extracts motion patterns, while a symbolic layer applies first-order logic (FOL) rules based on PD symptoms. Final predictions combine neural and symbolic outputs for accurate, interpretable motion deficit detection.

2.1 Neuro-symbolic Model

To effectively detect motion deficit in PD patients, neuro-symbolic model was designed that combines deep learning with interpretable symbolic reasoning. Let each motion segment be represented as an input tensor $X_i \in \mathbb{R}^{m \times n}$ where m is the number of time steps and n refers to the number of input features. The model predicts a binary label $y_i \in \{0, 1\}$, indicating the presence or absence of motion deficit.

The neural component $f_\theta(X_i)$ is implemented using a convolutional neural network followed by fully connected layers that yield a sigmoid-activated scalar output

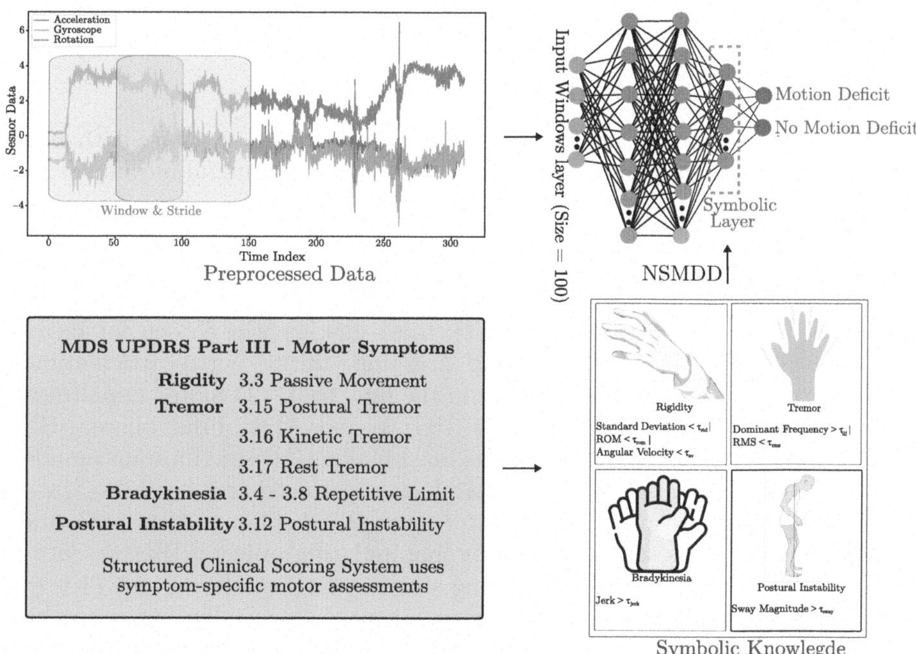

Fig. 1. NSMDD Framework Overview: IMU signals (acceleration, gyroscope, rotation) are segmented with a sliding window, linked to MDS-UPDRS Part III. Threshold-based symbolic rules for each symptom are applied and combined in the final neuro-symbolic layer to detect motion deficit.

$$\hat{y}_{\text{neural}} = \sigma(f_\theta(X_i)), \tag{1}$$

which represents the probability of motion deficit based on learned temporal patterns.

In parallel, symbolic reasoning function, $R(X_i)$, consisting of a four hand-crafted binary rules $r_1, r_2, r_3, r_4 \in \{0, 1\}$, each capturing specific motion-based indicators. These are combined using weighted aggregation:

$$\hat{y}_{\text{symbolic}} = \frac{1}{\sum_j w_r^{(j)}} \sum_{j=1}^{4} w_r^{(j)} r_j(\mathbf{X}_i), \tag{2}$$

where $w_r^{(j)}$ are tunable weights emphasizing clinically meaningful rules. This symbolic output encodes interpretable domain knowledge through weighted binary conditions and the final decision $\hat{y}_i$ was computed as a weighted fusion of the neural and symbolic outputs:

$$\hat{y}_i = \sigma(\mathrm{W}_{\text{neural}}\hat{y}_{\text{neural}} + \mathrm{W}_{\text{symbolic}}\hat{y}_{\text{symbolic}}), \tag{3}$$

where $\mathrm{W}_{\text{neural}}$ and $\mathrm{W}_{\text{symbolic}}$ are scalar weights controlling the contributions of each pathway. This fusion allows the model to balance statistical learning with rule-based interpretability and model was optimized using the binary cross-entropy loss:

$$\mathcal{L} = -\left[y \log(\hat{y}) + (1-y)\log(1-\hat{y})\right]. \tag{4}$$

This formulation enables the model to balance statistical learning with interpretable, rule-based reasoning grounded in clinically meaningful movement patterns.

2.2 Symbolic Knowledge Representation

Among the ADLs (cardigan, key, toast), toast-making was chosen for its rich motion profile that involves reaching, grasping, lifting, wrist articulation—capturing spontaneous motor behavior in the first trial. PD motor impairments from dopamine loss manifest as rigidity (RG), tremor (TR), bradykinesia (BK), and postural instability (PI). During the toast making, these symptoms manifest in distinct and observable ways. RG manifests as reduced arm flexibility during fine-motor actions like pressing a toaster lever. TR is observed as involuntary shaking or oscillations while holding or manipulating objects. BK presents as delayed or hesitant movements including slow reaching or slicing and PI is evidenced by exaggerated sway in the horizontal plane, especially during reaching or returning to an upright position. These observable deficits were captured by wearable IMUs, enabling direct mapping between real-world motor behavior and symbolic detection rules. Symbolic rules were formulated in FOL using MDS-UPDRS Part III and literature. From toast-making data averaged across IMUs, RG was evaluated by resistance to passive movement and ROM, further influenced by AV and joint amplitude [2]. These features align with the motion based indicators manifestation of RG and correspond to Item 3.3 of the scale. To represent this symptom quantitatively, three core features were selected: SD of gyroscope y-axis(to capture motion variability), ROM from orientation matrices (to reflect limb flexibility), and AV magnitude (for limb rotation).

Among the gyroscope axes, the y-axis showed the clearest separation between PD and healthy subjects as shown in subfigure (a) of Fig. 2. Accordingly, the mean SD of the gyroscope y-axis across sensors was used to capture limb movement variability. ROM was obtained by converting 3 × 3 orientation matrices $\mathbb{R}^{3\times3}$ into Euler angles and computing angular displacements along x, y, and z. AV magnitude was derived from tri-axial gyroscope signals to reflect rotational intensity. These three indicators were then combined to construct the symbolic rule for detecting RG as:

$$\forall X,\ \mathrm{RG}(X) \leftrightarrow (\mathrm{SD}(X) < \tau_{\mathrm{std}} \lor \mathrm{ROM}(X) < \tau_{\mathrm{rom}} \lor \mathrm{AV}(X) < \tau_{\mathrm{av}}) \tag{5}$$

where τ_{std}, τ_{rom}, and τ_{av} are the threshold values for SD, ROM, and AV respectively, and X denotes a participant. An RG label is assigned if any feature falls below its threshold. For example, $\tau_{std} = 0.2978$ was set as the minimum mean SD of the gyroscope y-axis among healthy participants during toast 1, serving as a conservative lower bound for pathological reductions in limb movement

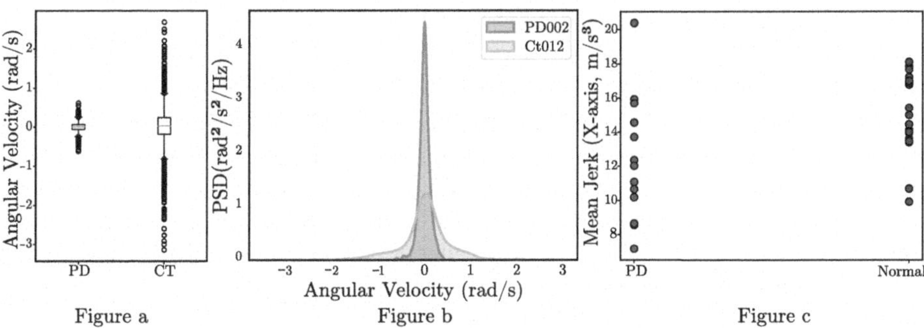

Fig. 2. (a) Boxplot of gyroscope y-axis AV (rad/s) for PD and CT groups (x-axis: groups, y-axis: AV with median, IQR, outliers). (b) Line plot of gyroscope y-axis PSD for PD002 (red) and Ct012 (blue), x-axis: frequency (Hz), y-axis: PSD ($rad^2/s^2/Hz$). (c) Scatter plot of accelerometer x-axis mean jerk (m/s^3) for PD (red) and Normal (blue), y-axis: jerk values per subject. (Color figure online)

variability. Using the minimum healthy baseline enforces a clinically grounded standard, as healthy subjects exhibit natural variability, and consistent deviations below this suggest RG or stiffness. Similarly, τ_{rom}= 110.5759° was defined as the minimum mean ROM in healthy participants, marking the lowest acceptable joint mobility; persistent restriction below this indicates impaired flexibility, consistent with RG.

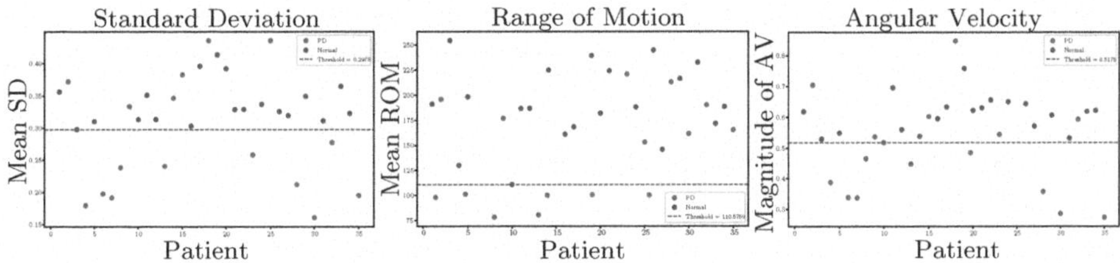

Fig. 3. Kinematic indicators of RG. Distributions of SD, ROM, and AV used in the RG rule are shown for PD (red) and Normal (blue) participants, with green dashed lines marking clinically derived thresholds separating normal and abnormal ranges. (Color figure online)

The AV threshold was set to $\tau_{av} = 0.5175$ rad/s, equal to the minimum mean AV observed among healthy participants, providing a conservative lower bound for normal joint rotation. Consistent with clinical observations that RG involves slower, restricted rotation, a mean AV below this cutoff indicates reduced motor flexibility and stiffness hallmark indicators of RG in PD as shown in Fig. 3. Because the cutoff is empirically derived from controls, it preserves clinical relevance and data-driven precision, enabling the symbolic rule to distinguish physiologically normal from pathologically impaired rotational behavior.

TR was quantified using DF and RMS of acceleration, features widely used in wearable sensor research to characterize TR rhythmicity and amplitude. Prior studies [7] have demonstrated that these features effectively capture the characteristics of rest, postural, and kinetic tremors,(MDS-UPDRS Part III Items 3.15–3.17). Both were derived from x-axis gyroscope signals during toast-making, chosen via spectral analysis, which revealed stronger oscillatory activity along this axis compared to the y and z directions in both PD and healthy subjects, as shown in subfigure (b) of Fig. 2. RMS reflects oscillation amplitude and serves as a robust indicator of tremor abnormalities. These features were then used to construct the symbolic rule for TR, defined as:

$$\forall X,\ \mathrm{TR}(X) \leftrightarrow (DF(X) > \tau_{\mathrm{df}} \vee \mathrm{RMS}(X) < \tau_{\mathrm{rms}}) \tag{6}$$

A participant X is classified as exhibiting TR if DF $>\tau_{df}$ or RMS $< \tau_{rms}$. The DF threshold $\tau_{df} = 2.85$ was set as the maximum DF in healthy individuals, consistent with PD patients' elevated tremor frequencies (4–8 Hz). DF was estimated using Welch's method, with the peak of the PSD curve as the value. RMS, measuring oscillation amplitude and relevant for kinetic tremor, used a threshold of $\tau_{rms} = 0.4785$, the minimum RMS among healthy subjects during toast-making. Clinically, lower RMS indicates dampened voluntary motion or irregular tremors, while data-driven use of the healthy baseline improves sensitivity and specificity by flagging deviations from normal performance.

By combining frequency and amplitude based indicators in a single rule, the model is equipped to capture a more nuanced and clinically comprehensive profile of TR even during complex tasks like toast-making, ensuring subtle but clinically significant motor deviations are not overlooked and enhancing diagnostic utility. BK was quantified using jerk from y-axis acceleration, reflecting vertical movements such as reaching, lifting, and spreading. Clinically, BK corresponds to slowed, irregular motion with reduced smoothness and variability. Jerk, validated in prior studies [4], was therefore adopted to construct the symbolic rule for BK, defined as:

$$\forall X,\ \mathrm{BK}(X) \leftrightarrow (\mathrm{J}(X) > \tau_{\mathrm{jerk}}) \tag{7}$$

The jerk threshold $\tau_{jerk} = 26.0013$, set as the minimum mean jerk in healthy individuals, differentiates normal from pathological dynamics. A participant with mean jerk below this value is classified as exhibiting BK, reflecting reduced fluidity and hesitations characteristic of PD. PI was quantified using sway magnitude (SM) from horizontal-plane accelerations (x, y), capturing lateral and anterior–posterior body sway during tasks. Clinically, PI indicates impaired balance and fall risk, with SM chosen based on prior research demonstrating its effectiveness in characterizing PD-related balance deficits [1] The symbolic rule to detect PI was defined as:

$$\forall X,\ \mathrm{PI}(X) \leftrightarrow (\mathrm{SM}(X) > \tau_{\mathrm{sway}}) \tag{8}$$

The sway threshold $\tau_{sway} = 5.3245$, set as the maximum SM in healthy participants, distinguishes stable from unstable posture and values above this indicate

PI, consistent with clinical observations of increased sway and balance deficits in PD.

All thresholds were empirically derived from the dataset, using minimum or maximum values from healthy participants to keep rules clinically grounded and aligned with normative behavior. After defining rules for RG, TR, BK, and PI, motion deficit was determined using a composite FOL rule, where the presence of any one symptom indicates impairment, consistent with MDS-UPDRS guidelines. This unified rule defines motion deficit detection in our framework as:

$$\forall X,\ \mathrm{MD}(X) \leftrightarrow \mathrm{R}G(X) \vee \mathrm{TR}(X) \vee \mathrm{BK}(X) \vee \mathrm{PI}(X). \tag{9}$$

The rule identifies motion deficit by labeling a participant impaired if any indicator exceeds its threshold, consistent with clinical reasoning that a single symptom can affect functional ability. As PD is heterogeneous, not all symptoms appear in every task; missing thresholds may reflect disease stage, medication, or task demands. Hence, the rules detect symptom-specific impairments rather than enforce a universal PD classification.

2.3 Training Strategy and Implementation Details

To improve robustness and reduce overfitting, Gaussian noise $\mathcal{N}(0, 0.01)$ was added for data augmentation, doubling the training set while preserving labels. A weighted loss addressed class imbalance. Data were segmented into overlapping windows (size m, stride n) and labeled using symbolic rules from clinically grounded thresholds. The NSMDD was implemented in TensorFlow with Adam optimizer, learning rate scheduling, and early stopping. All experiments used consistent settings for reproducibility and clinical applicability.

3 Experiments

To assess generalizability, the NSMDD framework was evaluated using a cross-subject validation protocol with non-overlapping training, validation, and testing groups. This mimics real-world clinical scenarios, testing the model's ability to detect PD symptoms across unseen individuals. Such a setup ensures clinical relevance and gauges deployment readiness. The following sections detail training setup, evaluation metrics, baseline comparisons, and performance results.

3.1 Experiment Setup

This study uses a public dataset [10] with motion recordings from 34 participants (15 PD, 19 controls) using five 9-axis IMUs on the upper/lower arms and head. Participants performed three ADLs, each repeated three times, with accelerometer, gyroscope, and orientation data yielding 18 features per trial.

Data Preprocessing and Feature Extraction. Sensor data were organized into five sheets (18 features each: 9 motion + 9 orientation), yielding 90 features per trial and 810 per participant across nine trials. A binary label (0: healthy, 1: PD) was added. To improve interpretability, seven symbolic indicators (SD, ROM, RMS, AV magnitude, DF, J, SM) from the first toast trial were included, expanding the dataset to 817 features. Data were windowed (size 100, stride 50) for training.

3.2 Quantitative and Comparative Analysis

Five independent runs with different seeds and splits were performed to avoid bias, following best practices recommending multiple seeds [5]. The test set was fixed with seven unseen patients to simulate real-world generalization.

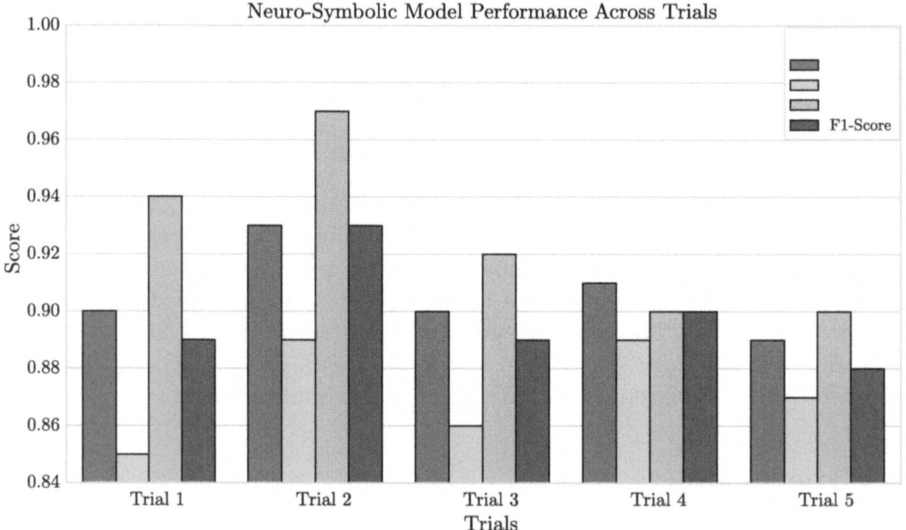

Fig. 4. Performance of the neuro-symbolic model across five independent training trials, showing accuracy, precision, recall, and F1-score variations (89%–93%). Despite fluctuations from random seeds, metrics remained consistently high, demonstrating robustness and reliability in detecting PD motor symptoms.

Across five trials, accuracy, precision, recall, and F1-score remained stable, with test accuracy 89–93% (mean 91%) as shown in Fig. 4, Sensitivity analysis with varied train-validation splits (30–45%) and 462–588 windows confirmed consistent performance, demonstrating robustness for real-world clinical deployment.

We selected SVM and CNN as baselines for their relevance in biomedical signal analysis and PD research. SVMs perform well even with small datasets [6] and achieved $\geq$ 80% accuracy in IMU-based PD detection, outperforming

Table 1. Comparative Performance of SVM, CNN, and Neuro-Symbolic Models on Hold out set

Model	Accuracy	Precision	Recall	F1-Score
SVM [9]	0.61	0.63	0.33	0.43
CNN	0.58	0.53	0.60	0.56
Neuro-Symbolic	0.92	0.86	0.96	0.91

ANN, decision trees, and random forests [11]. CNNs are widely used in time-series and activity recognition, making them effective for our (100×810) IMU windows. In contrast, more advanced architectures such as transformers, though powerful, require much larger datasets; with limited data (∼2,000 windows per split), they risk overfitting. As shown in Table 1, SVM and CNN struggled on the hold-out test set, In contrast, the proposed neuro-symbolic framework embeds clinically meaningful symbolic rules—based on seven motion-based indicators—into its decision-making process, enabling interpretable and symptom-specific predictions. By combining neural representations with data-derived thresholds for RG, TR, BK, and PI, the model remains both data-adaptive and clinically grounded. Unlike conventional models that often fail with real-world variability, our approach anchors predictions in structured clinical knowledge aligned with MDS-UPDRS scoring. As a result, the neuro-symbolic model delivers scalable, explainable, and clinically actionable motion deficit detection—bridging the gap between computational outputs and clinical expectations.

The considered dataset was modest in size, limiting generalizability but consistent with exploratory studies. Toast-making was emphasized as it elicited richer PD symptoms than key or cardigan tasks, improving interpretability though reducing coverage of other ADLs. Finally, as validation relied on an existing dataset rather than prospective trials, future work should include larger, more diverse, longitudinal cohorts in clinical settings.

4 Conclusion

This study have proposed the NSMDD framework, which integrates data-driven learning with symbolic reasoning to detect motion deficit in PD patients using IMU sensor data. The resulting neuro-symbolic model achieved a test accuracy of 92%, bridging the gap between automated analysis and clinical interpretability.

References

1. Engel, D., et al.: Sway frequencies may predict postural instability in Parkinson's disease: a novel convolutional neural network approach. J. Neuroeng. Rehabil. **22**(1), 29 (2025)
2. del Rosario Ferreira-Sánchez, M., Moreno-Verdú, M., Cano-de-la Cuerda, R.: Quantitative measurement of rigidity in Parkinson's disease: a systematic review. Sensors **20**(3), 880 (2020)

3. Goetz, C.G.: The history of Parkinson's disease: Early clinical descriptions and neurological therapies. Cold Spring Harb. Perspect. Med. **1**(1), a008862–a008862 (2011)
4. Habets, J.G.V., et al.: Rapid dynamic naturalistic monitoring of bradykinesia in Parkinson's disease using a wrist-worn accelerometer. Sensors **21**(23), 7876 (2021)
5. Henderson, P., Islam, R., Bachman, P., Pineau, J., Precup, D., Meger, D.: Deep reinforcement learning that matters. In: Proceedings of the AAAI Conference on Artificial Intelligence, vol. 32(1), 3207–3214 (2018)
6. Kirchner, A., Signorino, C.S.: Using support vector machines for survey research. Surv. Pract. **11**(1), 1–14 (2018)
7. Lukšys, D., Jonaitis, G., Griškevičius, J.: Quantitative analysis of parkinsonian tremor in a clinical setting using inertial measurement units. Parkinson's Disease **2018**(1), 1–7 (2018)
8. Mahlknecht, P., Marini, K., Werkmann, M., Poewe, W., Seppi, K.: Prodromal Parkinson's disease: hype or hope for disease-modification trials? Transl. Neurodegenerat. **11**(1), 11 (2022)
9. Ricci, M., Di Lazzaro, G., Pisani, A., Mercuri, N.B., Giannini, F., Saggio, G.: Assessment of motor impairments in early untreated Parkinson's disease patients: the wearable electronics impact. IEEE J. Biomed. Health Inform. **24**(1), 120–130 (2020)
10. Russell, J., Inches, J., Carroll, C., Bergmann, J.: A five-sensor IMU-based Parkinson's disease patient and control dataset including three activities of daily living [dataset]. Dryad (2023)
11. Trabassi, D., et al.: Machine learning approach to support the detection of Parkinson's disease in IMU-based gait analysis. Sensors **22**(10), 3700 (2022)
12. Yan, F., Gong, J., Zhang, Q., He, H.: Learning motion primitives for the quantification and diagnosis of mobility deficits. IEEE Trans. Biomed. Eng. **71**(12), 3339–3349 (2024)
13. Yan, F., Wang, D., He, H.: Robotic understanding of spatial relationships using neural-logic learning. In: 2020 IEEE/RSJ International Conference on Intelligent Robots and Systems (IROS), pp. 8358–8365. IEEE (2020)
14. Yan, F., Wang, D., He, H.: Comprehension of spatial constraints by neural logic learning from a single RGB-D scan. In: 2021 IEEE/RSJ International Conference on Intelligent Robots and Systems (IROS), pp. 9008–9013. IEEE (2021)

Omnisurface: Intention Awareness and Touch-Based Query for Human–Robot Teaming

Akhlak Uz Zaman, Hui Li, Tianjun Xu, and Hongsheng He(✉)

The University of Alabama, Tuscaloosa, AL 35487, USA
hongsheng.he@ua.edu

Abstract. Effective communication of robot intentions is essential for safe and efficient human–robot teaming. Nevertheless, existing visual and auditory interfaces often fail to provide clear and shared situational awareness in dynamic environments. Current projection-based interfaces improve visibility but suffer from geometric distortions on non-planar or deformable surfaces and rarely support real-time, bidirectional interaction. This paper introduces a unified framework that combines intention awareness with touch-based query response to enable distortion-free, interactive projection in collaborative workspaces. The system dynamically visualizes robot intentions and allows users to respond directly through on-surface touch gestures. Experiments across diverse surface geometries demonstrate precise spatial consistency and reliable real-time responsiveness. Furthermore, a user study reveals notable improvements in intuitiveness, effectiveness, and overall user satisfaction compared with conventional graphical interfaces.

Keywords: human–robot teaming · interactive projection · intention communication · real-time collaboration

1 Introduction

Human–robot teaming is increasingly adopted to enhance productivity and adaptability across diverse environments. In these collaborative settings, humans and robots work side by side, integrating their complementary capabilities. Effective coordination requires that human partners maintain clear situational awareness of the robot's current state, planned actions, and underlying intentions. A lack of such awareness can lead to misinterpretation of robot behavior and jeopardize both safety and overall performance [1,2].

Traditional approaches to conveying robot intent, such as head-mounted displays or audio cues, have notable limitations. Wearable devices are often designed for individual use and may obscure the broader workspace, while audio cues lack spatial precision [3]. In contrast, projector-based visualization presents a compelling alternative by directly embedding visual cues into the shared physical

This research was funded by NSF grants #2420355.

S. S. Ge et al. (Eds.): ICSR + BioMed 2025, LNAI 16435, pp. 225–237, 2026.
https://doi.org/10.1007/978-981-95-7538-1_20

environment. This approach allows all team members to simultaneously perceive the robot's intentions without personal devices, fostering a more inclusive and collaborative setting [7].

Despite these advantages, implementing projector-based visualization in real-world collaborative environments remains challenging. Workspaces are rarely static or perfectly planar; rather, they are dynamic, irregular, and often involve deformable surfaces. These geometric complexities introduce projection distortions that, if uncorrected, can obscure visual information and diminish the clarity of robot intention communication [11].

Establishing clear intention communication between humans and robots is a prerequisite for trust, safety, and fluid coordination in shared workspaces. When a robot's goals and actions are transparently projected and easily interpretable, human partners can anticipate its behavior and make informed decisions, thereby reducing cognitive load and improving collaboration. Conversely, unclear or delayed intention cues compel operators to infer robot states from motion alone, increasing mental effort and reducing efficiency. By making robot actions both visible and interactive within the shared workspace, the proposed framework fosters transparency and establishes a trust-based foundation for safe and effective human–robot interaction.

The proposed framework combines visual intention projection with touch-driven interaction to create a natural, bidirectional communication loop. Robots convey their planned actions and context-aware queries directly onto the workspace, while a 3D depth camera detects fingertip responses even on uneven or deformable surfaces. A real-time distortion-compensation technique ensures geometrically accurate projection on dynamic, non-planar surfaces. The main contributions of this paper are as follows:

1. Establishment of a real-time, distortion-compensated projection framework for intention awareness, enabling clear and geometrically accurate visualization of robot intentions on complex and dynamic surfaces.
2. Integration of a touch-based query interaction module using depth-guided fingertip detection, establishing an intuitive and responsive two-way communication interface that enhances human–robot collaboration.

2 Related Work

Research on human–robot teaming has explored various strategies to enhance mutual understanding, transparency, and coordination between humans and robots. Existing studies can broadly be categorized into three domains: (1) methods for conveying robot intent through motion and multimodal cues, (2) visualization techniques that leverage projection to communicate planned actions in the shared workspace, and (3) interactive systems that enable users to provide feedback or responses through touch or gesture. This section reviews key developments in these areas, emphasizing their technical contributions and identifying limitations that motivate the proposed real-time framework for intention awareness and touch-based interaction.

2.1 Conveying Robot Intent

Early research on human–robot interaction focused on modifying robot motion to enhance the legibility of trajectories, thereby making actions more predictable and intuitive for human collaborators [1]. Subsequent studies incorporated additional modalities such as audio and verbal cues to provide continuous feedback on robot state and progress [3,4]. Reviews in the field further highlight the advantages of multimodal interaction for maintaining situational awareness and improving team coordination [5,6].

2.2 Projection-Based Visualization

Projection-based visualization has emerged as a compelling alternative to wearable or auditory interfaces by embedding digital cues directly into the shared workspace. This approach offers a common, real-time visual reference accessible to all team members, thereby enhancing collaboration and situational awareness [7]. Prior studies demonstrated that projecting visual information onto the environment can align a robot's internal decision-making with human interpretation, improving transparency and task coordination [8–10]. However, most existing systems assume static and planar surfaces, limiting their applicability in dynamic or irregular workspaces where geometric distortions degrade projection accuracy.

2.3 Projection Mapping on Uneven Surfaces

In practical human–robot teaming scenarios, workspace surfaces are rarely planar, leading to geometric distortions that hinder accurate projection and interpretation of visual cues. Dynamic projection mapping techniques have been developed to adapt projected imagery in real time based on the target surface geometry [11]. Building on these advances, recent studies have integrated projection and touch-based interactivity to create more intuitive collaboration between humans and robots [12,13]. These systems demonstrate how augmented projections can align digital content with irregular surfaces and enable direct user interaction. However, most existing methods remain limited to static or simplified surfaces and lack the robustness required for real-time performance on deformable or dynamically changing workspaces.

2.4 Interactive Query Projection and Touch-Based Response

Recent work in projection-based interfaces has explored interactive systems that enable direct touch-based interactions with visualized content. He et al. [14] developed a touch-sensitive interactive projection system that allowed users to manipulate projected information through finger touches, thereby establishing a natural, two-way communication between the display and the user. Building on similar principles, Ntelidakis et al. [15] presented a method for accurate touch detection on planar interactive displays by utilizing lateral depth views. More recently, Lokhande et al. [16] demonstrated a machine learning-based approach for converting projector outputs into smart board interactions, highlighting the potential for enhanced user engagement in interactive projection systems. This work extends these concepts by integrating interactive query projection into a real-time robot intention visualization framework. In this system, queries are dynamically projected onto the shared workspace, and users provide responses by simply touching the projected options.

Overall, while previous research has made significant contributions in each of these areas, a gap remains in integrating these advances into a practical, real-time system for dynamic environments. The work presented in this paper aims to bridge that gap by combining accessible hardware with advanced distortion compensation techniques to ensure clear and undistorted visualization of robot intent. Moreover, this framework extends prior interactive systems by incorporating query projection and precise finger touch-based response detection to support natural two-way communication and multiuser collaboration.

3 Intention Awareness and Touch-Based Query Framework

The proposed framework establishes a unified system for visual intention awareness and touch-based interaction in human–robot teaming. It integrates a 3D depth camera and a projector that operate cooperatively to capture surface geometry and render geometrically consistent visual projections. The depth sensor acquires the three-dimensional structure of the target workspace, from which refined depth information is derived. Using this data, an inverse projection transformation maps two-dimensional image coordinates onto the corresponding three-dimensional world coordinates. A pre-warped image is then generated to correct geometric distortions arising from non-planar or irregular surfaces. This distortion-compensated projection serves as the foundation for both the robot's intention visualization and the interactive, touch-based query response mechanism described in the following subsections.

Figure 1 illustrates the intention awareness and touch-based query framework designed for intuitive human–robot interaction. The system integrates visual intention projection with touch-based feedback in a unified loop. From right to left, the robot system generates motion plans and task intentions, which are geometrically mapped onto the environment through inverse projection and distortion compensation. The human operator perceives these projected cues and responds directly on the surface via touch. Depth sensing and fingertip detection capture these responses, closing the communication loop and enabling real-time, bidirectional collaboration between human and robot.

3.1 Inverse Projection Transformation on Arbitrary Surfaces

Accurate projection of visual cues onto real-world surfaces is essential for maintaining geometric consistency in intention visualization. In practical human–robot teaming environments, the workspace surfaces are often non-planar, irregular, or deformable, resulting in nonlinear geometric distortions in projected imagery. To mitigate these distortions, the proposed framework employs an inverse projection transformation that reconstructs a 3D surface model from

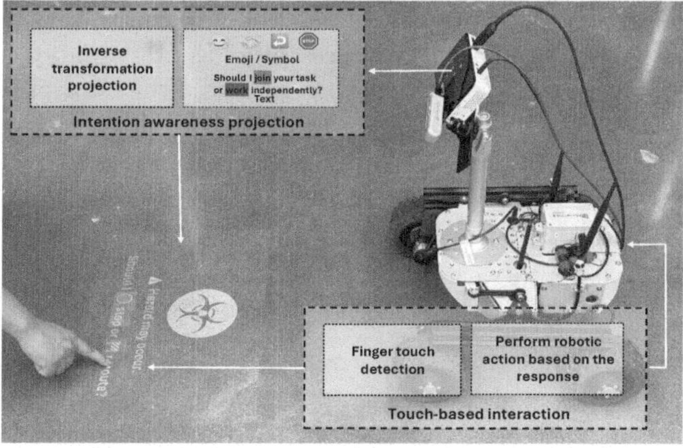

Fig. 1. The proposed omnisurface framework for intention awareness and touch-based query in human–robot interaction. The system integrates depth sensing, inverse projection, and interactive touch-based feedback to enable real-time communication between human operators and robots within a shared workspace.

depth data and pre-warps the projected image to ensure spatial accuracy. The depth array captured by the 3D depth camera serves as the primary data source for the proposed framework. Let $Z(i, j)$ denote the raw depth value at pixel coordinates (i, j) captured by the 3D depth camera. The refined depth map $Z'(i, j)$ is computed as $Z'(i, j) = \mathcal{R}(Z, i, j, \omega)$ where the recursive interpolation function $\mathcal{R}$ is defined by

$$\mathcal{R}(Z, i, j, \omega) = \frac{\sum_{k=-K}^{K} \omega(k)\, Z(i+k, j)}{\sum_{k=-K}^{K} \omega(k)}.$$

Here K is the half-size of the Gaussian kernel, and the Gaussian weights $\omega(k)$ are computed as $\omega(k) = \frac{1}{\sqrt{2\pi}\,\sigma} \exp\left(-\frac{k^2}{2\sigma^2}\right)$ where σ represents the standard deviation of the kernel.

To project a 2D image onto an arbitrary 3D surface, it determines the inverse projection transformation from image coordinates to 3D world coordinates. Let $p = [u\ v\ 1]^T$ denote the homogeneous coordinates of a pixel in the image, and let $P = [X\ Y\ Z\ 1]^T$ denote the homogeneous coordinates of the corresponding 3D world point. The standard pinhole camera model is given by $p = K\,[R\,t]\,P$, where $K \in \mathbb{R}^{3\times3}$ is the intrinsic matrix containing the camera's internal parameters (e.g., focal lengths and the principal point), $R \in \mathbb{R}^{3\times3}$ is the rotation matrix representing the orientation of the camera relative to the world coordinate system, and $t \in \mathbb{R}^{3\times1}$ is the translation vector representing the position of the camera in the world coordinate system. The inverse transformation that recovers the world coordinates P from the image coordinates p is given by

$$P = \begin{bmatrix} R^T & -R^T t \\ 0^T & 1 \end{bmatrix} K^{-1} p.$$

The refined depth map Z' is used in conjunction with this inverse projection to generate a calibrated 3D point cloud representing the target surface.

To correct geometric distortions on non-planar surfaces, a pre-warped projection image is generated using the reconstructed depth field. The valid depth range $[Z_{\text{min}}, Z_{\text{max}}]$ is first estimated, and an opposite depth map $Z''(i,j)$ is computed as

$$Z''(i,j) = Z_{\text{max}} - (Z(i,j) - Z_{\text{min}}),$$

which reverses local depth variations to compensate for surface curvature. The transformed depth values are then incorporated into the inverse projection model

$$P'' = \begin{bmatrix} R^T & -R^T t \\ 0^T & 1 \end{bmatrix} K^{-1} p,$$

producing a geometrically aligned 3D point cloud. The resulting 2D projection yields a pre-warped image that preserves spatial fidelity and enables distortion-free visualization across irregular and deformable workspaces.

The inverse projection transformation establishes the foundation for accurate, distortion-free visualization in dynamic and non-planar workspaces. By reconstructing a calibrated 3D surface model and generating a pre-warped projection image aligned with real-world geometry, the system ensures that visual cues remain spatially consistent regardless of surface irregularities. This precise geometric alignment not only enhances the fidelity of intention projection but also enables reliable localization of user interactions on the projected surface. Building on this foundation, the next subsection introduces a touch-based query response mechanism that leverages the refined depth data to detect fingertip contact and facilitate interactive communication between humans and robots.

3.2 Touch-Based Query

While the inverse projection ensures geometric accuracy of visual cues, effective human–robot collaboration further requires an intuitive and responsive means of interaction. In dynamic environments, traditional input devices such as keyboards or tablets are impractical, and conventional vision-based methods often fail on uneven or reflective surfaces. To overcome these limitations, the proposed system incorporates a touch-based interaction module that detects fingertip contact directly on the projected surface. By integrating depth sensing and visual hand-tracking, this module enables human operators to respond to projected queries through natural touch gestures, thereby establishing a seamless and bidirectional communication channel within the shared workspace. The system captures the surface depth and refines it according to Subsect. 3.1 to enable reliable fingertip contact detection. Hand and finger landmarks are identified using MediaPipe [17], from which the index fingertip landmark is extracted in normalized image coordinates $(\tilde{x}_{\text{tip}}, \tilde{y}_{\text{tip}})$ and mapped to projector-space pixels as

$$u_{\text{tip}} = \lfloor \tilde{x}_{\text{tip}} W \rfloor, \quad v_{\text{tip}} = \lfloor \tilde{y}_{\text{tip}} H \rfloor.$$

The corresponding fingertip depth is read from the refined depth map, $Z_{\text{tip}} = D'(u_{\text{tip}}, v_{\text{tip}})$. To obtain a stable surface reference, the mean depth $\bar{Z}_{\text{ROI}}$ is computed over a local window Ω of $N \times N$ pixels surrounding the fingertip, excluding pixels belonging to the finger region,

$$\bar{Z}_{\text{ROI}} = \frac{1}{|\Omega|} \sum_{(i,j)\in\Omega} D'(i,j), \quad |\Omega| = N^2.$$

A touch event is registered when the depth difference $\Delta Z = \bar{Z}_{\text{ROI}} - Z_{\text{tip}} < \tau$, where τ denotes the threshold distance between the fingertip and the surface.

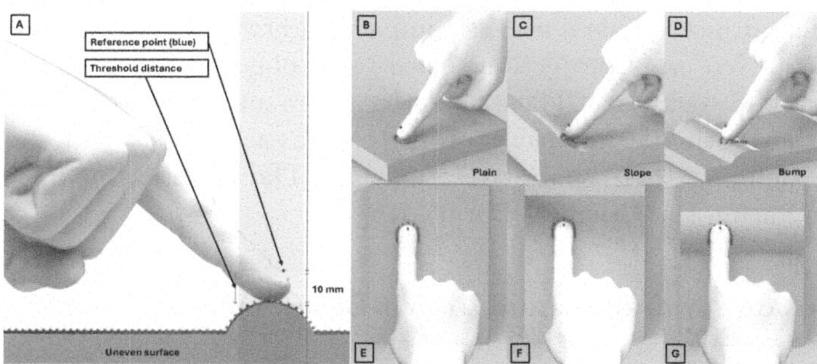

Fig. 2. Touch detection on uneven surfaces. (A) illustrates the fingertip approaching the reference point with a threshold distance applied for reliable contact recognition. (B–G) show detection mechanism across plain, sloped, and bumped surfaces, demonstrating consistent fingertip identification under varying geometries.

Figure 2 illustrates the fingertip detection process across multiple surface geometries in the touch-based query framework. Subfigure (A) shows the fingertip approaching a reference point (blue) within a threshold distance used for contact recognition. Subfigures (B–G) demonstrate that the system maintains consistent fingertip localization across plain, sloped, and bumped surfaces. In this case, the framework evaluates depth variations across a small neighborhood of surrounding pixels instead of relying on a single depth value to confirm touch contact. This combination of local depth analysis and MediaPipe-based landmark detection ensures accurate and stable interaction on uneven or deformable surfaces.

The robot's queries are projected toward the human operator using emojis, symbols, and text elements. Human operators respond by touching the interactive region B_j embedded within the projected query, where

$$B_j = \{(x_1^j, y_1^j), (x_2^j, y_2^j), \ldots, (x_n^j, y_n^j)\}, \quad j \in \{1, 2, \ldots, m\},$$

represents the set of pixel coordinates corresponding to the jth selectable query region. Upon detecting a touch event at $(u_{\text{tip}}, v_{\text{tip}})$, the system evaluates the membership condition

$$(u_{\text{tip}}, v_{\text{tip}}) \in B_j \Rightarrow Q_{\text{active}} = j,$$

where Q_{active} denotes the currently selected query index. This mapping allows precise detection of user selections across uneven or deformable surfaces. This approach enables reliable touch detection on arbitrary geometries, including sloped, bumped, or irregular surfaces, by minimizing false positives caused by finger occlusion.

4 Experiment

4.1 Experiment Setup

An "Intel RealSense D435" 3D depth camera is employed to capture the depth of non-planar surfaces. This sensor is compact, lightweight, and economical. The "AAXM P300 Neo" miniprojector is used to display the rectified image within the human-robot workspace. The 3D depth camera and projector were calibrated by considering both the intrinsic parameters of each device and the extrinsic parameters defining their spatial relationship. The calibration procedure was implemented using the OpenCV library [18].

4.2 Intention Awareness and Touch-Based Query

The depth map of the projection surface was captured and refined to support reliable touch detection. A real-time hand-tracking framework was utilized to locate the user's index fingertip in projector coordinates. Touch events were detected by comparing the measured distance of the fingertip from the surface with the average distance of the surrounding area. Upon touch registration, the system determines which button region contains the fingertip position and records that selection as the user's response. This pipeline operates at 20 to 30 frames per second on uneven surfaces, enabling smooth, accurate, touch-based interaction with projected queries.

Surface data captured by the 3D depth camera typically contains some invalid values (e.g., zeros). In this experiment, zero values are replaced with the median to reduce noise, and recursive Gaussian interpolation is applied to smooth the surface. The value of the standard deviation sigma is 0.1, and the size of the kernel, K = 10. The surface depth data were captured and refined to build an accurate 3D model of the projection target. The inverse projection transformation and pre-warping were implemented using the Open3D library [19]. The prewarped cues were projected onto the real-world surface using a calibrated projection system. This ensured that, despite surface irregularities and varying angles, the visual indicators remained correctly aligned and undistorted from the observer's viewpoint.

Figure 3 illustrates six representative scenarios demonstrating the proposed intention awareness and touch-based query framework in human–robot teaming. Each scenario depicts the robot projecting task-related queries directly onto the shared workspace and the human operator responding via touch interaction on the projected interface. The transition from the initial query display to the

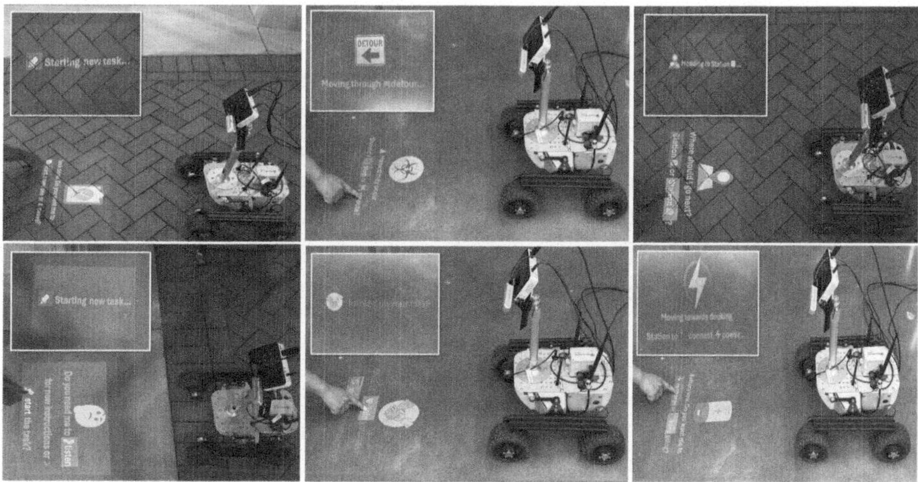

Fig. 3. Six representative scenarios of human–robot teaming demonstrating the proposed intention awareness and touch-based query framework. Each scenario illustrates the projected interface and the corresponding state after a touch interaction is performed on the in-line query options.

post-touch response highlights the system's ability to recognize fingertip contact accurately and update the visual feedback in real time. These examples collectively validate the effectiveness of the framework in enabling intuitive, low-latency communication between humans and robots across varying interaction contexts and surface geometries.

4.3 Performance

To evaluate the distortion-compensation pipeline, projection accuracy was measured on four surface types (flat, curved, inclined, and deformable). For each surface, twenty random target coordinates $\mathbf{y}_i = [u_i, v_i]^T$ were defined in the projector's image space and projected onto the corresponding physical surface. A 3D depth camera subsequently captured the projected pattern, from which the measured coordinates $\hat{\mathbf{y}}_i$ of each point were extracted. Accuracy was quantified using the root-mean-square error (RMSE):

$$\varepsilon = \sqrt{\frac{1}{n}\sum_{i=1}^{n}\left\|\mathbf{y}_i - \hat{\mathbf{y}}_i\right\|^2},$$

where $\|\cdot\|$ denotes the Euclidean distance in projector space and $n = 20$ for each surface. This metric captures the average spatial deviation introduced by surface irregularities and validates the effectiveness of the proposed prewarping and geometric correction procedures.

Table 1. Point-projection accuracy for static, dynamic, and deformable surfaces

	RMSE (mm)			Avg. Error (%)		
Surface	Static	Dynamic	Deformable	Static	Dynamic	Deformable
Flat	0.77	1.08	0.95	0.20	0.25	0.23
Curved	2.70	3.25	3.00	0.34	0.43	0.38
Inclined	3.00	3.60	3.20	0.38	0.48	0.40
Freeform	3.40	4.00	3.65	0.45	0.53	0.48
Average	**2.47**	**2.86**	**2.83**	**0.34**	**0.42**	**0.37**

Table 1 presents the quantitative evaluation of the proposed framework across four representative surface types under static, dynamic, and deformable conditions. The results demonstrate consistently low projection errors, with average RMSE values remaining below 3 mm and mean spatial deviations under 0.5%. Flat surfaces show the highest precision due to minimal curvature effects, while curved and freeform geometries exhibit slightly larger deviations caused by increased local depth variation. Overall, these results confirm that the prewarping and geometric correction process effectively preserves spatial fidelity across diverse real-world surface geometries.

To verify that the proposed intention–projection and touch-based query framework operates in real time, the system latency and throughput were evaluated under diverse surface conditions. Latency was measured from the moment of depth capture to the corresponding projector update and touch-event response, encompassing all intermediate stages such as depth refinement, fingertip detection, projection mapping, and rendering. Each component was timed using a monotonic clock synchronized with camera hardware timestamps. Latency distributions are reported in terms of the 50th (P50), 95th (P95), and 99th (P99) percentiles, representing the median, near-worst-case, and worst-case response times, respectively. The system was tested on flat, curved, inclined, and freeform surfaces to assess robustness under realistic workspace geometries.

Table 2. Real-time performance of the proposed framework across different surface geometries

	Latency (ms)			Throughput (Hz)		
Surface	P50	P95	P99	Static	Dynamic	Deformable
Flat	21.8	35.1	46.7	32	31	29
Curved	24.5	38.6	49.9	29	28	27
Inclined	25.2	39.4	51.0	28	27	26
Freeform	27.1	41.2	52.4	27	26	25
Average	**24.7**	**38.6**	**50.0**	**29**	**28**	**27**

Table 2 summarizes the quantitative performance. Across all scenarios, the framework consistently maintained a median latency below the 50 ms soft real-time threshold, corresponding to an effective update rate above 25 Hz. The low jitter and deadline-miss rates demonstrate stable performance suitable for continuous visual feedback and responsive human interaction. Overall, the framework achieved low-latency performance suitable for real-time intention awareness and interactive touch-based querying in collaborative human–robot environments.

4.4 User Acceptance

Twenty participants with diverse technical backgrounds performed predefined navigation and task-selection scenarios using two interaction modes: (1) a conventional graphical user interface (GUI) on a computer, and (2) our projector-3D camera-based intention visualization with touch-enabled query response on the shared workspace. After each mode, they rated seven acceptance criteria on a 1–5 Likert scale: *Correctness*, defined as the accuracy with which participants could interpret and convey the robot's intended action; *Ambiguity*, the degree of precision and unambiguity in instruction; *Effectiveness*, how well the method supported task completion compared to traditional programming or button panels; *Complexity*, the perceived operational difficulty relative to other interfaces; *Visibility*, the clarity and legibility of visual cues under typical indoor lighting and against varied surface conditions; *Intuitiveness*, the naturalness with which participants understood and used the interface without extensive training; and *Overall Satisfaction*, their holistic preference for the interaction method.

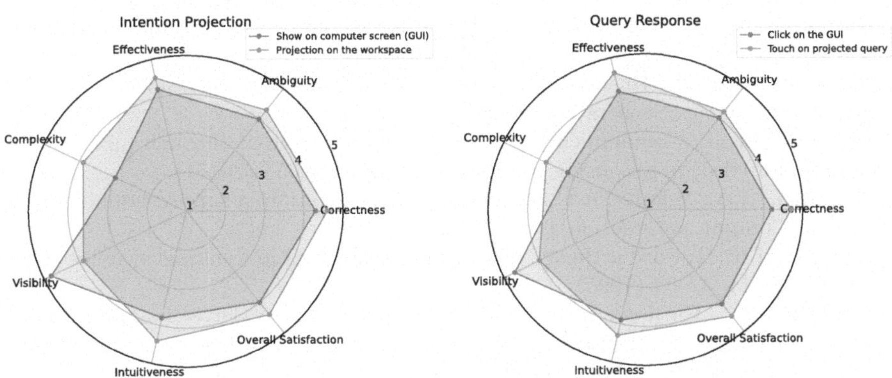

Fig. 4. Radar charts comparing mean user acceptance scores (1–5) for traditional GUIs versus our projection-and-touch system across seven evaluation criteria: (left) intention projection and (right) query response.

Figure 4 shows side-by-side radar charts comparing GUI versus projection for intention communication (left) and GUI versus touch for query response (right).

While the GUI scored highest in Visibility and maintained strong Correctness, our projection-and-touch system achieved superior Intuitiveness, Effectiveness, and Overall Satisfaction, illustrating its benefits for effective human–robot collaboration.

5 Conclusion

This paper presented a real-time framework for distortion-free projection of robot intentions on dynamic and deformable surfaces. By compensating for geometric variations, the system maintains spatial accuracy and clarity in complex workspaces. The resulting shared visual interface enhances situational awareness and transforms robots from passive tools into proactive teammates capable of transparent, human-centered communication. Furthermore, the integration of touch-based query interaction enables intuitive, bidirectional exchange between humans and robots without additional sensing hardware. Experimental results across static, dynamic, and deformable surfaces demonstrated substantial improvements in visual consistency, responsiveness, and collaborative fluency. Future work will focus on enhancing touch-detection precision, incorporating multimodal feedback, and extending the framework to multi-robot teams where shared intention projection could facilitate collective task coordination and human oversight.

References

1. Dragan, A.D., Bauman, S., Forlizzi, J., Srinivasa, S.S.: Effects of robot motion on human–robot collaboration. In: Proceedings of the 10th ACM/IEEE International Conference on Human-Robot Interaction (HRI), pp. 51–58 (2015)
2. Natarajan, M., Seraj, E., Altundas, B., et al.: Human-robot teaming: grand challenges. Current Robot. Rep. **4**(4), 279–289 (2023)
3. Mamone, V., et al.: Head-mounted projector for manual precision tasks: performance assessment. Sensors **23**(9) (2023)
4. Rosen, E., et al.: Communicating robot arm motion intent through mixed reality head-mounted displays, arXiv preprint arXiv:1708.03655 (2017)
5. Goodrich, M.A., Schultz, A.C.: Human-robot interaction: a survey. Found. Trends Human Comput. Interaction **1**(3), 203–275 (2007)
6. Endsley, M.R.: Toward a theory of situation awareness in dynamic systems. Hum. Factors **37**(1), 32–64 (1995)
7. Ganesan, R.K., Rathore, Y.K., Ross, H.M., Amor, H.B.: Better teaming through visual cues: how projecting imagery in a workspace can improve human-robot collaboration. IEEE Robot. Autom. Mag. **25**(2), 59–71 (2018)
8. Andersen, R.S., Madsen, O., Moeslund, T.B., Amor, H.B.: Projecting robot intentions into human environments. In: Proceedings of the 25th IEEE International Symposium on Robot and Human Interactive Communication (RO-MAN), pp. 294–301 (2016)
9. Chadalavada, R.T., Andreasson, H., Krug, R., Lilienthal, A.J.: That's on my mind! robot to human intention communication through on-board projection on shared floor space. In: Proceedings of the European Conference on Mobile Robots (ECMR), pp. 1–6 (2015)

10. Ruffaldi, E., Brizzi, F., Tecchia, F., Bacinelli, S.: Third point of view augmented reality for robot intentions visualization In: Proceedings of the IEEE International Symposium on Mixed and Augmented Reality (ISMAR), pp. 471–478 (2016)
11. Narita, G., Watanabe, Y., Ishikawa, M.: Dynamic projection mapping onto deforming non-rigid surfaces using deformable dot cluster markers. IEEE Trans. Visual Comput. Graphics **23**(3), 1235–1248 (2017)
12. Zaman, A.U., Li, H., Yan, F., Zhang, Y., He, H.: Omnisurface: common reality for intuitive human-robot collaboration. In: International Conference on Social Robotics, pp. 334–345. Springer (2024)
13. Yan, F., Chavez, E., Yihun, Y., He, H.: Touch detection in augmented Omni-surface for human-robot teaming. J. Manag. Eng. Integr. **15**(2) (2022)
14. He, M., Cheng, J., Tao, D.: Touch-sensitive interactive projection system. In: Proceedings of the 2014 IEEE International Conference on Security, Pattern Analysis, and Cybernetics (SPAC), pp. 436–441 (2014). https://doi.org/10.1109/SPAC.2014.6982729.
15. Ntelidakis, A., et al.: Touch detection for planar interactive displays based on lateral depth views. Multimedia Tools Appl. **76**, 12683–12707 (2017). https://doi.org/10.1007/s11042-016-3695-5
16. Lokhande, U., Jaiswal, N., William, J., Malik, M.M.A., Sonar, S.: ML based projector to smart board conversion. In: Proceedings of the 2024 Second International Conference on Inventive Computing and Informatics (ICICI), pp. 342–351 (2024). https://doi.org/10.1109/ICICI62254.2024.00063.
17. Zhang, F., et al.: MediaPipe Hands: On-device Real-time Hand Tracking, arXiv preprint arXiv:2006.10214 (2020). https://arxiv.org/abs/2006.10214
18. Camera Calibration and 3D Reconstruction (2025). OpenCV.org, https://docs.opencv.org/4.x/d9/d0c/group__calib3d.html, Accessed 17 April 2025
19. Zhou, Q.Y., Park, J., Koltun, V.: Open3D: A modern library for 3D data processing. arXiv preprint arXiv:1801.09847 (2018). https://arxiv.org/abs/1801.09847

Personalized Resistance Control Method for Wrist Rehabilitation Robots in Isotonic and Isokinetic Training

Weiwei Yu[1(✉)], Donglai Lu[1(✉)], Sixiang Fei[2], and Abderraouf Benali[3]

[1] School of Mechanical Engineering, Northwestern Polytechnical University, Xi'an 710072, China
yuweiwei@nwpu.edu.cn, ludonglai@mail.nwpu.edu.cn
[2] Hebei University of Technology, Tianjin, China
[3] Laboratoire d'Ingéniérie Systèmes Versailles, Université de Versailles Saint Quentin en Yvelines, Paris, France

Abstract. This study proposes a personalized resistance training control method for wrist rehabilitation robots to address the need for individualized isotonic and isokinetic training in late-stage rehabilitation. Using the NPU-WRIST robot, fuzzy rules were constructed based on joint torque and range of motion to generate personalized resistance and speed parameters. Comparative experiments showed that the personalized scheme achieved significantly higher training efficiency (90.1% for isotonic, 95.3% for isokinetic) than the fixed-parameter scheme (30.5% and 24.8% respectively), verifying its effectiveness.

Keywords: wrist rehabilitation · personalized resistance training · fuzzy rules · isotonic training · isokinetic training · rehabilitation robot

1 Introduction

Studies have shown that many rehabilitation individuals have upper limb motor dysfunction [1,2]. As the wrist is key for human dexterous movements and daily life, targeted wrist rehabilitation is crucial for regaining motor abilities.

Brunnstrom theory notes that late-stage rehabilitation patients have improved active motor ability (with recovered muscle tone) but still low muscle strength and poor joint movement speed/accuracy [3]. Resistance training (e.g., isotonic, isokinetic [4]) is commonly used: isotonic training (dynamic, constant resistance) effectively trains dynamic muscle strength consistently across joint range [5]; isokinetic training (constant resistance/angular velocity, near-max muscle force) enhances strength, avoids injury, and comprehensively improves muscle function by enabling max strength output at any joint position [6].

For dynamic training such as isotonic training and isokinetic training, the core lies in the setting of resistance and speed. One type of research focuses on setting through adaptive strategies. For instance, Tanishka Goyal et al. proposed a stiffness-observer-based adaptive controller: the stiffness-observer learns

S. S. Ge et al. (Eds.): ICSR + BioMed 2025, LNAI 16435, pp. 238–249, 2026.
https://doi.org/10.1007/978-981-95-7538-1_21

subject-specific wrist stiffness to modify the robot's reference trajectory, and the adaptive controller coordinates four BMAs to meet dynamic training's resistance and trajectory adaptation needs [7]; Fumin Guo et al. developed the MWOA with adaptive strategies (e.g., adaptive inertia weight), which optimizes upper extremity exoskeleton's isokinetic trajectory to keep joint speed stable, achieving adaptive speed control for isokinetic training [8]. Another type of research involves setting parameters with reference to joint parameters of healthy individuals. For example, MinKi Sin et al. set the resistance and speed required for isotonic and isokinetic training based on joint torque and movement speed of healthy individuals [9]. However, due to differences in muscle strength levels and joint ranges of motion among different patients, the settings of resistance and speed in existing isotonic and isokinetic training are mostly universal modes, which are difficult to meet the needs of personalized rehabilitation training.

In summary, personalized resistance/speed for isotonic/isokinetic training is urgently needed. This study thus designed a personalized wrist robot control method for resistance training and conducted feasibility experiments.

2 Experimental Platform

The experimental platform is called NPU-WRIST wrist rehabilitation robot, with three active degrees of freedom corresponding to the wrist's supination-pronation, ulnar-radial deviation, and flexion-extension. As resistance training's key is identifying wrist force generation and movement intention, its handle has a six-axis force/torque sensor to detect human-robot interaction forces/torques [10,11]. The robot also has adjustable dimensional mechanisms for stroke patients with different wrist sizes. Its physical prototype, structural schematic, and modified DH parameters are shown in Fig. 1 and Table 1.

(a) Physical prototype

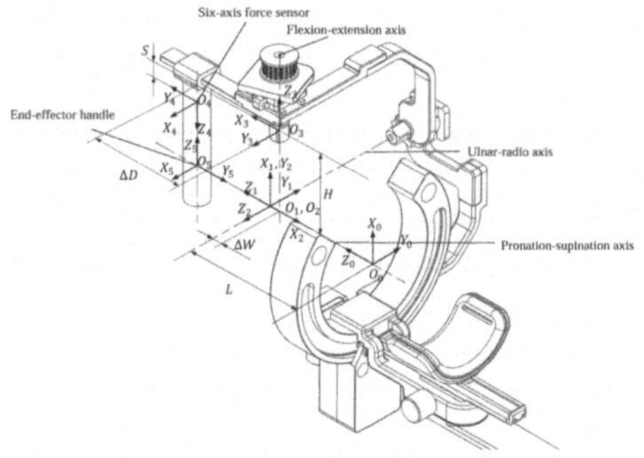

(b) Schematic diagram

Fig. 1. NPU-WRIST.

Table 1. Modified DH Parameter of NPU-WRIST

i	α_{i-1}	a_{i-1}	θ_i	d_i
1	0	0	θ_{sp}	L
2	$\frac{\pi}{2}$	0	$\theta_{urd} - \frac{\pi}{2}$	0
3	$-\frac{\pi}{2}$	ΔW	$\theta_{fe} + \pi$	H
4	π	ΔD	$-\frac{\pi}{2}$	S

θ_{sp} represents the rotation angle for the forearm pronation/supination motion,
θ_{urd} represents the rotation angle for the ulnar/radial deviation motion,
θ_{fe} represents the rotation angle for the flexion/extension motion.

To detect the force direction of wrist, the first step is to obtain the joint torques of the three degrees of freedom of the wrist joint movements. The handle of the experimental platform NPU-WRIST used in this paper is equipped with a six - dimensional force sensor, which can collect the force and torque exerted by the wrist joint on the handle. The measurement position and orientation coincide with Coordinate System 4. To decouple the force and torque collected by the sensor into joint torques, it is necessary to solve for the Jacobian matrix, whose structure is shown in Eq. (1):

$$\mathbf{J} = \begin{bmatrix} \mathbf{J}_v \\ \mathbf{J}_\omega \end{bmatrix} \tag{1}$$

Among them, the velocity Jacobian matrix is:

$$\mathbf{J}_v = \begin{bmatrix} \frac{\partial {}^0_4\boldsymbol{p}}{\partial \theta_{sp}} & \frac{\partial {}^0_4\boldsymbol{p}}{\partial \theta_{urd}} & \frac{\partial {}^0_4\boldsymbol{p}}{\partial \theta_{fe}} \end{bmatrix} \tag{2}$$

The angular velocity Jacobian matrix, on the other hand, is:

$$\mathbf{J}_\omega = \begin{bmatrix} \boldsymbol{z}_{sp} \ \boldsymbol{z}_{urd} \ \boldsymbol{z}_{fe} \end{bmatrix} \tag{3}$$

In Eq. (3), $\boldsymbol{z}_{sp}$, $\boldsymbol{z}_{urd}$, and $\boldsymbol{z}_{fe}$ represent the unit vectors in the direction of the new Z-axis in the rotated coordinate system. Each of these vectors corresponds to the third column of the rotation matrices ${}^0_1\mathbf{R}$, ${}^0_2\mathbf{R}$, and ${}^0_3\mathbf{R}$, respectively.

According to the principle of virtual work, it can be obtained that:

$$\boldsymbol{T}^T \Delta\boldsymbol{\theta} + (-\boldsymbol{F}^T)\Delta\boldsymbol{x} + (-\boldsymbol{M}^T)\Delta\boldsymbol{q} = \boldsymbol{0} \tag{4}$$

In Eq. (4), $\boldsymbol{T}$ represents the joint torque of the robot, $\boldsymbol{F}$ represents the force in the workspace collected by the robot's end-effector six-dimensional force sensor, $\boldsymbol{M}$ represents the torque in the workspace collected by the end-effector six-dimensional force sensor, $\Delta\boldsymbol{\theta}$ represents the virtual displacement angle of the joint in the joint space, $\Delta\boldsymbol{x}$ represents the virtual displacement in the workspace, and $\Delta\boldsymbol{q}$ represents the virtual displacement angle in the workspace. Since:

$$\boldsymbol{x} = \mathbf{J}_v \Delta\boldsymbol{\theta} \tag{5}$$

$$\boldsymbol{\Delta q} = \mathbf{J}_\omega \boldsymbol{\Delta\theta} \tag{6}$$

And since the directions of the force and torque collected by the six-dimensional force sensor are fixed to the sensor's coordinate system rather than the workspace, it is necessary to map the force and torque collected by the sensor into the workspace:

$$\boldsymbol{F} = {}_4^0\mathbf{R} \times \boldsymbol{F}_{sensor} \tag{7}$$

$$\boldsymbol{M} = {}_4^0\mathbf{R} \times \boldsymbol{M}_{sensor} \tag{8}$$

After arrangement, we finally obtain:

$$\boldsymbol{T} = \mathbf{J}_v^T \times {}_4^0\mathbf{R} \times \boldsymbol{F}_{sensor} + \mathbf{J}_\omega^T \times {}_4^0\mathbf{R} \times \boldsymbol{M}_{sensor} \tag{9}$$

Through Eq. (9), the force and torque exerted by the wrist joint on the robot handle, which are collected by the six - dimensional force sensor, can be converted into joint torques. In this way, the direction and magnitude of the force exerted by the wrist joint can be accurately identified.

3 Personalized Resistance Training Method Realized with Wrist Rehabilitation Robot

3.1 Planning and Control Method for Isotonic and Isokinetic Training

Patients differ in muscle strength, endurance, and rehabilitation progress. To develop individualized isotonic/isokinetic resistance training methods for their personalized needs, two core issues need solving: first, personalized isotonic training requires differentiated programs per subject's condition; second, personalized isokinetic training needs suitable muscle strength thresholds and joint angular velocities for individuals. Given patients' large differences in muscle strength and motor ability, reasonable thresholds/difficulty maintain optimal force generation during training, while suitable velocities improve movement smoothness and coordination.

To solve these issues, this chapter uses joint torque (reflecting force-generating capacity) and motion range (indicating flexibility/mobility) to build personalized programs. Fuzzy rules enable the wrist robot's control strategy to adapt to individual torque and motion range, ultimately realizing individualized resistance training.

Construction of Fuzzy Rules for Personalized Rehabilitation. To meet the needs of personalized rehabilitation, this subsection plans the resistance and joint velocity required for isotonic and isokinetic resistance training based on physiological parameters. To achieve this goal, it is first necessary to establish a set of fuzzy rules. The establishment process of the fuzzy rules is shown in Fig. 2.

First, it is necessary to define the fuzzy sets. As mentioned earlier, to address the differentiated and personalized rehabilitation needs of different individuals, distinct training programs must be developed based on two parameters—joint torque and range of joint motion—among varying individuals. Therefore, the fuzzy sets used to describe the physiological parameters of different individuals include:

(1) Joint Torque: This refers to the torque in the directions of the three degrees of freedom of movement of the wrist joint, influencing the joint's motor capacity and stability.

(2) Range of Joint Motion: It denotes the maximum and minimum angles that the wrist joint can achieve across its three degrees of freedom of movement.

Fig. 2. Fuzzy Rules.

For the elements in the fuzzy set, this subsection makes the following settings, as shown in Table 2:

Table 2. Physiological Parameter Fuzzy Set Elements

Physiological Parameter Fuzzy Set Elements	
Wrist Joint Torque	Wrist Joint Range of Motion
Small	Small
Medium	Medium
Large	Large

Note that in Table 2, each element corresponds to the wrist's three degrees of freedom (supination-pronation, ulnar-radial deviation, flexion-extension); only flexion-extension is presented herein to save space.

After determining fuzzy sets, membership functions (quantifying physiological parameters' membership to fuzzy sets) need constructing. Due to large individual differences in maximum joint torque and ROM, membership functions rely on subjects' unaffected hand data for personalized rehabilitation: for torque, use the unaffected hand's single-DOF maximum isometric contraction torque (collected pre-training at neutral position); for ROM, use the unaffected hand's single-DOF motion range. Their membership functions are shown in Fig. 3a and Fig. 3b, respectively.

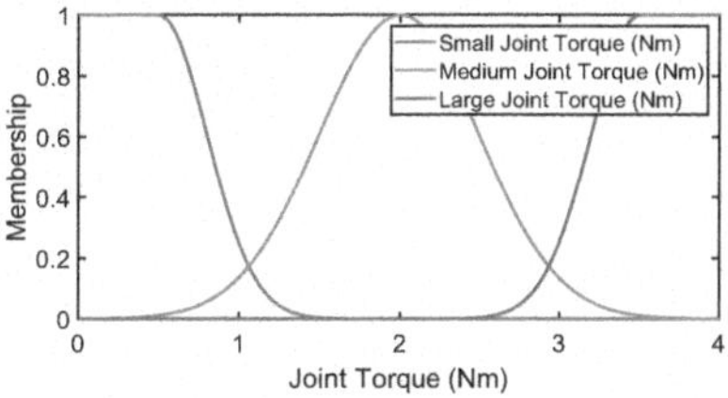

(a) An example of wrist torque (flexion-extension DOF) membership function

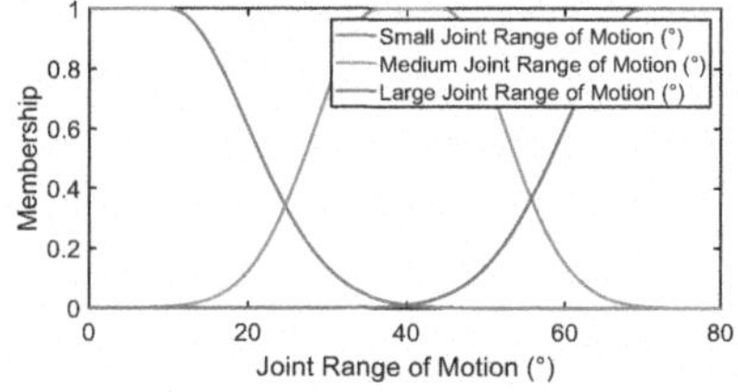

(b) An example of wrist ROM (flexion-extension DOF) membership function

Fig. 3. Membership functions for physiological parameters.

After completing the construction of membership functions for physiological parameters, the next step is to construct fuzzy rules. This process is crucial, as fuzzy rules can link different input parameters with corresponding output results, thereby enabling more precise decision support. Specifically, it is necessary to set a series of fuzzy rules based on the characteristics of joint torque and range of motion, such as the fuzzy rule tables for resistance and speed, as shown in Table 3 and Table 4 respectively.

After designing fuzzy rule tables, the next step is to construct membership functions for resistance and speed in isotonic/isokinetic training. Defining these functions maps physiological parameters to fuzzy sets, providing a basis for subsequent decision-making. The membership functions are shown in Fig. 4a and Fig. 4b

Table 3. Fuzzy Rule Table for Resistance

ROM	Joint Torque		
	Small Torque	Medium Torque	Large Torque
Small Range	Small Resistance	Small Resistance	Medium Resistance
Medium Range	Small Resistance	Small Resistance	Medium Resistance
Large Range	Small Resistance	Medium Resistance	Large Resistance

Table 4. Fuzzy Rule Table for Speed

ROM	Joint Torque		
	Small Torque	Medium Torque	Large Torque
Small Range	Slow Speed	Slow Speed	Slow Speed
Medium Range	Medium Speed	Medium Speed	Medium Speed
Large Range	Medium Speed	Fast Speed	Fast Speed

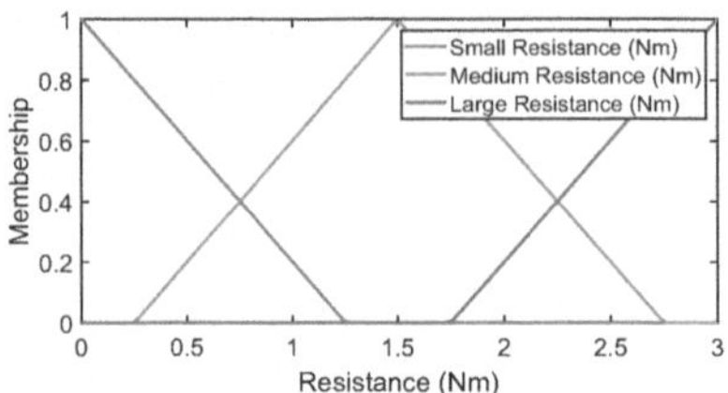

(a) An example of resistance (flexion-extension DOF) membership function

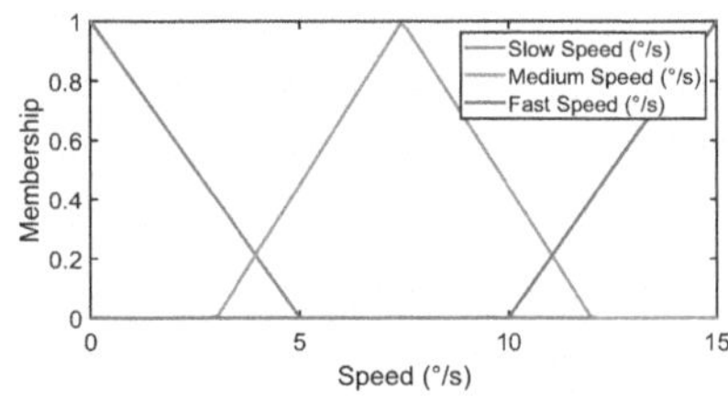

(b) An example of angular velocity (flexion-extension DOF) membership function

Fig. 4. Membership functions for resistance training.

After constructing fuzzy rules, resistance and speed for isotonic/isokinetic training can be determined via wrist joint torque and range of motion (ROM). Torque reflects the force patients should exert, while ROM provides their safe training motion range. Combining these two, fuzzy rule-based evaluation and center-of-gravity defuzzification (calculating the fuzzy set's geometric center to convert reasoning results to specific values) yield precise resistance and speed.

$$x^* = \frac{\int_a^b x \cdot \mu(x)\,\mathrm{d}x}{\int_a^b \mu(x)\,\mathrm{d}x} \tag{10}$$

Here, x^* is the defuzzified precise value, $\mu(x)$ the fuzzy set's membership function, and a, b its domain. Fuzzy rule-generated resistance and speed surfaces are shown in Fig. 5a and Fig. 5b; these convert patients' torque/ROM to training resistance/speed, enabling personalized programs for stroke patients and precise, scientific rehabilitation.

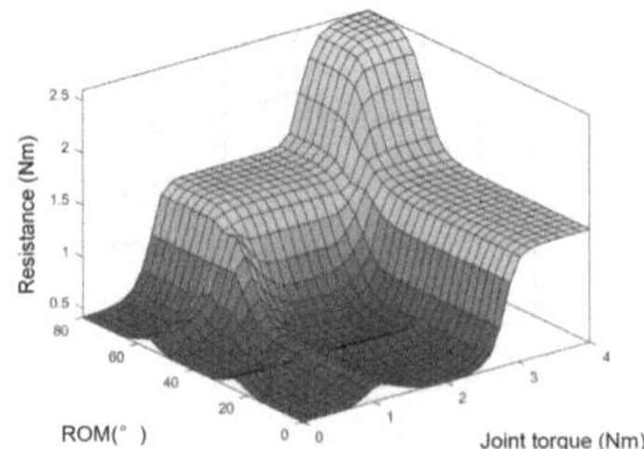

(a) An example of fuzzy rule-based resistance surface (flexion-extension DOF)

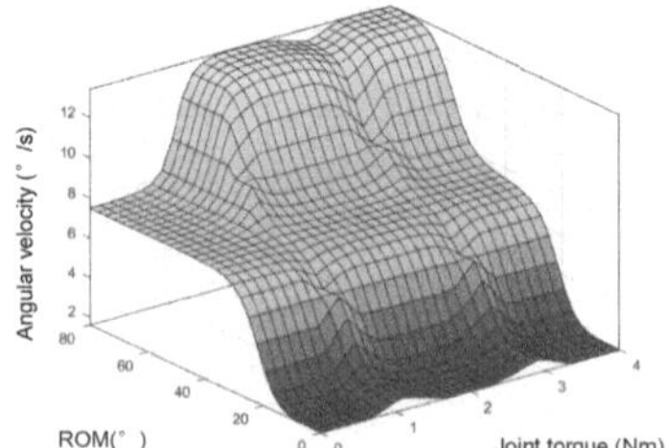

(b) An example of fuzzy rule-based angular velocity surface (flexion-extension DOF)

Fig. 5. Fuzzy rule-based surface.

Control Method for Isotonic and Isokinetic Controllers of Wrist Joint Rehabilitation Robots. This section establishes isotonic and isokinetic resistance training control methods for stroke patients' post-rehabilitation needs, based on generated resistance and speed.

The core of impedance control is the robot's real-time tracking of wrist motion and constant resistance application—activating only when the patient's force exceeds a predefined threshold. In practice, it delivers fuzzy rule-based constant resistance matching patients' muscle strength and joint range, enabling personalized, safe, and effective training.

For isotonic training, a 6D force sensor decouples the subject's force/torque on the handle to derive torque for each wrist DOF (capturing motion intent and guiding the robot along the force direction). Constant resistance is ensured via impedance control: $T_{resisted}$ (fuzzy rule-generated from joint torque/ROM) remains constant and opposes wrist motion direction.

$$\mathbf{B}(\dot{\boldsymbol{\theta}}-\dot{\boldsymbol{\theta}}_d)+\mathbf{K}(\boldsymbol{\theta}-\boldsymbol{\theta}_d) = \mathbf{J}_v^T \times {}_4^0\mathbf{R} \times \boldsymbol{F}_{sensor} + \mathbf{J}_\omega^T \times {}_4^0\mathbf{R} \times \boldsymbol{M}_{sensor} - \boldsymbol{T}_{resisted} \quad (11)$$

Isokinetic training adds speed constraints to the above framework: patients must overcome constant resistance *and* maintain constant speed (better simulating daily movement demands). Speed constraints are added to Eq. 11, with Eqs. 12 and 13 integrating force and speed for precise control.

$$\mathbf{K}(\boldsymbol{\theta}-\boldsymbol{\theta}_d) = \mathbf{J}_v^T \times {}_4^0\mathbf{R} \times \boldsymbol{F}_{sensor} + \mathbf{J}_\omega^T \times {}_4^0\mathbf{R} \times \boldsymbol{M}_{sensor} - \boldsymbol{T}_{resisted} \quad (12)$$

$$\dot{\boldsymbol{\theta}} = \dot{\boldsymbol{\theta}}_{fuzzy} \quad (13)$$

Here, T_{resisted} (training resistance) and $\dot{\theta}_{\text{fuzzy}}$ (constant speed) are fuzzy rule-generated with personalized settings (based on individual joint torque/ROM), ensuring the robot maintains constant speed to drive patients' uniform motion.

4 Experimental Protocol

The previous section constructed late-stage rehabilitation personalized training methods (including personalized training program generation and wrist robot control methods). To verify their effectiveness, a controlled experiment was conducted. Due to rehabilitation training being high-load active force-generating training, for safety (avoiding irreversible patient harm) and adhering to medical ethics' "minimum risk" principle, this study used healthy individuals as subjects first.

For the experimental group: Pre-experiment: measure subjects' wrist neutral position torque and joint range of motion; generate personalized rehabilitation resistance and speed via fuzzy rules. Then perform single-degree-of-freedom (e.g., flexion-extension) isotonic and isokinetic training via the wrist rehabilitation robot.

For the control group: The resistance and speed of isotonic and isokinetic training were fixed, and the training was performed directly.

5 Results

5.1 Efficiency of Isotonic and Isokinetic Training

Table 5 shows subjects' physiological parameters and fuzzy rule-generated resistance training parameters.

Figure 6 presents the experimental group's (flexion-extension DOF) training results: blue = personalized resistance, red = subjects' joint torque, black dashed = isokinetic set speed, green = actual angular velocity. Differences in required resistance across subjects confirm individual physiological/motor differences, and subjects' torque overcoming resistance to drive the robot verifies the control method's effectiveness. In isokinetic training (Fig. 6b), angular velocity stably follows the set value, meeting isokinetic requirements.

Table 5. Physiological Parameters and Personalized Rehabilitation Program Parameters (Flexion-Extension DOF)

Subject ID	Isometric Torque (N·m)	ROM	Resistance (N·m)	Angular Velocity
1	1.49	+54°/−54°	1.11	8.83°/s
2	2.18	+61°/−61°	1.45	11.5°/s
3	2.52	+70°/−70°	1.5	12.9°/s

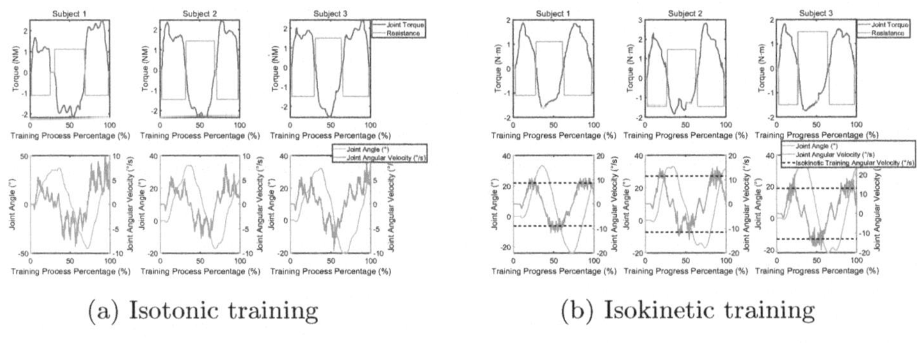

(a) Isotonic training

(b) Isokinetic training

Fig. 6. Experimental Group Results (Flexion-Extension DOF): Personalized Training Performance. Red: Wrist torque; Blue: Robot impedance torque; Yellow: Joint angle; Green: Joint velocity; Black dashed: Isokinetic set speed. (Color figure online)

Figure 7 shows the control group's results (fixed parameters: isotonic resistance 2 N·m, isokinetic speed 15o/s). When subjects' torque fails to reach resistance, the robot does not move (invalid training).

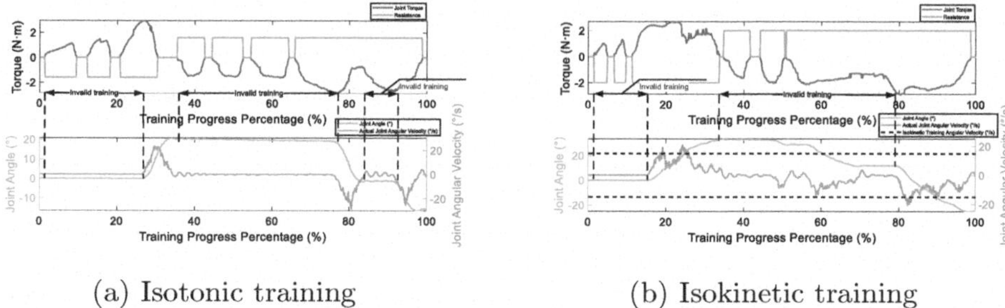

(a) Isotonic training (b) Isokinetic training

Fig. 7. Results of control group (flexion-extension DOF). When the subject's joint torque is greater than the set resistance, the robot can move (green curve, which represents the robot's joint velocity $\neq 0$), and this situation is regarded as effective training.

Effective training is measured by $R = \Delta t/T$ (Eq. 15), where Δt = time torque $>$ resistance (non-zero velocity) and T = total training time. Table 6 shows the experimental group's efficiency (isotonic 90.1%, isokinetic 95.3%) is far higher than the control group's (isotonic 30.5%, isokinetic 24.8%).

$$\begin{cases} v \neq 0, \left| \mathbf{J}_v^T \times {}_4^0\mathbf{R} \times \boldsymbol{F}_{sensor} + \mathbf{J}_\omega^T \times {}_4^0\mathbf{R} \times \boldsymbol{M}_{sensor} \right| > \left| \boldsymbol{T}_{resisted} \right| \\ v = 0, \left| \mathbf{J}_v^T \times {}_4^0\mathbf{R} \times \boldsymbol{F}_{sensor} + \mathbf{J}_\omega^T \times {}_4^0\mathbf{R} \times \boldsymbol{M}_{sensor} \right| \leq \left| \boldsymbol{T}_{resisted} \right| \end{cases} \tag{14}$$

$$R = \frac{\Delta t}{T} \tag{15}$$

Table 6. Training Efficiency of Experimental and Control Groups

Efficiency Training Type	Experimental Group Personalized Scheme	Control Group Fixed-parameter Scheme
Isotonic Training	90.1%	30.5%
Isokinetic Training	95.3%	24.8%

The personalized scheme considers individual joint torque and motion range (appropriate resistance/speed), boosting participation; fixed parameters lack adjustments, reducing efficiency. This verifies the personalized program's advantages and provides empirical support for future rehabilitation design.

6 Discussion

Aiming at late-stage rehabilitation patients' personalized resistance training needs, this study proposes a fuzzy rule-based intelligent control method for wrist rehabilitation robots—integrating multi-dimensional wrist-hand physiological parameters to build a fuzzy rule base, dynamically adjusting joint torque and motion range thresholds for personalized isotonic/isokinetic training parameter adaptation.

To clarify its position in adaptive control, it is compared with typical methods (ML, MPC): 1) Data dependency: ML needs large-scale labeled data, while this method only uses pre-measured unaffected hand parameters (max isometric torque, ROM) to build membership functions, reducing data burden. 2) Real-time performance/safety: MPC's online optimization delays motion, but this method maps torque/range to resistance/speed via pre-established rule tables (Table 3, Table 4) and center-of-gravity defuzzification, achieving millisecond-level adjustment and lower overload risks. 3) Clinical interpretability: ML (e.g., black-box neural networks) lacks transparent logic, while this method's rules directly link "torque (small/medium/large) + range (small/medium/large)" to resistance/speed levels, intuitive for clinicians.

A comparative experiment (same subjects, personalized vs. fixed-parameter schemes) verified effectiveness: personalized scheme's isotonic/isokinetic effective rates (90.1%, 95.3%) are significantly higher than fixed-parameter's (30.5%, 24.8%). This shows fuzzy inference-based personalized regulation improves rehabilitation biomechanical adaptability (balancing real-time performance, data efficiency, interpretability vs. ML/MPC), providing a theoretical basis for subsequent large-scale clinical verification.

Acknowledgments. This study was funded by National High-end Foreign Experts Project (Grant No. G2023183021L) and Key Research & Development of Shaanxi Province (Grant No.2020SF152).

References

1. Gandolfi, M., et al.: eXplainable AI allows predicting upper limb rehabilitation outcomes in sub-acute stroke patients. IEEE J. Biomed. Health Inf. **27**(1), 263–273. IEEE (2022)
2. Lawrence, E.S., et al.: Estimates of the prevalence of acute stroke impairments and disability in a multiethnic population. Stroke **32**(6), 1279–1284 (2001)
3. Zhang, Z., Fang, Q., Gu, X.: Fuzzy inference system based automatic Brunnstrom stage classification for upper-extremity rehabilitation. Expert Syst. Appl. **41**(4), 1973–1980 (2014)
4. Lee, S.E.K., de Lira, C.A.B., Nouailhetas, V.L.A., Vancini, R.L., Andrade, M.S.: Do isometric, isotonic and/or isokinetic strength trainings produce different strength outcomes? J. Bodywork Mov. Ther. **22**(2), 430–437 (2018)
5. Tanaka, H., et al.: Improvement in muscle strength with low-load isotonic training depends on fascicle length but not joint angle. Muscle Nerve **57**(1), 83–89 (2018)
6. Petrucci, A., Guglielmino, D., Pecci, J., Pareja-Galeano, H.: The effects of isokinetic training in athletes after knee surgery: a systematic review. Physician Sportsmedicine **52**(4), 309–316 (2024)

7. Goyal, T., Hussain, S., Martinez-Marroquin, E., Brown, N.AT, Jamwal, P.K.: Stiffness-observer-based adaptive control of an intrinsically compliant parallel wrist rehabilitation robot. IEEE Trans. Hum. Mach. Syst. **53**(1), 65–74 (2022)
8. Guo, F., Zhang, H., Xu, Y., Xiong, G., Zeng, C.: Isokinetic rehabilitation trajectory planning of an upper extremity exoskeleton rehabilitation robot based on a multistrategy improved whale optimization algorithm. Symmetry **15**(1) 232 (2023)
9. Sin, M.K., Park, D.G., Cho, K.-J.: Comparison and evaluation of robotic strength rehabilitation algorithms: isokinetic, isotonic and shared control method. In: The 2011 International Conference on Advanced Mechatronic Systems, Zhengzhou, China, pp. 438–441. IEEE (2011)
10. Chen, Y., Yu, W., Zhi, J., Benali, A., Wang, R.: Integrating human factors in the systematic mechanical design of NPU-Wrist Rehabilitation Robot. In: AHFE International Conference on Applied Human Factors Ergonomics, San Francisco, CA, USA, pp. 50–61 (2023)
11. Yu, R., et al.: Achieving personalized wrist training: apply human factors in the control strategy of rehabilitation robot. In: AHFE International Conference on Applied Human Factors Ergonomics, San Francisco, CA, USA (2023)

Research on Cloud Edge Collaborative Algorithm for Surgical Robots Based on Model Predictive Control

Yinghao Zhao[1,2], Yaoxing Hu[1,2], Hao Zeng[1,2], Fan Feng[1,2], Xinyu Zhang[1,2], and Yingchao Song[1,2](✉)

[1] Department of Industry Engineering, School of Mechanical Engineering, Northwestern Polytechnical University, Xi'an 710072, China
songyc@mail.nwpu.edu.cn

[2] Bio-Additive Manufacturing University-Enterprise Joint Research Center of Shaanxi Province, Northwestern Polytechnical University, Xi'an 710072, China

Abstract. With the development of 5G remote communication technology, surgical robot technology, and artificial intelligence, telesurgery has overcome the limitations of space and time on surgical procedures. However, telesurgery still faces issues such as data transmission delay, surgical robot delay, and stability. To reduce the latency of surgical robots, virtual controllers are designed using cloud-edge collaboration technology, and model predictive control algorithms are employed to enhance the data processing capabilities at the edge and reduce the computational resource usage of the cloud. By reasonably allocating tasks between cloud computing and edge computing, the information transmission time can be effectively reduced, thereby decreasing the latency of surgical robots.

Keywords: Telesurgery · Cloud-Edge Collaboration · Surgical Robots · Model Predictive Control

1 Introduction

Since the inception of the biomedical industry, the premise for doctors to treat patients has often been that both are in the same place at the same time. However, real-world constraints mean that sometimes there is a significant spatial distance between doctors and patients in urgent need of treatment. This situation is often seen with surgical patients [1]. For example, soldiers on the battlefield, residents of underdeveloped areas, and survivors of accidents such as plane crashes and shipwrecks often lose their lives because they cannot receive timely medical treatment. According to the World Health Organization, about 5 billion people worldwide do not have access to safe, affordable basic surgical care.

To address this issue, telesurgery technology and related equipment have emerged. Telesurgery is an important concept within telemedicine, referring to surgeries performed by an operator using remote communication technology and robotic surgical systems without direct physical contact with the patient [2]. During the surgery, the surgeon

S. S. Ge et al. (Eds.): ICSR + BioMed 2025, LNAI 16435, pp. 250–259, 2026.
https://doi.org/10.1007/978-981-95-7538-1_22

performs routine surgical actions from a distance, with the control of surgical instruments and the execution of surgical procedures being synchronized by an electronic system that manages the robotic arms.

The development of telesurgery fundamentally relies on remote communication technology and surgical robotic arms, both of which depend on networks for data transmission. However, network-based data transmission causes operational delays in both local and remote surgical robots [3, 4]. The length of these delays significantly impacts the surgical outcome and the success of the procedure.

Research indicates that the maximum acceptable overall delay for surgeons is 300 ms; however, considering factors such as the motion characteristics of robotic arms, the effectiveness of complex surgical operations, and dynamic environments, the most suitable overall delay should be within 200 ms [5]. Excessive delay can prolong the surgery duration and impose significant psychological pressure on surgeons, thereby increasing the risk of surgery [6].

This study investigates how to reduce the latency time of telesurgery robots.

Network-based data transmission causes operational delays in both local and remote surgical robots. Currently, telesurgery uses wireless network transmission based on 5G technology [7]. Due to the shared and competitive nature of data transmission, the waiting and processing times of data can dynamically change as it passes through multiple nodes. This affects the stability of data transmission, resulting in delays for surgical robots.

Therefore, the key to reducing the latency of surgical robots is to reduce the waiting and processing times of data transmission [8]. This paper proposes the use of cloud-edge collaboration technology to design virtual controllers: applying model predictive control algorithms to enhance the data processing capabilities at the edge of the network, reducing data processing time, and lowering the computational resource usage of the cloud. This approach frees up computational power on cloud servers, allowing for the allocation of more computing resources to data transmission, thereby reducing data waiting time.

2 Related Works

The three most widely used robotic systems in telesurgery are the Da Vinci Minimally Invasive Surgical System, the Zeus Robotic Surgical System, and the Aesop Voice-Controlled Robotic Surgical Assistant System.

(1) The Da Vinci Minimally Invasive Surgical System is a widely used intelligent surgical platform worldwide, mainly consisting of a console system, manipulator system, and imaging system [9].
(2) The Zeus Robotic Surgical System mainly comprises several components: the Aesop Voice-Controlled Endoscope Positioner, the Hermes Voice-Controlled Center, the Zeus Robotic Surgical System (including left and right robotic arms, surgeon's operating console, and video control console), and the Socrates Remote Collaboration System.
(3) The Aesop Voice-Controlled Robotic Surgical Assistant System primarily consists of mechanical hands, robotic arms, mechanical body, and a computer voice recognition system. It is also one of the earliest successfully developed remote surgical systems (Fig. 1).

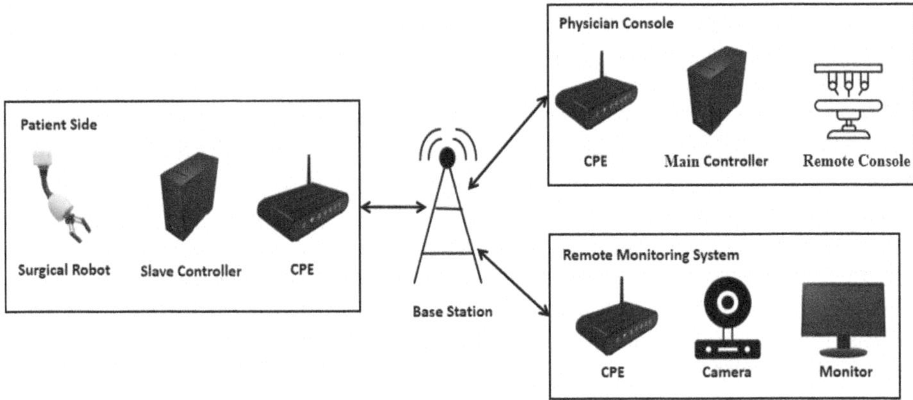

Fig. 1. Telesurgery Robot System

Many experts and scholars have embarked on exploratory research to address the latency issues of these three robotic surgical systems.

Researchers have constructed recursive neural network latency prediction models from an algorithmic perspective, providing different functions to compute cell states and obtain predicted latency values [10, 11]. This effort offers crucial data support for subsequent latency reduction, enhancing the responsiveness of telesurgery robots. However, predicted values may be subject to dynamic changes due to information flow interference, making it difficult to accurately reflect real-time conditions during surgery.

Many scholars have also explored various communication methods to reduce latency, such as dedicated fiber-optic lines and the internet. Fiber-optic lines offer minimal latency but significantly increase surgical costs [12]. On the other hand, using cost-effective commercial internet transmission is heavily influenced by network bandwidth conditions and poses risks related to network competition and data security [13].

In summary, there is a need to find a method that is secure, reliable, real-time, and highly fault-tolerant to reduce the latency of surgical robots while ensuring their stability.

This paper proposes the use of cloud-edge collaboration technology to design virtual controllers: applying model predictive control algorithms to enhance the data processing capabilities at the edge of the network, reducing data processing time, and lowering the computational resource usage of the cloud. This approach frees up computational power on cloud servers, allowing for the allocation of more computing resources to data transmission, thereby reducing data waiting time.

3 Methodology

3.1 Existing Problems

The implementation of telesurgery can be decomposed into three modules: the surgeon's control end (edge-side robot), the patient's surgical end (edge-side robot), and the remote communication system (cloud-side server).

The latency of surgical robots mainly manifests in two aspects: data processing time and waiting time.

(1) Data processing time

The inherent delays in surgical robots, such as reaction time of robotic arms, graphics processing delays, and video encoding/decoding delays, contribute to the overall latency [14].

Theoretically, the operation of surgical robots involves the following steps: High-definition cameras capture images, which are then transmitted to the cloud-side server. The server performs encoding and decoding tasks and transfers the images to the main surgical robot [15]. The main robot receives the surgeon's commands and uploads them to the cloud-side server. The server performs encoding and decoding tasks and transmits the motion commands to the slave robots. The slave robots move according to the received commands.

In this process, the cloud-side server continuously receives data from both the main and slave robots and performs tasks such as encoding, decoding, and data exchange [16]. This significantly consumes the server's computational resources. Additionally, due to limitations in computational resources and processing power, all data processing tasks are centralized on the cloud-side server, prolonging the data processing time.

(2) Data waiting time

With the advancement of remote communication technology, an increasing number of telesurgery procedures are no longer reliant on inefficient and high-latency physical links but are instead utilizing wireless network data transmission. Particularly in recent years, with the development of 5G technology, data waiting times have been significantly reduced [17, 18]. In 2019, Dr. Liu Rong from the Hepatobiliary and Pancreatic Surgery Department at the 301 Hospital in Beijing, China, successfully performed the world's first animal surgery experiment using 5G technology for telesurgery [19].

However, due to the nature of network-based data transmission not being "point-to-point," there are issues with data sharing and competition. When data is transmitted via cables or wireless signal towers to devices or machines, waiting delays occur. The longer the waiting delay, the longer it takes for this data to be sent. This results in dynamic changes between real-time data and historical data. How to reduce data waiting delay time is an important issue for maintaining the safety of telesurgery.

3.2 Solution

Using a cloud-edge collaboration solution, computing and encoding/decoding services are moved from the cloud to the local network for processing, enabling faster response times for surgical robots. Edge computing allows data collection and analysis to be performed on the device side (surgical robot) to ensure data security and provide optimal service to users.

Cloud-based edge computing has become mainstream, and migrating data to the cloud can significantly reduce the response time of surgical robots.

As mentioned earlier, like many experts and scholars, addressing the latency issues of surgical robots can be approached from an algorithmic perspective [20]. On one hand, optimizing data flow transmission algorithms can reduce data transmission time. On the other hand, building dedicated lines or exclusive network spaces can ensure data transmission without waiting time (Fig. 2).

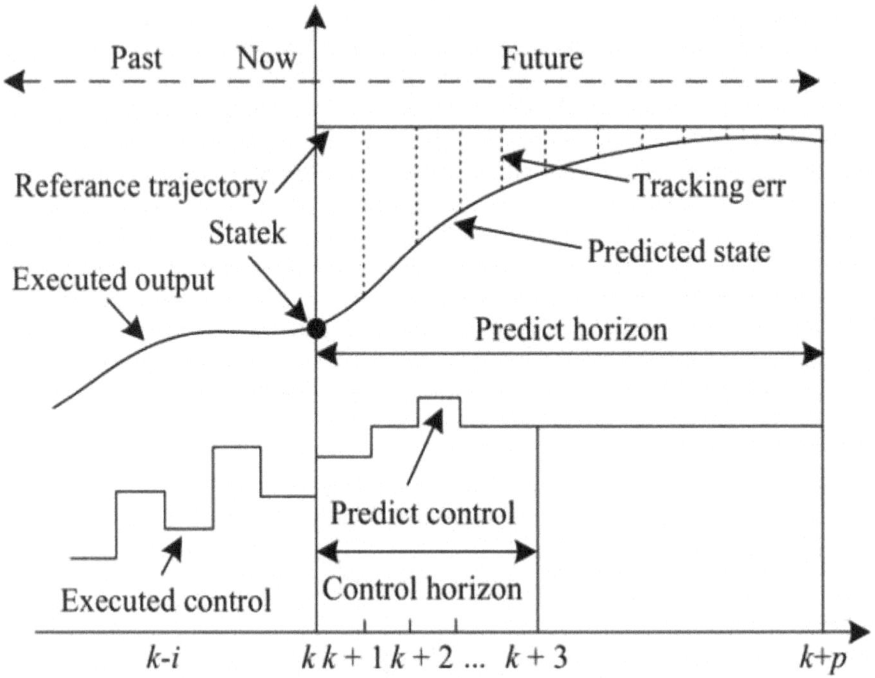

Fig. 2. Model Predictive Control Mechanism

To address the latency of surgical robots, this paper will utilize cloud-edge collaboration technology to design a virtual controller. It will apply model predictive control algorithms to enhance the data processing capabilities of surgical robots at the edge, reducing data processing time and lowering the computational resource usage of the cloud. This approach will free up computational power on cloud servers, allowing for the allocation of more computing resources to data transmission, thereby reducing data waiting time.

(1) Edge end - surgical robot

Edge computing is a distributed computing architecture that differs from cloud computing. It decomposes tasks previously handled by central servers and distributes these decomposed task fragments to the edge of the network, where edge devices are responsible for computation.

Edge computing reduces the transmission time of relevant information and decreases latency.

However, the control algorithms used in telesurgery robotic systems are typically PID (Proportional-Integral-Derivative) algorithms. PID controllers have advantages such as simplicity, strong adaptability, and high precision. However, they also have disadvantages, including difficulties in parameter tuning and strong reliance on system models [21].

In practical work, due to the complexity of parameter tuning methods, conventional PID controllers often have poorly tuned parameters and unsatisfactory performance, resulting in poor adaptability to operating conditions. This can significantly consume edge computing resources, necessitating the search for more efficient, accurate, and stable control algorithms.

Model Predictive Control (MPC) is a special type of control that obtains the current control action by solving a finite-time open-loop optimal control problem at each sampling instant. Compared to PID control, it can simultaneously control multiple variables, thus improving control efficiency (Fig. 3).

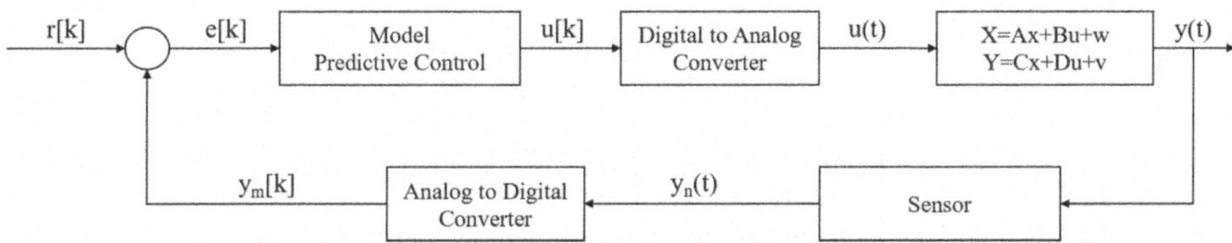

Fig. 3. Model Predictive Control System

Applying the model predictive control method can speed up edge computing and effectively reduce the latency of surgical robots.

Firstly, the kinematic model of the main robot and the slave robot needs to be established. The Denavit-Hartenberg method is commonly used to establish the model.

The transformation relationship between the link coordinate systems is as follows:

$$A_i = Rot(z_i, \theta_i)Trans(z_i, d_i)Trans(x_{i-1}, \alpha_{i-1})Rot(x_{i-1}, \alpha_{i-1}) \tag{1}$$

The general form of A_i is:

$$A_i = \begin{bmatrix} cos\theta_i & -sin\theta_i cos\alpha_{i-1} & sin\theta_i sin\alpha_{i-1} 0 & \alpha_{i-1} cos\theta_i \\ sin\theta_i & cos\theta_i cos\alpha_{i-1} & 0 & \alpha_{i-1} sin\theta_i \\ 0 & sin\alpha_{i-1} & -cos\theta_i sin\alpha_{i-1} & d_i \\ 0 & 0 & 0 & 1 \end{bmatrix} \tag{2}$$

Multiplying the transformation matrices of each link together yields the arm transformation matrix:

$$A_N = A_1 A_2 A_3 A_4 A_5 \ldots\ldots A_n \tag{3}$$

When the joint angle information of the surgical robot's robotic arm is known, the end position of the robotic arm can be calculated using Eq. (3).

Next, based on the principle of model predictive control, at time k, the system state information is read to obtain the system output y(k).

Applying the control input u(k|k) to the system, the system's performance is predicted as y(k + 1|k). At time k + 1, applying a control input u(k + 1|k) to the system, the system's performance is predicted as y(k + 2|k). This process is repeated continuously to obtain future outputs:

$$Y_k = \left[\ y_k(k+1|k)\ y_k(k+2|k)\ \ldots\ldots\ y_k(k+N|k)\ \right]^T \tag{4}$$

The control input is:

$$U_k = \left[\ u(k|k)\ u(k+1|k)\ \ldots\ldots\ u(k+N-1|k)\ \right]^T \tag{5}$$

The objective function is:

$$minJy(k), U(k) = \sum_{i=k+1}^{k+N} (r(i) - y(i|k))^2 \tag{6}$$

Finally, at time k, the optimal control sequence U_k calculated using Eq. (6) is obtained, and only u(k|k) is applied to the system.

By applying the model predictive control method, the computational capabilities at the device edge can be effectively enhanced.

(2) Cloud – Server

By using data such as images obtained through high-definition cameras, there is no need to upload them to the cloud server. Instead, local networks can be used for the surgical robot to directly decode, encode, and process data. The surgical robot can process the acquired data locally and directly receive instructions for movement operations [22]. This reduces the physical space required by the server, allowing for better data processing and faster response to user needs.

Due to the partial offloading of data processing tasks to the edge computing on the device side, the computational load on the cloud server is reduced. The surplus computational resources can be allocated to data transmission, thereby reducing waiting time.

Furthermore, although many computing tasks can be completed on the device side, data still needs to be backed up to the server. This effectively enhances data security, and data backup can prevent unexpected events such as network disconnections or packet loss, ensuring the safety of telesurgery.

4 Discussion

This paper adopts cloud-edge collaboration technology to design a virtual controller, applying model predictive control algorithms to enhance the data processing capabilities of surgical robots at the edge. This reduces data processing time and lowers the computational resource usage of the cloud. By freeing up computational power on cloud servers, more computing resources can be allocated to data transmission, thereby reducing data waiting time.

Compared to PID control, model predictive control is adept at handling multi-input multi-output systems and can simultaneously control multiple variables, reducing data processing time. Additionally, because model predictive control solves the controller's actions by constructing an optimization problem, constraints can be naturally incorporated into the optimization problem to ensure compliance. Furthermore, model predictive control considers future time domains, effectively avoiding the occurrence of unexpected accidents.

However, the research presented in this paper is still in the theoretical stage and has not yet been experimentally validated. Additionally, many input parameters are difficult to measure accurately or are subject to natural fluctuations, leading to uncertainties in the model output.

To address these limitations, we plan to further optimize the model predictive control algorithm by incorporating a double-layer structure predictive control algorithm, thereby advancing the practical application of model predictive control.

5 Conclusion

Network-based data transmission causes operational delays in both local and remote surgical robots. Currently, the data transmission method used in telesurgery is wireless network transmission based on 5G technology. Due to the shared and competitive nature of data transmission, the waiting and processing times of data dynamically change as it passes through multiple nodes. This affects the stability of data transmission, leading to delays in the surgical robots.

This paper adopts cloud-edge collaboration technology to design a virtual controller, applying model predictive control algorithms to enhance the data processing capabilities of surgical robots at the edge. This approach reduces data processing time and lowers the computational resource usage of the cloud. By freeing up computational power on cloud servers, more computing resources can be allocated to data transmission, thereby reducing data waiting time.

Acknowledgments. This study was funded by the National Key R&D Plan (2022YFB3304000). Fig. 1 was modified from Servier Medical Art (http://smart.servier.com/), licensed under a Creative Common Attribution 3.0 Generic License (https://creativecommons.org/licenses/by/3.0/).

Disclosure of Interests. The authors have no competing interests to declare that are relevant to the content of this article.

References

1. Aiken, A.R.A., Lohr, P.A., Lord, J., Ghosh, N., Starling, J.: Effectiveness, safety and acceptability of no-test medical abortion (termination of pregnancy) provided via telemedicine: a national cohort study. BJOG Int. J. Obstet. Gynaecol. **128**, 1464–1474 (2021). https://doi.org/10.1111/1471-0528.16668
2. Battineni, G., Sirignano, A., Amenta, F., Ricci, G.: Telemedicine practice: review of the current ethical and legal challenges. Telemed. E-Health. (2020). https://doi.org/10.1089/tmj.2019.0158

3. Friedman, A.B., Gervasi, S., Song, H., Bond, A.M., Chen, A.T., Bergman, A., David, G., Bailey, J.M., Brooks, R., Smith-McLallen, A.: Telemedicine catches on: changes in the utilization of telemedicine services during the COVID-19 pandemic. Am. J. Manag. Care. **28**, E1–E6 (2022). https://doi.org/10.37765/AJMC.2022.88771
4. Kim, Y., Genevriere, E., Harker, P., Choe, J., Balicki, M., Regenhardt, R.W., Vranic, J.E., Dmytriw, A.A., Patel, A.B., Zhao, X.: Telerobotic neurovascular interventions with magnetic manipulation. Sci. Robot. **7**, (2022). https://doi.org/10.1126/scirobotics.abg9907
5. Su, H., Mariani, A., Ovur, S.E., Menciassi, A., Ferrigno, G., De Momi, E.: Toward teaching by demonstration for robot-assisted minimally invasive surgery. IEEE Trans. Autom. Sci. Eng. **18**, 484–494 (2021). https://doi.org/10.1109/TASE.2020.3045655
6. Zarbock, A., et al.: Effect of remote ischemic preconditioning on kidney injury among high-risk patients undergoing cardiac surgery: a randomized clinical trial. JAMA J. Am. Med. Assoc. **313**, 2133–2141 (2015). https://doi.org/10.1001/jama.2015.4189
7. Gopura, R.A.R.C., Bandara, D.S.V., Kiguchi, K., Mann, G.K.I.: Developments in hardware systems of active upper-limb exoskeleton robots: a review. Robot. Auton. Syst. **75**, 203–220 (2016). https://doi.org/10.1016/j.robot.2015.10.001
8. Saeidi, H., Opfermann, J.D., Kam, M., Wei, S., Leonard, S., Hsieh, M.H., Kang, J.U., Krieger, A.: Autonomous robotic laparoscopic surgery for intestinal anastomosis. Sci. Robot. **7** (2022). https://doi.org/10.1126/scirobotics.abj2908
9. Peters, B.S., Armijo, P.R., Krause, C., Choudhury, S.A., Oleynikov, D.: Review of emerging surgical robotic technology. Surg. Endosc. **32**, 1636–1655 (2018). https://doi.org/10.1007/s00464-018-6079-2
10. Shugaba, A., Lambert, J.E., Bampouras, T.M., Nuttall, H.E., Gaffney, C.J., Subar, D.A.: Should all minimal access surgery be robot-assisted? A systematic review into the musculoskeletal and cognitive demands of laparoscopic and robot-assisted laparoscopic surgery. J. Gastrointest. Surg. **26**, 1520–1530 (2022). https://doi.org/10.1007/s11605-022-05319-8
11. Lum, M.J.H., et al.: The RAVEN: design and validation of a telesurgery system. Int. J. Robot. Res. **28**, 1183–1197 (2009). https://doi.org/10.1177/0278364909101795
12. Boal, M., et al.: Evaluation status of current and emerging minimally invasive robotic surgical platforms. Surg. Endosc. **38**, 554–585 (2024). https://doi.org/10.1007/s00464-023-10554-4
13. Sedef, M., Samur, E., Basdogan, C.: Real-time finite-element simulation of linear viscoelastic tissue behavior based on experimental data. IEEE Comput. Graph. Appl. **26**, 58–68 (2006). https://doi.org/10.1109/MCG.2006.135
14. Su, H., Qi, W., Schmirander, Y., Ovur, S.E., Cai, S., Xiong, X.: A human activity-aware shared control solution for medical human–robot interaction. Assem. Autom. **42**, 388–394 (2022). https://doi.org/10.1108/AA-12-2021-0174
15. Marescaux, J., et al.: Transcontinental robot-assisted remote telesurgery: feasibility and potential applications. Ann. Surg. **235**, 487–492 (2002). https://doi.org/10.1097/00000658-200204000-00005
16. Gladilin, E., Zachow, S., Deuflhard, P., Hege, H.-C.: On constitutive modeling of soft tissue for the long-term prediction of cranio-maxillofacial surgery outcome. Int. Congr. Ser. **1256**, 343–348 (2003). https://doi.org/10.1016/S0531-5131(03)00500-4
17. Mendoza-Azpur, G., de la Fuente, A., Chavez, E., Valdivia, E., Khouly, I.: Horizontal ridge augmentation with guided bone regeneration using particulate xenogenic bone substitutes with or without autogenous block grafts: a randomized controlled trial. Clin. Implant Dent. Relat. Res. **21**, 521–530 (2019). https://doi.org/10.1111/cid.12740
18. Tolman, D.E.: Advanced residual ridge resorption: surgical management. Int. J. Prosthodont. **6**, 118–125 (1993)
19. Chiapasco, M., Zaniboni, M.: Clinical outcomes of GBR procedures to correct peri-implant dehiscences and fenestrations: a systematic review. Clin. Oral Implants Res. **20**, 113–123 (2009). https://doi.org/10.1111/j.1600-0501.2009.01781.x

20. Rochat, P.: Five levels of self-awareness as they unfold early in life. In: Conscious Cogn, pp. 717–731. Academic Press Inc (2003). https://doi.org/10.1016/S1053-8100(03)00081-3
21. Zong, L., Luo, J., Wang, M., Yuan, J.: Obstacle avoidance handling and mixed integer predictive control for space robots. Adv. Space Res. **61**, 1997–2009 (2018). https://doi.org/10.1016/j.asr.2018.01.025
22. Estrada, E., Yu, W., Li, X.: Stable bilateral teleoperation with phase transition and haptic feedback. J. Frankl. Inst. **358**, 1940–1956 (2021). https://doi.org/10.1016/j.jfranklin.2020.12.027

Research on the Application of Additive Manufacturing Technology in Precision Electronic Components

Sidra Aslam[1(✉)], Chi Zhang[1,2], Nasar Ali[1], Ghulam Hassan Askari[2], Aamir Shehzad[1], and Maimoona Afzal[2]

[1] School of Mechanical Engineering, Northwestern Polytechnical University, Xi'an, China
sidraaslam@mail.nwpu.edu.cn

[2] Bio-Additive Manufacturing University-Enterprise Joint Research Center of Shaanxi Province, Northwestern Polytechnical University, Xi'an 710072, China

Abstract. Recent advancements in manufacturing and materials science have greatly heightened the demand for intelligent precision components in electronics. Additive manufacturing (AM), especially 3D printing, gives designers more freedom than ever before and lets them quickly make prototypes of complex, functional shapes. This has led to the creation of advanced smart elements in precision electronics. For example, 3D-printed sensors, interconnects, and microelectronic modules are now used in aerospace, telecommunications, and robotics. AM is also very active in the medical field, where it makes custom diagnostic probes and implants that can both sense and act. Also, AM makes it possible to print flexible micro-batteries, which leads to new ideas in battery technology. The main benefits of 3D printing are that it can do many different things with shapes, it cuts down on the time it takes to go from design to prototype, and it can combine different functions into one structure. Even though there are problems with large-scale fabrication and long-term reliability, future improvements in multi-material printing and AI-driven optimization could make it possible to use AM to its full potential to make smart, highly integrated and precise electronic systems.

Keywords: Additive Manufacturing · 3D printed Piezoelectric · 3D printed medical implants · sensors · electronic components

1 Introduction

Additive manufacturing (AM) greatly enhances the performance of precision electronic components, characterized by their requirement for high accuracy and precise specifications [3]. Additive manufacturing (AM) greatly enhances the performance of precision electronic components, characterized by their requirement for high accuracy and precise specifications [1]. Additive manufacturing (AM) gives designers more freedom and better integration options, which leads to better precision electronics. The main goals of using AM in this field are to get better functionality, more design options, and faster production. This means directly making active parts like transistors, LEDs, and batteries.

S. S. Ge et al. (Eds.): ICSR + BioMed 2025, LNAI 16435, pp. 260–272, 2026.
https://doi.org/10.1007/978-981-95-7538-1_23

A key goal is to meet the size, design, and cost requirements for mass production, as well as to make sure that quality control is in place from lab research to large-scale production [6]. AM also makes it possible to design parts with the best topologies, which can greatly improve performance [1]. AM can make electronic systems that fit on complex, curved surfaces, unlike traditional planar circuit boards [2]. This has led to the creation of "structural electronics," which lets hundreds of parts fit into one printed piece. This cuts down on assembly time and failure rates [3]. It can be hard for traditional manufacturing methods to make complicated designs or get the fine resolutions that precision parts need [10]. AM also changes the way batteries are made by allowing for more complex shapes, better materials, and lower costs [20].

This review will explain the materials and types of 3D printing technologies used to fabricate a range of precision electronic components, including sensors, piezoelectric materials, and devices for medical applications. The discussion will also cover the manufacturing of batteries, PCBs, as well as the creation of circuits, microstructures, and high-performance electronics like TENGs. Challenges in additive manufacturing, material selection, and future perspectives for these applications will be examined in detail.

2 3D Printing Materials for Precision Electronic Components

The additive manufacturing (AM) process requires materials with specific properties, enabling the printing of a wide range of functional materials.

Structural Materials (Metals, Polymers, and Composites): Metals are a popular choice for 3D printing in the aerospace, automotive, and medical fields because they are very flexible, resistant to corrosion, and light. Cobalt, aluminum, stainless steel, and titanium alloys are some of the most common metals used in these industries to make parts [4]. Polymers are also used a lot, from basic prototypes to complex functional structures. Thermoplastics like polylactic acid (PLA) and acrylonitrile butadiene styrene (ABS) are often used in printing mechanisms that use extrusion. Polymers are great for biomedical devices and electronics because they melt at low temperatures, are light, and are cheap [5]. People like composites because they are light, strong, and resistant to corrosion. People use these materials, like glass fibre, carbon fibre, and natural fiber-reinforced polymers, in many different industries. **Advanced and Functional Materials (Ceramics and Smart Materials):** Ceramics are strong, long-lasting, and fire-resistant materials that can be used to make 3D-printed objects with no big holes or cracks [6]. Because they can turn into liquid before solidifying, they can make complex shapes. Ceramics with better mechanical properties are used in scaffolds and bone research. Smart materials can change their shape, size, or color when they come into contact with things like heat or water [7]. The commercial impact of AM has increased markedly since the late 1980s [8].

3 3D Printing Techniques for Precision Electronic Components

Selective Laser Sintering: Selective Laser Sintering (SLS) Selective Laser Sintering (SLS) is an additive manufacturing (AM) method that uses a laser to turn powdered materials into a solid 3D part.

The blade puts down layers of powder one after the other, and the laser then selectively sinters them based on a CAD model. The size of the powder particles has a direct effect on the surface finish and spatial resolution of the final part. SLS is very flexible and can work with a lot of different materials, such as metals, ceramics, and polymers like Polystyrene, PVC, and ABS [37] (Fig. 1).

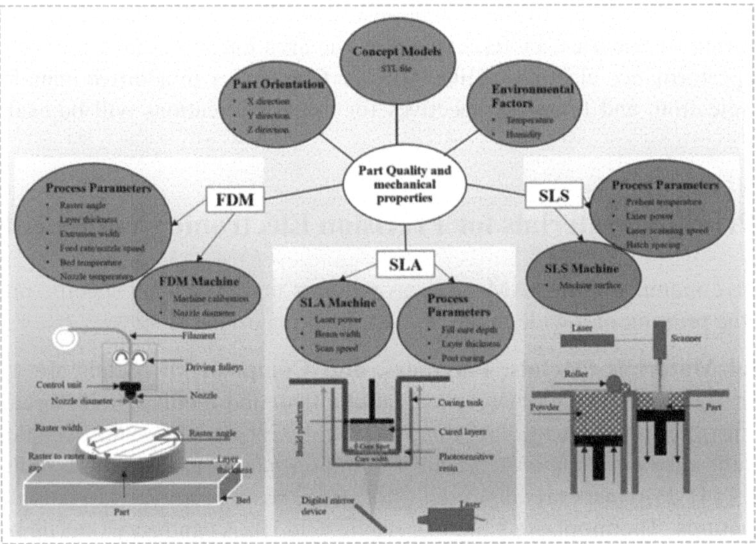

Fig. 1. Diagrams illustrating how different vat photopolymerization and inkjet printing setups work. (a) Set up FDM. (b) To set up the SLA [9]. (c) To set up the SLS [10]. Copyright CC

Stereolithography: An additive manufacturing (AM) process called stereolithography (SLA) uses an ultraviolet (UV) laser to photopolymerize and cure layers of a liquid resin. Chuck Hull came up with the process in 1984. It uses a platform that moves down to let new layers of resin be added. Photo-initiators and UV absorbers in the resin control the reaction [11]. **Digital Light Processing:** Digital Light Processing (DLP) is an additive manufacturing (AM) process that uses a digital projector to harden whole layers of photosensitive resin at once, just like Stereolithography (SLA). DLP is less likely to be affected by oxygen inhibition than SLA because the resin is not exposed to air at the bottom of the vat. A Digital Micromirror Device (DMD) shows a black-and-white picture of the model one layer at a time. As each layer hardens, the build platform rises until the model is finished. This process gives a high resolution, usually between 10 and 50 μm [9]. **Inkjet Printing (IJP):** Inkjet 3D printing is a type of additive manufacturing

(AM) that uses a print head to place liquid materials on top of each other. This method uses low pressure and low temperature. Texas Instruments and Brother Industries were the first to use this method, which uses a print head with micro-heaters to quickly melt and shoot droplets of liquid thermoset resin or a binder onto a powder bed. The fluid physics, such as the Ohnesorge, Reynolds, Weber, and Bond numbers, determine the size and shape of the droplets that are ejected. There are three steps in the interaction between the binder droplets and the powder particles: impact, capillary relaxation, and final balance [43]. **Fused Deposition Modelling (FDM):** Fused Deposition Modeling (FDM) is a widely used additive manufacturing (AM) process that creates 3D objects by extruding a heated thermoplastic filament layer by layer [12]. It is one of the most common 3D printing methods due to its cost-effectiveness, energy efficiency, and a wide variety of available materials [12, 13]. The process involves a heated nozzle that melts the filament and deposits it onto a build plate to form a component [49]. Key parameters, such as layer thickness, infill percentage, printing speed, and extrusion temperature, are critical for optimizing the quality of the print [52].

Direct Ink Writing (DIW): Direct Ink Writing (DIW) is a type of additive manufacturing (AM) that uses a thick, gooey slurry to make complicated 3D structures out of more than one material. The process depends on the ink's exact rheological properties to flow through a nozzle, which makes it possible to make things quickly and in an environmentally friendly way [14]. DIW can hold a lot of different types of ceramics and polymers and can extrude materials at room temperature all the time. The size of the nozzle determines the print resolution. The process depends on the ink's ability to be continuously extruded and quickly harden after being deposited. This is done by using shear-thinning fluid properties to keep the dimensions and shape accurate [15].

4 AM Application in Precision Electronics Components

4.1 Additive Manufacturing of Piezoelectric

Different additive manufacturing (AM) methods, such as Direct Ink Writing (DIW), Fused Deposition Modeling (FDM), and Selective Laser Sintering (SLS), are being used to make well-known piezoelectric ceramics like barium titanate ($BaTiO_3$), lead zirconate titanate (PZT), and potassium sodium niobate (KNN) [16]. For flexible uses, polymers like polyvinylidene fluoride (PVDF) and its copolymers are used with AM methods to increase their beta-phase content, which is necessary for piezoelectricity. In-situ polarization has resulted in a phase content exceeding 55%, yielding an output current of 0.106 nA [17] (Fig. 2).

Specialized printing techniques are used to line up nanowires like ZnO and $BaTiO_3$ so that they respond better to electricity and magnetism. A $BaTiO_3$ nanowire composite generated 15.3 nW of power, which is 273% more than randomly oriented nanocrystals. These materials are important for biomedical and soft electronics. A silk fibroin-enhanced PVDF composite is a new type of biocompatible material that can be used in medical implants and wearables. This material had a Young's modulus of 2.77 GPa and a three-fold increase in energy conversion efficiency when made with NFES, which is better than regular PVDF [19]. DIW has also been used with inks that contain silver

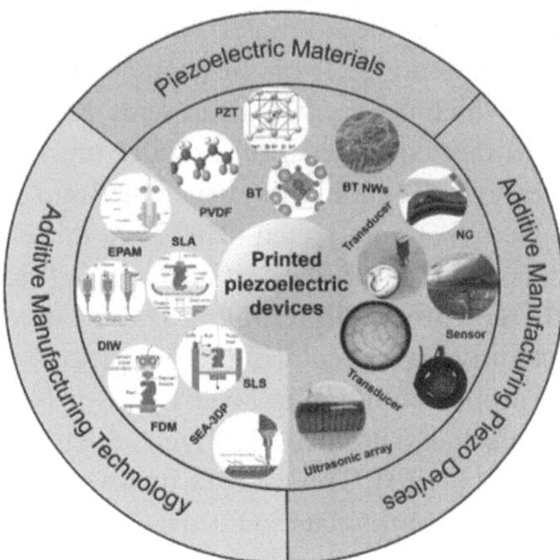

Fig. 2. Additive manufacturing of piezoelectric materials and piezoelectric devices [18]. Copyright 2019 WILEY

nanowires (AgNWs) and carbon nanotubes (CNTs). These inks have shown a charge output increase of about 300% and better long-term stability [20].

4.2 3D-Printed Stretchable and Self-healing Material

Materials that are stretchable and self-healing are necessary for wearable technology. By mixing a polymer surfactant with a PEDOT:PSS and DMSO mixture, we created a thermoelectric composite. This composite is more resilient to repeated bending because it can stretch by roughly 35% and self heal after being cut. This material can be used to 3D print a thermoelectric generator that, even after damage, retains more than 85% of its initial output [21, 22] (Figs. 3 and 4).

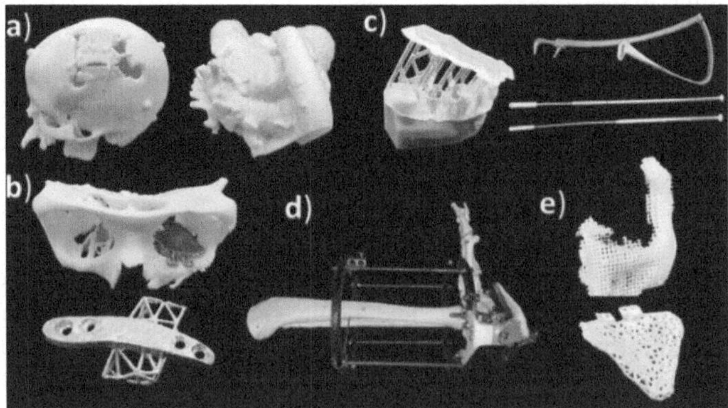

Fig. 3. (a) Medical models; (b) implants; (c) tools, instruments and parts for medical devices; (d) medical aids, supportive guides, splints and prostheses; (e) biomanufacturing [23]. Copyright CC.

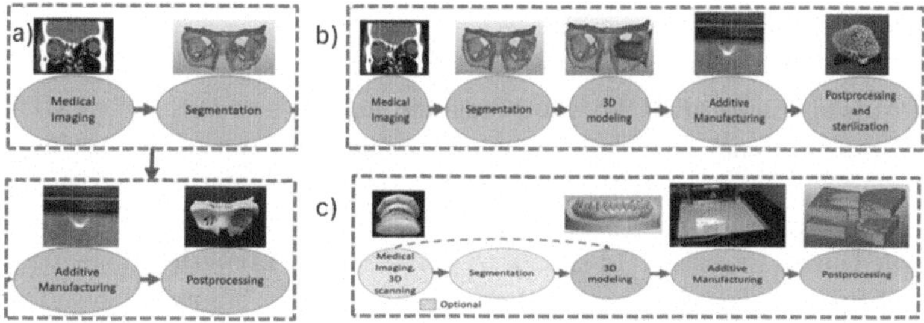

Fig. 4. (a) Typical process flow for medical models. (b) Typical process flow for implants. (c) Typical process flow for tools, instruments and parts for medical devices [23]. Copyright CC

4.3 Additive Manufacturing of Batteries

3D printing used to create complex and specific geometries, such as woodpile-like and interdigital electrodes, as well as flexible fiber batteries. These images highlight the technological progress in utilizing AM to fabricate intricate, next-generation electronic components with precise structural control (Fig. 5).

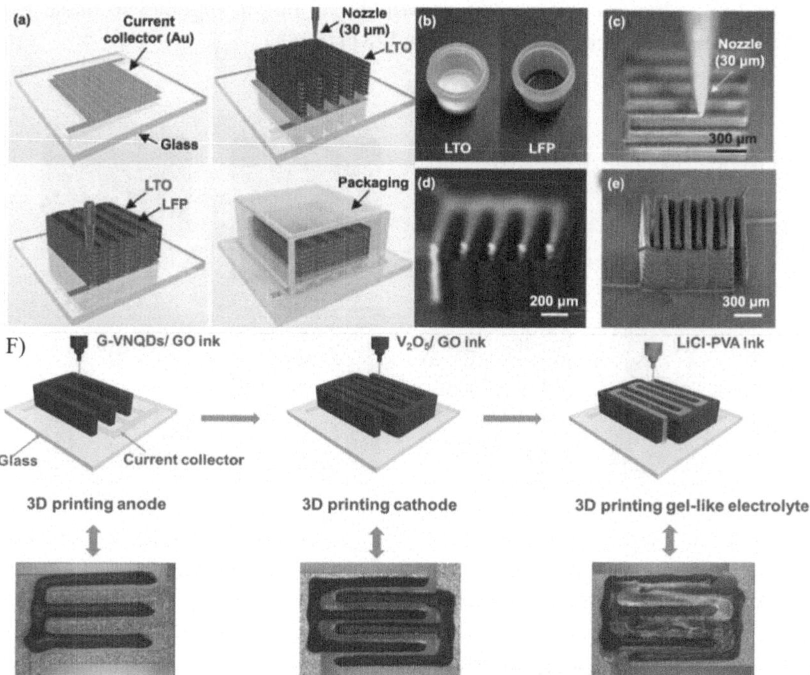

Fig. 5. 3D printing of lithium-ion battery components: a) schematic of LTO/LFP cathodes; b–e) images and performance of LTO-LFP electrode [24]. Copyright 2013 WILEY. f) 3D-printed asymmetric MSC with interdigitated electrodes; g) layer-by-layer printing of VNQDs/GO anode, V_2O_5/GO cathode, and gel electrolyte [25]. Copyright 2018 WILEY.

4.4 3D-Printed Power Electronics

Thermal Management of PCB: The Managing heat in power-electronics PCBs is a big problem. Traditional fabrication is good for making a lot of things, but additive manufacturing (AM) gives you more design freedom and better thermal performance. This method makes products run cooler, which shows that AM techniques work to lower thermal stress in real-world situations [75]. **Power Magnetic:** Magnetic parts are important for power electronics converters, but they can be big and heavy. Traditional manufacturing is costly and restricts the production of intricate geometries that could improve performance. Additive manufacturing (AM) solves these problems by allowing for quick prototyping and one-of-a-kind shaping. Engineers can now make parts up to 4 mm high with a relative permeability of 63–103 and a high resonance frequency by making a UV-curable ferrite paste and sintering printed parts at temperatures below 1000 °C. This makes designs more flexible and efficient [26, 27].

Creation of Circuits: 3D print electronic parts with conductive thermoplastic filaments using a dual-material fused filament fabrication process. The resistance of these filaments can be very precisely controlled by changing the filler material. This makes it possible to make resistors with a wide range of values. This method has also been used to make other parts, like inductors and capacitors, which can be put together to make working 3D-printed circuits, such as high-pass filters [28] (Fig. 6).

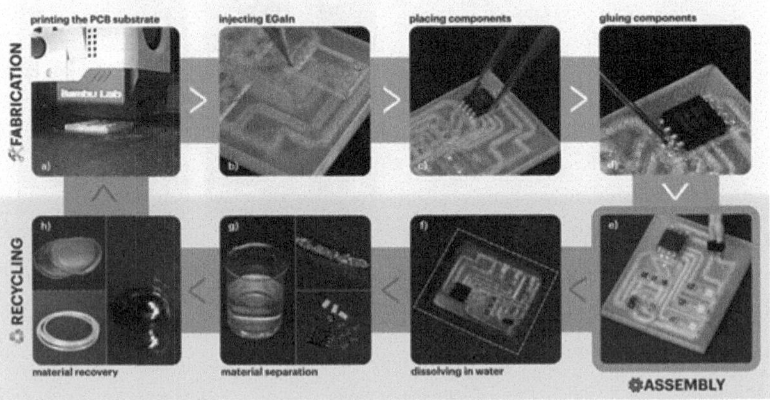

Fig. 6. Fabrication and recycling of DissolvPCB: a) 3D-printed base; b) liquid metal injection; c) component assembly; d) PVA sealing; e) finished circuit; f) dissolution in water; g) separated materials; h) recovered PVA and EGaIn [29]. Copyright CC.

4.5 Wearable Electronics via 3D-Printed

TENG via 3D-Printed: Triboelectric Nanogenerators (TENGs) use the triboelectric effect to turn mechanical energy into electrical energy. To solve the problems with oil-based TENGs that don't break down in the environment, a new 3D-printed, biodegradable, and renewable TENG has been made. This TENG has electrodes and triboelectric parts made of Poly Glycerol Sebacate (PGS) and Carbon Nanotubes (CNTs). A flexible PGS framework lets the TENG respond to biomechanical movements, which makes it produce a lot of energy. The Direct-Ink-Writing (DIW) process makes the device in one step. This process makes complex, multi-layered porous structures that are hard to make with traditional moulding methods [30]. **Wearable Antenna System:** You can make flexible antenna systems for radio services with 3D printing. You can print these antennas on leather, plastic, paper, and fabric, which are not normal substrates. They are made with new conductive materials like graphene ink and stretchable silver conductors, as well as their rigid, traditionally made counterparts. This shows that additive manufacturing has a bright future in electronics [31].

Smart Electronics Eyeglasses: Electronic smart glasses are a promising new technology that could give us more control over what we do and give us more information about what's going on around us. These new smart glasses are like smartwatches in that they can be 3D-printed and personalized to give the wearer information directly from their body. These smart glasses can also sort the data they collect for dynamic human-machine interaction (HMI) apps. They have delicate, highly conductive composite electrodes that let them record physiological activities reliably and continuously [32]. **Microstructure:** The microstructure had good light transmittance and flexibility because it was made of silicon. These results show that simple microprinting methods can be used to make 3D flexible hardware, which could also be used to make other 3D structures for testing mechanical and electrical systems [33] (Fig. 7).

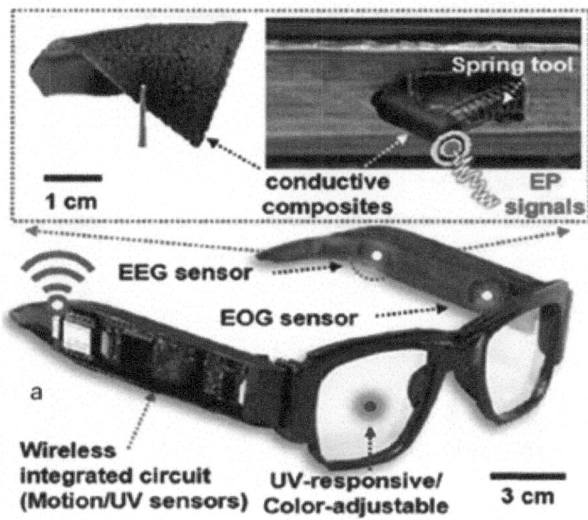

Fig. 7. (a) The 3D printed smart electronic glasses [32]. Copyright 2020 ACS

4.6 Sensors

Sensors are very important in modern science. 3D printing (3DP) makes it easier to make them by letting you make complicated shapes without a clean room. The use of electronic devices in sensing of different parameters such as displacement, force, strain and pressure has been widespread in latest science and technologies. The sensor has been used in rampant manner with numerous applications. Sensors play a vital role in academics, industries and research [34]. Materials are chosen based on how they will be used. For example, thermoplastic polymers and metal nanoparticles that meet certain temperature requirements are common choices [35]. People like ABS and PLA because they are strong and easy to work with [36]. FDM is a cheap way to make sensors and actuators. Kim et al. utilized. FDM to fabricate a monolithic multiaxial force sensor from TPU and CNT-infused TPU [37].

Petroni et al. employed FDM to fabricate an electrochemical sensor utilizing a graphite/ABS composite. Hong et al. created an FDM-based FBG sensor using PLA to measure pressures [38]. Joseph et al. utilized Direct Ink Writing (DIW) for the development of stretchable strain sensors integrated into wearable devices [39]. The research also involves stretchable strain sensors made from a cheap, carbon-based composite dough. Using ionic hydrogels that are highly conductive and biocompatible, additive manufacturing was used to make a hydrogen-based deformation sensor for lungs [40]. It is possible to make a flexible 3D-printed force sensor out of PLA and a silicone rubber spacer. The sensor detects force by measuring changes in inductance [41].

Lastly, flexible tactile sensors made with multi-material 3D printing can sense human movement and pulse. They have a high compressive gauge factor of 180, which makes them perfect for wearable devices [42]. The impact of extruded PLA on FBG sensor has avoided the structural deformation due to shrinkage (Fig. 8).

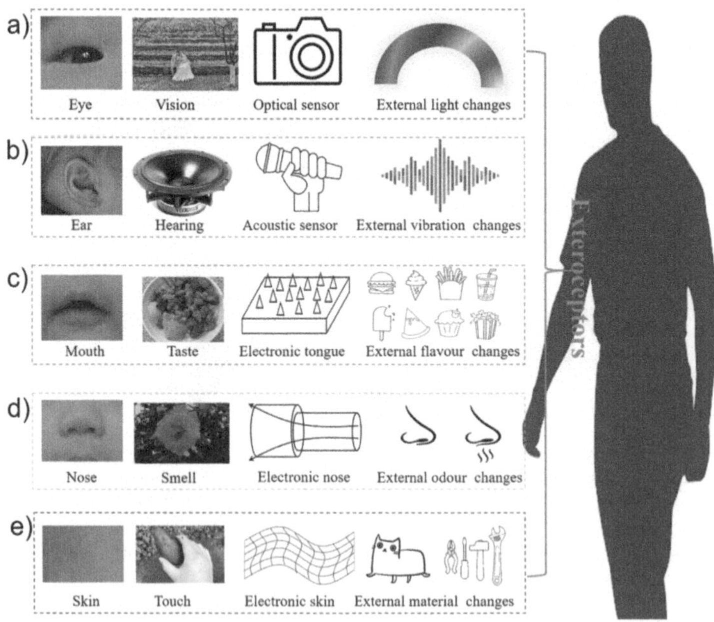

Fig. 8. Human sensory systems and their artificial counterparts: a) Eyes → optical sensors; b) Ears → acoustic sensors; c) Tongue → electronic tongue; d) Nose → electronic nose; e) Skin → flexible electronic skin sensors [43]. Copyright CC Open Access

5 Conclusion

In conclusion, this review paper has examined the revolutionary influence of additive manufacturing (AM) on the production of precision electronic components. By co-depositing conductive inks and polymers, it is possible to directly combine complex 3D circuits, conformal sensors, and embedded actuators. This makes it possible to make small, flexible devices.

Even though AM has a lot of potential, there are still some big problems that are keeping it from being widely used. One of the main problems is that multi-material systems can't be used as much because of problems like poor interfacial bonding and materials that don't work well together. Also, functional materials that can be printed often don't work as well or last as long as materials that are made in a traditional way. Scaling production down to the micro-level is still a big problem, which means that the technology is mostly limited to prototyping and low-volume production. To get past these problems, we need to make progress in material innovation, create hybrid manufacturing techniques, and combine AI-assisted design and digital manufacturing platforms. This will make it possible for AM to be fully commercialized and standardized in high-performance electronics.

In the end, the ongoing development of this technology will change how electronic parts are made and designed, resulting in smarter, more connected, and more personalized devices.

Disclosure of Interests. The authors have no competing interests to declare that are relevant to the content of this article.

References

1. Zhang, Z., Yuan, X.: Applications and future of automated and additive manufacturing for power electronics components and converters. IEEE J. Emerg. Sel. Top. Power Electron. **10**(4), 4509–4525 (2022). https://doi.org/10.1109/JESTPE.2021.3135285
2. Luo, X., Wang, J., Dooner, M., Clarke, J.: Overview of current development in electrical energy storage technologies and the application potential in power system operation. Appl. Energy **137**, 511–536 (2015). https://doi.org/10.1016/j.apenergy.2014.09.081
3. McGrath, M.P., Rowland, F.S.: Ideal gas thermodynamic properties of HOBr. J. Phys. Chem. **98**(18), 4773–4775 (1994). https://doi.org/10.1021/j100069a001
4. Gnanavel, M., Bhattacharyya, A.J.: Utilizing carbon nanotubes to enhance rate capability of lithium iron phosphate for high power lithium-ion batteries (2012). https://doi.org/10.1149/ma2012-01/9/501
5. Ligon, S.C., Liska, R., Stampfl, J., Gurr, M., Mülhaupt, R.: Polymers for 3D printing and customized additive manufacturing. Chem. Rev. **117**(15), 10212–10290 (2017). https://doi.org/10.1021/acs.chemrev.7b00074
6. Farrell, E.S., et al.: 3D-printing of ceramic aerogels by spatial photopolymerization. Appl. Mater. Today **24**, 101083 (2021). https://doi.org/10.1016/j.apmt.2021.101083
7. Choong, Y.Y.C., Maleksaeedi, S., Eng, H., Yu, S., Wei, J., Su, P.C.: High speed 4D printing of shape memory polymers with nanosilica. Appl. Mater. Today **18**, 100515 (2020). https://doi.org/10.1016/j.apmt.2019.100515

8. Nazir, A., et al.: The rise of 3D printing entangled with smart computer aided design during COVID-19 era. J. Manuf. Syst. **60**(43), 774–786 (2021). https://doi.org/10.1016/j.jmsy.2020.10.009
9. Ge, L., Dong, L., Wang, D., Ge, Q., Gu, G.: A digital light processing 3D printer for fast and high-precision fabrication of soft pneumatic actuators. Sens. Actuators A Phys. **273**, 285–292 (2018). https://doi.org/10.1016/j.sna.2018.02.041
10. Kafle, A., Luis, E., Silwal, R., Pan, H.M., Shrestha, P.L., Bastola, A.K.: 3D/4D printing of polymers: fused deposition modelling (FDM). Polymers (Basel) **13**, 1–37 (2021). https://doi.org/10.3390/polym13183101
11. Zhou, P., et al.: Direct-write nanocomposite sensor array for ultrasonic imaging of composites. Compos. Commun. **28**, 100937 (2021). https://doi.org/10.1016/j.coco.2021.100937
12. Wang, J., Mubarak, S., Dhamodharan, D., Divakaran, N., Wu, L., Zhang, X.: Fabrication of thermoplastic functionally gradient composite parts with anisotropic thermal conductive properties based on multicomponent fused deposition modeling 3D printing. Compos. Commun. **19**, 142–146 (2020). https://doi.org/10.1016/j.coco.2020.03.012
13. Hu, X., et al.: 3D-printed thermoplastic polyurethane electrodes for customizable, flexible lithium-ion batteries with an ultra-long lifetime. Small **19**(34), 1–10 (2023). https://doi.org/10.1002/smll.202301604
14. Lewis, J.A., Smay, J.E., Stuecker, J., Cesarano, J.: Direct ink writing of three-dimensional ceramic structures. J. Am. Ceram. Soc. **89**(12), 3599–3609 (2006). https://doi.org/10.1111/j.1551-2916.2006.01382.x
15. Yuk, H.D., Kim, J.K., Jeong, C.W., Kwak, C., Kim, H.H., Ku, J.H.: Differences in pathologic results of repeat transurethral resection of bladder tumor (TURBT) according to institution performing the initial TURBT: comparative analyses between referred and nonreferred group. Biomed. Res. Int. **2018** (2018). https://doi.org/10.1155/2018/9432606
16. Gaytan, S.M., et al.: Fabrication of barium titanate by binder jetting additive manufacturing technology. Ceram. Int. **41**(5), 6610–6619 (2015). https://doi.org/10.1016/j.ceramint.2015.01.108
17. Malakooti, M.H., Julé, F., Sodano, H.A.: Printed nanocomposite energy harvesters with controlled alignment of barium titanate nanowires. ACS Appl. Mater. Interfaces **10**(44), 38359–38367 (2018). https://doi.org/10.1021/acsami.8b13643
18. Pang, Y., et al.: Additive manufacturing of batteries. Adv. Funct. Mater. **30**(1), 1–22 (2020). https://doi.org/10.1002/adfm.201906244
19. Pan, C.-T., et al.: Significant piezoelectric and energy harvesting enhancement of poly(vinylidene fluoride)/polypeptide fiber composites prepared through near-field electrospinning. J. Mater. Chem. A **3**(13), 6835–6843 (2015). https://doi.org/10.1039/C5TA00147A
20. Bodkhe, S., Rajesh, P.S.M., Gosselin, F.P., Therriault, D.: Simultaneous 3D printing and poling of PVDF and its nanocomposites. ACS Appl. Energy Mater. **1**(6), 2474–2482 (2018). https://doi.org/10.1021/acsaem.7b00337
21. Kee, S., Haque, M.A., Corzo, D., Alshareef, H.N., Baran, D.: Self-healing and stretchable 3D-printed organic thermoelectrics. Adv. Funct. Mater. **29**(51) (2019). https://doi.org/10.1002/adfm.201905426
22. Someya, T., Bao, Z., Malliaras, G.G.: The rise of plastic bioelectronics. Nature **540**(7633), 379–385 (2016). https://doi.org/10.1038/nature21004
23. Salmi, M.: Additive manufacturing processes in medical applications. Materials (Basel) **14**(1), 1–16 (2021). https://doi.org/10.3390/ma14010191
24. Sun, K., Wei, T.-S., Ahn, B.Y., Seo, J.Y., Dillon, S.J., Lewis, J.A.: 3D printing of interdigitated Li-ion microbattery architectures. Adv. Mater. **25**(33), 4539–4543 (2013). https://doi.org/10.1002/adma.201301036

25. Shen, K., Ding, J., Yang, S.: 3D printing quasi-solid-state asymmetric micro-supercapacitors with ultrahigh areal energy density. Adv. Energy Mater. **8**(20), 1–7 (2018). https://doi.org/10.1002/aenm.201800408
26. Liu, L., Ge, T., Ngo, K.D.T., Mei, Y., Lu, G.Q.: Ferrite paste cured with ultraviolet light for additive manufacturing of magnetic components for power electronics. IEEE Magn. Lett. **9**, 1–5 (2018). https://doi.org/10.1109/LMAG.2018.2822622
27. Cui, H., Ngo, K.D.T., Moss, J., Lim, M.H.F., Rey, E.: Inductor geometry with improved energy density. IEEE Trans. Power Electron. **29**(10), 5446–5453 (2014). https://doi.org/10.1109/TPEL.2013.2289926
28. Flowers, P.F., Reyes, C., Ye, S., Kim, M.J., Wiley, B.J.: 3D printing electronic components and circuits with conductive thermoplastic filament. Addit. Manuf. **18**(2017), 156–163 (2017). https://doi.org/10.1016/j.addma.2017.10.002
29. Yan, Z., Hong, S., Hester, J., Cheng, T., Peng, H.: DissolvPCB: fully recyclable 3D-printed electronics with liquid metal conductors and PVA substrates (2025). https://doi.org/10.1145/3746059.3747604
30. Chen, S., et al.: A single integrated 3D-printing process customizes elastic and sustainable triboelectric nanogenerators for wearable electronics. Adv. Funct. Mater. **28**(46), 1–8 (2018). https://doi.org/10.1002/adfm.201805108
31. Cook, B.S., Shamim, A.: Inkjet printing of novel wideband and high gain antennas on low-cost paper substrate. IEEE Trans. Antennas Propag. **60**(9), 4148–4156 (2012). https://doi.org/10.1109/TAP.2012.2207079
32. Lee, J.H., et al.: 3D printed, customizable, and multifunctional smart electronic eyeglasses for wearable healthcare systems and human–machine interfaces. ACS Appl. Mater. Interfaces **12**(19), 21424–21432 (2020). https://doi.org/10.1021/acsami.0c03110
33. Liu, Y., et al.: 3D printed microstructures for flexible electronic devices. Nanotechnology **30**(41) (2019). https://doi.org/10.1088/1361-6528/ab2d5d
34. Kenda, M., Klobčar, D., Bračun, D.: Condition based maintenance of the two-beam laser welding in high volume manufacturing of piezoelectric pressure sensor. J. Manuf. Syst. **59**, 117–126 (2021). https://doi.org/10.1016/j.jmsy.2021.02.007
35. Güdür, C., Türkoğlu, T., Eren, İ.: Eriyik yiğma modelleme ile üretilen PLA, ABS VE PETG polimerlerinin özellikleri üzerinde kafes tasarimi ve proses parametrelerinin etkisi (2023). https://doi.org/10.55546/jmm.1357217
36. Abueidda, D.W., Elhebeary, M., Shiang, C.S., Pang, S., Al-Rub, R.K.A., Jasiuk, I.: Mechanical properties of 3D printed polymeric gyroid cellular structures: experimental and finite element study (2019). https://doi.org/10.1016/j.matdes.2019.107597
37. Kim, K., Park, J., Hoon Suh, J., Kim, M., Jeong, Y., Park, I.: 3D printing of multiaxial force sensors using carbon nanotube (CNT)/thermoplastic polyurethane (TPU) filaments. Sens. Actuators A Phys. **263**, 493–500 (2017). https://doi.org/10.1016/j.sna.2017.07.020
38. Hong, C., Yuan, Y., Yang, Y., Zhang, Y., Abro, Z.A.: A simple FBG pressure sensor fabricated using fused deposition modelling process. Sens. Actuators A Phys. **285**, 269–274 (2019). https://doi.org/10.1016/j.sna.2018.11.024
39. Muth, J.T., et al.: Embedded 3D printing of strain sensors within highly stretchable elastomers. Adv. Mater. **26**(36), 6307–6312 (2014). https://doi.org/10.1002/adma.201400334
40. Zhu, Z., Park, H.S., McAlpine, M.C.: 3D printed deformable sensors. Sci. Adv. **6**(25), 1–10 (2020). https://doi.org/10.1126/sciadv.aba5575
41. Kisić, M., Živanov, L., Blaž, N., Stefanov, A., Menićanin, A.: Investigation of dielectric properties of printed material for capacitor application. In: 2020 43rd International Spring Seminar on Electronics Technology (ISSE), pp. 1–5 (2020). https://doi.org/10.1109/ISSE49702.2020.9120980

42. Guo, S.Z., Qiu, K., Meng, F., Park, S.H., McAlpine, M.C.: 3D printed stretchable tactile sensors. Adv. Mater. **29**(27), 1–8 (2017). https://doi.org/10.1002/adma.201701218
43. Chen, D., Han, Z., Zhang, J., Xue, L., Liu, S.: Additive manufacturing provides infinite possibilities for self-sensing technology. Adv. Sci. **11**(28), 1–22 (2024). https://doi.org/10.1002/advs.202400816

The Competency Assessment of UAV Operators Based on Human-Machine Collaboration

Shanshan Wu[1,2], Weiwei Yu[3], Peng Hu[1,2](✉), Xiang Zou[1,2], Yichuan Yang[1,2], and Huan Liu[1,2]

[1] The Second Research Institute of Civil Aviation Administration of China, No. 17 Eerhuanlu Nanerduan, Chengdu 610041, China
hupengbaby@163.com

[2] Low-Altitude Traffic Intelligent Management and Control Key Laboratory of Sichuan Province, No. 17 Eerhuanlu Nanerduan, Chengdu 610041, China

[3] Northwestern Polytechnical University, Youyi Xilu 127hao, Xi'an 710072, China

Abstract. Effective collaboration between UAV operators and intelligent control systems is crucial for the successful completion of tasks. To address the operational safety risks of UAVs during the expansion of the low-altitude economy, this study proposes and establishes a hierarchical competency assessment system for UAV operators. The system is based on the competency framework for operators proposed in the "Regulations on the Management of Civil Unmanned Aerial Vehicle Operators," and, considering the differing competency requirements for micro/small, medium, and large UAVs in typical scenarios, 12 core competency indicators are identified. Grey relational analysis and the Delphi method are used for comprehensive weighting, and the Lagrange operator is introduced to integrate subjective and objective weights, creating a comprehensive weight model. The results show that the core competencies for mainframe operators are focused on problem decision-making and team leadership. Medium UAV operators emphasize program execution and automated management, while micro/mini UAV operators focus on situational awareness and anomaly handling. This research provides theoretical support for differentiated training assessments and lays the foundation for the industry to establish a dynamic competency evaluation mechanism that integrates human-machine collaboration.

Keywords: Drone Operator · Competency Model · Grey Relational Analysis · Delphi Method · Weight Fusion

1 Introduction

With the rapid development of the low-altitude economy, the application of drone technology is becoming increasingly widespread, especially in fields such as healthcare and rescue, where it plays a key role in improving operational efficiency and safety. In practical applications, the interaction and collaboration between UAV operators and intelligent

This research was funded by the National Key R&D Program of China (No. 2023YFB2604100) and Natural Science Foundation of Sichuan Province (2025ZNSFSCO394).

S. S. Ge et al. (Eds.): ICSR + BioMed 2025, LNAI 16435, pp. 273–283, 2026.
https://doi.org/10.1007/978-981-95-7538-1_24

control systems are crucial to the successful completion of tasks. However, at present, the industry lacks systematic competency standards for the training and evaluation of operators, which leads to limited efficiency of talent selection and training, and may even lead to operational errors or safety accidents.

As a classic tool in human resource management, the competency model provides a scientific framework for job competency evaluation by integrating core elements such as knowledge, skills, and attitudes [1]. In the field of aviation, foreign research has shifted from "general models" to "contextual adaptation". McClelland's [2] "iceberg model" only provides a classification of competency levels, but it is difficult to explain the sources of performance differences in complex routes. After Spencer and Spencer [3] operationalized it, the FAA incorporated it into the pilot selection criteria in the form of AC 120-54B, laying the foundation for the "General Framework" stage. In 2013, ICAO Doc 9868 first proposed the nine core competencies (4 technical and 5 non-technical), and subsequently added "Adaptive Competency" in Doc 10119 (2020), emphasizing the dynamic moderating role of task situations [4]. Mansikka et al. [5] confirmed through a combined eye-motion-EEG experiment that "adaptive competency" significantly regulates situational awareness in high-workload situations, introducing the neuroergonomic paradigm to competency research. In China, before 2010, domestic research was in the stage of concept introduction. After Zhang [6] systematically translated the iceberg model, Gao et al. [7] used the complexity of the aircraft system as a moderating variable and found that the weight of the 'fault diagnosis' of the maintenance personnel decreased with the increase of redundancy. In 2016, Li [8] added the dimension of "hypoxia cognitive ability" based on the BEI data of 72 high-altitude pilots, increasing the validity. After the release of the "PLM Roadmap" in 2021, operational big data such as QAR and LOSA were used to correct competency weights in real time, achieving synchronous evolution of models and systems [9].

Although this model has mature applications in the aviation field, research on the emerging occupation of unmanned aerial vehicle operators is still insufficient. Most existing studies focus on a single technical capability, while neglecting the dynamic capability requirements in a multi-task environment. In addition, the high iterativeness of unmanned aerial vehicle (UAV) technology poses new requirements for the continuous learning ability of operators, and traditional competency models urgently need to be expanded and optimized.

2 Classification and Operation Scenario Analysis of Unmanned Aerial Vehicles

Drones are classified into micro, small, medium and large types based on their maximum takeoff weight. Based on practical application scenarios, this paper systematically analyzes the competency requirements of operators for micro, small, medium and large unmanned aerial vehicles, providing a theoretical basis for the subsequent construction of competency models.

2.1 Micro and Small Unmanned Aerial Vehicles

Micro and small unmanned aerial vehicles (UAVs) (weight $\leq$ 25 kg) face complex environmental challenges in scenarios such as agricultural plant protection, power inspection, and disaster emergency mapping. Operators are required to have high situational awareness, accurate track control, and emergency response capabilities.

2.2 Medium-Sized Unmanned Aerial Vehicle

Medium-sized UAV (25 kg $<$ maximum take-off weight $\leq$ 150 kg) is suitable for urban low-altitude logistics and emergency material delivery. It requires the operator to have professional program execution, complex airspace track management, problem analysis and decision-making, and cross-unit communication and coordination capabilities.

2.3 Large Unmanned Aerial Vehicle

Large UAVs (maximum take-off weight $>$ 150 kg) have obvious advantages in long-distance and complex meteorological conditions, such as wide-area border patrol and inter-provincial logistics transportation. Operators are required to have the ability of crew resource management, transfer coordination, complex system monitoring and emergency decision-making.

3 Build a Core Competence System

Based on the "Regulations for the Management of Civil Unmanned Aircraft Operators" Annex M: Adjusted Competency Model [10], combined with the analysis of the operating scenarios in Chapter 2, the competency models of large, medium and small UAV operators are extracted respectively [11–14], as listed in Table 1.

Table 1. Competency models for various types of drone operators.

Types of unmanned aerial vehicles	Operator competence
Large unmanned aerial vehicle	Leadership, teamwork and self-management skills (C1)
	Communication skills (C2)
	Problem-solving and decision-making abilities (C3)
	Flight path management and automation of remote-controlled aircraft (C4)
Medium-sized unmanned aerial vehicle	The application of the program (C5)
	Flight path management and automation of remote-controlled aircraft (C6)

(continued)

Table 1. (*continued*)

Types of unmanned aerial vehicles	Operator competence
	Problem-solving and decision-making abilities (C7)
	Coordination and handover capabilities (C8)
Micro and small unmanned aerial vehicles	Situational awareness (C9)
	Workload management (C10)
	Flight path management and automation of remote-controlled aircraft (C11)
	The ability to manage abnormal situations (C12)

4 Weight Calculation Model

4.1 Calculation of Index Weights Using the Grey Relational Analysis Method

Grey relational analysis is a systematic analysis method used to measure the degree of association between factors. By comparing the degree of association between each index sequence and the ideal reference sequence (or target sequence), the contribution of the index to the overall evaluation is determined, thereby determining the weight. The calculation steps are as follows:

1. Suppose there are m samples and n indicators, and the data matrix is $X = \left(x_{ij}\right)_{m\times n}$.
2. Determine the reference sequence X_0: Take thc ideal reference sequence composed of the optimal values of all indicators.
3. Data preprocessing (normalization): To eliminate the influence of dimensions, the data is generally normalized first to make it dimensionless. The range method is commonly used for normalization, and the calculation formula is as follows:

$$y_{ij} = \frac{x_{ij} - min_i x_{ij}}{max_i x_{ij} - min_i x_{ij}} \tag{1}$$

4. Calculate the grey correlation coefficient

   Calculate the absolute difference between the j indicator of the i sample and the reference sequence:

$$\Delta_{ij} = \left|y_{0j} - y_{ij}\right| \tag{2}$$

   Then find the maximum and minimum values of all the Δ_{ij}:

$$\Delta_{max} = \max_{i,j} \Delta_{ij},\ \Delta_{min} = \min_{i,j} \Delta_{ij} \tag{3}$$

   The correlation coefficient is defined as:

$$\xi_{ij} = \frac{\Delta_{min} + \rho\Delta_{max}}{\Delta_{ij} + \rho\Delta_{max}} \tag{4}$$

Among them, $\rho \in (0, 1)$ is the resolution coefficient, usually taken as 0.5, which is used to adjust the correlation sensitivity.

5. Calculate the grey correlation degree

   For each sample, calculate the correlation degree between its index and the reference sequence:

$$\gamma_i = \frac{1}{n}\sum_{j=1}^{n}\xi_{ij} \tag{5}$$

6. Determine the index weights

   Calculate the average correlation coefficient of each indicator for all samples, and then normalize to obtain the weight:

$$w_j = \frac{\sum_{i=1}^{m}\xi_{ij}}{\sum_{j=1}^{n}\sum_{i=1}^{m}\xi_{ij}} \tag{6}$$

4.2 Delphi Method Index Weight Calculation

(1) Expert selection

The study will invite five professionals from civil aviation universities, institutions directly under the National Civil Aviation Administration or other related fields as consultants. The criteria for the inclusion of experts must simultaneously meet the following conditions: ① The industry they are engaged in is related to civil aviation; ② Master's degree or above; ③ Intermediate or above professional title; ④ Be willing to participate in multiple rounds of expert inquiries.

(2) Expert inquiry by letter. Expert opinions were solicited through questionnaires, and two rounds of expert inquiries were carried out in total.

The content of the first round of inquiries:

1. First, determine the expert authority coefficient. It is determined based on the basic information of the experts, their familiarity with the experts and the basis for judgment. The experts' familiarity with the research topic of this study is divided into five levels: very familiar, relatively familiar, generally familiar, unfamiliar, and very unfamiliar, which are respectively awarded 1, 0.8, 0.5, 0.2, and 0 points. The basis for judgment is divided into four aspects: theoretical analysis, practical experience, understanding of domestic and foreign peers, and intuitive perception. The degree of influence is classified as large, medium, and small, and different scores are assigned to each. Theoretical analysis is (0.3, 0.2, 0.1), practical experience is (0.5, 0.4, 0.3), understanding by domestic and foreign peers is (0.1, 0.1, 0.1), and intuitive perception is (0.1, 0.1, 0.1). The expert authority coefficient is calculated based on familiarity and judgment basis, and the formula is

$$Cr = \frac{Ca + Cs}{2} \tag{7}$$

   The Cr value ranges from 0 to 1. The closer it is to 1, the higher the authority of the expert. Generally, it is considered that when $Cr \geq 0.7$, the authority level is acceptable.

2. Consultation on the importance of indicators. The importance score of the indicator is based on the Likert 5-level scoring method, which classifies the importance as very important (5 points), relatively important (4 points), generally important (3 points), not important (2 points), and very not important (1 point). Kendall's Coefficient of Harmony (W) is used to evaluate the consistency of experts' opinions on the importance of each indicator. The W value ranges from 0 to 1. The larger the value, the better the coordination and the more consistent the experts' opinions tend to be. After the first round of questionnaire collection, statistical analysis was conducted on the inquiry results, following the screening principles of an average importance score of ≥ 3.50 points, a coefficient of variation of ≤ 0.25, and a full score rate of $\geq 20\%$.

After the first round of expert consultation, the second round of questionnaire was formulated according to the feedback of experts, including the specific adjustment of the first round of revision suggestions, the revised index definition and importance evaluation. The whole process needs two rounds of exchange of views, and the experts reach a basic consensus.

4.3 Application of the Comprehensive Weighting Method

This paper refers to some model examples and introduces the Lagrange operator to calculate the comprehensive weights. After obtaining the weights W1 and W2 under the two methods, the Lagrange operator is used to combine the weights to meet the practical need for the subjective and objective consistency of the evaluation model. The calculation method of the comprehensive weight is shown in the formula (8).

$$W_j = \frac{(\alpha_j \beta_j)^{\frac{1}{2}}}{\sum_{j=1}^{m} (\alpha_j \beta_j)^{\frac{1}{2}}} \tag{8}$$

Among them, α_j is the subjective weight, that is, the weight obtained by the gray-scale correlation method; β_j is the objective weight, that is, the weight obtained by the Delphi method; j is the index ordinal number. The weight value W_1 obtained by the gray-scale correlation method, the weight value W_2 obtained by the Delphi method, and the weight value W_3 obtained through the synthesis of the Lagrange operator.

5 Calculation of Competency Levels

5.1 Determination of Index Weights by Grey Relational Analysis Method

Based on the historical data of the industry [11–14], this study uses the normal distribution random generation method to construct the competency analysis data set, and the median value of the ability score is set to $\mu = 5$. According to the characteristics of different UAV operator groups, set parameters: large UAV operators due to the CCAR-92 mandatory qualification certification constraints, the ability to converge, set the low dispersion parameter $\sigma^2 = 2$; the medium-sized UAV operator group covers professional flying hands and industry users, with medium capacity fluctuations, using $\sigma^2 = 4$; the micro UAV is mainly used for entertainment applications, with loose training requirements and significant differences in skills. The high discrete parameter $\sigma^2 = 6$ is set. Generate 100 sets of data, eliminate samples that do not meet $0 \leq x \leq 10$ and regenerate them to ensure that the samples meet the distribution characteristics and meet the interval restrictions, and the values retain a decimal number.

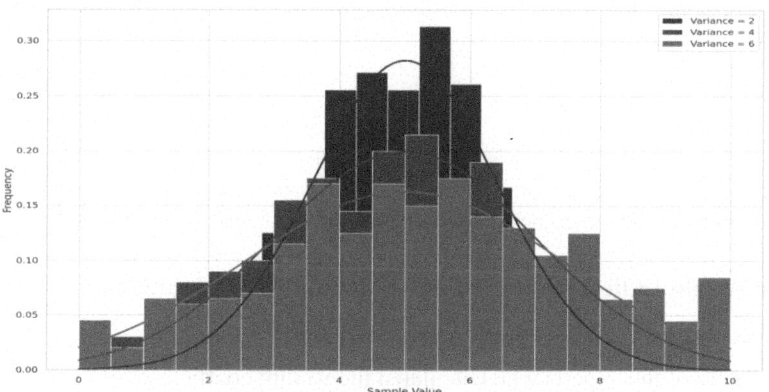

Fig. 1. Sample data distribution

To construct a competency analysis dataset with engineering credibility, this study uses a normal distribution random generation method based on historical industry data to simulate the competency level of operators, and selects the median of the competency score $\mu = 5$ as the core parameter of the normal distribution. The operators of large unmanned aerial vehicles are subject to the mandatory qualification certification of Part CCAR-92. After standardized training, their capabilities tend to be similar. Therefore, the low dispersion parameter $\sigma^2 = 2$ is set. The group of medium-sized drone operators includes professional pilots and industry users, with moderate fluctuations in their capabilities. $\sigma^2 = 4$ is adopted; Micro and small unmanned aerial vehicles (UAVs) are mainly used for entertainment purposes. The training requirements are lenient, and there are significant differences in skills. A high discrete parameter $\sigma^2 = 6$ is set. Subsequently, 100 sets of data were randomly generated using this distribution; During the data generation process, samples that do not meet the value range constraints ($0 \leq x \leq 10$) are excluded and regenerated randomly using the same distribution parameters until all data fall within the specified range. This ensures that the samples not only conform to the specified distribution characteristics but also satisfy the range restrictions, with values retained to one decimal place.

The data distribution is as shown in Fig. 1.

The weight distribution of key indicators of large, medium and small unmanned aerial vehicle systems calculated by the Grey Relational Analysis (GRA) method is shown in the following Table 3 (Fig. 2).

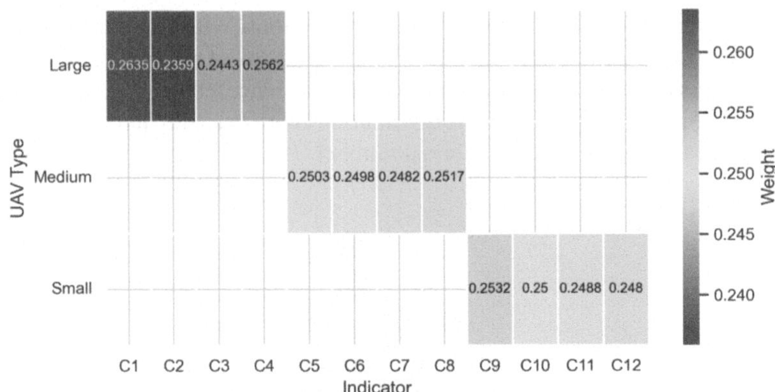

Fig. 2. The weight heatmap based on Grey Relational Analysis (GRA)

5.2 The Weight Indicators of the Delphi Method Are Determined

5.2.1 Calculation of Expert Authority Coefficient

The familiarity of the experts who calculated the weight coefficients of the five experts, the basis for judgment, and the final calculated authority coefficients are shown in the following Table 2.

Table 2. Calculation table of expert authority coefficient.

	Degree of familiarity	Theoretical analysis	Practical experience	Domestic and foreign peers understand	Intuitive perception	Expert authority coefficient
Expert 1	Relatively familiar	Big	Middle	Big	Big	0.85
Expert 2	Very familiar	Big	Big	Middle	Big	1
Expert 3	Very familiar	Big	Small	Big	Big	0.8
Expert 4	Very familiar	Middle	Middle	Big	Middle	0.9
Expert 5	Relatively familiar	Small	Big	Big	Big	0.8

After normalization, the authority coefficients of the five experts were 0.1954, 0.2299, 0.1839, 0.2069, and 0.1839 respectively.

5.2.2 Calculation of Indicator Importance

The scores given by five experts to drone operators are as follows (Extremely important-E, more important-M, less important-L, completely unimportant-C) (Table 3).

Table 3. Score of the ability evaluation index for drone operators.

Types of unmanned aerial vehicles	Evaluation index	Expert 1 score	Expert 2 score	Expert 3 score	Expert 4 score	Expert 5 score	Final score of the indicator
Large unmanned aerial vehicle	C1	E	M	M	M	E	4.3793
	C2	E	M	M	E	L	4.2184
	C3	E	E	M	M	E	4.6092
	C4	M	M	M	E	E	4.3908
Medium-sized unmanned aerial vehicle	C5	M	E	E	M	M	4.4138
	C6	M	M	M	M	E	4.1839
	C7	E	E	E	E	M	4.8161
	C8	L	M	M	E	E	4.1954
Micro and small unmanned aerial vehicles	C9	E	E	E	E	M	4.8161
	C10	E	M	M	E	E	4.5862
	C11	M	E	M	E	E	4.6207
	C12	M	E	E	E	M	4.6207

The scores given by five experts to drone operators are as shown in Fig. 3.

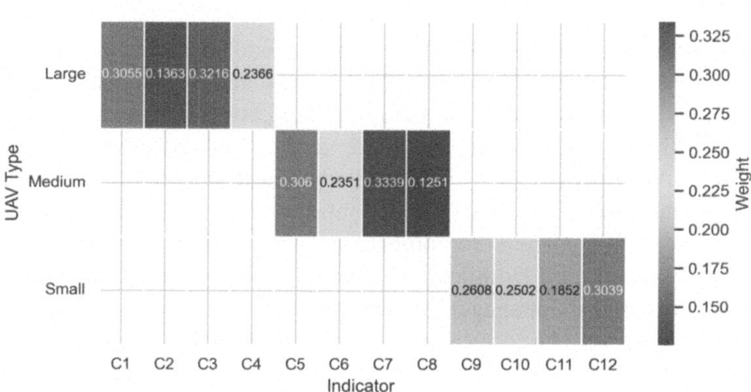

Fig. 3. The weight heatmap based on the Del method.

5.3 Calculate the Comprehensive Weight

By introducing the Lagrange operator to combine the subjective weights (generated by the Delphi method) and the objective weights (generated by the gray-scale correlation method), the final comprehensive weight distribution is shown in Table 4 (Fig. 4).

Table 4. The result of the comprehensive weight distribution.

Indicator	C1	C2	C3	C4	C5	C6	C7	C8	C9	C10	C11	C12
Comprehensive weight	0.2851	0.1808	0.2891	0.2451	0.2868	0.2443	0.2918	0.1771	0.2548	0.2479	0.2158	0.2805

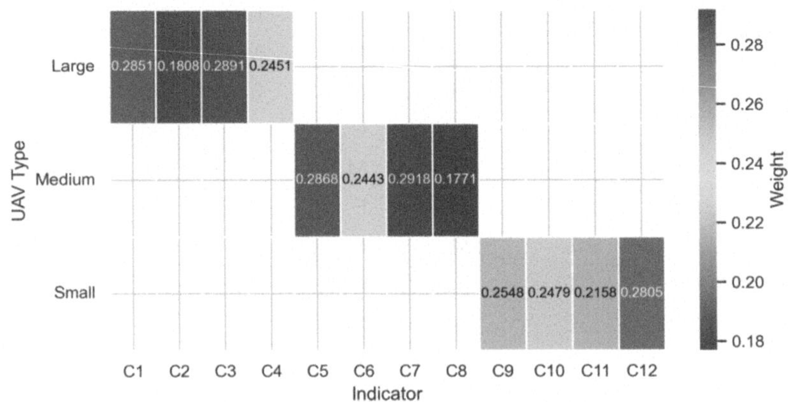

Fig. 4. Heat map of comprehensive weight distribution

6 Summary

This study, by constructing a comprehensive weight model that integrates subjective and objective elements, systematically reveals the differentiated weight distribution patterns of the competency of micro/small, medium and large unmanned aerial vehicle (UAV) operators. The empirical results show that the core competencies of large unmanned aerial vehicle (UAV) operators are mainly reflected in leadership, teamwork and self-management capabilities (28.51%), remote control of aircraft flight path management and automation (28.91%). The core competencies of medium-sized unmanned aerial vehicle (UAV) operators are significantly inclined towards the application ability of programs (28.68%) and the management and automation of flight paths for remotely piloted aircraft (24.43%). The core capabilities of micro/small drone operators focus on situational awareness (25.48%) and the ability to manage abnormal situations (28.05%).

References

1. Lv, S.: Research on the Construction and Application of the Job Competence Model for Police UAV Pilots. People's Public Security University of China (2022)
2. McClelland, D.C.: Testing for competence rather than for "intelligence." Am. Psychol. **28**(1), 1–14 (1973)
3. Spencer, L.M., Spencer, S.M.: Competence at Work: Models for Superior Performance. Wiley, New York (1993)
4. ICAO: Procedures for Air Navigation Services—Training (Doc 9868). ICAO, Montréal (2020)

5. Mansikka, H., Harris, D., Virtanen, K.: Adaptive competencies in commercial aviation: a neuroergonomic approach. Hum. Factors **61**(4), 621–635 (2019)
6. Zhang, L.: A review of competence theory and its application in civil aviation. Adv. Psychol. Sci. **18**(4), 692–700 (2010)
7. Gao, K., Li, X., Wang, Y.: Competence model of aviation maintenance personnel for complex systems. Acta Aeronaut. Astronaut. Sin. **36**(4), 1099–1108 (2015)
8. Li, H.: Construction and Validation of the Competence Model for High-Plateau Route Pilots. Civil Aviation University of China, Tianjin (2016)
9. Civil Aviation Administration of China: Implementation Roadmap for the Construction of the Full Life Cycle Management System of Transport Airline Pilot Skills. Civil Aviation Administration of China, Beijing (2021)
10. Civil Aviation Administration of China: Regulations on the Management of Civil Unmanned Aerial Vehicle Operators. Civil Aviation Administration of China Flight Standards Department (2021)
11. Zhao, T., Zhou, C., Hu, K.: Analysis of UAV operation capability evaluation models. Electron. Technol. **51**(12), 32–33 (2022)
12. Li, Y.: Research on the Air Situation Awareness Competence Assessment Method for Large UAV Operators. Civil Aviation Flight University of China (2025)
13. Zhao, T.: Research on the Transfield Control Competence of Medium and Large-Sized Trunk Line Logistics UAV Pilots. Civil Aviation Flight University of China (2023)
14. Zhou, C., Li, Y., Huo, G., et al.: Competence assessment of large UAV operators based on improved AHP. Autom. Appl. **66**(06), 1–5 (2025)

Schlieren-Based Monitoring and Deep Learning Detection for Volumetric Additive Manufacturing

Miaomiao Yuan, Yifei Wang, and Xiaoxiao Han(✉)

HNU College of Mechanical and Vehicle Engineering, Hunan University, Changsha 410082, China
xiaoxiaohan@hnu.edu.cn

Abstract. Volumetric additive manufacturing (VAM) has emerged as a promising strategy for fabricating biomedical devices owing to its capacity to produce complex architectures in a single step. This technique requires precise spatial regulation of light dose and meticulous control over exposure time. However, conventional exposure timing methods still rely heavily on operator subjectivity, leading to labour-intensive workflows and inconsistent printing reproducibility. To address these challenges, this study introduces an integrated volumetric printing system featuring in-situ monitoring functionality, coupled with an intelligent visual inspection framework that combines schlieren imaging with deep learning. Through systematic optimisation of the viscosity of refractive index-matching solutions and background illumination parameters, substantial enhancements were achieved in both quality and stability of real-time imaging, enabling the acquisition of extensive image datasets throughout the fabrication process. A convolutional neural network based on ResNet18 was then employed to accurately recognize and classify different printing stages. Experimental results indicate that when using a refractive index-matching solution with a viscosity below 650 mPa s under 1000 lx background illuminance, the system captures high-contrast, low-noise schlieren images that clearly elucidate dynamic solidification behaviour. The integration of deep learning further underscores its potential for AI-driven interpretation and quality assurance in VAM. These outcomes provide crucial technical foundations for real-time monitoring and closed-loop control in VAM, underscoring new opportunities in precision manufacturing and biomedical applications.

Keywords: Volumetric Additive Manufacturing · in-situ monitoring · Deep Learning

1 Introduction

The emergence of volumetric additive manufacturing (VAM) represents a significant paradigm shift within the field of additive manufacturing [1, 2]. Its core characteristic lies in the departure from traditional layer-by-layer deposition approaches, enabling holistic solidification of material in three-dimensional space and direct fabrication of

S. S. Ge et al. (Eds.): ICSR + BioMed 2025, LNAI 16435, pp. 284–295, 2026.
https://doi.org/10.1007/978-981-95-7538-1_25

target structures. This technology demonstrates remarkable rapid prototyping capabilities and substantially enhanced manufacturing efficiency. Inspired by the principles of computed tomography (CT), VAM operates by projecting a series of two-dimensional images in the form of light energy onto a rotating vial containing photosensitive resin from multiple angles, achieving spatial energy superposition and control [3, 4]. When the accumulated energy absorbed by the material exceeds its polymerisation threshold, the desired three-dimensional shape is formed. Leveraging this unique forming mechanism, VAM effectively overcomes inherent limitations associated with conventional layer-based printing technologies—such as fused deposition modelling (FDM), stereolithography (SLA), and digital light processing (DLP)—including prolonged printing time, weak interlayer adhesion, and the need for support structures for overhanging features [4, 5]. In contrast, VAM's volumetric approach circumvents these drawbacks, offering a novel solution for efficient fabrication of complex architectures. Notably, VAM exhibits exceptional advantages in printing speed—typically completing the entire structure within minutes or even seconds. This attribute renders it particularly promising for highly time- and environment-sensitive applications, such as bioprinting of living cells [6–8].

During the VAM process, the polymerisation kinetics are governed by both light dose distribution—affected by vial rotation speed, projection area, and intensity—and material photoresponse, influenced by position, temperature, and oxygen concentration. These interdependent variables challenge process stability and consistency. Exposure time serves as a macroscopically adjustable parameter that indirectly integrates light-material interactions, offering a practical means to achieve printing precision. However, its current reliance on empirical determination impedes accurate print termination and reproducibility. Notably, exposure times may vary by up to 40% even under consistent material conditions, necessitating recalibration and undermining VAM's rapid manufacturing advantage. The central constraint in VAM precision is thus insufficient process controllability, exacerbated by the absence of real-time curing monitoring and feedback. Implementing compatible in-situ monitoring systems to dynamically track solidification and regulate printing endpoints is essential to improve accuracy, stability, and repeatability.

Numerous researchers have actively explored this direction. Loterie et al. [10] improved the printing accuracy of models by developing a low-étendue illumination system combined with an open-loop control strategy, demonstrating the potential of this technology in fabricating functional structures. Optical approaches have provided new pathways to address resolution and accuracy limitations in VAM. For instance, in the same year, Li et al. [11] proposed a system based on three-dimensional refractive index monitoring, which employs tomographic reconstruction of colour schlieren images to track polymerisation changes, thereby enhancing print fidelity and reducing the debugging cycle for new material development. Bhattacharya et al. [12] developed a projection optimisation method to determine the optimal light dose distribution and integrated a shadowgraph imaging system to monitor object formation, ultimately improving print quality. To achieve true in-situ shape monitoring, Orth et al. [13] developed an Optical Scattering Tomography (OST) system that leverages the significant increase in light scattering during resin curing to enable real-time 3D imaging and quantitative modelling during the printing process. This work laid the foundation for next-generation rapid prototyping technologies capable of real-time defect identification and correction. More recently, the same team built upon the OST system by calibrating scattering thresholds to enable automatic determination of exposure parameters [9]. Although these studies have made significant progress in optical optimisation, in-situ monitoring, and feedback control, current VAM technologies still face challenges such as complex monitoring systems, limited material applicability, insufficient intelligence, and high experimental costs. Meanwhile, deep learning techniques have shown great potential in defect recognition and process monitoring, yet their application in the VAM domain remains in its early stages.

Addressing the current limitations, this study proposes an intelligent visual monitoring solution for VAM to enhance the visualisation and intelligence of the printing process. First, an in-situ monitoring system based on schlieren technology is established to capture dynamic images resulting from refractive index changes during printing. Second, the optical parameters of the material are optimised to improve image contrast and resolution, ensuring the reliability and stability of the monitoring data. Finally, preliminary exploration of deep learning methods is conducted using the acquired image data to verify the feasibility of intelligent defect detection and process evaluation based on image information. Through this systematic investigation, the study aims to advance quality assurance and intelligent control in VAM, laying the foundation for real-time feedback and adaptive printing. This effort is expected to further expand the application of VAM technology in high-precision manufacturing, medical devices, and personalised biofabrication.

2 Methods and Materials

2.1 Materials

The photosensitive resins used in this study were composed of Urethane-dimethacrylate (UDMA) and phenyl bis (2,4,6-trimethyl benzoyl)-phosphine oxide (I819), which served as monomers and photoinitiator, respectively. In addition, glycerol, poly(ethylene glycol) diacrylate (PEGDA), and polydimethylsiloxane (PDMS) are used as refractive index matching solutions due to their high light transmittance, closely matched refractive indices, and stable physicochemical properties, thereby improving printing quality and imaging clarity. All the materials mentioned above were purchased from Aladdin Company.

2.2 Characterisation of Material Viscosity Properties

To evaluate the effect of viscosity of refractive index-matching solutions on imaging quality, this study employed a rotational rheometer (MCR 302e, Anton Paar) to measure the viscosity of the solutions at 25 °C. Each solution was tested three times, and the average value was taken to minimise random errors. The tests were conducted in shear rate sweep mode (range: 0–200 s^{-1}), and the steady-state viscosity values were recorded to analyse the potential influence of the flow behaviour of the solutions on printing imaging and to determine the applicable viscosity window for the system. Furthermore, the viscosity variation of glycerol over the temperature range of 20–100 °C was investigated to explore the feasibility of optimising imaging performance by adjusting viscosity through temperature control.

2.3 In-Situ Monitoring System for Volumetric Additive Manufacturing

The in-situ monitoring system for VAM developed in this study is illustrated in Fig. 1a. The system consists of two main modules: the VAM module and the in-situ monitoring module. The VAM module primarily includes a 405 nm wavelength projector (PDC-03, GVINDA, China), a transparent rectangular glass tank (serving as a refractive index-matching device), a transparent cylindrical glass vial, and a set of motor-driven rotating fixtures. The patterned light emitted by the projector is corrected by the refractive index-matching tank to eliminate radial distortion caused by the curved surface of the vial. This ensures that the light beam is incident onto the central region of the vial in a collimated form, thereby improving the uniformity of the projected energy distribution and enhancing printing accuracy and process stability [2] (Fig. 1b).

The in-situ monitoring module is based on the schlieren technique, which visualises the printing process by converting light ray deflection caused by refractive index gradients within the medium into contrast variations in the images [14]. The imaging optical path of this module consists of the following components: a 5 W collimated white LED light source, an adjustable aperture for regulating light intensity and imaging clarity, a set of high-quality plano-convex lenses (Goldenvue GL31-050B-180-VIS) for beam shaping, and a camera (Canon EOS 6D Mark II) equipped with a 100 mm macro lens for image acquisition. The test area is located within the optical path between the lens assemblies. The light beam passes vertically through the refractive index-matching tank and the vial, arranged orthogonally to the VAM optical path. The tank effectively eliminates surface-induced distortion, providing the monitoring system with an imaging environment characterised by minimal aberration and high clarity (Fig. 1c).

2.4 Printing Process of VAM

All CAD models were designed using 3D modeling software (SolidWorks 2021) and exported as STL files. The conversion from 3D STL files to 2D tomographic slices was performed using the open-source CAL algorithm package developed by Kelly et al. [4] to generate a sequence of 2D patterns. These patterns were then projected sequentially at a light intensity of 7 mW/cm^2. Throughout the printing process, real-time monitoring was conducted via a camera to visually track printing progress and completion. Before projection began, the vial was ensured to be fully within the camera's field of view to prevent recording failures. It is important to note that the container was rotated for several minutes prior to projection to allow the resin to reach the same angular velocity as the cavity, thereby avoiding relative motion between them. After printing, the printed part was promptly cleaned and post-cured to ensure structural integrity and material performance.

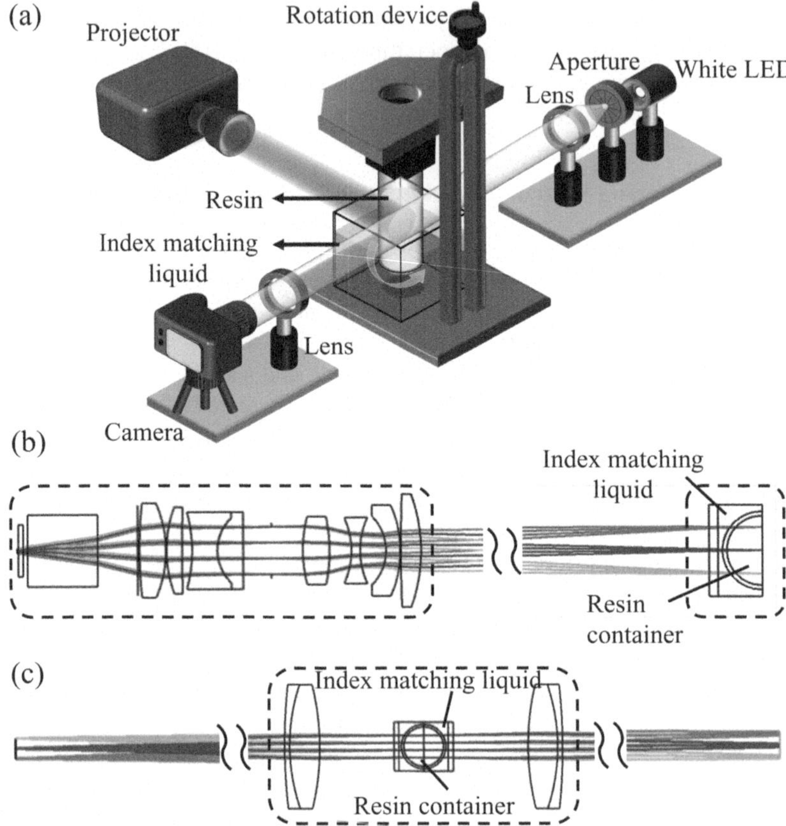

Fig. 1. (a) In-situ monitoring system for volumetric additive manufacturing. (b) Optical pathway diagram of the VAM system. (c) Optical pathway diagram of the in-situ monitoring system.

2.5 Image Processing Methodology

Real-time video was captured during printing using a Canon EOS 6D Mark II camera in black-and-white mode (1080p resolution, 25 fps). Under consistent lighting, a localised region within the vial was selected as the region of interest (ROI) to minimise edge effects on grayscale analysis. Quantitative evaluation of the ROI included mean grayscale, standard deviation, and gradient variance to characterise optical disturbances and image quality.

3 Results and Discussion

3.1 Viscosity–Imaging Compatibility

In volumetric printing with UDMA resin, glycerol, PEGDA, and PDMS are commonly used as refractive index-matching solutions to reduce optical distortion. However, during in-situ monitoring, glycerol under vial rotation produced persistent irregular streaks

(Fig. 2a), which disturbed both projection and background light, impairing print quality and image clarity. No such streaks occurred with PEGDA or PDMS. This difference is attributed to flow behaviour: high-viscosity liquids like glycerol require more energy for molecular displacement and exhibit slower recovery to steady state, leading to prolonged perturbation relaxation.

To validate the aforementioned hypothesis, this study measured the viscosities of various refractive index-matching solutions (Fig. 2b) and quantitatively analysed the grayscale standard deviation of images captured under both static and dynamic vial conditions (Fig. 2c). The results indicated that the viscosities of glycerol, PEGDA, and PDMS were approximately 14,850 mPa s, 650 mPa s, and 6 mPa s, respectively, with no significant variation observed across different shear rates. Experimental findings demonstrated that replacing glycerol with PEGDA or PDMS as the refractive index-matching solution significantly reduced image disturbances and markedly improved system stability. Based on these results, this study proposes that the applicable viscosity window for optical correction devices should not exceed 650 mPa s, with the viscosity of PEGDA serving as the upper reference limit. Furthermore, considering the temperature sensitivity of liquid viscosity, the variation in glycerol viscosity at different temperatures was investigated (Fig. 2d). The results revealed that when the temperature of glycerol was raised to 65 °C under a printing rotation speed of 24°/s, its viscosity decreased to approximately 650 mPa s. At this viscosity, the grayscale standard deviation of the images showed significant improvement compared to the values obtained at 20 °C (Fig. 2e–f). These consistent findings confirm that viscosity is a critical parameter influencing image disturbances and experimentally validate the feasibility of optimising imaging quality through viscosity control.

3.2 Light Source–Imaging Compatibility

To determine the optimal matching relationship between the illumination conditions in schlieren imaging and the optical properties of UDMA material for achieving high-quality and stable imaging performance, this study systematically evaluated the influence of varying background light intensities (in lx) on the grayscale and clarity of UDMA sample images (Fig. 3a). Experimental results demonstrated that, within the tested illumination range, the grayscale of the UDMA region exhibited a linear relationship with light intensity (Fig. 3b), indicating that grayscale variations primarily originated from the inherent optical response of the material rather than significant interference or bias introduced by the imaging system. This consistency ensures the reliability of subsequent image analysis. Furthermore, three image clarity evaluation algorithms based on grayscale gradient variance were employed to quantitatively analyse the printed shapes (Fig. 3c). All three methods consistently indicated that the sharpness of UDMA images reached an optimum at an illumination level of 1000 lx, suggesting this intensity as the ideal light source parameter for schlieren imaging of UDMA.

Under optimised parameters (PEGDA refractive index-matching solution, 1000 lx background illumination), in-situ schlieren monitoring successfully captured microscale solid formation during initial printing stages. Prior to exceeding the curing threshold, the resin maintained uniform refractive distribution with no observable changes. Once

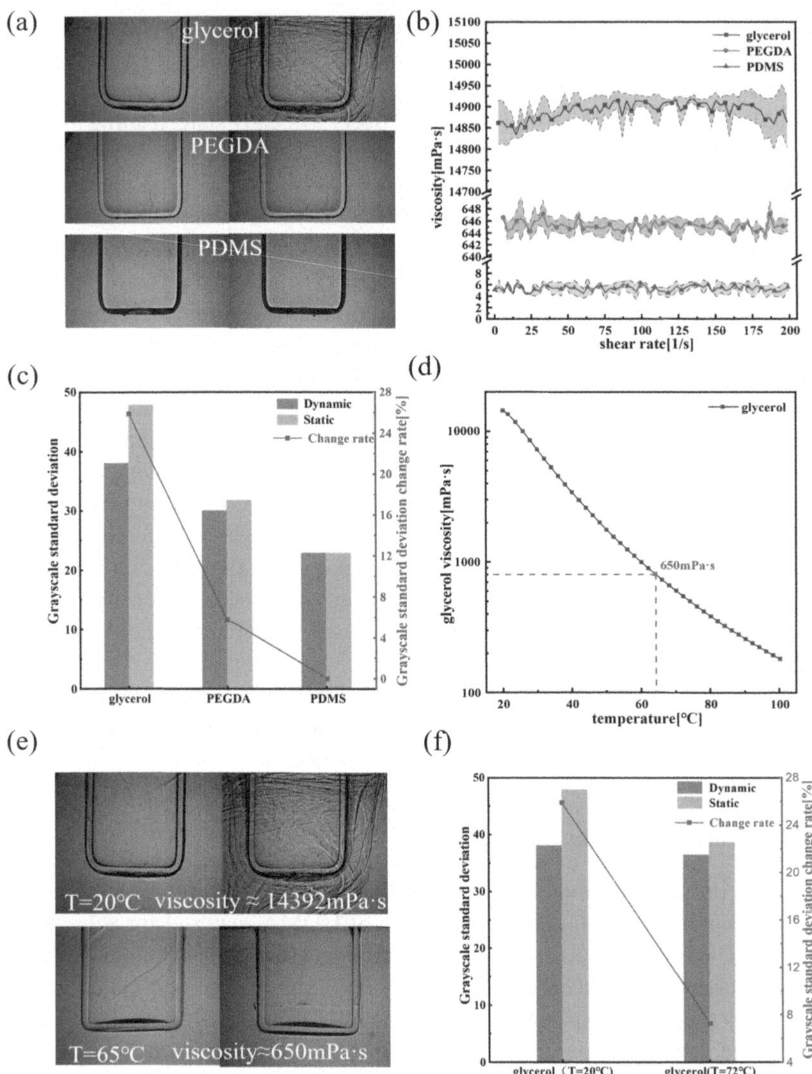

Fig. 2. (a) Image comparison of refractive index-matching solutions with varying viscosities (left: static, right: rotating; sampling condition: vial rotated at 24°/s for 1 min). (b) Viscosity curves of different refractive index-matching solutions. (c) Comparison of grayscale standard deviation for refractive index-matching solutions with varying viscosities. (d) Variation curve of glycerol viscosity with temperature. (e) Comparison of glycerol images at different temperatures (left: static, right: rotating; printing rotation speed: 24°/s). (f) Comparison of grayscale standard deviation for glycerol images at different temperatures.

the threshold was surpassed, liquid-to-solid transition commenced with progressively distinct refractive contrast, yielding clearly defined curing regions (Fig. 3d).

The in-situ monitoring system successfully captures real-time refractive index dynamics during printing, revealing detailed liquid-to-solid transition characteristics. This validates its effectiveness for real-time process observation and provides an experimental basis for precision control and curing endpoint determination. The high-quality, stable schlieren images offer a reliable data source for deep learning-based analysis, significantly improving the accuracy of image-based process monitoring and evaluation.

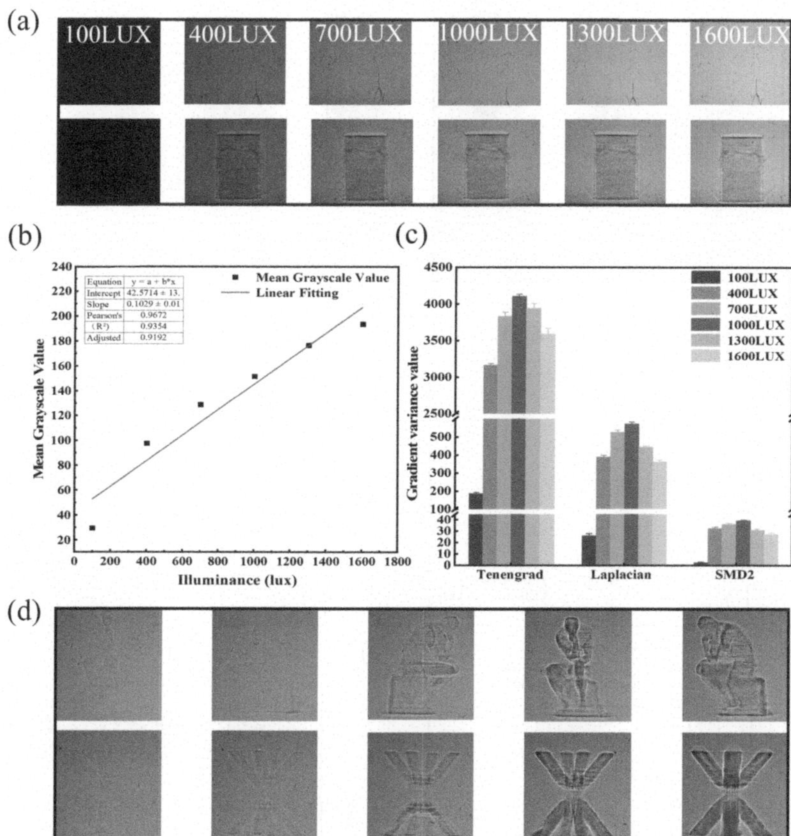

Fig. 3. (a) Schlieren images of UDMA ink during printing under varying illumination intensities (using PEGDA as refractive index-matching solution; vial rotation speed: 24°/s). (b) Illumination intensity and grayscale variation curves for UDMA. (c) Histogram of image clarity evaluation for UDMA. (d) Example schlieren image captured by the camera during the printing process.

3.3 Application of Deep Learning

Deep learning demonstrates an advantage in automatically extracting subtle feature differences in image recognition [15]. Building on this, the present study introduces it into the intelligent monitoring of the VAM process, aiming to perform feature identification and analysis of images at different printing stages to support intelligent evaluation and feedback during printing. A lightweight convolutional neural network, ResNet18, is selected as the base model [16], which maintains strong feature extraction capabilities while offering high training efficiency, moderate parameters, and low computational demands—making it suitable for applications in closed-loop control and real-time detection.

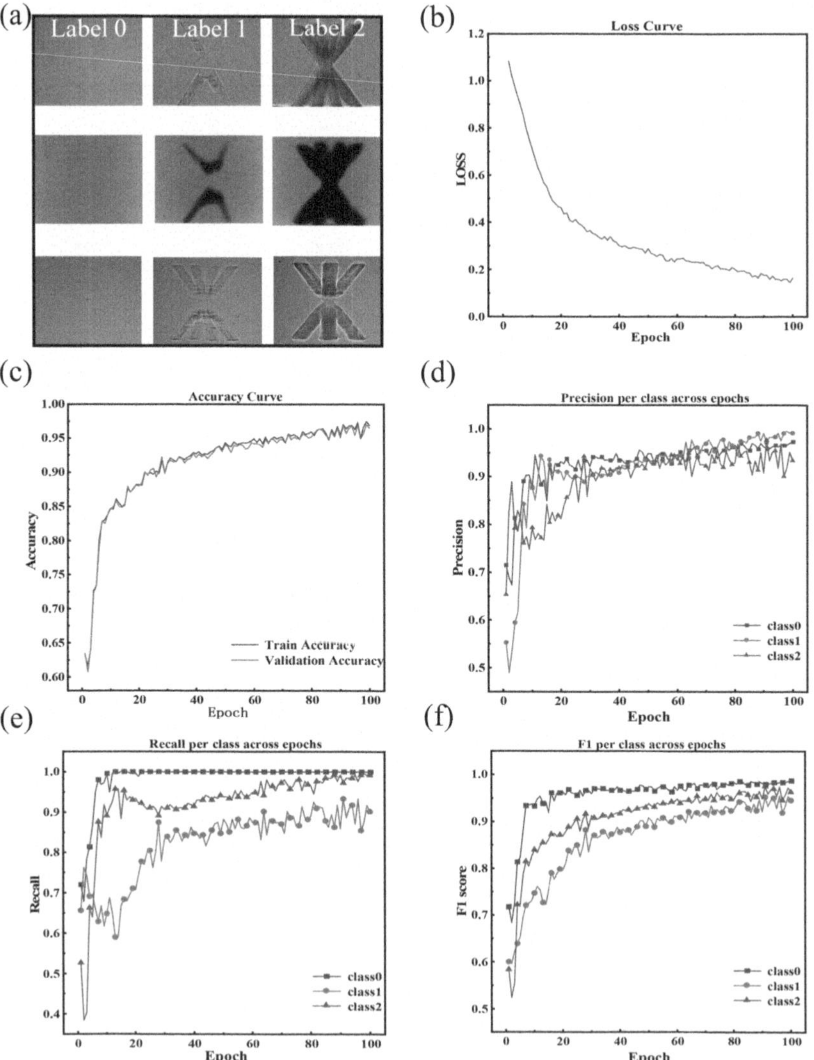

Fig. 4. (a) Dataset (Label 1: Uncured; Label 2: Curing; Label 3: Fully Cured). (b) ResNet18 loss curve. (c) ResNet18 accuracy curves. (d–f) ResNet18 accuracy, recall, and F1-score.

Based on the ResNet18 architecture, this study constructed an image dataset encompassing pre-printing (uncured), printing (curing), and post-printing (fully cured) stages (Fig. 4a) to characterize structural evolution during liquid-to-solid transformation. All images, obtained from an in-situ monitoring system, were processed through frame extraction, screening, and annotation. The resulting 3871 images were uniformly cropped to 512 × 512 pixels and divided into training and validation sets at an 8:2 ratio (3099 and 772 images), with balanced class distribution. Preliminary training and validation were performed to assess the feasibility of the proposed method for stage recognition and intelligent detection in the printing process.

Preliminary results show that the model achieved stable convergence, with training loss decreasing progressively. Both training and validation accuracy increased steadily, reaching approximately 0.97 (Fig. 4b–c). Evaluation further revealed Precision and Recall values above 0.90, with the F1-score exceeding 0.95, demonstrating strong discriminative power and balanced performance across classes (Fig. 4d–f). These findings confirm the effectiveness of the lightweight convolutional neural network in feature identification throughout the printing stages, underscoring the promise of deep learning for intelligent detection in volumetric additive manufacturing. It should be emphasised that the present results are derived from offline analysis, and real-time detection has yet to be realised. Nonetheless, the model's lightweight architecture provides a sound basis for future deployment.

Although this study remains exploratory and exhibits certain limitations—such as a lack of systematic testing, limited coverage of complex defect types, and absence of integration with an adaptive control system—future work will focus on expanding the dataset to incorporate greater diversity and scale, improving software-hardware coordination, and advancing system integration and validation. Building on these efforts, we aim to develop real-time adaptive closed-loop control strategies to enhance the practicality, robustness, and generalisability of the system within real-world volumetric additive manufacturing scenarios. These developments are expected to facilitate the progression of deep learning applications from real-time monitoring towards comprehensive intelligent closed-loop regulation.

4 Conclusion

This study presents an intelligent vision-based monitoring solution for VAM, which integrates schlieren imaging technology with deep learning algorithms to overcome the limitations of conventional process visualisation and quality control methods. We have successfully developed an integrated VAM system with in-situ monitoring capability, employing schlieren technology to achieve high-quality real-time imaging of refractive index dynamics during printing, thereby providing a reliable data foundation for intelligent analysis. Through systematic investigation of the effects of refractive index-matching solution viscosity and background illumination parameters on imaging quality, an optimal process window was established—with a viscosity not exceeding 650 mPa s (using PEGDA as reference) and an illuminance of 1000 lx—significantly enhancing image contrast and stability. The research also developed a model describing the coupling relationship between imaging quality and light–material parameters, offering an experimental basis for parameter optimisation and broader applicability of the monitoring system. In terms of intelligent application, this study conducted preliminary exploration into deep learning for state recognition in VAM processes. A network model based on

ResNet18 accurately distinguished among the three stages—"uncured", "curing", and "fully cured"—achieving an F1-score exceeding 0.95, demonstrating strong potential for intelligent interpretation and quality assessment. Although the study has made substantive progress in visualisation and intelligent recognition, the model still requires systematic validation with independent test sets, and closed-loop control capabilities remain to be further developed.

In summary, this study presents an integrated solution combining visual monitoring and intelligent detection, offering an effective technical pathway for real-time monitoring, precision assurance, and adaptive control in VAM. Future work will focus on enhancing the generalisation capability and robustness of the deep learning model, extending applicability to multi-material systems, and advancing closed-loop feedback control from state recognition to adaptive printing. These developments will ultimately enable quality-assured and intelligent manufacturing across the entire VAM process, laying a solid foundation for its application in biomedical engineering, precision devices, and other high-value fields.

References

1. Whyte, D.J., Doeven, E.H., Sutti, A., Kouzani, A.Z., Adams, S.D.: Volumetric additive manufacturing: a new frontier in layer-less 3D printing. Addit. Manuf. **84**, 104094 (2024)
2. Shusteff, M., et al.: One-step volumetric additive manufacturing of complex polymer structures. Sci. Adv. **3**(12), eaao5496 (2017)
3. Madrid-Wolff, J., et al.: A review of materials used in tomographic volumetric additive manufacturing. MRS Commun. **13**(5), 764–785 (2023)
4. Kelly, B.E., Bhattacharya, I., Heidari, H., Shusteff, M., Spadaccini, C.M., Taylor, H.K.: Volumetric additive manufacturing via tomographic reconstruction. Science **363**(6431), 1075–1079 (2019)
5. Thijssen, Q., Toombs, J., Li, C.C., Taylor, H., Van Vlierberghe, S.: From pixels to voxels: a mechanistic perspective on volumetric 3D-printing. Prog. Polym. Sci. **147**, 101755 (2023)
6. Mathur, V., Dsouza, V., Srinivasan, V., Vasanthan, K.S.: Volumetric additive manufacturing for cell printing: bridging industry adaptation and regulatory frontiers. ACS Biomater. Sci. Eng. **11**(1), 16–181 (2025)
7. Bernal, P.N., et al.: Volumetric bioprinting of complex living-tissue constructs within seconds. Adv. Mater. **31**(42), 1904209 (2019)
8. Jing, S., et al.: Advances in volumetric bioprinting. Biofabrication **16**(1), 012004 (2023)
9. Orth, A., et al.: Automatic exposure volumetric additive manufacturing. Adv. Mater. Technol. e02168 (2025)
10. Loterie, D., Delrot, P., Moser, C.: High-resolution tomographic volumetric additive manufacturing. Nat. Commun. **11**(1), 852 (2020)
11. Chung Li, C., Toombs, J., Taylor, H.: Tomographic color Schlieren refractive index mapping for computed axial lithography. In: Proceedings of the 5th Annual ACM Symposium on Computational Fabrication. LNCS, pp. 1–7 (2020)
12. Bhattacharya, I., Toombs, J., Taylor, H.: High fidelity volumetric additive manufacturing. Addit. Manuf. **47**, 102299 (2021)
13. Orth, A., et al.: On-the-fly 3D metrology of volumetric additive manufacturing. Addit. Manuf. **56** (2022)
14. Vogel, A., Apitz, I., Freidank, S., Dijkink, R.: Sensitive high-resolution white-light Schlieren technique with a large dynamic range for the investigation of ablation dynamics. Opt. Lett. **31**(12), 1812–1814 (2006)

15. Fujiyoshi, H., Hirakawa, T., Yamashita, T.: Deep learning-based image recognition for autonomous driving. IATSS Res. **43**(4), 244–252 (2019)
16. He, K., Zhang, X., Ren, S., Sun, J.: Deep residual learning for image recognition. In: Proceedings of the IEEE Conference on Computer Vision and Pattern Recognition, pp. 770–778 (2016)

3D Printed Microstructure Hydrogel for Wearable Sensors and Triboelectric Nanogenerator

Tuanjie Chen[1(✉)], Hongxue Xu[2], and Caijuan Li[3]

[1] Lanzhou No. 63 Middle School, Lanzhou, Gansu 730060, People's Republic of China
chentuanjie2025@163.com

[2] Lanzhou Bowen College of Science and Technology, Lanzhou, Gansu 730101, People's Republic of China

[3] Lanzhou Institute of Technology, Lanzhou, Gansu 730050, People's Republic of China

Abstract. This study addresses the urgent demand for high-performance conductive materials in flexible wearable devices by designing a dual-network structure PAAm/SA/LiCl hydrogel. This material exhibits excellent mechanical properties (200% elongation at break), anti-freezing (− 35.4 °C) and high conductivity (117.6 S/cm). A triboelectric nanogenerator (TENG) assembled from 3D-printed micro-conical hydrogel structures generates an open-circuit voltage of up to 112.4 V and illuminates 35 LED lights. The devices demonstrate a sensitive response to human movements such as finger and knee flexion, which is promising for applications in self-powered sensors and flexible wearable devices.

Keywords: TENG · Sensor · 3D printing

1 Introduction

Sensors represent a significant application area for hydrogel materials [1, 2]. Hydrogels possess high biocompatibility, softness, breathability and strong affinity with skin, making them unlikely to cause rejection or irritation in the human body [3]. They can be fabricated into forms such as electrodes or electronic skin, which are widely employed in monitoring human movement, heartbeat, respiration, and other physiological signals [4].

In recent years, hydrogel electrodes with microstructured surfaces fabricated using 3D printing technology have been shown to significantly improve their sensitivity [5]. Following encapsulation, these electrodes can be integrated into triboelectric nanogenerator (TENG) structures. In these structures, charge transfer occurs between the hydrogel electrode and the encapsulation layer during contact, separation, or friction, thereby converting external mechanical energy into electrical energy [6, 7]. When subjected to pressure of varying magnitude or frequency, this structure outputs corresponding electrical signals, thereby combining sensing and power generation capabilities.

Compared to conventional strain sensors, hydrogel-based TENG sensors offer significant advantages [8]. Firstly, they require no external power source, substantially

S. S. Ge et al. (Eds.): ICSR + BioMed 2025, LNAI 16435, pp. 296–307, 2026.
https://doi.org/10.1007/978-981-95-7538-1_26

simplifying circuitry and reducing interference with human movement, thereby capturing more accurate motion signals. Secondly, this structure can harvest mechanical energy generated by bodily motion and convert it into electrical energy, enabling energy reuse. For instance, Li et al. [9] constructed a self-powered, self-healing TENG (SS-TENG) by sandwiching a PAAm/carrageenan hydrogel between two layers of glycerol-hydroxyethyl cellulose elastomer (GHEC). They further developed a 3 × 3 transparent touch sensor array, offering a viable solution for self-powered flexible screen sensors. Sun et al. [10] employed a sandwich-structured PAAm/gelatin/PEDOT:PSS (MGP) hydrogel to fabricate a stretchable TENG (STENG). This device not only detects human motion but also illuminates LED arrays, charges capacitors, and even directly powers portable electronic devices. This self-power generation capability significantly expands the application value of TENG sensors in human motion sensing.

In this study, we employed polyacrylamide (PAAm) as the primary network and sodium alginate (SA) as the secondary network. Lithium chloride (LiCl) was incorporated as the conductive medium, while LAP was incorporated to prepare PAAm/SA/LiCl hydrogels via photopolymerisation. The chemical composition and microstructure of the hydrogel were characterised using FT-IR and SEM, and its anti-freezing, mechanical, electrical, and sensing and output characteristics as a TENG were systematically evaluated.

2 Materials and Methods

2.1 Materials

Lithium chloride (LiCl) was purchased from Shanghai Acmec Biochemical Technology Co. Ltd. Acrylamide (AAm), Sodium alginate (SA) and N, N′-methylenebisacrylamide (MBA) were purchased from Shanghai McLean Biotechnology Ltd. Lithium phenyl (2,4,6-trimethylbenzoyl) phosphate (LAP) was obtained from Shanghai Shifeng Biotechnology Co., Ltd. (Shanghai, China).

2.2 Preparation of the Hydrogels

First, acrylamide AAm (9 g) and LiCl (2.5 g) were dissolved in deionised water at 60 °C. SA (2 g) was then added to this solution and stirred vigorously at 60 °C for 2 h. Subsequently, add MBA (37.5 mg) and LAP (0.12 g) and stir for 10 min to obtain the PAAm/SA/LiCl hydrogel precursor solution. The precursor solution within the mould was photopolymerised using ultraviolet light at a wavelength of 405 nm (5–20 s), ultimately obtaining a PAAm/SA/LiCl hydrogel. The specific composition design of the PAAm/SA/LiCl hydrogel precursor solution is detailed in Table 1.

Table 1. Composition of hydrogel precursor

Hydrogels	AAm	SA	LiCl	H_2O	MBA (mg)	LAP (g)
PAAm	9	0	0	50.84	37.5	0.12
PAAm/SA	9	2	0	48.84	37.5	0.12
PAAm/SA/LiCl	9	2	2.5	42.12	37.5	0.12

2.3 Characterization

Fourier transform infrared spectroscopy was measured using an FT-IR spectrometer (BRUKER, Germany). Cross-sectional morphology of the hydrogel was analysed using a Tescan Vega4 tungsten filament electron microscope (TESCAN, Czech Republic). The hydrogel material underwent dehydration and freeze-drying via a TF-FD-27 vacuum freeze-dryer (Shanghai Tianfeng, China) prior to electron microscopy imaging, with the fracture surfaces of the specimens subjected to gold spraying. Tensile properties of the hydrogel were tested using a CTM2500 tensile testing machine (Xieqiang Instruments, China) at a measurement speed of 50 mm/min. Anti-freezing performance was investigated using a DSC 214 differential scanning calorimeter (NETZSCH, Germany). The electrical resistance of the PAAm/SA/LiCl hydrogel was measured using a DMM6500 digital multimeter (Keithley, USA), with conductivity subsequently calculated. The electrical output performance of the TENG was assessed using a 6514 electrometer (Keithley, USA).

3 Results and Discussion

3.1 Microtopography of Hydrogels

Figure 1a and b respectively display the cross-sectional morphology of the PAAm/SA hydrogel and the PAAm/SA/LiCl hydrogel. As evident from the figures, both double-network composite hydrogels exhibit three-dimensional porous structures. In comparison, the addition of LiCl results in a marked reduction in pore size within the PAAm/SA/LiCl hydrogel. This alteration may stem from LiCl enhancing intermolecular interactions between polymer chains (such as hydrogen bonding), thereby promoting the formation of a denser, finer pore architecture.

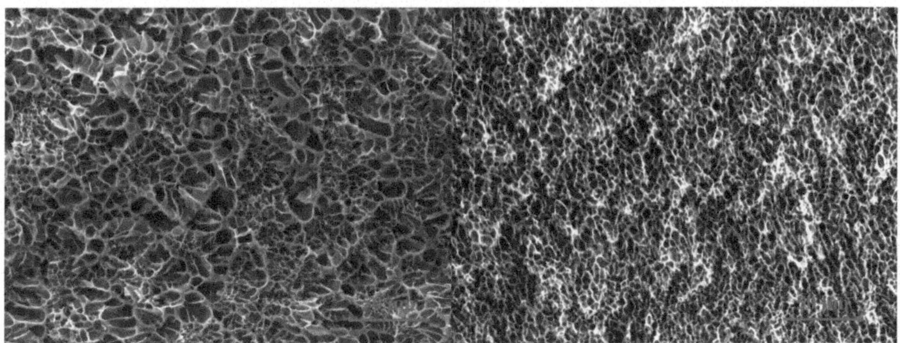

Fig. 1. The SEM images of (a) PAAm/SA and (b) PAAm/SA/LiCl hydrogel.

3.2 FTIR of the PAAm/SA/LiCl Hydrogel

Figure 2 displays the Fourier transform infrared (FTIR) spectrum of the PAAm/SA/LiCl hydrogel. In the PAAm spectrum, the broad absorption peak at 3296 cm^{-1} is attributed to N–H stretching vibrations. The peak at 1596 cm^{-1} corresponds to N–H bending vibrations, while the peak at 1026 cm^{-1} represents $-NH_2$ rocking vibrations. The peak at 1654 cm^{-1} corresponds to the stretching vibration of the C=O bond in the amide I band. In the SA spectrum, the absorption peak at 3412 cm^{-1} is attributed to O–H stretching vibration. The peaks at 1611 cm^{-1} and 1413 cm^{-1} correspond to the asymmetric and symmetric stretching vibrations of the carboxyl group (–COO–), respectively, while the peak at 1031 cm^{-1} represents C–O stretching vibration.

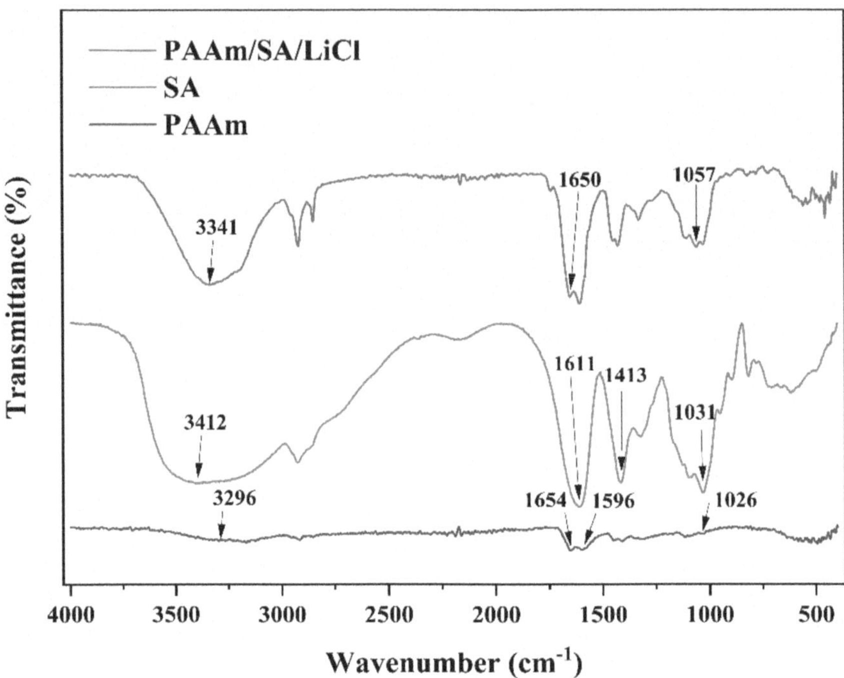

Fig. 2. The FT-IR spectra of SA, PAAm, PAAm/SA/LiCl hydrogels.

In the PAAm/SA/LiCl composite hydrogel, the N–H stretching vibration peak shifted to 3341 cm^{-1} and exhibited significant broadening, indicating the formation of hydrogen bonds between PAAm and SA. Furthermore, due to the combined effects of hydrogen bonding and van der Waals forces between PAAm and SA, the C=O stretching vibration peak within the amide I band also shifted from 1654 cm^{-1} to 1650 cm^{-1}.

3.3 Anti-freezing Property of Hydrogels

The anti-freezing properties of different hydrogels were characterised via differential scanning calorimetry (DSC) (Fig. 3). The freezing point of the PAAm/SA hydrogel was approximately − 11.9 °C, whereas the PAAm/SA/LiCl hydrogel remained unfrozen down to − 35.4 °C following LiCl incorporation. This phenomenon can be attributed to two mechanisms. Firstly, LiCl increases the content of bound water within the system through hydration. Secondly, the ionic coordination between Li^+ ions and the COO^- groups on the SA chains also helps constrain water molecule movement, thereby significantly enhancing the anti-freezing performance of the hydrogel. These results indicate that the PAAm/SA/LiCl hydrogel possesses excellent application potential in extreme low-temperature environments.

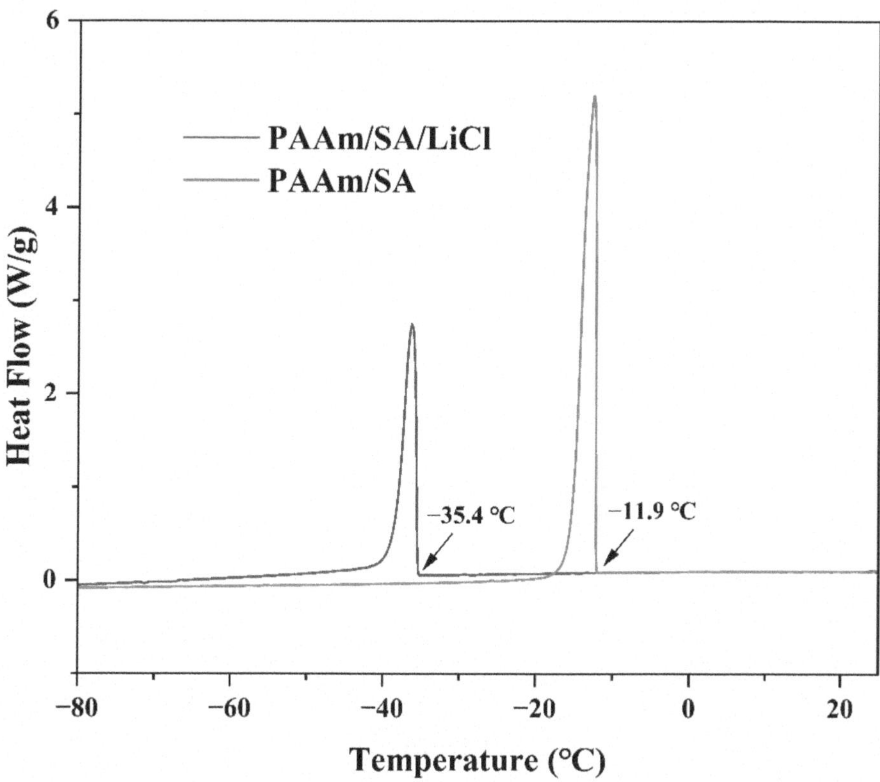

Fig. 3. The DSC curves of PAAm/SA and PAAm/SA/LiCl hydrogels.

3.4 Mechanical Property of Hydrogels

The flexibility and stretchability of hydrogels are key mechanical properties enabling their multifunctional applications. As shown in Fig. 4, the PAAm/SA hydrogel exhibits a fracture stress of 24.1 kPa and a fracture elongation of 200%. This is primarily attributed to its internally highly ordered porous three-dimensional structure and the hydrogen bonding interactions formed between PAAm and SA molecular chains.

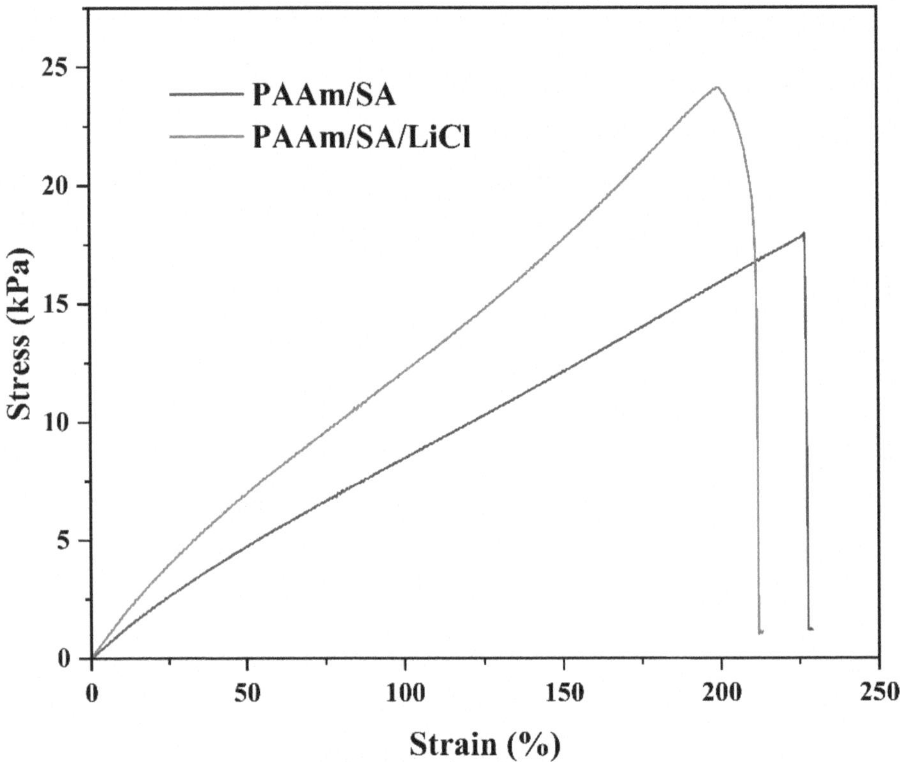

Fig. 4. The tensile curves of PAAm/SA and PAAm/SA/LiCl hydrogels.

In contrast, the fracture stress of the PAAm/SA/LiCl hydrogel decreased to 17.9 kPa, whilst the fracture elongation increased to 226%. The alteration in mechanical properties may be attributed to the incorporation of LiCl. On the one hand, ionic interactions between Li^+ and SA may induce flocculation, forming chemically cross-linked structures that partially impede the uniform distribution of SA molecules within the gel network. On the other hand, this interaction also enhances molecular chain flexibility, thereby improving the material's stretchability. Overall, the addition of LiCl enhances extensibility while somewhat diminishing the strength of the PAAm/SA/LiC hydrogel.

3.5 Conductive Properties of Hydrogels

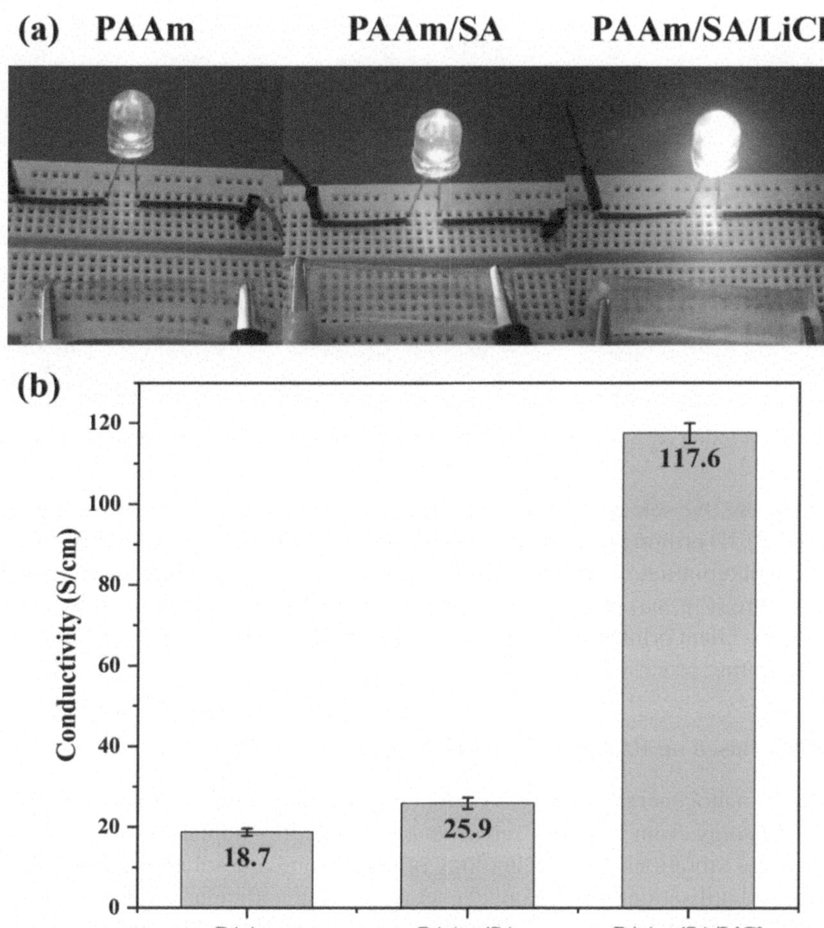

Fig. 5. (a) LED brightness when hydrogel is connected to 5 V circuit; (b) the conductivity of PAAm, PAAm/SA and PAAm/SA/LiCl hydrogels.

Figure 5a compares the electrical conductivity of the three hydrogels and the brightness of the LED illuminated in a 5 V circuit. It can be observed that the conductive properties of the hydrogels progressively enhance with the addition of SA and LiCl. The specific data in Fig. 5b reveal that the conductivity of the PAAm hydrogel and PAAm/SA hydrogel is 18.7 S/cm and 25.9 S/cm respectively, whereas the conductivity of the PAAm/SA/LiCl hydrogel increases significantly to 117.6 S/cm upon LiCl addition. This outstanding conductivity can be attributed to the directional migration of Li^+, Na^+, and Cl^- ions under the influence of an electric field, thereby forming effective electrical pathways.

3.6 3D Printing of PAAm/SA/LiCl Hydrogels

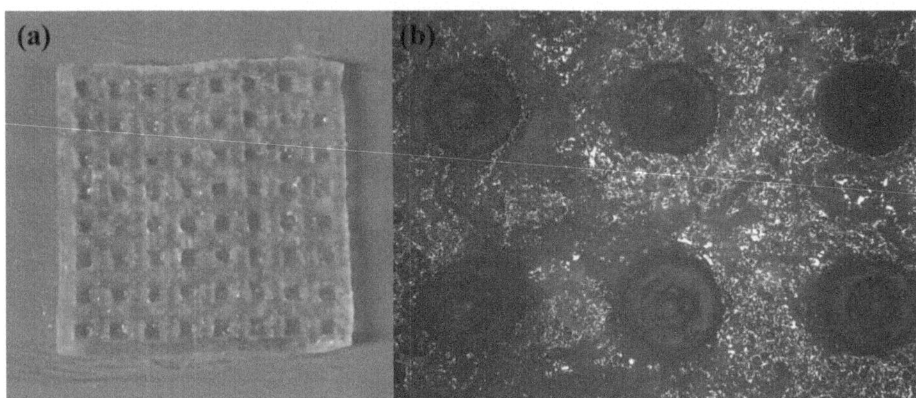

Fig. 6. 3D printing (a) 8 × 8 grid structure hydrogel, (b) conical microstructure hydrogel.

Furthermore, we selected a PAAm/SA/LiCl precursor solution for digital light processing (DLP) 3D printing tests, leveraging the photopolymerisation capability provided by LAP as a photoinitiator. We successfully printed a 10-layer scaffold featuring an 8 × 8 grid structure (Fig. 6a) alongside an array of micro-conical structures, fully demonstrating the excellent printability of this hydrogel and the high-resolution characteristics of the 3D printing process.

3.7 TENG Based on PAAm/SA/LiCl Hydrogel

Triboelectric nanogenerators (TENG) efficiently capture diverse forms of dispersed mechanical energy from everyday environments, including human activity and ambient mechanical vibrations. This technology offers a promising solution for the efficient harvesting and utilisation of mechanical energy, proving particularly suitable for applications such as energy harvesting, self-powered sensing, and flexible wearable electronics. PAAm/SA/LiCl hydrogels exhibit both exceptional flexibility and high conductivity, making them ideal materials for constructing single-electrode mode TENGs. The TENG structure based on PAAm/SA/LiCl hydrogel (PAAm/SA/LiCl-TENG) is illustrated in Fig. 7a. The conical microstructure hydrogel (Fig. 6b) serves as the electrode encapsulated between two PDMS films, with the electrodes connected via copper wires. As shown in Fig. 7b, the fabricated PAAm/SA/LiCl-TENG successfully illuminated a "five-pointed star" pattern composed of 35 LEDs, demonstrating excellent energy output performance.

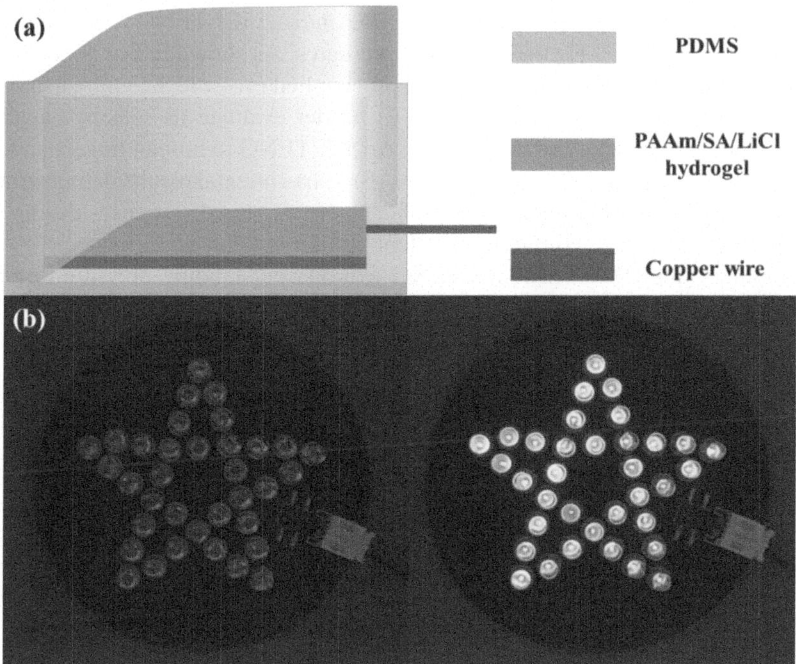

Fig. 7. (a) The structure of PAAm/SA/LiCl-TENG; (b) LED pattern powered by PAAm/SA/LiCl-TENG.

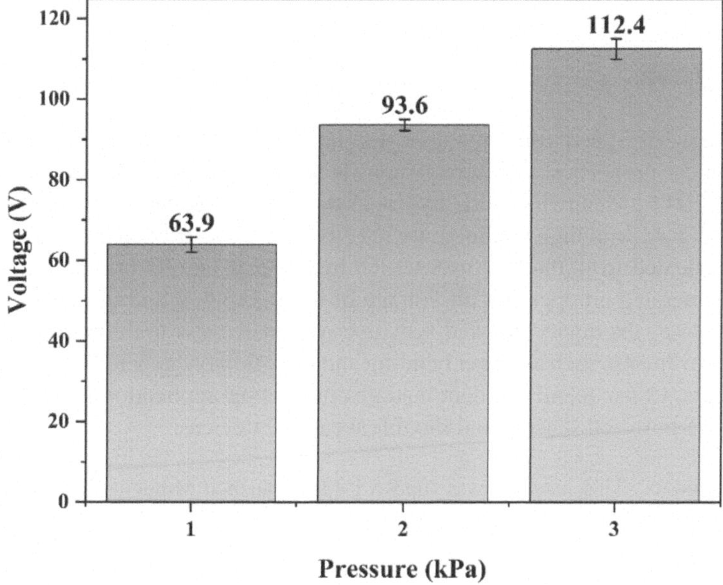

Fig. 8. Open circuit voltage generated by PAAm/SA/LiCl-TENG at different pressure

The power generation performance of the PAAm/SA/LiCl-TENG was further investigated at a frequency of 1 Hz under varying pressures. As shown in Fig. 8, the device's output voltage increases significantly with rising applied pressure, reaching a maximum open-circuit voltage of 112.4 V at 3 kPa. To further evaluate its sensing capabilities in practical scenes, we attached the PAAm/SA/LiCl-TENG to human fingers and knees and measured its open-circuit voltage (Fig. 9a–b). Experimental results demonstrate that the device generates highly regular and stable electrical signal responses during finger flexion and knee bending, exhibiting excellent motion sensing performance.

In summary, the PAAm/SA/LiCl-TENG exhibits outstanding pressure-responsive performance and efficient energy conversion capabilities, demonstrating significant application potential in the fields of flexible energy harvesting and self-powered sensing.

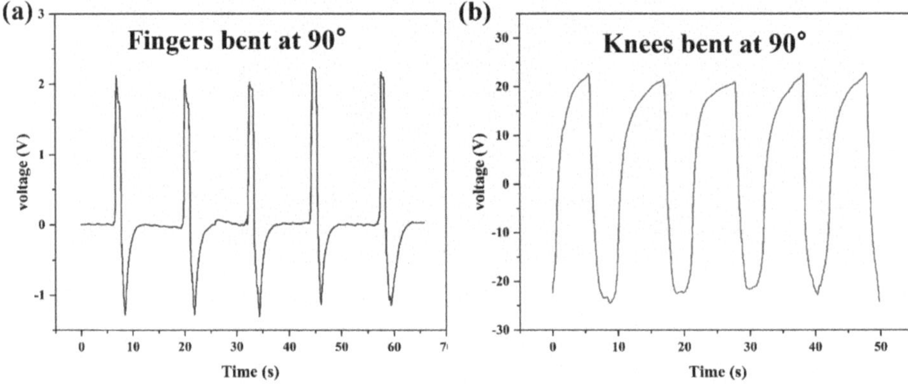

Fig. 9. Voltage curve generated by PAAm/SA/LiCl-TENG (a) when the finger is bent at 90°, (b) when the knee is bent at 90°.

4 Conclusions

In this study, we designed a dual-network structure PAAm/SA/LiCl hydrogel with excellent mechanical properties, which has a tensile strength of 24.1 kPa and an elongation at break of 200%. Meanwhile, this hydrogel possesses excellent anti-freezing performance (– 35.4 °C) and high conductivity (117.6 S/cm). The triboelectric nanogenerator (TENG) fabricated from the PAAm/SA/LiCl hydrogel using 3D-printed micro-conical structures generated an open-circuit voltage of up to 112.4 V and illuminated 35 LED lights. Moreover, the device showed sensitive responsiveness to deformations induced by human movements such as finger bending and knee flexion, generating clear electrical signal outputs. Consequently, it demonstrates promising application potential in fields including self-powered sensors and flexible wearable devices.

Acknowledgments. This research was funded by the Lanzhou Municipal Education Science '14th Five-Year Plan' Project (LZ[2024]GH0074).

Disclosure of Interests. The authors have no competing interests to declare that are relevant to the content of this article.

References

1. Cui, C., Fu, Q., Meng, L., Hao, S., Dai, R., Yang, J.: Recent progress in natural biopolymers conductive hydrogels for flexible wearable sensors and energy devices: materials, structures, and performance. ACS Appl. Bio Mater. **4**, 85–121 (2021). https://doi.org/10.1021/acsabm.0c00807
2. Tavakoli, J., Tang, Y.: Hydrogel based sensors for biomedical applications: an updated review. Polymers **9**, 364 (2017). https://doi.org/10.3390/polym9080364
3. Wang, Z., Wei, H., Huang, Y., Wei, Y., Chen, J.: Naturally sourced hydrogels: emerging fundamental materials for next-generation healthcare sensing. Chem. Soc. Rev. **52**, 2992–3034 (2023). https://doi.org/10.1039/D2CS00813K
4. Zhu, Y., et al.: Recent advances in conductive hydrogels for electronic skin and healthcare monitoring. Biosensors (Basel) **15**, 463 (2025). https://doi.org/10.3390/bios15070463
5. Yang, R., Chen, X., Zheng, Y., Chen, K., Zeng, W., Wu, X.: Recent advances in the 3D printing of electrically conductive hydrogels for flexible electronics. J. Mater. Chem. C **10**, 5380–5399 (2022). https://doi.org/10.1039/D1TC06162C
6. Gu, Y., et al.: Empowering human-machine interfaces: self-powered hydrogel sensors for flexible and intelligent systems. Adv. Funct. Mater. e09085. https://doi.org/10.1002/adfm.202509085
7. Qin, J., et al.: Flexible and stretchable capacitive sensors with different microstructures. Adv. Mater. **33**, 2008267 (2021). https://doi.org/10.1002/adma.202008267
8. Luo, Y., et al.: Highly sensitive strain sensor and self-powered triboelectric nanogenerator using a fully physical crosslinked double-network conductive hydrogel. Nano Energy **104**, 107955 (2022). https://doi.org/10.1016/j.nanoen.2022.107955
9. Li, X., et al.: Stretchable, self-healing, transparent macromolecular elastomeric gel and PAM/carrageenan hydrogel for self-powered touch sensors. Mater. Sci. Eng. B **283**, 115832 (2022). https://doi.org/10.1016/j.mseb.2022.115832
10. Sun, H., et al.: Ultra-stretchable, durable and conductive hydrogel with hybrid double network as high performance strain sensor and stretchable triboelectric nanogenerator. Nano Energy **76**, 105035 (2020). https://doi.org/10.1016/j.nanoen.2020.105035

4D Printed CNT-Ag/PLLA/TPU Bone Scaffold Having Enhanced Electro-Responsive Shape Memory Properties

Feng Yang, Jiye Jia, and Pei Feng(✉)

State Key Laboratory of Precision Manufacturing for Extreme Service Performance, College of Mechanical and Electrical Engineering, Central South University, Changsha, China
fengpei@csu.edu.cn

Abstract. Herein, Ag-modified carbon nanotube (CNT-Ag)/ poly(L-lactic acid) (PLLA)/thermoplastic polyurethane (TPU) scaffold was fabricated by selective laser sintering (SLS) for bone defect repair, and Ag was in-situ grown on CNT for promoting dispersion and conductivity for effective electrothermal conversion. The dispersion state of CNT was improved by the introduction of Ag onto CNT, and the scaffold containing 1.5 wt% CNT-Ag exhibited a higher electrical conductivity of 244.6 ds/m than that of 26.7 ds/m for the scaffold containing 1.5 wt% CNT, and consequently exhibited an enhanced electro-responsive shape memory R_r of 96.1%. In addition, the composite scaffold possessed good biocompatibility, which was expected to be applied in bone defect repair.

Keywords: Electro-responsive shape memory · Selective laser sintering · Bone scaffold

1 Introduction

The application of 4D printing that achieved by 3D printing shape memory material [1] in minimally invasive surgery is blossoming [2]. Shape memory poly(L-lactic acid) (PLLA)/thermoplastic polyurethane (TPU) composite scaffold is eye-catching for its good biocompatibility and complementary mechanical properties in the application of bone defect repair [3]. In the PLLA/TPU composite scaffold, PLLA usually works as switch segments to fix the temporary shape and TPU acts as netpoints to remember the permanent shape. The key to realizing the shape memory effect for PLLA/TPU composite scaffold is the glass transition of PLLA. In other words, the temporary shape fixation and the transformation between the temporary shape and the permanent shape are triggered by the conversion between the glassy state and the highly elastic state of PLLA [4]. Considering that the glass transition of PLLA is triggered by thermal stimulation [5], it is crucial to choose a suitable way to generate heat to match the service environment of the bone scaffold. Electrothermal stimulation is fast, remote and controlled, and it was reported that the electrical stimulation was conducive to promoting cell adhesion [6], which might be a suitable for bone scaffold.

S. S. Ge et al. (Eds.): ICSR + BioMed 2025, LNAI 16435, pp. 308–317, 2026.
https://doi.org/10.1007/978-981-95-7538-1_27

Carbon nanotube (CNT) is eye-catching as a functional filler to endow the scaffold with electrothermally responsive behavior, due to its excellent electrical and thermal conductivity [7]. However, the application of the composite scaffold containing CNT is still obscured. In detail, the conductive network formed by CNT is based on the percolation theory, and only when the content of CNT reaches a percolation threshold can the conductivity of the scaffold be significantly improved and exhibit effective electrothermal conversion [8]. However, CNT is easy to agglomerate even at a lower loading, resulting in poor mechanical properties of the scaffold [9], therefore, it is necessary to improve the electrical conductivity of CNT and promote its dispersion in polymer. This could be addressed by in-situ growing highly conductive nanoparticles such as Ag on CNT surface, where the introduction of Ag is expected to not only improve the conductivity of CNT, but also promote its dispersion in the polymer, endowing the scaffold with enhanced comprehensive properties.

Herein, PLLA/TPU composite scaffold was fabricated by selective laser sintering (SLS), and Ag nanoparticles were in-situ growth on the surface of CNT to enhance the electrothermally responsive behavior of scaffold. Ag nanoparticles were introduced into CNT to further improve the electro-responsive shape memory behavior of the scaffold, and the biocompatibility of the scaffold was evaluated.

2 Materials and Methods

2.1 Materials

TPU powder was supplied by LEHVOSS Chemical Trading Co., Ltd. (China). PLLA powder was purchased from Polymtek Co., Ltd. (China). CNT with carboxyl group content of 2.5 wt% was supplied by Chengdu Organic Chemicals Co., Ltd. (China). Deionized water and phosphate buffered solution (PBS) were procured from Sino-pharm Chemical Reagent Co., Ltd. (China). Ammonium hydroxide (NH_4OH) was obtained from Guangdong Guanghua Sci-Tech Co., Ltd. (China). $AgNO_3$ was obtained from the Shanghai Institute of Fine Chemical Materials (China).

2.2 Synthesis of CNT-Ag

Ag was in-situ growth on the surface of CNT to obtain the nanohybrids (denoted as CNT-Ag), and the synthetic process was as follows [10]. Firstly, 0.03 g CNT was dispersed in 100 mL deionized water, and then subjected to ultrasonic for 1 h to obtain a uniformly dispersed suspension. Secondly, 100 mL $AgNO_3$ with a concentration of 0.25 mol/L was added into the suspension and then stirred for 3 h. Thirdly, the pH of the obtained solution was adjusted to approximately 10 by adding NH_4OH, and then poured into a Teflon-lined hydrothermal autoclave under a vacuum at 120 °C for 6, 9 and 12 h respectively. Finally, the CNT-Ag nanohybrids were obtained by centrifugation, washing and drying, and the obtained nanohybrids under the hydrothermal reaction of 6, 9 and 12 h were denoted as CNT-Ag6, CNT-Ag9 and CNT-Ag12, respectively.

2.3 Characterization of CNT-Ag

Fourier transform infrared spectroscopy (FTIR, China) was carried out to examine the functional groups of the CNT and CNT-Ag9. X-ray diffractometer (XRD, Netherlands) was performed to analyze the crystal structure of CNT and CNT-Ag9. Scanning electron microscopy (SEM, Netherlands) and transmission electron microscopy (TEM, USA) was performed to observe the morphologies of the CNT-Ag, and the distribution of elements was detected via an energy-dispersive spectrometer (EDS, USA) equipped with TEM.

2.4 Preparation of Composite Powder and Scaffold

For the preparation of composite powders, a typical process was illustrated with the case of PLLA containing 1.5 wt% CNT: 0.045 g CNT was dispersed in deionized water by ultrasonication for 30 min, then adding 2.955 g PLLA powders followed by stirring. After the mixture had been filtered and dried, the composite powder was obtained. The obtained composite powder was denoted as 1.5cPLLA, where 1.5 represented the content of the nanofiller, c represented the nanofiller of CNT, and PLLA represented the matrix. The PLLA-based composite powders containing 1.5 wt% CNT-Ag6, 1.5 wt% CNT-Ag9 and 1.5 wt%CNT-Ag12 were prepared, and were denoted as c-Ag@6PLLA, c-Ag@9PLLA and c-Ag@12PLLA, respectively. Then the composite scaffold was fabricated by SLS. Typically, 1.5cPLLA powder was evenly spread and selectively sintered according to the three-dimensional model of the scaffold. Then a new layer of TPU powder was evenly spread and selectively sintered. A designed scaffold with the layered co-continuous structure was fabricated after repeating the above procedures, and was denoted as TPU/cPLLA. c-Ag@6, c-Ag@9 and c-Ag@12 were also obtained by conducting the same procedure.

2.5 Characterization of Composite Scaffold

SEM was performed to investigate the cross-section of the composite scaffold with a layered co-continuous structure. Tensile tests were carried out to evaluate the mechanical properties of composite scaffold using a universal testing machine, and size of the composite scaffold was 12 mm × 3 mm × 3 mm. An insulation resistance tester was employed to measure the direct current electrical resistivity (ρ) of the composite scaffold with the dimension of Φ12 mm × 0.9 mm. A closed circuit was applied to the composite scaffold using a direct current (DC, China) source of 20 V, and a thermocouple was utilized to record the surface temperature evolution of the scaffold to evaluate the electrothermal conversion properties.

2.6 Shape Memory Properties

U-shape bending experiment was carried out to study the thermo-responsive and electro-responsive shape memory properties, and the dimension of sample was 20 mm × 5 mm × 1.5 mm. The experiments consisted of the following four steps: firstly, the sample with an initial angle of 180° was heated above 80 °C by immersion in hot water. Secondly, the sample was bent into θ_1 by applying an external force, the external force was kept and held for 3 min after the sample was put into a freezer to cool down. After the external force was removed, the angle of sample was recorded as θ_2. Thirdly, for the thermo-responsive shape recovery, the sample was heated again by immersion in hot water. For the electro-responsive shape recovery, the sample was connected to a DC source, exerting a voltage of 20 V. The obtained angle of sample was recorded as θ_3 after the thermo-responsive shape recovery or electro-responsive shape recovery. The R_f could be obtained based on the equation: $R_f = (180 - \theta_2)/(180 - \theta_1)$, and the R_r could be obtained based on the equation: $R_r = \theta_3/180$ [11].

2.7 Cell Culture

MG-63 cells were incubated in 24 well-plate containing Dulbecco's Modified Eagle's Medium (DMEM). And then the cells were seeded on scaffold and cultured for 1, 4 and 7 d under standard conditions. After cultured, the scaffold was then treated with glutaraldehyde, PBS and ethanol to make the cell fixed and dehydrate. SEM was carried out to observe the cell adhesion. In addition, the live and dead cells were stained with green and red fluorescence, respectively, and then a fluorescence microscope was used to image the live and dead cells to assess the cell viability. The ImageJ software was utilized to obtain the statistics of cell-spreading area and cell density.

2.8 Statistical Analysis

All experiments in the study were conducted in quintuplicate unless otherwise specified. Statistical Package for the Social Science (SPSS) was used for the experimental data analysis, and * and ** were marked as significant when $p < 0.05$ and marked as very significant when $p < 0.01$.

3 Results and Discussions

The effect of the hydrothermal reaction time on the morphologies of CNT-Ag was studied. As shown in Fig. 1a1, a2, a large number of rod-like nanotubes were intertwined with each other for pure CNT. White particles could be found on the surface of CNT for CNT-Ag6, CNT-Ag9 and CNT-Ag12, where the white particles might be Ag nanoparticles. And there were more white particles on the surface of CNT-Ag9 with better dispersion. The white particles on surface of CNT-Ag12 were larger and agglomerated together, which may not be conducive to the dispersion of CNT-Ag in PLLA. The micromorphology of CNT-Ag9 was further characterized by TEM, and it could be found that the size of white particles was 5–30 nm, as shown in Fig. 1e1–e3. And two different lattices with lattice fringes of 0.256 and 0.235 nm were observed in the high-resolution TEM, which corresponded to C(002) and Ag(111), respectively [12]. The SAED diagram showed the typical mirrors of Ag and C, and the EDS result further validated the existence of Ag particles, as shown in Fig. 1f1–f4, indicating that Ag had grown successfully on the surface of CNT.

The FTIR and XRD were carried out to further analysis the phase composition, and the results were shown in Fig. 1g, h. In the FTIR spectrum, it was found that both CNT and CNT-Ag exhibited two peaks at 3410 cm^{-1} and 1721 cm^{-1} corresponding to the tensile vibration of O–H and the bending vibration of C=O, respectively, which was the typical absorption peaks of CNT [13]. And CNT-Ag exhibited a new absorption peak at 661 cm^{-1}, which was related to Ag [14]. In the XRD spectrum, a typical peak of CNT at 27.2° was found, which corresponded to the (002) plane of CNT. New peaks at 39.8°,44.2°, 64.3°and 78.2° were found, which were attributed to the Ag, indicating the successful synthesis of CNT-Ag [15].

Composite scaffold samples of c-Ag@6, c-Ag@9 and c-Ag@12 were then prepared, and the thermal response shape memory properties were evaluated by U-shaped experiment with the 1.5cPLLA/TPU scaffold sample as the control group. R_f and thermo-responsive R_r of scaffold samples were calculated and the results were shown in Fig. 2a. It could be found that the sample containing CNT-Ag exhibited better R_f and thermo-responsive R_r compared with the sample containing pure CNT. And c-Ag@9 showed the best R_f and R_r of 98.2% and 96.1%, respectively. The thermo-responsive shape memory properties of c-Ag@9 increased slightly compared with that of c-Ag@12, which might attributed to the in-situ growth of Ag on the surface of CNT promoted the dispersion of CNT and beneficial to the stress transfer [16]. In other words, a large number of Ag particles grew on the surface of CNT-Ag9 without agglomeration for the CNT-Ag9, making the corresponding scaffold good thermo-responsive shape memory properties.

The effect of CNT-Ag on the electro-responsive shape memory properties of composite scaffolds was then studied, and the electrical conductivity (σ) was tested, as shown in Fig. 2b. The electrical conductivity of c-Ag@6 ($\sigma = 112.4$ ds/m), c-Ag@9 ($\sigma = 244.6$ ds/m) and c-Ag@12 ($\sigma = 198.2$ ds/m) were significantly higher than that of 1.5cPLLA/CNT ($\sigma = 26.7$ ds/m), indicating that Ag with appropriate size on the surface of CNT could not only improve the dispersion of CNT, but also further improve the conductivity, promoting the formation of the conductive path in matrix [17]. The electrothermal conversion of composite scaffolds was then investigated, with the evolution of surface temperature for the composite scaffolds shown in Fig. 2c. It was found that the surface temperature of scaffolds increased rapidly within 100 s, where c-Ag@9 exhibited a faster heating rate and a higher temperature of about 74 °C after energized for 500 s. The addition of CNT-Ag could improve the electrical conductivity and electrothermal conversion efficiency of composite scaffolds, which was attributed to that the in-situ growth of Ag could reduce the contact resistance among CNT. Ag could also promote the dispersion of CNT in matrix and facilitate the formation of conductive networks. This would lead to the Joule heat being dispersed more evenly in the composite scaffold to obtain a good electro-responsive shape memory behavior. This was also verified by U-shaped experiment, and the electro-responsive R_r of c-Ag@6, c-Ag@9 and c-Ag@12 were 90.2%, 93.6% and 91.5%, respectively, as shown in Fig. 2d.

The mechanism of the electro-responsive shape memory of composite scaffold might be as follows. When the temperature was higher than the T_g of PLLA, composite scaffold could be easily deformed to obtain a predetermined temporary shape after applying the external force. After cooling, PLLA became rigid and could ensure the stability of the temporary shape after the external force was removed, with the rebound force stored in elastic TPU. When the composite scaffold was electrified, the conductive path formed in the composite scaffold by CNT-Ag would convert electrical into heat energy through the

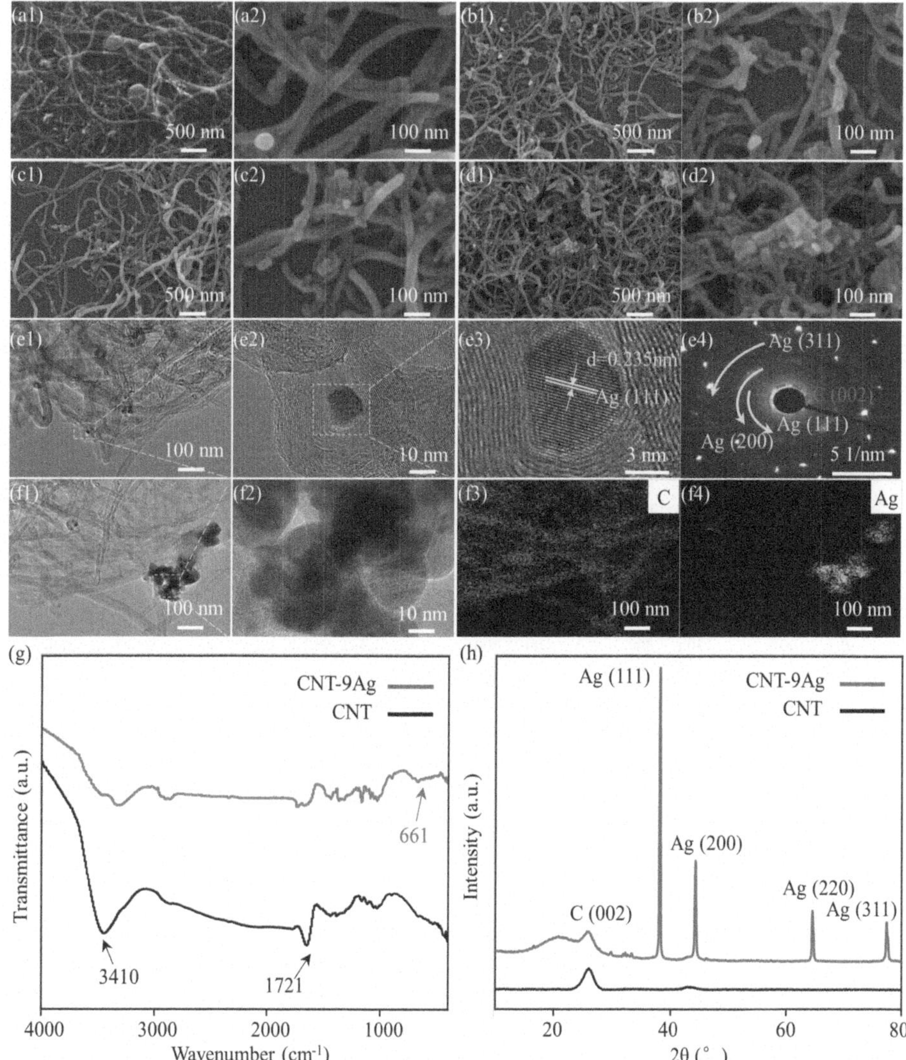

Fig. 1. SEM images for CNT (a1, a2), CNT-6Ag (b1, b2), CNT-9Ag (c1, c2) and CNT-12Ag (d1, d2) at different multiples. TEM image (e1) and high-resolution TEM (e2–e3) of CNT-9Ag. TEM image of CNT-9Ag with the corresponding elemental mapping images (f1–f4). XRD (g) and FTIR (h) of CNT and CNT-9Ag.

Joule effect, so that the rigid PLLA would be easily deformed again. At the same time, the rebound force stored in TPU would promote the shape recovery of the composite scaffold.

The cytocompatibility of the scaffold was investigated by choosing the c-Ag@9 with the best comprehensive properties, and the results were shown in Fig. 3. SEM was used to study the morphologies of cell adhesion [18, 19]. It was found that the number of

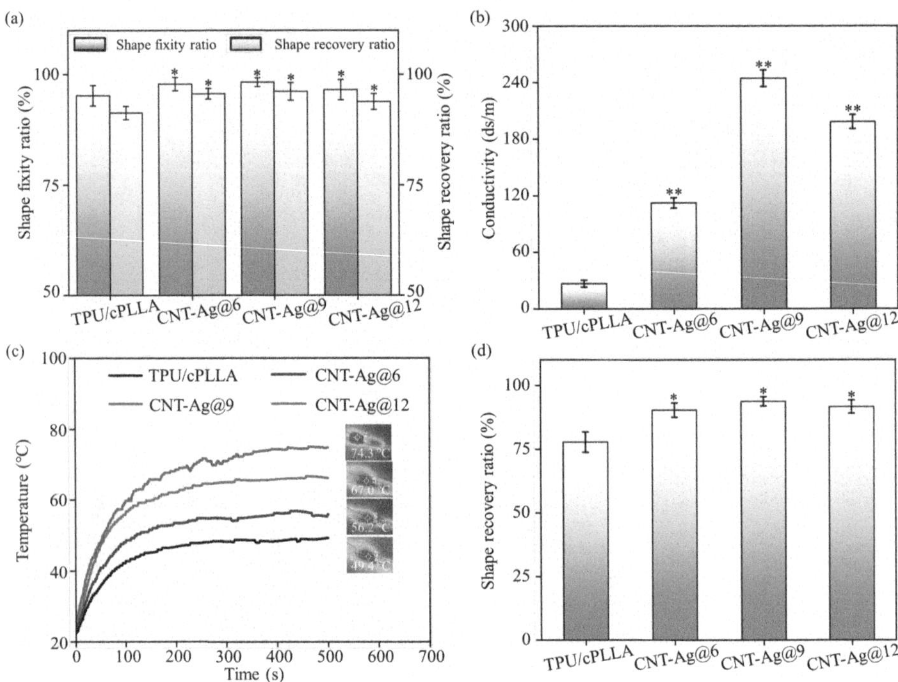

Fig. 2. Digital images of the thermo-responsive shape memory progress of the composite scaffolds (a). Shape fixity ratio and thermal-actuated shape recovery ratio of the composite scaffolds (b). Conductivity of the composite scaffolds (c). Surface temperature evolution of the composite scaffolds with conduction at 20 V (d). Electro-actuate shape recovery ratio of the composite scaffolds (e). Schematic of electro-actuated shape memory process (f). (The error bar represents the SD. * and ** represent $p < 0.05$ and $p < 0.01$ compared with TPU/cPLLA scaffold, respectively).

MG-63 cells increased with the increase in culturing time, as displayed in Figs. 3a–c. MG-63 cells were spindle-shaped with filamentous pseudopodia after culturing for 1 d, while the cells almost covered the whole scaffold with superposition of multi-cell layers after culturing for 7 d. And the area of cell-spreading increased from 14.85% to 81.78% as displayed in Fig. 3g. The result of cell fluorescence also showed that with the extension of cultivation time, the number of living cells increased with the cell density increase from 130 cells/mm^2 to 767 cells/mm^2 shown in Fig. 3h, and the shape of cells gradually changed from spherical to rhomboid without dead cells, as shown in Figs. 3d–f. In conclusion, the addition of CNT-Ag9 into the scaffold exhibited no cytotoxic effect, and the c-Ag@9 scaffold possessed good cell activity and was expected to be used in bone tissue engineering [20, 21].

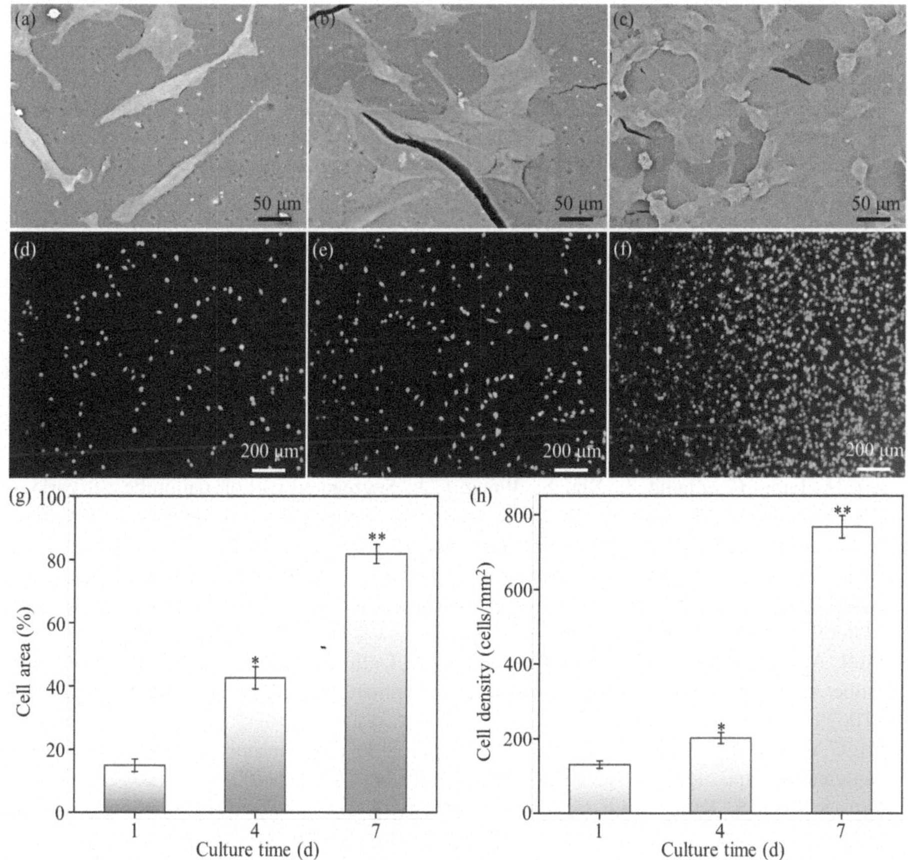

Fig. 3. SEM of cell cultured on CNT@Ag9 scaffold for 1 d (a), 4 d (b) and 7d (c). Fluorescence images of cell cultured on the CNT@Ag9 scaffold for 1 d (d), 4 d (e) and 7d (f). The corresponding statistical of cell-spreading area (g) and cell density (h). (The error bar represents the SD. * and ** represent $p < 0.05$ and $p < 0.01$ compared with CNT@Ag9 scaffold culturing for 1 d, respectively).

4 Conclusion

In this study, the CNT/PLLA/TPU composite scaffolds were fabricated by SL, and the conductivity and Joule thermal effect of the composite scaffolds were further improved by in-situ growth of Ag on the surface of CNT, leading to an enhanced electro-responsive R_r of 96.1% for c-Ag@9. The *in vitro* experiments showed that c-Ag@9 possessed good biocompatibility, which was expected to be applied in bone tissue engineering.

References

1. Lyu, Z., Wang, J., Chen, Y.: 4D printing: interdisciplinary integration of smart materials, structural design, and new functionality. Int. J. Extreme Manuf. **5**(3), 032011 (2023)

2. Feng, P., Yang, F., Jia, J., Zhang, J., Tan, W., Shuai, C.: Mechanism and manufacturing of 4D printing: derived and beyond the combination of 3D printing and shape memory material. Int. J. Extreme Manuf. **6**(6), 062011 (2024)
3. Shuai, C., Xu, W., He, H., Yang, F., Liu, J., Feng, P.: Layered co-continuous structure in bone scaffold fabricated by laser additive manufacturing for enhancing electro-responsive shape memory properties. J. Mater. Res. Technol. **30**, 61–69 (2024)
4. Jiang, Y., Leng, J., Zhang, J.: A high-efficiency way to improve the shape memory property of 4D-printed polyurethane/polylactide composite by forming in situ microfibers during extrusion-based additive manufacturing. Addit. Manuf. **38**, 101718 (2021)
5. Liu, H., Wang, F., Wu, W., Dong, X., Sang, L.: 4D printing of mechanically robust PLA/TPU/Fe_3O_4 magneto-responsive shape memory polymers for smart structures. Compos. Part B-Eng. **248**, 110382 (2023)
6. Cui, L., et al.: Electroactive composite scaffold with locally expressed osteoinductive factor for synergistic bone repair upon electrical stimulation. Biomaterials **230**, 119617 (2020)
7. da Silva, M.M., Proença, M.P., Covas, J.A., Paiva, M.C.: Shape-memory polymers based on carbon nanotube composites. Micromachines **15**(6), 748 (2024)
8. Du, H., Fang, C., Zhang, J., Xia, X., Weng, G.J.: Segregated carbon nanotube networks in CNT-polymer nanocomposites for higher electrical conductivity and dielectric permittivity, and lower percolation threshold. Int. J. Eng. Sci. **173**, 103650 (2022)
9. Hoseini, A.H.A., Arjmand, M., Sundararaj, U., Trifkovic, M.: Significance of interfacial interaction and agglomerates on electrical properties of polymer-carbon nanotube nanocomposites. Mater. Design **125**, 126–134 (2017)
10. Jatoi, A.W., Ogasawara, H., Kim, I.S., Ni, Q.-Q.: Cellulose acetate/multi-wall carbon nanotube/Ag nanofiber composite for antibacterial applications. Mater. Sci. Eng. C-Mater. **110**, 110679 (2020)
11. Fu, C.Y., Chuang, W.T., Hsu, S.H.: A biodegradable chitosan-polyurethane cryogel with switchable shape memory. ACS Appl. Mater. Interfaces **13**(8), 9702–9713 (2021)
12. Kim, S., Park, S., Kim, D., Jin, C.: Thermal diffusivity of Ag/CNT-added Ag nanocomposites prepared by spark plasma sintering. Int. J. Precis. Eng. Manuf. **21**(7), 1357–1362 (2020)
13. Kaur Billing, B., Agnihotri, P.K., Singh, N.: Fabrication of branched nanostructures for CNT@Ag nano-hybrids: application in CO_2 gas detection. J. Mater. Chem. C **5**(17), 4226–4235 (2017)
14. Perez-Gonzalez, R., et al.: Carbon nanotube anodes decorated with Ag NWs/Ni$(OH)_2$ NWs for efficient semitransparent flexible solid state supercapacitors. Electrochim. Acta **354**, 36684 (2020)
15. Osman, A.M., Abulkibash, A.M., Atieh, M.A.: Fabrication of a CNT/Ag potentiometric sensor for redox reactions via catalytic chemical vapor deposition. Electrochem. Commun. **119**, 106806 (2020)
16. Rangari, V.K., et al.: Synthesis of Ag/CNT hybrid nanoparticles and fabrication of their nylon-6 polymer nanocomposite fibers for antimicrobial applications. Nanotechnology **21**(9), 095102 (2010)
17. Li, S., et al.: A tough flexible cellulose nanofiber air cathode for oxygen reduction reaction with silver nanoparticles and carbon nanotubes in rechargeable zinc-air batteries. Energy Fuel **35**(10), 9017–9028 (2021)
18. Yang, W., et al.: Defect engineering synergistically boosts the catalytic activity of Fe-MoO(v) for highly efficient breast mesh antitumor therapy. J. Colloid Interf. Sci. **678**, 260–271 (2025)
19. Qi, F., et al.: Reactive oxygen species responsive nitric oxide release for rnhanced photodynamic antibacterial therapy of scaffolds. ACS Appl. Polym. Mater. **6**(11), 6581–6593 (2024)

20. De Mori, A., et al.: Evaluation of antibacterial and cytotoxicity properties of silver nanowires and their composites with carbon nanotubes for biomedical applications. Int. J. Mol. Sci. **21**(7), 2303 (2020)
21. Nie, C., et al.: Bioinspired and biocompatible carbon nanotube-Ag nanohybrid coatings for robust antibacterial applications. Acta Biomater. **51**, 479–494 (2017)

Author Index

A
Afzal, Maimoona 54, 260
Ai, Yi 120
Ali, Nasar 54, 260
Arif, Sarah 151
Askari, Ghulam Hassan 54, 260
Aslam, Sidra 54, 260

B
Benali, Abderraouf 23, 238

C
Cabibihan, John-John 151
Chang, Honglong 35
Chen, Chunliang 95
Chen, Tuanjie 108, 296
Chen, Xiaohu 43, 95
Cheng, Xian 141

F
Fei, Sixiang 23, 238
Feng, Fan 250
Feng, Pei 308

G
Guo, Yixiao 43

H
Han, Xiaoxiao 284
He, Hongsheng 131, 215, 225
Hong, Zhang 12
Hu, Peng 120, 273
Hu, Yaoxing 1, 192, 250

J
Jia, Jiye 308
Jia, Zhongyu 181
Jia, Zonghai 181

L
Li, Caijuan 108, 204, 296
Li, Hui 225
Li, Xinpei 65
Liang, Gaofeng 181
Liu, Huan 273
Liu, Minyan 43
Liu, Zhewei 65
Liu, Zhisheng 43, 95
Lu, Donglai 23, 238
Lu, Yi 80

M
Muneer, Muhsina 151

P
Ponnada, Ajay Kishore 131

Q
Qiang, Zhang 12

R
Ren, Bo 43

S
Shehzad, Aamir 54, 260
Shen, Jiawei 169
Shen, Shangyi 35
Song, Yingchao 43, 250
Srivastava, Gautam 169

S. S. Ge et al. (Eds.): ICSR + BioMed 2025, LNAI 16435, pp. 319–320, 2026.
https://doi.org/10.1007/978-981-95-7538-1

T

Thota, Sai Leela Harika 215

W

Wang, Mengjie 95
Wang, Ruoyu 169
Wang, Yanen 43, 95
Wang, Yifei 284
Wang, Yihui 35
Wenxiu, Wang 12
Wu, Rili 80
Wu, Shanshan 273
Wu, Xiru 80

X

Xiaojie, Wang 12
Xin, Li 12
Xu, Aoliang 80
Xu, Hongxue 204, 296
Xu, Tianjun 225

Y

Yan, Fujian 131, 215
Yang, Feng 308
Yang, Lijun 108
Yang, Yanqing 141
Yang, Yichuan 120, 273
Yang, Zhenqi 35
Yi, Pang 12
Yin, Huijun 35
Yu, Ting 35
Yu, Weiwei 23, 120, 169, 238, 273
Yuan, Miaomiao 284
Yuan, Xun 141

Z

Zaman, Akhlak Uz 225
Zeng, Hao 1, 192, 250
Zhang, Chi 54, 65, 95, 181, 260
Zhang, Guangyuan 120
Zhang, Haonan 43, 95
Zhang, Xinyu 250
Zhang, Yakuang 65
Zhao, Haitao 35
Zhao, Yinghao 95, 250
Zheng, Xiaolu 141
Zhong, Yuhai 80
Zhou, Junchen 141
Zhu, Wei 141
Zou, Xiang 120, 273

The manufacturer's authorised representative in the EU is Springer Nature Customer Service Centre GmbH, Europaplatz 3, 69115 Heidelberg, Germany. If you have any concerns regarding our products, please contact ProductSafety@springernature.com

Printed and bound by CPI Group (UK) Ltd, Croydon, CR0 4YY
07/07/2026
02160917-0009